MW00997336

Liber Malorum Spirituum seu Goetia

Theurgia-Goetia

Ars Paulina

Ars Almadel

Lemegeton Clavicula Salomonis

"The demons are enticed by men to work marvels, not by offerings of food, as if they were animals, but by symbols which conform to the individual taste of each as a spirit, namely, various stones, plants, trees, animals, incantations, and ceremonies."

- St. Augustine, *De Civitate Dei*, XXI, 6.

Sourceworks of Ceremonial Magic Series

In the same series:

Volume I – The Practical Angel Magic of John Dee's Enochian Tables - ISBN 978-0-9547639-0-9

Volume II – The Keys to the Gateway of Magic: Summoning the Solomonic Archangels & Demonic Princes – ISBN 978-0-9547639-1-6

Volume III – The Goetia of Dr Rudd: The Angels & Demons of *Liber Malorum Spirituum seu Goetia* – ISBN 978-0-9547639-2-3

Volume IV – The Veritable Key of Solomon– ISBN 978-0-7378-1453-0 (cloth) - ISBN 978-0-9547639-8-5 (limited leather)

Volume V – The Grimoire of Saint Cyprian: *Clavis Inferni* - ISBN 978-0-9557387-1-5 (cloth) – ISBN 978-0-9557387-4-6 (limited leather)

Volume VI – *Sepher Raziel: Liber Salomonis* – ISBN 978-0-9557387-3-9 (cloth) – ISBN 978-0-9557387-5-3 (limited leather)

Volume VII - *Liber Lunæ & Sepher ha-Levanah* - ISBN 978-0-9557387-2-1 (cloth) - ISBN 978-0-9557387-3-8 (limited leather)

Volume VIII - The Magical Treatise of Solomon, or *Hygromanteia* - ISBN 978-0-9568285-0-7 (cloth) - ISBN 978-0-9568285-1-4 (limited leather)

For further details of forthcoming volumes in this series edited from classic magical manuscripts see www.GoldenHoard.com

Other Books by David Rankine

Books on the Western Esoteric Tradition by David Rankine

Avalonia's Book of Chakras (with Sorita d'Este) - Avalonia
Becoming Magick - Mandrake
Book of Gold (with Paul Harry Barron) - Avalonia
Book of Treasure Spirits - Avalonia
Circle of Fire (with Sorita d'Este) - Avalonia
Climbing the Tree of Life - Avalonia
Collection of Magical Secrets (with Stephen Skinner) - Avalonia
Complete Grimoire of Pope Honorius (with Paul Harry Barron) - Avalonia
Cosmic Shekinah (with Sorita d'Este) - Avalonia
Crystals: Healing & Folklore - Avalonia
Fairie Queen (with Sorita d'Este) - Avalonia
Goetia of Dr Rudd: Liber Malorum Spirituum (with Stephen Skinner) – Golden Hoard
Grimoire of Arthur Gauntlet - Avalonia
Grimoire of Saint Cyprian: Clavis Inferni (with Stephen Skinner) – Golden Hoard
Guises of the Morrigan (with Sorita d'Este) - Avalonia
Heka: Ancient Egyptian Magic - Avalonia
Hekate Liminal Rites (with Sorita d'Este) - Avalonia
Horns of Power (with Sorita d'Este) - Avalonia
Isles of the Many Gods (with Sorita d'Este) - Avalonia
Keys to the Gateway of Magic (with Stephen Skinner) – Golden Hoard
Magick Without Peers (with Ariadne Rainbird) - Capall Bann
Practical Angel Magic of Dr. Dee (with Stephen Skinner) – Golden Hoard
Practical Elemental Magick (with Sorita d'Este) - Avalonia
Practical Planetary Magick (with Sorita d'Este) - Avalonia
Practical Qabalah Magic (with Sorita d'Este) - Avalonia
Veritable Key of Solomon (with Stephen Skinner) – Golden Hoard
Visions of the Cailleach (with Sorita d'Este) - Avalonia
Wicca Magickal Beginnings (with Sorita d'Este) - Avalonia

Other Books by Stephen Skinner

Books on the Western Esoteric Tradition by Stephen Skinner

Agrippa's Fourth Book of Occult Philosophy (edited) – Askin, Ibis
Aleister Crowley's Astrology (edited) – Spearman, Ibis
Complete Magician's Tables – Golden Hoard, Llewellyn
Dr John Dee's Spiritual Diaries: the fully revised and corrected edition of 'a True & Faithful Relation of what passed…between Dr John Dee…& some Spirits' – Golden Hoard
Geomancy in Theory & Practice – Golden Hoard, Llewellyn
Goetia of Dr Rudd: Liber Malorum Spirituum (with David Rankine) – Golden Hoard
Grimoire of Saint Cyprian: Clavis Inferni (with David Rankine) – Golden Hoard
Key to the Latin of Dr John Dee's Spiritual Diaries - Golden Hoard, Llewellyn
Keys to the Gateway of Magic (with David Rankine) – Golden Hoard
Magical Diaries of Aleister Crowley (edited) – Spearman, RedWheel Weiser
Michael Psellus 'On the Operation of Daimones' - Golden Hoard
Millennium Prophecies: Apocalypse 2000 - Carlton
Nostradamus (with Francis King) – Carlton
Oracle of Geomancy – Warner Destiny, Prism
Practical Angel Magic of Dr. Dee (with David Rankine) – Golden Hoard
Sacred Geometry – Gaia, Hamlyn
Search for Abraxas (with Nevill Drury) – Spearman, Salamander
Sepher Raziel: Liber Salomonis (with Don[e] Karr) – Golden Hoard
Techniques of Graeco-Egyptian Magic – Golden Hoard, Llewellyn
Techniques of Solomonic Magic – Golden Hoard, Llewellyn
Techniques of High Magic (with Francis King) – Daniels, Inner Traditions, Askin
Terrestrial Astrology: Divination by Geomancy – Routledge
Veritable Key of Solomon (with David Rankine) – Golden Hoard, Llewellyn

Books on Feng Shui by Stephen Skinner

Advanced Flying Star Feng Shui – Golden Hoard
Feng Shui Before & After - Haldane Mason, Tuttle
Feng Shui for Everyday Living aka *Feng Shui for Modern Living* - Cico
Feng Shui History: the Story of Classical Feng Shui in China & the West – Golden Hoard
Feng Shui Style - Periplus
Feng Shui the Traditional Oriental Way - Haldane Mason
Feng Shui: the Living Earth Manual - Tuttle
Flying Star Feng Shui - Tuttle
Guide to the Feng Shui Compass – Golden Hoard
K.I.S.S. Guide to Feng Shui (Keep it Simple Series) – Penguin, DK
Key San He Feng Shui Formulae – Golden Hoard
Living Earth Manual of Feng Shui – RKP, Penguin, Arkana
Mountain Dragon – Golden Hoard
Original Eight Mansion Formula – Golden Hoard
Practical Makeovers Using Feng Shui – Haldane Mason, Tuttle
Water Dragon – Golden Hoard

The *Goetia* of Dr Rudd

Lemegeton Clavicula Salomonis

including

Ars Almadel
Ars Paulina
Theurgia-Goetia
Liber Malorum Spirituum seu Goetia

with a study of the techniques of evocation in the context of the angel magic tradition of the seventeenth century

being a transcription of Dr Rudd's 'Liber Malorum Spirituum seu Goetia' from Harley MS 6483, with other pertinent extracts from manuscripts Harley MS 6482, Sloane MS 3824 and Wellcome MS 3203

Edited by

Stephen Skinner & David Rankine

Golden Hoard Press

2017

Published by Golden Hoard Press Pte Ltd
PO Box 1073
Robinson Road PO
Singapore 902123

www.GoldenHoard.com

First Edition - Fourth Printing

ISBN: 978-0-9547639-2-3

Printed in Malaysia

Dedicated to Helene Hodge and Sorita D'Este
the two magical ladies
who have helped to make it all possible

Acknowledgements

Illustrations of the *Lemegeton* seals and sigils (including Figures 6, 7, 8, 9, 13, 14, and 15) from Harley MS 6483; of Peter Smart's engraving of Solomon's Brass Vessel (Figure 5) and Rudd's version of the *Tabula Sancta* (Figure 14) from Harley MS 6482; the Spirit Compass Rose (Figure 10) from Sloane MS 3825; of a magician evoking a spirit from within a Circle from Cotton MS Tiberius A VII, folio 44 (the dust jacket and Figure 2); of the magician 'Canoaster', with grimoire, admonishing two demons from Additional MS 39844, folio 51 (Figure 3); and the variant forms of the Circle from Sloane MS 3824 (Figure 17) have been reproduced with the kind permission of the Trustees of the British Library.

The illustrations (including Figures 10, 11 and 17) from Wellcome MS 3203 have been reproduced with the kind permission of the Wellcome Trust, for which we are also duly grateful.

Our thanks to Adam McLean for the illustration of the Seals of the Patriarchs (Figure 4) from his *Magical Calendar.* We are also grateful for the painstaking work of restoring and cleaning the seals by Dianthus and Valentina Kim and Er Choon Haw. And last but not least to Joseph Peterson for having done the definitive version of the *Lemegeton* in the first place.

Contents

List of Tables

List of Illustrations

"Like angels, they [the demons] have wings and fly from one end of the world to the other, and know the future; and like men they eat, propagate, and die"

- *Hagaddah* 16b; Ab. R. N. xxxvii.

Introduction

This book is based on Dr Thomas Rudd's manuscript version of the *Lemegeton,* or *Lesser Key of Solomon* as it appears in British Library Harley MS 6483. This version is mentioned by Joseph Peterson in his excellent *The Lesser Key of Solomon,* but he understandably dismisses it as being the least reliable version, due to its apparent lateness (1712-13) and to its inclusion of additional material from Peter de Abano's *Heptameron.*

However although he reproduces three of the sigils from Rudd's manuscript in Appendix 4 of his work, Joseph Peterson does not discuss the immense practical significance of Harley MS 6483.[1]

The *Lemegeton* is divided into five books, of which the most discussed is the first book, the *Goetia.* To fully appreciate the revolutionary nature of this particular version of the *Goetia,* one needs to place it in the context of Rudd's other work.

Harley MS 6482, also by Rudd, contains amongst other material the *Nine Keys*[2] and *Tabula Sancta cum Tabulis Enochi* (see Appendix 3) and discusses the interconnected-ness of the different categories of 'spiritual creatures'. Here there is a highly significant reference to the Goetic demons and their connection with Enochian magic, and the associated use of the Shem ha-Mephorash angels.

In Harley MS 6483 the genius of Rudd becomes clear, for the 72 double-seals given by him for working with the 72 Goetic demons also contain the 72 corresponding Shem ha-Mephorash angels, and their associated Biblical verses from *Psalms.* The Shem ha-Mephorash angels are, as we will show, used to control the Goetic demons, transforming the nature of Goetic magic into a much more accessible and somewhat safer form of practice.

We have included Rudd's translation of the Biblical verses and their provenance on the same pages as their respective seals for the benefit of the reader. Some of this material comes from Harley MS 6482, but needs to be seen together with Rudd's manuscript Harley MS 6483, to fully contextualise it.

---

[1] Peterson, Joseph. (editor), *The Lesser Key of Solomon: Lemegeton Clavicula Salomonis*, Weiser Books, Maine, 2001, page xii and Figures 12-14, 17, 20, 22 on pages 263-8.

[2] See *The Keys to the Gateway of Magic* by Stephen Skinner & David Rankine, for the full text of *The Nine Keys* and a discussion of its significance.

That Rudd was heavily influenced by Peter de Abano's *Heptameron* is evident, but more importantly all the invocations of the *Goetia* (in every manuscript version) also draw heavily on that important work. Other key points in the *Heptameron,* such as the wearing of the pentacle as a lamen on the chest, are important aspects of the procedure of the *Goetia.* By wearing the seal with the reverse side bearing the appropriate controlling Shem ha-Mephorash angel facing towards his heart, the magician is more protected from the wiles, or malice, of the demon he has summoned.

We have only footnoted some of the differences in the names of the spirits between other manuscripts and Rudd's *Goetia* of Harley MS 6483, rather than repeating the excellent comparative work done by Joseph Peterson in the footnotes of his edition of the *The Lesser Key of Solomon.*

Wellcome MS 3203

We have included material and illustrations from Ebenezer Sibley's relatively late copy of the *Lemegeton,* whose history will be detailed at greater length in the history chapter.

Sloane MS 3824

We have also included in Appendix 1, material found in Sloane MS 3824, which is a collection of items which make up a sort of proto-*Lemegeton,* as this manuscript contains many of the items that later made up the *Lemegeton,* but in many cases in a more complete state. There are two general invocations of infernal spirits which seem to be missing from the usually accepted texts of the Lemegeton, one of which refers to Lucifer, Beelzebub and Satan. There are also invocations of the Wandering spirits or Princes of the *Theurgia-Goetia,* which we have reproduced in Appendix 1, and which do not appear elsewhere in print. From the initial part of the text it is clear this was originally part of a more complete *Theurgia-Goetia.* A fascinating inclusion in this material is a Spirit Contract with the spirit Padiel which was meant to be used during the all important *ligatio* part of the evocation.

Raison d'Être

One of the continuing aims of this Volume in the present series is to show how interconnected the scholarly practice of angel magic was with the magic of the grimoires, and to rescue the grimoires from the stigma of being mere sorcerer's handbooks, as A E Waite suggested, and to show that they are indeed an integral part of the traditions of ceremonial magic, and were often utilised by such acknowledged luminaries as Trithemius, Agrippa, Dee, and de Abano.

This Volume contains material from four separate manuscripts. It is consequently difficult to give this Volume a simple title, so we have had to resort to a slightly misleading short title, followed by a longer subtitle, which was typical of seventeenth century books. For whilst this volume is derived from Dr Rudd's magical manuscripts it contains much more than just his *Goetia.*

Of the manuscripts, Harley MS 6483 which is entitled *Liber Malorum Spirituum seu Goetia* is transcribed in full, with the exception of its fifth section the *Ars Notoria.* Additional material is also taken from Harley MS 6482, Wellcome MS 3203 and Sloane MS 3824. These other manuscripts are clearly referenced by, or connected with the main manuscript, and in doing so we have taken whole 'items' or sections from these manuscripts. However we need to expand our deceptively short book title to give the reader an idea of what complete works are actually included in this volume:

Lemegeton, Clavicula Salomonis Regis, The Lesser Key of Solomon (all of which titles describe the same book, and are used interchangeably by many writers). This collection of grimoires comprises five books which are grouped into three categories:

Goetia (the first book which deals with 72 evil spirits),
Theurgia-Goetia (the second book which deals with spirits of mixed nature),
Theurgia (the third, fourth and fifth books which deal with good spirits and angels).

These five constituent grimoires are:

a. *Liber Malorum Spirituum seu Goetia*
b. *Theurgia-Goetia*
c. *The Art Pauline [I and II] of Solomon [Theurgia]*
d. *The Art Almadel of Solomon [Theurgia]*
e. *The Notory Art of Solomon [Theurgia]* [1]

We have added to these a number of smaller connected items transcribed in the Appendices such as Rudd's extrapolation and expansion of Dee's *Tabula Sancta cum Tabulis Enochi.*

Why another edition of the Lemegeton?

The first question any reader will ask is 'why do we need yet another edition of the *Lemegeton,* and especially of its first part the *Goetia,* which has been printed many times since it was first transcribed by S L MacGregor Mathers

[1] This book is sometimes missing from manuscripts of the *Lemegeton.* It is very interesting in its own right, but we will not be considering it in this volume, because of its size and because it really requires a volume of its own to explain its techniques adequately. *Ars Notoria* was actually printed at around the same time as most of the manuscripts of the *Lemegeton* were written (1657). In fact the manuscript versions were actually copied from the printed translation of Robert Turner, rather than the other way around. But even the printed book is unworkably incomplete, as the method cannot be used without the elaborate illustrations or *notae* which are completely missing from the printed version and all seventeenth century manuscripts. Ben Jonson, the Elizabethan playwright, owned a copy of the *Ars Notoria.* On its opening and closing folios is written the word 'Theurgia'.

over 100 years ago?' It is in fact a question we both asked each other when we first planned to issue this volume, especially when the definitive edition of the *Lemegeton* has been already been excellently edited by Joseph Peterson[1].

There are a number of manuscripts of the *Lemegeton*, each with its own faults and virtues. Peterson used as his prime text Sloane MS 3825 which possibly dates from 1641. We have selected Harley MS 6483 as our prime text. Although the manuscript is dated 1712-1714 it is a transcription of a much earlier manuscript written or owned by Dr Thomas Rudd (1583-1656).

Given that Rudd died in 1656, and that the manuscript contains some material taken from the 1655 English edition of Peter de Abano's *Heptameron* we can probably date the original Rudd manuscript fairly accurately as 1655/6. Therefore this version falls 15 years after the probably date of the manuscript used by Joseph Peterson. We will refer to it simply as the original Rudd MS.

The answer to the question 'why another edition?' is fivefold:

1. This manuscript contains much additional material which no other version does. As Joseph Peterson says, 'Harley MS 6483...contains much additional material, with extracts from de Abano's *Heptameron* replacing [and sometimes amplifying] much of the instructions included in Book 1 [the *Goetia*] of the other manuscripts'.[2]

2. We wanted to show how the system of magic in the *Lemegeton* was developed and actually practiced by working magicians in the seventeenth century. As well as examining the earliest texts available, we deliberately chose the most fully expanded text used by working magicians as our prime text.

3. The seals in this manuscript are beautiful and more carefully drawn than in any other manuscript. Moreover they are completely unique because they show Hebrew names of the demons (albeit as surmised by Rudd), and each is drawn with its corresponding angelic seal, angel name in Hebrew, and its Latin invocational Psalm text, all of which do not appear in any other manuscript or printed version, in this form.[3] They do however have copyist errors (which we have noted), and they don't always agree with those of other manuscripts.

4. This version explains the preparation and protection of the magician, specifically what precise angel he should use to compel each individual demon, and the use of the Brass Vessel. These key practical details are not

[1] Peterson, Joseph, *The Lesser Key of Solomon: Lemegeton Clavicula Salomonis*, Weiser, Maine, 2001.
[2] Joseph Peterson, *ibid*, page xii.
[3] Except for just three examples printed in Appendix 4 of Peterson, *ibid*.

present in any other edition or manuscript of the *Goetia*.[1]

5. We wanted to trace where the *Lemegeton* material comes from and to demonstrate that its roots reach back at least to the thirteenth century, and the connections between angel magicians and those evoking in the grimoire tradition, which in the case of this manuscript proves to be identical. We hope this will help heal the divisive dualism which was introduced into magic by the church, and reassert that magic, as a working definition, consists in dealing with 'spiritual creatures'[2] of whatever hue, be they spirits, angels or demons. In fact the terms 'spirit' and 'demon' have been used almost interchangeably throughout this volume. This may seem theologically sloppy, but many of the magicians and scholars who dealt with them, also used these terms interchangeably.

We originally thought just to present the new material and explain the techniques presented, but it rapidly became clear that we would be constantly referring the reader back to the text of the *Lemegeton*, and so it was decided to reproduce in entirety the first four books of the *Lemegeton*, in fact the whole of Harley MS 6483 (except for the *Ars Notoria)* so that the reader would have everything needful right in front of him.

Our reason for omitting the *Ars Notoria*, is that it is not a workable system in the form it appears in these manuscripts, without its *notae*. To add these in, and provide a commentary that makes the system usable, including the keys, would result in a large book in its own right. It is therefore beyond the scope of this volume.

Before beginning it is worth clearing up the confusion between *necromantia* (which is divination by the invocation of the spirit of a dead person) and *nigromantia* (divination by the invocation of demons) which terms became a little confused after the Middle Ages. Several modern academic works use the term 'necromancy' when in fact they are dealing with nigromancy. Here we deal only with the invocation of spiritual creatures such as spirits, angels, and demons. Necromancy, or its modern equivalent of spiritist séances, is not at all relevant to the current work.

Throughout the course of this work the term 'spiritual creatures' will be used to apply collectively to angels, demons, spirits, elementals, fairies, or other non-human entities. As pointed out elsewhere, if the doctrine of the Fall is accepted then demons are but fallen angels. In practice, Dr John Dee and others often found it difficult to tell if the spiritual creatures they invoked and

[1] Except for Carroll Runyon's *The Book of Solomon's Magick*, CHS, Silverado, 2003 which takes its lead from the present Rudd manuscript.

[2] A term often used by Dr John Dee to encompass angels, demons, spirit or any of a number of other discarnate entities.

saw in their crystals were angels, demons masquerading as angels, or simply mischievous spirits. Although there is a difference between demons and spirits, in the present text the 72 demons of the *Goetia* will sometimes be referred to as spirits, and so these terms have been used interchangeably.

Finally, because there are so many spirit names, which belong to a rather complicated hierarchy, we decided to import the relevant Tables from *The Complete Magician's Tables*, as a way of providing a tabular reference to the first four books of the *Lemegeton*.[1] These appear in Appendix 2 and 7.

1 Skinner, Stephen, *The Complete Magician's Tables*, Golden Hoard Press, London & Singapore, 2006 and Llewellyn, Woodbury, 2006.

History and Origins

Liber Malorum Spirituum seu Goetia

The *Goetia* as a distinct book dates back at least to the fifteenth century, but its techniques and purpose date back at least two and maybe three thousand years. We wouldn't, as MacGregor Mathers seemed to, assert that the present text was actually written by King Solomon, but we are convinced that the magical technology behind it may date back to the time of that King. So we propose to briefly trace the transmission of some of these techniques, as they throw considerable light on how the *Goetia* (and the other books of the *Lemegeton*) were meant to be used.

King Solomon, his Temple & the Jinn

King Solomon (who reigned 977-927 BCE) had a reputation for being a consummate magician. Many sources, Christian, Jewish and Islamic contain stories of King Solomon's god-given skills in calling and binding demons. These skills included interrogating them, imprisoning them, and finally forcing them to obey him, even to the point of doing heavy physical work like hewing stones and timber for the construction of his famous temple in Jerusalem. Living as he did well before the advent of Christianity, and without its dualist view of the spiritual worlds, Solomon had no qualms about dealing with both angels and demons; in fact he clearly saw it as part of his duties to curb the power of the latter, thereby reducing the amount of wickedness on the loose in this world.

Who did Solomon leave his secrets to? The four magicians usually quoted are Fortunatus, Eleazar, Macarus and Toz Grecus, who are sometimes called the *quartet annulus*. Of these, there are many manuscripts extant on magic reputedly written by Toz Grecus (which some writers suggest may mean 'the Greek Thoth'). There are also records of a much later Eleazar using his master's methods of dealing with spirits, and we will look further at his story in the section on the *Testament of Solomon*.

The Temple of Solomon was destroyed and rebuilt several times, and each time there were manifestations and phenomena which suggest that Solomon had not only used demonic powers effectively to build it, but had bound some of these into the very structure of the Temple itself. This procedure was not part of Solomon's later religious defection to the foreign gods of his many wives, but an integral part of his use of magic in building the Temple for the Lord, so that it became truly a magical place.

All that is left of the Temple now is a massive platform that takes up a considerable part of the South Eastern corner of the old city of Jerusalem, looking out over the valley of Kedron. The western wall of this platform constitutes what the Jews refer to as the Wailing Wall, being the closest wall of the Temple platform to the Jewish quarter of Jerusalem. On top of this platform (which is now considered to be part of the Muslim quarter of the city) has been built the al-Aksa Mosque. Also on this platform is the Dome of the Rock, a large octagonal building built over an extraordinary and huge unhewn natural rock from which Muhammad was supposed to have ascended into heaven. The emphasis is upon *unhewn;* as such natural rock is still connected directly with the earth, and hence is of greater magical efficacy. This rock may also been part of the 'threshing floor' that King David originally purchased as the future site for the Temple later built by his son Solomon. Recently there has been considerable controversy over Jewish efforts to investigate the tunnels under this massive platform, which undoubtedly still hold some of Solomon's secrets, both religious and magical.

Strange phenomenon attended the demolition and rebuilding of the Temple. The first time the Temple was destroyed was by the armies of Babylon in 587 BCE. King Herod replaced it with a larger temple just a few years before the Christian era. In 70 CE the Romans under Titus destroyed the Temple completely, taking many of the sacred golden temple implements back to Rome with them, where they were either melted down, or disappeared.

A third and last attempt at rebuilding the Temple has been given very little attention. It took place under the reign of Julian, the last pagan Roman Emperor (reigned 360-363 CE) who decreed that all pagan temples should be rebuilt, including the great Temple of Solomon. Julian ruled after the Emperor Constantine made Christianity the official religion of the Roman Empire. Julian, often called 'the Apostate' had been brought up a Christian, but discovered that the pagan beliefs of his forefathers were more to his taste, and much more intellectually satisfying than those of the 'Gallileans', which is how he referred to Christians. In many ways Julian was bound to fail, as he tried in just three short years to put the clock back, unseat Christianity and restore pagan worship. Already many pagan temples had been destroyed or converted to secular use. When Julian died, so did paganism, and the tide of Christianity swept over what was left of the Roman Empire.

As Rome had destroyed the Temple of Solomon (or more accurately its second incarnation as reconstruction by Herod) so Julian decreed that Rome would also have to pay to restore it. Julian even referred to it as the 'new Temple of the Most High God'. He saw it as a pagan temple, and an important one at that. Work began in 363 CE with the clearing of the existing foundations on the platform, and it was funded by the Imperial treasury as a high priority project.

Because of the sacred nature of the site, the Rabbis decreed that all the mattocks, shovels and baskets should be made of silver and not iron, which the Romans duly did. This was in accordance with Jewish law, but there is a clear echo in this provision not only of the religious law, but also of the distaste of demons for iron. Accordingly, the Romans were required to work without any iron tools:

> "Thou shalt build the altar of the Lord thy God, an altar of stones: thou shalt not lift up *any* iron *tool* upon them. Thou shalt build the altar of the Lord thy God of whole [unhewn] stones"[1]

During construction there were a number of inexplicable accidents, and mysterious balls of fire were seen in the second half of May 363 CE. Finally as if even the earth resented the intrusion, there was a substantial earthquake that caused many fatalities and destroyed much of the surrounding area, but interestingly not the Temple Mount platform itself. [2]

The Knights Templar, founded in 1118 were given the 'stables of Solomon' on the Temple platform as their headquarters, by the then King of Jerusalem. This location is approximately where the al-Aksa Mosque stands today. The Knights were very interested in Solomon, and almost certainly excavated under the platform of the old Temple during the years they were based there. Josephus confirms that there were arched structures and cisterns under the platform not just rock fill. The Templars reputedly found something in the tunnels underneath, which may have become the basis for their considerable power and rapidly acquired wealth.

We don't know what was discovered there, but it has sometimes romantically been asserted to be the Ark of the Covenant, hidden there when the temple was sacked. This 'instrument of the Lord' was inherited by Solomon and certainly appears to have had very real magical powers, being able to indiscriminately kill careless or unprepared people even at a distance. It was even dangerous to look too closely at the Ark.

> "And he [the Lord] smote the men of Beth-shemesh, because they looked into the ark of the Lord, even he smote of the people fifty thousand and threescore and ten men."[3]

Touching the Ark even with the best of intentions, to steady it or prevent it from falling, could also be fatal:

> "and when they came to Nachon's threshing floor, Uzzah put forth his hand to the ark of God, and took hold of it; for the oxen shook it. And the anger of the Lord was kindled against Uzzah; and God smote him there for his error; and

[1] *Deuteronomy* 27:5-6.

[2] St Cyril of Jerusalem wrote a letter about these events very shortly after they took place, and a 6th century Syriac copy of this letter still exists, so we can be fairly sure that the details have not been too distorted by the accretion of myth.

[3] In 1 *Samuel* 6:19. 'Beth-Shemesh' incidentally literally means 'house of the Sun.'

> there he died by the ark of God."[1]

This suggests that the punishment meted out was not a moral one, but something which was as objective as the result of touching a live electricity cable.

Only the properly prepared priests wearing the necessary breastplates, or lamens were able to approach the Ark, and even they would be careful not to touch it. The preparations which enabled the priests to go near the Ark were very like the rules of purity imposed upon a karcist before he undertakes a magical operation. That is not to imply any connection between the Ark and evocation, simply to point out that the Ark is definitely another example of Solomon's use of magical technology, a technology whose effects were very real and very physical, and not at all imaginary or airy-fairy.

Our point is that there was much more to the construction of Solomon's Temple than just simply wood, gold and masonry, and that some of the magical work done by Solomon, in for example imprisoning demons there, or constructing the Ark, was quite physical and still had considerable effect, even centuries later.

Strange phenomena were again experienced in 1536, when Sultan Suleiman the Magnificent ordered extensive restorations on the Temple Mount. He converted the church which had been built on Mount Zion by the Crusaders into the al-Aksa Mosque, which still stands today. By building this mosque, Suleiman magically linked himself with his namesake King Solomon, the son of David. On the walls which be built around Jerusalem at the same time are stone decorations in the form of the two interlaced triangles of the Star of David, known to Muslims as *Khatam Suleiman* and to Jews as *Khatam Shlomo* (King Solomon's Seal). Their function was to protect the city. This same symbol occurs later in the *Goetia* as the Hexagram, a protection to be worn on the breast.

Testament of Solomon

Let us look more closely at Solomon's methods. King Solomon's procedures are most specifically outlined in the third Century CE *Testament of Solomon*, perhaps the earliest and most archetypal grimoire. These procedures are sometimes spoken formulae, but more often very specific physical methods, and it is these methods that have in part been lost or become scrambled by the time we reach the grimoires of the thirteenth to eighteenth centuries. So that by the time we reach the current manuscripts of the *Goetia*, the emphasis is upon listing the spirits rather than explaining the method, which occurs only in abbreviated note form at the end of the book.

[1] See 2 *Samuel* 6:6-7. The 1981 Indiana Jones film *Raiders of the Lost Ark* treated this theme in a fictional, but well researched manner, showing the dangerous nature of the force locked in the Ark.

In this text Solomon interrogates and binds no less than 60 demons. He starts with the demon Ornias, who he discovers has been vampirising one of his servants. With the help of prayers and a magic ring given to him by the archangel Michael, he binds this demon. From Ornias he extracts enough information and help to call and bind a whole succession of demons, one at a time. The procedure is still exactly the same today: the magician starts with a minor demon that may eventually become a 'familiar', and with his help works up to binding other and more powerful demons. Solomon was also helped to bind the demons by the archangel Michael.

In fact the technique of using angels to control demons, found in the *Testament,* is one of the techniques that Rudd expands upon in his rendering of the *Goetia.* We will look at these methods in detail in a later chapter.

Despite the overlap in method, it is a bit disappointing to only find a minimal overlap between the names of the demons in the *Goetia* with those in the *Testament of Solomon.* In fact the only obvious overlap is the demon Asmodeus (number 32 in the *Goetia*) and perhaps Ornias/Orias (number 59 in the *Goetia*).

Unlike the late mediaeval Church view that supposed that magical powers were *only* granted by the Devil, Solomon was one magician who clearly derived his power and formulas directly from God and his archangels, with no hint of any commerce with the Devil. Even a cursory inspection of any grimoire[1] will show that this is still true, and that the words of command in most grimoires are angelic or Godnames, and that the signing away of one's soul is simply a Romantic invention which occurs with much greater frequency in gothic novels than in grimoires.

Solomon practiced magic as a high art in the service of God, with the aim of taming and chaining up the chaotic forces, or alternatively of putting them to good use. Of course, as a matter of techniques, once a senior demon has been bound, then his name may be used to control lesser demons. But this in no sense implies subservience by the magician to that senior demon.

Flavius Josephus (c. 37 – c. 100 CE)

Josephus lived a few years after Jesus Christ, and wrote at length about Jewish history. His works are perhaps the most significant extra-biblical writings of the first century of the Christian era. His comments on Solomon's methods are quite enlightening:[2]

---

[1] With the exception of a couple of late and romantic grimoires which have absorbed the literary tradition of a soul-endangering pact.

[2] Flavius Josephus (translated by William Whiston), *Antiquities of the Jews*, Hendrickson Publishers, Peabody, 1987, Book 8 Chapter 2:5, verse 42-49.

"42) Now the sagacity and wisdom which God had bestowed upon Solomon was so great, that he exceeded the ancients, insomuch that he was no way inferior to the Egyptians, who are said to have been beyond all men in understanding; nay, indeed, it is evident that their sagacity was very much inferior to that of the king's.

43) He also excelled and distinguished himself in wisdom above those who were most eminent among the Hebrews at that time for shrewdness: those I mean were Ethan, and Heman, and Chalcol, and Darda, the sons of Mahol.

44) He also composed books of odes and songs, a thousand and five; of parables and similitudes, three thousand; for he spake a parable upon every sort of tree, from the hyssop to the cedar; and in like manner also about beasts, about all sorts of living creatures...

45) God also enabled him [Solomon] to learn that skill which expels demons, which is a science useful and sanative [healthful] to men. He composed such incantations also by which distempers [illnesses] are alleviated. And he left behind him the manner of using exorcisms, by which they drive away demons, so that they never return,

(46) and this method of cure is of great force unto this day; for I have seen a certain man of my own country whose name was Eleazar, releasing people that were demoniacal [possessed] in the presence of [the Roman Emperor] Vespasian [reigned 69-79 CE], and his sons, and his captains, and the whole multitude of his soldiers. The manner of the cure was this:-

47) He put a ring that had a root of one of those sorts mentioned by Solomon to the nostrils of the demoniac [the possessed man], after which he drew out the demon through his nostrils; and when the man fell down immediately, he abjured him [the demon] to return into him [the possessed man] no more, making still [further] mention of Solomon, and reciting the incantations which he [Solomon] composed.

48) And when Eleazar would persuade and demonstrate to the spectators that he had such a power, he set a little way off a cup or basin full of water, and commanded the demon, as he went out of the man, to overturn it, and thereby to let the spectators know that he had left the man;

(49) and when this was done, the skill and wisdom of Solomon was shown very manifestly; for which reason it is, that all men may know the vastness of Solomon's abilities, and how he was beloved of God, and that the extraordinary virtues of every kind with which this king was endowed may not be unknown to any people under the sun..."

It is interesting to see that the demon was required to do a specific physical act, overturning the basin of water, rather than just some impalpable act. It is also significant that this was a bowl of water, given that water was often used in restraining demons. The witnesses were very credible, and the event took place during Josephus' life. But anyway, such exorcism was a commonplace in those days, and might be just as common today if those techniques were still known. Other instructive clues in this passage include the use of the magical Ring, which was used by Solomon, and which appears also in the *Goetia*. Interestingly, it mentions that the root *barra* was enclosed in the Ring. It is possible that the purpose of placing it under the nose of the possessed, was that the root *barra* may have had psychoactive properties.

Nag Hammadi

In one of the Nag Hammadi gospels[1] written in Alexandria, Egypt, between 190 and 300 CE, there is an account of the sacking of the Temple of Solomon in Jerusalem by Titus and his Roman troops in 70 CE. In it there is a matter of fact reference to the breaking of water pots set up by Solomon to restrain the demons he had captured, and how as a result the demons were released into the world. We will be looking at this account, and its implications, in greater detail later.

Alf Laylah wa Laylah

There are a number of accounts in both Hebrew and Arabic sources (particularly in the *Alf Laylah wa Laylah* or 'One Thousand and One Nights') of Solomon and his interaction with demons or jinn. These stories have passed in a rather corrupt state into Mediaeval myth and legend. Of all the stories perhaps the most persistent is the sealing of spirits in the Brass Vessel by Solomon which was then thrown by him into the sea or a lake. The drawing of what purports to be both this Brass Vessel and its all important stopper (inscribed with the Secret Seal of Solomon) turns up in a number of later grimoires especially the *Goetia*, where it forms an important part of the technique.

The Advent of Christianity

It is only with the advent of the Christianity that magic begins to be seen as something derived from the Devil, rather than an art used to *control* demons for the benefit of the magus and of mankind. Even Jesus exorcised demons, and was thought by many with good reason to be a magician. No particular censure was attached to this view of Jesus, by his contemporaries, as he was obviously a wonder-worker, and therefore this was expected of him.

In fact Jesus was even accused of using a specific demon's name, Beelzebub, to order and control spirits. In *Matthew* 12:24-27 he speaks of using this demon's name for this purpose, and asks the Pharisees, in a very matter of fact way, which name they used. The passage is a striking testament to the general knowledge of one of the accepted techniques of demon control in that period.

---

[1] The *Testimony of Truth* (IX, 3) in James Robinson, *Nag Hammadi Library in English*, Brill, Leyden, 1977.

24: "But when the Pharisees heard it, they said, 'This fellow doth not cast out devils, but [except] by Beelzebub the prince of devils'.

25: And Jesus knew their thoughts, and said unto them...

27: 'And if I by Beelzebub cast out devils, by whom [in what name] do your children cast them out?' "

Of course the heavy irony will not have been lost on the Pharisees. The important thing is that the technique of using a senior demon's name to control lesser ones was accepted as a commonplace by both Jesus and the Pharisees. In the last analysis it does not matter who used the name of Beelzebub to control lesser demons, the important point is that it was seen as an acceptable procedure, used by holy men, and not a damnable one, and this procedure is definitely a part of Solomonic magic. Interestingly, it was the sect of the Pharisees and not the Sadducees who believed in demons, and in resurrection:[1]

"For the Sadducees say there is no resurrection, neither angel, nor spirit: but the Pharisees confess [believe in] both."

In due course Jesus' name was itself used in the same way by others to control demons:[2]

13. "Then certain of the vagabond Jews, exorcists, took upon themselves to call over [exorcise] them which had evil spirits [in them, by] the name of the Lord Jesus, saying, 'We adjure you by Jesus whom Paul [the Apostle] preacheth'.

14. And there were seven sons of one Sceva, a Jew, chief of the priests, which did so.

15. And the evil spirit answered and said, 'Jesus I know, and Paul I know; but who are you?'

16. And the man in whom the evil spirit was, leaped upon them [the would-be exorcists], and overcame them, and prevailed against them, so that they fled out of that house naked and wounded."

This may have been one of the first times that 'Jesus' (or even 'Paul') was used as a name of power in its own right.[3] It is interesting that the demon acknowledged that he knew both Jesus and Paul. In this case the exorcism was attempted by the children of Sceva, a Jewish high priest, albeit unsuccessfully. The children of Sceva were obviously hoping for a bit of the reflected glory and ability of their father, but in the end came off much the worse for wear.

---

[1] *Acts* 23:8.

[2] *Acts* 19:13-16.

[3] For further examples of the use of 'Jesus' as a commemorative word of power, see Geller, M J, "Jesus' Theurgic Powers: Parallels in the Talmud and Incantation Bowls", *Journal of Jewish Studies*, Oxford, 28, pages 141-55.

A contemporary of Sceva was Eleazar, who we mentioned earlier, and who used the name of 'Solomon' and was notably more successful at exorcism. Thus the names of those who demonstrably had power over demons was seen to be effective over other demons, which is why commemoration of the names of magicians of the past is often used as part of conjurations. The full procedure of conjuration also included the exorcist looking up to heaven, sighing or groaning, making signs with his right hand,[1] spitting, invoking the deity, using words of power, and calling out strings of vowels in the Greek fashion, according to one contemporary Church Father.

The Early Church Fathers

Whilst Jesus seems to have had no problem with acknowledging that he was able to converse with and control demons, his followers apparently did, and early on the Church began to harden its view of magic, and attempt to draw a theoretical distinction between one kind of miracle and another.

However the early Church Fathers had their work cut out trying to claim that Jesus' miracles were different from the miracles of any other wonderworker, such as Simon Magus for example. Either Jesus practiced the magic of Egypt and of his [Hebrew] forefathers, or other magicians had the same access to miracles as did Jesus. Either way the Church Fathers had some explaining to do to their congregations. For those readers who think it strange that we refer to the life and acts of Jesus in a book on the *Goetia*, reflect that Jesus was a true 'son of David' whose magical techniques were part of the direct line of transmission from Solomon, the very first 'son of David'.

Origen (c.185-254 CE) responded to the view that Jesus and his disciples performed their miracles through demonic means, with the assertion that their resort to miracle working was of secondary importance to their 'rare piety of soul', an argument that could hardly be seen as persuasive. To remove the taint of magic, Origen even went as far as to say that the miracles of Jesus and the saints were 'superfluous'.

St. Augustine (354-430 CE) also tried to wash the magic out of miracles by maintaining that the miracles of Jesus "occurred in order to encourage the worship of the one true God...and were wrought by simple faith and pious trust, not by spells and incantations inspired by the sacrilegious curiosity of the art of magic - vulgarly called *goetia* and, more politely, *theurgy*."[2] Jesus obviously *did* need miracles to encourage converts, but to say that he worked simply by 'pious trust' is just not credible. In the same sentence Augustine gives away what he was really thinking of...*goetia* and *theurgy*.

[1] Making 'signs' with the *left* hand was actually at this time a fineable offence.

[2] St Augustine, *The City of God* (in Migne, *PL* 41:291).

When Simon Magus, a well known contemporary magician, offered money to the disciples to buy the secrets of Jesus' magic, we can safely assume that he was certain that there *were* real magical secrets to buy. As the saying goes "it takes one to know one". The disciples were offended by this and spurned his offer, and perhaps this was the beginning of a hardening of attitude by the nascent Church, for which miracles were both a blessing and an embarrassment.

The clearest example of the change from the ancient view of magic (or even Jesus' own view of magic) to the view of magic of the newly founded Christian religion is reported in the Gnostic *Acts of St. Peter.* This describes a magical tournament between the apostles St Peter and St Paul on one hand, and Simon Magus on the other, in front of the Emperor Nero (who reigned 54-68 CE) and all his court.

Simon was quite happy to display his considerable magical powers by levitating. The saints did not attempt to demonstrate their powers at all, but simply took the easy course, and spitefully prayed against Simon, disturbing the fine balance of his magic, rather like deliberately distracting a tightrope walker, so that he fell from a height and broke his legs. With this act of malice they felt that they, and their new religion, had been fully vindicated. It is not recorded what the Emperor thought, but if it had been favourable then no doubt it would have been recorded in the gospels. It wasn't.

The theme of magical contests between Christians and pagans was continued in 433 CE with Saint Patrick and his follower Saint Benin performed 'miracles' to combat the magic of the druids. This could more accurately be described as magic rather than miracles, though the Church would of course disagree!

> "So saying, the Chief Druid set fire to the pile, and, accompanied by two other Druids and some guards, proceeded till he came to where the saint and his assistants, in their white robes, were chanting their psalms. 'What mean these incantations?' tried the Druid, curiously glancing at the hooks so unlike their own wooden staves and tablets; 'or why this flame on the eve of Bealteiné, contrary to the orders of the Ard Righ and the Ard Druid?'[1]

The subsequent magical battle sees Saint Patrick banish the snow and darkness summoned by the druids. His companion Saint Benin undergoes the final combat, where he is unharmed by the flames of a burning tent, where the druids are burned to ash. Another magical duel saw Saint Patrick repeat the actions of Saint Peter by causing a levitating druid to fall and kill himself, without demonstrating any power of his own to levitate.[2]

---

[1] Patrick Kennedy, "St Patrick's Contest with the Druids" in *Legendary Fictions of the Irish Celts*, 1891.

[2] James Bonwick, *Irish Druids and Old Irish Religions*, 1894, page 28.

The Middle Ages

Throughout the next millennium there were many instances of magicians working with angels, and using the holy names of God, to bind demons to achieve their ends,[1] but the Church was determined to set its face against the very techniques that its founder had probably used to attract the first converts. It was Hincmar of Rheims (c.806-882 CE) who declared that magic, without exception, is accomplished through a diabolical agency. It was his type of thinking which resulted in the prosecution of magic being transferred from the secular to the religious courts. Previously in the secular courts magic was only prosecuted if it lead to death, or seriously affected some highborn person, but in the religious courts magic was increasingly construed as a crime in itself.

The key to this shift was the increasing identification of magic and witchcraft with heresy (a crime against God). One canon which is often quoted by twentieth century writers about witchcraft is the ninth century *Canon Episcopi,* which was incorporated by Gratian (fl. 1140) into his decretals. Gratian hinted that much of the events of the witches' sabbat might in fact have been more imaginary than real, and proposed simple expulsion from the parish as a penalty for any witch who confessed to attending the sabbat, rather than execution. But there was no doubt in his mind, or those of his successors, that such imaginings were caused by 'sporting demons'.

Up to 1258 the categories of sorcery and heresy were kept well apart, and Pope Alexander IV actually issued a canon forbidding inquisitors from getting involved in sorcery investigations, unless manifest heresy was also involved.

Finally in the fourteenth and fifteenth centuries, the thin line between sorcery and heresy was wiped out. It was Pope Innocent VIII's Bull, *Summis Desiderantes* (issued 5th December 1484) that finally declared witchcraft and the practice of magic a heresy, and therefore subject to the full weight of the Inquisition. Initially the inquisitors were only licensed in the dioceses of Mainz, Koln, Trier, Salzburg, and Bremen. One year later the *Malleus Maleficarum* was published, and it gave teeth to the Bull, and the Inquisition spread its tentacles across Europe. It was made into a permanent Church institution in 1542.[2]

In the darkest days of the Inquisition, magicians and witches were forced to 'confess' not only to heresy, but that they had made pacts selling their soul to

[1] Examples of which have already been recorded in Skinner & Rankine, *Keys to the Gateway of Magic*, Golden Hoard Press, London, 2005, pages 134-7.

[2] It is interesting to observe that the present Pope Benedict XVI, Joseph Ratzinger, was from 1981 till his papal elevation in 2005, the Prefect of the Congregation for the Doctrine of the Faith (or the Holy Office), which is the name now used by what used to be the Office of the Inquisition. So in effect the current Pope used to be the Head Inquisitor.

the dark side, a concept that probably would not have even remotely occurred to Solomon or to any of the magicians of pagan antiquity. If it had occurred to them, they would have though it totally laughable that any man would make himself beholden to a demon, rather than simply binding it. See the end of Appendix 1 for an example of a real Spirit Contract. Just one year before the proclamation of *Summis Desiderantes*, one of the most significant grimoires ever penned was published.

Peter de Abano (1250-1316)

His grimoire, the *Heptameron*, is very significant as it is the source of the main conjurations, and some of the techniques of the *Goetia.*

There is much scholarly debate about the exact author of the *Heptameron.* The usual reason for dismissing de Abano as its author is that "it is not like his other works". This of course is not a sufficient argument to discredit his attribution as author, and we will therefore continue to refer to this work as de Abano's *Heptameron* until a stronger candidate is proposed. De Abano's interest in magic is precisely what he was tried for by the Inquisition, twice, and therefore it seems quite a likely book topic for him to have penned, but one that probably circulated for a long time in manuscript only, before finally being finally printed in 1485. Furthermore he mentioned several grimoires in his *Lucidator* and was obviously quite familiar with them. The *Clavicula [Salomonis]* belonged to the treaties of magic mentioned in his *Lucidator*, whose drafting he re-examined in 1310.[1]

Trithemius in his *Antipalus Maleficiorum* (1508), refers to the *Clavicula* as the 'key made by Abano'. This is highly significant as the use of the word 'key' or 'Clavicule' echoes the name of the *Lemegeton*, the *Clavicula Salomonis.* Also Trithemius' own work was the intermediate source of at least two books of the *Lemegeton.* The *Heptameron* is the source of the invocations in the first book of the *Lemegeton*, the *Goetia*, not to mention other key bits, especially the circle in the present version of the *Goetia.* Therefore it seems quite probable that Abano was the author. After all, Trithemius of all people, writing just a few decades after the first publication of the *Heptameron*, should have known.

The reason why this book is mentioned here is that the *Goetia* draws its invocations, with very little changed, directly from the *Heptameron.*[2] So this important part of the *Goetia* dates from before 1310. The *Heptameron* is the direct parent of the *Goetia*'s conjurations, and in the case of the manuscript of the *Goetia* presented in this volume, it is also the parent of the form of its Circle.

---

[1] See Vescovini, *Pietro d' Abano, Tratatti di Astronomia: Lucidator Dubitalium Astronomiae.*

[2] One of the present authors, recognising its importance, published a facsimile of this key text back in 1978, and this is now available in a modern edition.

King Edward IV (reigned 1461-83)

An eighteenth century manuscript owned by Ebenezer Sibley and later by Frederick Hockley (both of whom we will look at in more detail later) contains a transcript of a Goetic evocation which claims to have been performed for the benefit of King Edward IV. If this was true, then the *Goetia* was significant enough to have been of interest to royalty in this period. Edward IV's motto was *modus et ordo*, or 'method and order'. Interestingly, *modus et ratio*, or 'method and reason' appears in the incipit of another manuscript on magic which was owned by King Henry VII (reigned 1485-1509) and read with considerable interest by Queen Elizabeth I (reigned 1558-1603) with the help of Dr John Dee.

Fifteenth Century Manuscript Grimoires

The Book of Abramelin

This major grimoire, supposedly written in 1427, originally translated by MacGregor Mathers from an incomplete French manuscript, has now been re-translated by George Dehn and Steven Guth from a much fuller German source. It lists out a hierarchy of spirits, of which one of the four Kings, Belial, also appears in the *Goetia*, and some of the eight Dukes or Sub-princes also correspond with the list in the *Goetia*, including Astaroth, Asmodai and Paimon.

Le Livre des Esperitz

This volume is only found as a parchment inserted in a bound collection of manuscripts in the library of Trinity College, Cambridge.[1] This fifteenth century French grimoire lists 47 spirits or demons. They are listed below, and where there is the same or a similar demon included in the *Goetia* we have added its *Goetia* number in square brackets.[2]

Governing demons:[3]

1. Lucifer [Sovereign]		
2. Bezlebuth		[Beelzebub]
3. Satan		

Four Princes of the four cardinal directions:

4. Orient, king	East	[Oriens]
5. Poymon, king	West	[Paymon] [9]
6. Aymoymon, king	South	[Amaymon]
?. Egin	North	[Egyn][1]

[1] Trinity College, Cambridge, MS 0.8.29, folios 179-182v.

[2] As shown in the second column of Table M15 in Appendix 2.

[3] For more about these three, Lucifer, Beelzebub and Satan, see Appendix 1.

The Rest of the Hierarchy:

7. Veal/Beal, King [1]
8. Agarat, duke
9. Barthas, prince
10. Bulfas, prince [3][2]
11. Amon, marquis [7]
12. Barbas, prince [5]
13. Gemen/Gemer, King[10]
14. Gazon, duke [11]
15. Artis, prince
16. Machin, duke [18?]
17. Dicision/Diusion, King
18. Abugor, duke [15?]
19. Vipos, count [22?]
20. Cerbere, marquis [24?]
21. Carmola, prince [25?]
22. Samatis, marquis
23. Goap/Coap, prince[33?]
24. Drap/Deas, duke
25. Asmoday, King [32]
26. Gaap/Caap, prince[33]
27. Bune, duke [26]
28. Bitur, marquis [12]
29. Lucubar, duke
30. Bugan, King [48?]
31. Parcas, prince
32. Flavos, duke [64?]
33. Vaal [Vual] [47]
34. Fenix, marquis [37]
35. Distolas, marquis [36]
36. Berteth, duke [28?]
37. Dam, count [40?]
38. Furfur, count [34]
39. Forcas, prince [31]
40. Malpharas, seigneur [39 or 6]
41. Gorsay/Gorsin, duke [11]
42. Samon, King
43. Tudiras Hoho *(sic)*, marquis
44. Oze, marquis [57]
45. Ducay, marquis
46. Bucal, duke

Other demons mentioned in passing, but not described in detail in the French manuscript include:

Zagon, King [61]

Andralfas, marquis [65]

The spirits total more than 30 matches in all. If you go beyond the name, and take the trouble to also match them up by their attributes and functions, as some of the names are deformed and unrecognizable, then most of the 47 demons in *Livre des Esperitz* can be found in the *Goetia*. For example, Gemer = Buer, Machin = Bathin, Bugan = Haagenti, and so on. But 12 demons of the *Livre des Esperitz* do not appear at all in the *Goetia* or *Pseudomonarchia Dæmonum*, and 31 demons of the *Pseudomonarchia* are not mentioned in the *Livre des Esperitz*, so the fit is not exact.

Therefore this manuscript is clearly a predecessor of the *Goetia*. It may be that the 72 spirit list originally comes from French sources, and that might be a fruitful direction for future research. This clearly shows that the list of demons of the *Goetia* dates back at least to the fifteenth century and probably a lot earlier.

---

[1] Egin has sometimes been incorrectly transcribed from this manuscript as 'Equi'. The numbering for Egin is also missing in the original manuscript.

[2] Only found in Weirus, and not in the *Goetia*, where it replaces Vassago.

Codex Latinus Monacensis 849

Another fifteenth century grimoire, but one with less spirit name overlap, is manuscript CLM 849.[1] Of the many spirits named in its conjurations, the more senior demons also occur later in the *Goetia*:

Alugor	[Eligos 15]
Astaroth	[Astaroth 29]
Baltim	[Bathin 18]
Barbarus	[Barbatos 8]
Belial	[Belial 68]
Berith	[Berith 28]
Cason	[Gusoin 11]
Curson	[Curson/Purson 20]
Gaeneron	[Gomory 56?]
Hanni	[Amy/Auns 58]
Otius	[Botis 17]
Paymon	[Paimon 9]
Taob	[Tap/Gaap 33]
Tuveries	[Cimeries 66?]
Volach	[Volac 62]

As you can see from this and the previous manuscript sources, the orthography and spelling of these names, in a period before there were any dictionaries and handwriting was often hard to decipher, fluctuates enormously. Hence the exercise of trying to convert the names back into Hebrew or Greek, or to assign numeric values to them, is fairly pointless. There are a few names where their Hebrew antecedents are very clear, like Belial or Astaroth, but for the most part Rudd's assignment of Hebrew forms is unfortunately mostly guesswork.

Johannes Trithemius (1462-1516)

The Abbot Johannes Trithemius is a key person in the history of the *Lemegeton*, as we can say with certainty that all five parts of that book existed in 1500 and all five were known to Trithemius, and in his library at Sponheim, indeed he probably wrote two of them. The key volume mentioned by Trithemius in his *Antipalus* (1508) is a work called *Composition of the Names and Characters of the Evil Spirits*. Although this book or manuscript has since been lost, it is fairly clear from the Latin title (*Liber Malorum Spirituum...)* that this is most likely to have been the source not only of the names, but also of the seals of the 72 Evil Spirits to be found in the *Goetia*. Unlike all the other manuscripts of the *Goetia*, Dr Rudd's copy is actually

[1] Published in Richard Kieckhefer, *Forbidden Rites: a Necromancer's Manual of the Fifteenth Century*, Sutton, Stroud, 1997.

entitled *Liber Malorum Spirituum*. So the first part, the *Goetia*, with its elaborate list of spirits and including its seals, already existed before 1508 in Trithemius' library.

Trithemius himself is the source of the demon names in the second (*Theurgia-Goetia)* and third (*Ars Paulina* Part 1) parts of the *Lemegeton*, which can be traced directly to his *Steganographia*. The *Steganographia* is an intriguing blend of magic and cryptography. We don't think it is a question of deciding if it is one or the other, because it is most decidedly both. In fact the essence of the cryptography in the *Steganographia* is that the spirit names are derived by using a semi-cryptographic process. This is precisely the same in Agrippa, where tables are used to derive spirit names.[1] The same tables that are used to encrypt also produced the spirit names. These spirit names are supposedly then used to transmit messages instantly and secretly to a distant receiver who has the key to both addressing the spirit who reveals the message, and for decrypting the message. Whimsically, you could look upon the methods outlined in the *Steganographia* as a sort of spirit-conveyed email.

Instead of trying to pointlessly separate the cryptography from the sorcery, as many commentators have attempted, we should instead recognise that the cryptography was an integral part of the sorcery. The huge tables drawn up by Dr John Dee, in imitation of Trithemius and Agrippa, were designed to be used to *derive* powerful and evocable spirit names. Using these tables to write letters to spies or potentates was less important, compared to this main use, even for Dee.

The second part of the *Lemegeton*, the *Theurgia-Goetia* is simply Book 1 of Trithemius' *Steganographia* recast in a more practical form with sigils. The third part of the *Lemegeton*, the *Ars Paulina* (Book 1) comes directly from Book 2 of the *Steganographia*.

The fourth part of the *Lemegeton*, the *Art Almadel*, uses a skrying method outlined by Trithemius, who obviously knew it well. The *Almadel* attributed to Solomon was also in his library. The technique involving wax tablet angel magic was something that Dr John Dee would also use almost 100 years later.

Finally the fifth part, the *Ars Notoria* is known in many different manuscripts, most of them missing the key illustrations or *notae*, with some dating from as early as 1300. At least one copy, probably more, was in Trithemius' extensive library.

You can see that all the separate parts of the *Lemegeton* already existed in 1500 and were most certainly all present in Trithemius' library. So Trithemius or his pupils look like the most likely persons to have brought them all together in one volume as the *Lemegeton*.

---

[1] Book III, Chapter XXVI.

Henry Cornelius Agrippa (1486-1533)

Agrippa was Trithemius' star pupil and would have had easy access to his library. Agrippa mentions by name four out of the five books of the *Lemegeton,* although the *Goetia* is not mentioned by him as a book *per se* because he must have known it under the name of *Liber Malorum Spirituum.* Likewise Agrippa does not mention the *Theurgia-Goetia* because he of course knew it as Book 1 of Trithemius' *Steganographia.* Although Agrippa covers a large part of the whole field of Western magic in his classic *Three Books of Occult Philosophy* (written in 1509 but not published till 1533), it isn't until the publication of his short *Of Magical Ceremonies* in the rather misleadingly titled *Fourth Book of Occult Philosophy,* that he goes into more detail about the generation of spirit names, and the procedures needed to make the books of the *Lemegeton* function. There he makes some very interesting points, and we will be taking these up when we consider the techniques of invocation and evocation. *Of Magical Ceremonies* is bound in *The Fourth Book of Occult Philosophy,* the same volume that, not coincidently, contains the *Heptameron.*

Wierus & the Pseudomonarchia Daemonum

The tradition passed from teacher to pupil, and then to his pupil. Johann Weyer (1515-1588) or Weir, or to give him his Latinised name, Ioannis Wieri or Wierus, was a young student of Agrippa. His *Praestigiis Daemonum* (first published in 1563) was partially a rebuttal of the hideously cruel witch hunter's handbook, *Malleus Maleficarum* or 'Hammer of the Witches'. His book includes many interesting items including biographical details of his teacher, Agrippa, and in turn Agrippa's teacher in magic the Abbott Trithemius and that archetypal magician, the original Dr. Faust (later immortalised by Goethe and Marlow).

Interestingly Sigmund Freud thought that Weir's *Praestigiis Daemonum* was one of the ten most significant books of all time. We don't know if that betrays a hidden interest in the demonic by Freud, or the fact that Weir could conceivably be credited with adopting, for the first time, a psychological approach to the hysteria surrounding both the practice and the persecution of witchcraft.

For our purposes the most significant part of this text is its Appendix. This Appendix was not published with the first edition and in fact did not appear in print until the 1583 edition of *Praestigiis Daemonum.* It consists of a catalogue of demons which Weir called the *Pseudomonarchia Daemonum,* which might be translated as 'the False Monarchy of Demons'. This catalogue of 69 demons is almost identical with the list of 72 demons to be found in the *Goetia.* Sadly the only modern English edition of Weir's monumental work[1]

[1] Strangely entitled *Witches, Devils, and Doctors in the Renaissance* edited by George Mora, Medieval & Renaissance Texts & Studies, New York, 1991.

omits this Appendix, probably because the interests of the editor were mainly medical and psychological. However fortunately a translation was published separately by Reginald Scot and is also reprinted in Peterson.[1]

What was Weir's source for this catalogue? We think it is quite likely to have been Trithemius' *Liber Malorum Spirituum.* Weir however referred to his source manuscript as *Liber Officiorum Spirituum, seu Liber dictus Empto[rium] Salomonis, de principibus & regibus dæmoniorum* (or 'Book of the Offices of Spirits, or the Book of Sayings received from Solomon concerning the Princes and Kings of the demons'). In Trithemius' 1508 list of books in his library, Solomon's *Liber Officiorum Spirituum* is listed almost immediately after *Liber Malorum Spirituum.*

Benoît Grévin suggests that *Liber dictus Empto. Salomonis* could be a deformed version of *Liber Emphoras Salomonis,* a title which would indicate a Solomonic grimoire dealing with the *Shem Ha-Mephorash,* the name of God which generates the 72 angel names. If this is so then this indicates that the association of the 72 demons with the 72 angels of the Shem Ha-Mephorash indeed goes back a long way, and Rudd's restitution or continuation of the association of the two is well founded. This is a most important point, but at this point can only be considered speculative.

The spelling of the demon names in the *Pseudomonarchia Daemonum* varies slightly from those in the *Goetia,* but is often phonetically similar. This similarity suggests that the author of the *Goetia* and Weir probably drew on a common source, rather than copying one from the other. Weir's catalogue does not include the 72 important and elaborate seals found in the *Goetia.* Another difference is that whilst Weir only gives a simple conjuration, the *Goetia* gives a more elaborate set of conjurations, which as we have mentioned, derives from the *Heptameron* of Peter de Abano.

The most striking difference between Weir and the *Goetia* however is the order of the spirits. The fact that the last three are missing strongly suggests a transcriptional error, rather than a conscious decision. Weir omits Vassago [3], Seere [70], Dantalion [71] and Andromalius [72], but includes Pruflas/Bufas giving a total of 69 demons.

This pseudo-monarchical hierarchy of demons comes with titles which include Rex (King), Dux (Duke), Princeps (Prince), Praeses (President), Marchio (Marques), Comes (Count or Earl), and just one 'miles' (usually translated 'soldier' or 'Knight'). It is possible that 'miles' was part of the description rather than a title in its own right, as we will see when we consider Furcas.

---

[1] Joseph Peterson, *The Lesser Key of Solomon*, Appendix 2: Johann Weyer, *Pseudomonarchia Daemonum*, pages 227-259.

Reginald Scot (1538-1599)

Scot was the author of *The Discoverie of Witchcraft*. The book was written to diminish the fear of, and belief in the supernatural powers of witches. Scot believed that the prosecution of those accused of witchcraft was irrational and un-Christian, and held the Inquisition and the Roman Catholic Church responsible. Scot's purpose in writing the book was to play down witchcraft, and introduce a more rational view. He found himself in direct opposition to the views of King James I who later ordered Scot's *Discoverie of Witchcraft* burned. James produced his own book, *Daemonologie* in 1597, which was designed to refute Scot and instead encouraged the prosecution of and burning of suspected witches. In the first year of his reign (after Scot's death) James I passed an Act which made any conjuration of an evil spirit "a crime punishable by death as a felon, the culprit losing all benefit of clergy and sanctuary". And so James I reversed the more humane and tolerant atmosphere which had grown under Elizabeth I, and been fostered by Scot.

Scot was very well read, and was aware of the individual grimoires which went to make up the *Lemegeton*. In Book xv, chapter xxxi of his *Discoverie of Witchcraft* he writes:

> "these conjurors carrie about at this daie, bookes intituled under the names of *Adam, Abel, Tobie, & Enoch...Abraham, Aaron* and *Salomon [Clavicula Salomonis]...Zacharie, Paule [Ars Paulina], Honorius, Cyprian* [probably *Clavis Inferni], Jerome, Jeremie, Albert* [Albertus Magnus], and *Thomas*: also of the angels, *Riziel, Razael,* and *Raphael...Ars Almadell, ars Notoria, ars Bulaphiae, ars Arthephi, ars Pomena, ars Revelationis, &c."*

In Book xv, chapter xlii he adds:

> "Hereunto belongeth the art of *Almadel,* the art of *Paule,* the art of Revelations, and the art Notarie (*sic*)."

This is quite a collection of grimoires, and includes three of the five books of the *Lemegeton.* Additional grimoire material was added to the edition of 1584 and augmented in the third edition of 1665, which is ironic as Scot had originally set out to debunk such beliefs, rather than to propagate them.

Amongst this material, Book xv is of most interest to us. The third chapter is called 'the houres wherein principall divels may be bound' and we have reproduced it in Appendix 13. The fourth chapter explains the 'forme of adjuring' and might be considered as part of the method missing from the *Goetia*: we have reproduced it as Appendix 15. The second chapter of Book xv, is the actual English translation of Weir's *Pseudomonarchia Daemonum,* effectively the text which parallels the list of spirits in the *Goetia,* with but a few minor differences. Scot appears to have taken the English translation from the work of a certain Master T. R.

Master T. R.

The chapter is entitled 'an inventarie of the names, shapes, powers, government, and effects of divels and spirits, of their severall segniories [titles] and degrees: a strange discourse worth the reading.' There is an intriguing note at the end of Scot's English version of the *Pseudomonarchia Daemonum* (Book xv, chapter ii) which states:

> "This was the work of one T.R. written in faire letters of red & blacke upon parchment, and made by him, Ann[o] 1570, to the maintenance of his living, the edifieng [*sic*] of the poore, and the glorie of gods holie name: as he himself saith."

This is a delightful justification for the translation of this grimoire; although the manuscript is not very clear how the poor will be edified by it. John Cokars assisted Master T. R. with his task.

This means that 14 years before the *Pseudomonarchia Daemonum* was actually printed, a certain 'T. R.' made a manuscript translation of it, and it is that manuscript copy (which may no longer to be extant), which Scot used for his English translation, bypassing the printed Latin *Pseudomonarchia Daemonum* altogether. The initials T.R. are highly suggestive of 'Thomas Rudd'. As the manuscript dates thirteen years before Dr Thomas Rudd's birth it can not have been him, but it is tempting to fantasise that this might have been translated by his father, who may have borne the same given name (a common practice in those days), and the same interest and expertise in magic, but this is only conjecture. If it were true however, it further demonstrates the very close knitted personal transmission of these magical techniques from teacher to pupil, or father to son.

Blaise de Vigenère (1523 - 1596)

Blaise de Vigenère was a French diplomat, cryptographer and magician. The Vigenère cipher is named after him, although it was incorrectly attributed to him in the nineteenth century. Blaise spent most of his working life in the diplomatic service, only retiring in 1570. Five years into his career he was sent to the Diet of Worms as a very junior secretary. It might be noteworthy that Worms was the hometown of Abraham, the author of the *Book of Abramelin.* At age 24, he entered the service of the Duke of Nevers. In 1549 he visited Rome on a two-year diplomatic mission, and again in 1566. On both trips, he came in to contact with books on both cryptography and magic, such as the *Steganographia* of Trithemius.

Vigenère was also intrigued by the 72-letter name of God, and the 72 angel names derived from it. Vigenère laid out the seals and associations of the 72 Shem ha-Mephorash angels in a manuscript still to be found in the Bibliothèque de l'Arsenal (now part of the Bibliothèque Nationale) in Paris.

Rudd used these seals as an integral part of the system in his *Goetia*. Mathers also used this manuscript when preparing papers which were given out to selected members of the Golden Dawn. It would be interesting to find Vigenère's source for these angelic seals.

It is amazing how often the worlds of magic and cryptography go hand in hand. Trithemius was probably one of the earliest, if not the first cryptographer, Blaise Vigenère was a well known cryptographer and Dr John Dee of course was also very much into cryptography, as an extension of his intelligence gathering activities for Queen Elizabeth I, as well as a need to keep some of his diaries secret.

Much of Blaise de Vigenère's work was preserved by his disciple Abel l'Angelier (1574-1610) and is to be found today in the Bibliothèque Nationale de France.

Dr John Dee (1527-1608)

Dee's indebtedness to Agrippa and in turn to Trithemius is well documented. Trithemius was doubly interesting to Dee as he was both a magician and a cryptographer. Dee's interest in angel magic dates from 1563, if not before. In that year, on the 16th February, Dee wrote to William Cecil that he had obtained a copy of Trithemius' *Steganographia* 'for which a Thowsand Crownes have be[e]n off[e]red, and yet could not be obteyned.' William Cecil, 1st Baron Burghley (1520 - 1598), was a very important man at the Elizabethan court, chief advisor of Queen Elizabeth I for most of her reign, Lord High Treasurer, and someone definitely not to be trifled with.

Cecil's interest might not have extended beyond cryptography, but Dee was obviously more excited, as this very rare manuscript gave him one of the keys to angel magic.[1] This manuscript, in due course turns up as a part of two books of the *Lemegeton*. Cecil might have also been interested in angel magic, as there is a persistent tradition of British aristocrats being involved at some depth in angel magic over the next couple of centuries.

In Appendix 3 we look at how the *Goetia*, the couterpointing of angels and demons, and Dee's magical practice come together with Rudd's strange interpretation of Dee's *Tabula Sancta cum Tabulis Enochi*.

Lemegeton precursors

We will look at the various manuscripts of the *Lemegeton* which date from the mid-1600s in the section on the manuscript. However there is one, Sloane MS 3824, which we need to examine at this point, as it is an important part of the history of the *Lemegeton*. See Appendix 1 for relevant extracts from it. This

---

[1] It was not published until 43 years later in 1606.

manuscript is a kind of proto-*Lemegeton*, as it contains many of the ingredients of the *Lemegeton*, but without its final form or its name. According to the annotation of a previous owner or of a librarian, it contains:

"fo. 1	Longobardus
fo. 29	Extract out of Cornelius Agrippa's *Occult Philosophy*
fo. 53	The Second Part of the *Art of King Solomon*
fo. 75	Circuli, Figurae Variae et Sigilla in re Magica
fo. 94	An Experiment to Call out Spirits that are Keepers of Treasure Trove
fo. 123	Trithemius Redivivus
fo. 133	The Magick and Magical Elements of the 7 dayes of the week"

It is not possible to date the whole volume as it is a collection of different manuscript items, but we can date some of the constituent items. Let us examine these items in turn:

i) *Longobardus*.[1] This interesting title precedes a number of invocations which although in the tone of the *Goetia*, include references to "L:B:S:". Here the scribe is being coy (or trying to protect himself) as these initials refer to 'Lucifer, Beelzebub and Satan', the ruling demons that have been left out of the manuscripts of the *Goetia*. We have seen that in fourteenth century manuscripts these three rule over the four Demon Princes, who in turn rule over the 72 lesser demons. So here is the connecting link between the older grimoires like the *Livre des Esperitz* and the mid seventeenth century manuscripts of the *Goetia*. The three ruling demons were probably cut out because of the dangers of listing them explicitly, even in the seventeenth century, and in practice the magician would never directly need to call them, but only need to use their names to constrain lesser spirits.

This item is in the handwriting of Elias Ashmole (1617-1692) and these pages can definitely be dated to 1649 or slightly later. Amongst the spells in this section is a spell to catch a thief, and the example given is someone who robbed John Rudd of Bedford in Kent, England.[2] This is almost certainly a relative of Thomas Rudd, thus making a link between Rudd and the manuscript's copyist Elias Ashmole. This is followed by various preparations, consecrations and benedictions, as also appear in the *Goetia*.[3]

ii) The extract from Agrippa is relevant, as it gives us several clues to date and provenance. It was also copied by Elias Ashmole, and dates from sometime after 1649.[4] Ashmole is obviously copying from Rudd's work, as he

[1] Folios 3-13. See Appendix 1 of the present Volume.
[2] This may be the John Rudd who was a scholar at Caius College, Cambridge in 1583-1584, and who subsequently transferred to St John's College in 1584.
[3] Folios 22-29v.
[4] We know that because Ashmole refers to an angelic working with Galvah, one of John Dee's angels, which took place in 1649.

uses the notes "noted by pages & capital Letters, where they were inserted by Dr: R:[Rudd]."[1] On that same page Ashmole confirms that the English translation of Agrippa's *Three Books of Occult Philosophy* was in fact made by Dr John French, rather than James Freake, who has recently been credited with it.

iii) *The Second part of the Art of King Solomon*[2] is in fact a version of the *Theurgia-Goetia*. This suggests that prior to the date of this manuscript the this book may have been called *The Art of King Solomon* rather than *Theurgia-Goetia*. The spelling of the four Emperors in this manuscript is much closer to the *Steganographia* than to other manuscripts of the *Lemegeton*. Part of this has been transcribed in Appendix 1.

iv) *Circuli, Figurae Variae et Sigilla in re Magica*

v) Experiment to Call out Spirits

vi) *Trithemius Redivivus.*[3] This item is important as it comprises a section from the *Steganographia*, in a form which is half way between Trithemius and their final form in the *Lemegeton*. Conjurations, which are present in Trithemius, but missing from all versions of the *Lemegeton*, are here included. We have added these conjurations back into the present text for the benefit of the reader, and they are clearly marked as such.

vii) *The Magical Elements.*[4] This is a version of Peter de Abano's *Magical Elements* or *Heptameron*. The highly significant thing about the existence of this item in Sloane MS 3824 is that Rudd's *Goetia* contains the de Abano material with its simple circle, whilst the other manuscripts of the *Goetia* do not, but instead have a more complex form of the magical Circle. This suggests that the Rudd MS may have been partly based on this manuscript.

As Sloane MS 3824 is a collection of items in different hands it is not possible to give it just *one* date. However Sloane MS 3824 is a significant step in the development of the *Lemegeton* and appears to be the link between the Rudd MS and the more ancient sources like Abano and Trithemius. The word *Lemegeton* does not occur in this manuscript, nor does it in the Rudd MS.

Interregnum

This period, which extended from the execution of King Charles I in January 1649 to the restoration of the monarchy and crowning of King Charles II in April 1661, saw a lot of activity in England relating to the *Goetia*.

---

[1] Folio 31.

[2] Folios 53-71. See Appendix 1 of the present Volume.

[3] Folios 121-130.

[4] Folios 133-140b.

During this short but fertile period of twelve years:
1649: Ashmole copies the first section of the proto-*Lemegeton* Sloane MS 3824;
1651: first English edition of Agrippa's *Three Books of Occult Philosophy* published;
1651: expanded second edition of Reginald Scot's *Discovery of Witchcraft* published, containing the English text of Weir's *Pseudomonarchia Daemonum;*
1651: Captain Thomas Rudd re-publishes Dee's *Mathematical Preface* to Euclid;
1655: the first English edition of Peter de Abano's *Heptameron* published in
1655: the first English edition of Agrippa's *Fourth Book of Occult Philosophy;*
1655/56: the original Rudd MS of the *Goetia* probably written;
1656: first English edition of Paracelsus *Of the Supreme Mysteries of Nature;*[1]
1656: Dr Thomas Rudd dies and passes on his manuscripts;
1657: Robert Turner publishes the first English edition of *Ars Notoria;*[2]
1659: Meric Casaubon publishes Dee's *True and Faithful Relation;*
1660: Weir's *Pseudomonarchia Daemonum* published in Latin;
1662: Dr Dee's four missing manuscripts found in a secret draw in Mr Wale's chest.

It would seem highly likely that many if not all the English manuscripts of the *Lemegeton* were penned during or circa this period of occult ferment.

Clavis Inferni

Another grimoire with a connection to the *Goetia* is the *Clavis Inferni,* or 'Key to Hell' which is by Cyprianus or pseudo-Cyprian. This book is sometimes referred to as the *Black Book,* and was supposed to be the sorcery textbook of the 'Black School of Wittenburg' a school of sorcery. The *Clavis Inferni* contains many of the words of power to be found in the *Goetia* invocations. This manuscript is strangely dated as MCCCCCCLLXVII, which is either a corruption of 1667 or possibly 1717. It is written and painted on parchment, but the form of the Latin contractions suggests a source of the early sixteenth century. Trithemius' library had a book on magic attributed to St. Cyprian.

One of its fascinations is that its detailed and beautiful colour illustrations show the four Demon Kings of the Quarters in animal guise, Maymon (as a black bird - King of the South), Egyn (or Ariton, as a bear - King of the North), Urieus (a red-crowned and winged serpent - as King of the East) and Paymon (as a black cat with horns, long whiskers and a tail - as King of the West). These are of course the standard names of the Demon Princes or Kings of the Quarters, but with the very interesting and startling exception that the King of the East is called Urieus, like the royal Egyptian serpent, rather than the more pedestrian Oriens (which was probably simply a corruption of the Latin for 'East').[3]

---

[1] Contained the original Zodiacal seals present in the *Art Pauline* (Book 2). Subsequently republished as *The Archidoxes of Magic*, Askin, London, 1975.

[2] The fifth book of the *Lemegeton.*

[3] Golden Hoard Press will be publishing a translation of the *Clavis Inferni* in due course.

Ebenezer Sibley (1752-99)

By the mid eighteenth century a lot of magical material was being copied by hand and passed on. From roughly 1750 to 1850 some of these manuscripts were copied and recopied many times; in fact the period could well be described as an 'Age of Grimoire Copying'.

Sibley was a key person in the transmission of magical material, and he probably introduced Francis Barrett to magic. His address in London in 1796 was Upper Titchfield Street which was in close proximity to Francis Barrett who lived just round the corner in 99 Norton (now Bolsover) Street, Marylebone, in fact their gardens may well have almost backed onto each other. Francis King has suggested quite reasonably, in the *Flying Sorcerer,*[1] that Sibley might well have been Barrett's mentor in things magical.

From the two brief entries in the *Dictionary of National Biography,* it can be seen that Ebenezer Sibley was primarily an astrologer who published a number of works on that subject. But he was also interested in alchemy and deeply into angelic and grimoire magic. He transcribed a number of grimoires, including *The Key of Solomon* and the *Goetia.* Sibley's interests in magic are less well documented than his interest in astrology, but it seems that several manuscripts of the *Key of Solomon* passed through his hands.[2]

Barrett of course was author of the *Magus,* a book on ceremonial and angel magic which was very influential and much sought after over the next 200 years, although most of its material was copied directly from Agrippa. Barrett died probably at a young age from a ballooning accident, and ironically the unbound sheets of his magnum opus fell into the hands of the Covent Garden bookseller Denley.

Ebenezer Sibley signs himself as 'M.D. F.R.H.S.' Sibley was a surgeon and medical doctor who took his MD at King's College, Aberdeen in 1792. The remaining initials, F.R.H.S. are not 'Fellow of the Royal Humane Society', as has been suggested by one commentator, but Fellow of the short-lived Harmoniac Philosophical Society in Paris. Sibley wrote at least one interesting

[1] Francis King, *The Flying Sorcerer*, Mandrake, Oxford, 1992.

[2] Sibley was very much into magic and owned and annotated a number of grimoires. One of these, currently residing in a private collection, has the following very long title: *The Clavis or Key to Unlock the Mysteries of Magic of Rabbi Solomon.* Translated from the Hebrew into French and from French into English with additions by Ebenezer Sibley M.D. Fellow of the Harmoniac Philosophical Society at Paris, Author of the *Complete Illustration of Astrology*, Editor of Culpepper's *Complete Herbal*, Placidus De Titus on *Elementary Philosophy*, etc. The whole enriched with Coloured Figures, Talismans, Pentacles, Circles, Characters, etc. 168 folios. Late 18th Century.
A second Sibley grimoire copy is to be found in the National Library of Scotland as MS. Crawford 158: *The Clavis or Key to unlock the Mysteries of Magick of Rabby (sic) Salomon.* Translated from the Hebrew into French and from French rendered into English with additions by Ebenezer Sibley, M.D… and enriched with Figures, Talismans, Pentacles, Circles, Characters, etc. London, No 18 Bartlett's Buildings, Holburn [Holborn], 7th August, 1789. 152 folios.

book on magic called *A New and Complete Illustration of the Occult Sciences*, of which Book 4 is the most interesting part. It listed the Harmoniac Philosophical Society as its publisher. In fact it was in this volume that the engraving showing Edward Kelly (and Paul Waring) raising spirits in a churchyard first appeared. Some later writers mistakenly captioned this engraving as Kelly and Dee raising spirits of the dead, something that Dee is most unlikely to have undertaken.

When Sibley died in 1799 he left his precious collection of manuscripts to his ungrateful nephew, who within a month had sold them all to Denley, the same Covent Garden bookseller who bought up the sheets of Barrett's *Magus*. Denley saw in this collection of manuscripts an opportunity for ongoing profit well beyond the sale of the original manuscripts.

Frederick Hockley (1808-1885)

Denley employed the young Frederick Hockley to act as his scribe and proceeded to have each manuscript copied a number of times. In fact so many of these copies were produced, that Hockley referred to them as his 'babes'. In a letter to Major F G Irwin (1823-1898), a fellow enthusiast, dated 18 June 1874 he wrote about one such copy, "*The Complete Book of Magic Science* is I presume from its title one of my particular babes, for at Denley's suggestion I made up the MS from other sources & made him several copies one after another." This is not to denigrate the content, which was copied faithfully enough by Hockley, but to show how it is that so many manuscripts survived. Amongst these manuscripts copied by Hockley was Sibley's copy of the *Lemegeton*.

In the nineteenth century Frederick Hockley tried many practical experiments in skrying and evocation, filling many volumes with the results. One experiment which he published[1] deals with an interesting combination of evocation and skrying. It demonstrates that a glass vessel made to the right size may be just as useful as a crystal for skrying. There is an additional element in this experiment, which is definitely not to be recommended, and that is the addition to the fluid condenser of his own blood.

Henry Dawson Lea

Henry Dawson Lea, not to be confused with Henry Charles Lea (1825-1909) the author of the excellent and massive *Materials Toward a History of Witchcraft* is the next link in the chain. In 1843 Henry Dawson Lea copied the first two books of the *Lemegeton* (including the *Goetia*) from Frederick Hockley's copy of the original manuscript of Ebenezer Sibley. This copy of the *Goetia* which

---

[1] Published in the *Spiritualist*, July 1880, then reprinted in the Theosophist's magazine *Lucifer*, Vol. 6, No. 31, March 1890, and finally in John Hamill, *The Rosicrucian Seer: Magical Writings of Frederick Hockley*, Aquarian, Wellingborough, 1986, pages 129-131.

has been hitherto ignored, finally found its resting place as Wellcome MS 3203.

Although this is rather late in the transmission of the text, we have included footnotes noting all major textual differences between it and our main text. As has already been discussed in our previous two volumes, Hockley was of immense importance in the transmission of a lot of magical material, and we felt it relevant to include the major differences in Lea's version which was copied direct from Hockley's working copy, even though this is relatively late material. In this context our present volume and Joseph Peterson's edition may be seen as complimentary, between them providing as complete a picture as we currently have of the origins and later development of the *Lemegeton.*

The interesting thing about Wellcome MS 3203 is that it leaves out 18 demons (from Leriac/Leraje to Foras inclusive) suggesting that some manuscript pages were missed from the Sibley/Hockley manuscript. One of the copyists ignored these 18, failed to number one at all (Beleth), and subsequently renumbered the rest of the demons, numbering the last one as 53 instead of the 54 which were present out of 72. The fact that exactly 18 demons are missing suggests that maybe three groups of 6 are missing. If this is so then the original manuscript (wherever that is) might have been paginated with 6 demons per page, or twelve pages in all, suggesting a division of the demons into the 12 signs of the Zodiac. If there was such an arrangement, it might have meant that the copyist omitted exactly three pages, the demons for Gemini, Cancer and Leo.

Also Wellcome MS 3203 only contains the first two parts of the *Lemegeton,* though reference is made to the supposed fifth part, the *'Ars Nota' (sic),* suggesting that originally all five parts existed in the original that this copy descends from. Although it is a defective copy, it is useful because it is bound with the 72 angels which are a key part of the system omitted from many other manuscripts. This also helps to demonstrate that Rudd was not alone in connecting the 72 angels directly with the 72 demons.

The manuscript also contains a transcript of a Goetic "Experiment of me J.W.[1] with the Spirits Birto, Agares, Baalphares & Vassago as hath often been proved at the Instant request of Edward the Fourth King of England" (who reigned 1461-1483). Assuming for a moment that this is true, and that the original manuscript recorded a real event, then some of the spirits of the *Goetia* were being conjured in the fifteenth century, for the pleasure of the then reigning monarch.

---

[1] It would be more than interesting if 'J.W.' turned out to be Johann Weir, but unlikely.

MacGregor Mathers (1854-1918)

S L MacGregor Mathers was the scholar-magician and Golden Dawn co-founder, who translated and published a number of important grimoires including *The Key of Solomon* and the *Book of Abramelin the Mage.* He drew attention to the importance of the *Lemegeton* towards the end of the nineteenth century. As far as we know he only transcribed the *Goetia,* the first book of the *Lemegeton,* as his notes tail off at the end of the *Goetia* with just a few diagrams (for example the Spirit Compass Rose) derived from the next book of the *Lemegeton.* Mathers was certainly very interested in the practical side of Goetic magic. When Aleister Crowley was refused advancement by the London lodge of the Golden Dawn, he went to see Mathers in person in Paris. Wisely or not, Mathers appointed him as his representative, and presumably authorised him to enter the lodge premises in London.

Aleister Crowley (1875-1947)

In April 1900, during his 'raid' on the Golden Dawn's headquarters in Blythe Road, Hammersmith, West London, Crowley 'acquired' various papers including the manuscript of the *Goetia,* as transcribed by Mathers. In fact Mathers' work on the manuscript was incomplete, as it incorporated a small part of the next book of the *Lemegeton,* and some quite unrelated Punic and Carthaginian symbols, which were not part of the *Goetia* at all, but just some of Mathers' research doodlings.

Aleister Crowley published Mathers' transcription of the *Goetia* in 1904 with redrawn sigils. Crowley's only contributions to the work were peripheral, and had very little to do with the *Goetia* itself. Crowley would have done a much greater service to the text if he had checked it against the manuscript and conscientiously completed Mathers' editing, but instead he just arranged to print it, adding various extraneous items. It would have been kinder to the reader if he had made it clear where these various extraneous elements included in 'his' edition of the *Goetia* actually came from. This material included:

i) A table of demon names entitled 'After the Hebrew of Dr. Rudd'. This consisted of the Hebrew orthography for the 72 demon names taken from each of the seals in the present manuscript.

ii) Extraneous diagrams. Various 'Punic' or Carthaginian symbols which have little if anything to do with the *Goetia.* They were printed out of order and mixed with genuine sigils. These were Mathers' very speculative notes on the origin of the Seal of Solomon and are numbered as illustrations 162-174 in Crowley's edition. In addition his illustrations 175-184 come from the first few pages of the *Theurgia-Goetia,* without any note to that effect, or even any corresponding text.

iii) A nasty Greek curse directed against Mathers[1]. It seems particularly childish of Crowley to print a curse against the very man who did the actual work of transcribing the *Goetia,* unless Crowley feared Mathers' revenge for his own wholesale appropriation of Mathers' copyright and work. This curse is accompanied by one of the incomplete squares taken, incredibly, from the *Book of Abramelin,* which was also translated by Mathers.

iv) The square drawn from the *Book of Abramelin.* The square is only partial and defectively drawn, but has nothing to do with the *Goetia.* On the basis of a quote from Crowley's autobiography this square has been identified as a magical square 'intended to prevent improper use of the book', but in Mathers' edition of *Abramelin* its purpose is 'to hinder any Necromantic or Magical Operations from taking effect…to undo any magic soever.'

This is interesting, as it suggests that Crowley either wanted to void all the magic made available in the *Goetia,* or to protect himself from an anticipated magical attack by Mathers. In fact the truth is a little more prosaic, for in the more complete German version of *Abramelin,* the square is simply designed to help the operator find rare astronomical books, although that is something that Crowley could not have known at the time.

v) A pompous Preface with Rosicrucian overtones which concludes with 'given forth from our Mountain of A[biegnus] this day of C[orpus] C[hristi] 1903 A. D.' which gives a spurious Rosicrucian imprimatur for Crowley's appropriation of Mathers' work. To imply that a work of evocation is a Rosicrucian official publication is even more confusing.[2] This Preface was written by Crowley, and contributes nothing to our understanding of the *Goetia.*

vi) The 'Preliminary Invocation' often referred to as the 'Bornless One'. Whilst this is a valuable and effective invocation, it does not occur in any manuscript of the *Goetia.* It is from a completely different tradition, of Graeco-Egyptian origin, and so has no place in this edition. This invocation (it was in fact an exorcism) is drawn from Charles Wycliffe Goodwin's (1817-1878) paper for the Cambridge Antiquarian Society, 1853, called *Fragment of a*

---

[1] A rough translation of this curse is as follows: "I call upon you, the Spirit of the void, terrible, invisible, omnipotent god, bringer of decay and desolation, you who hate an upstanding house, you who have come out of Egypt and the lands without. You are called the all-conquering and never defeated. I call upon you, Typhon, Seth, in fulfilment of your prophecies, in that I call you by your true name, whereby you cannot disobey Ioerbeth, Iopakerbeth, Iobolchoseth, Iopatathnax, Iosoro, Ioneboutosoualeth, Aktiophi, Ereschigal, Nebopooaleth, Aberamenthoou, Lerthexanax, Ethreluoth, Nemareba, Aemina, come altogether unto me and march and overthrow the terrible Mathers. With trembling and fire he has done injustice to a man, and has spilt his blood for his own pleasure. For this purpose I make these things known publicly."

[2] Although it is true that Rudd prefaced his work with some Rosicrucian sentiments, the *Goetia* is definitely not a Rosicrucian work. Rudd was friends with John Heydon who was promoting the Rosicrucian cause at the same time.

Græco-Egyptian Work upon Magic.[1] It was a favourite of Golden Dawn members especially Crowley, but it has nothing to do with the *Goetia*, being separated from it by at least 1500 years and a wide cultural gap.

vii) Crowley's essay 'The Initiated Interpretation of Ceremonial Magic.' This contains many of his tongue-in-cheek statements about evocation, including the ludicrous suggestion that, following Aldous Huxley, "the spirits of the Goetia are portions of the human brain". What makes this even more alarming is that Crowley undoubtedly knew the difference between the brain and the mind. He goes on to say that "Ceremonial Magic fines down, then, to a series of minute, though of course empirical, physiological experiments." The essay is hopefully a piece of over-rationalisation, and a product of its period, rather than what Crowley really thought. Instead of improving on Mathers' work, Crowley's tongue in cheek exposition of ceremonial magic has confused many generations of sincere students ever since, who in adhering to this very materialistic explanation of the phenomena of evocation have missed out on its true essence.

viii) The 'Explanation of Certain Names Used in this Book Lemegeton'. This does in fact occur in one manuscript of the *Goetia*, Sloane MS 2731, but is in another hand. As originally printed by Crowley (and in all subsequent printed editions) it is nonsense. This is because the text was transcribed by Mathers *across* the page when in fact it was originally written as two separate columns *down* the page. See Appendix 9, the *'Ars Nova': An Explanation of Certain Names used in the Figures of the Goetia,* where we have transcribed it in the original order. If it is read in this order it makes perfect sense, and will be seen to be a set of summary notes, listing Godnames, archangel and angel names, plus a prayer for each of the Sephiroth of the Tree of Life. It also lists the words used on the diagrams of the Circle, Triangle, Hexagram, and Pentagram. However, as transcribed by Mathers/Crowley, it reads like a set of nonsense definitions.

ix) A Compass Rose with the names of 31 spirits on it (see Figure 10). This does not belong to the *Goetia* at all, but is in fact an illustration which belongs to the next book, the *Theurgia-Goetia.* It was included in Mathers' notebook where he had begun his transcription of the next book of the *Theurgia-Goetia,* before breaking off without completing it, and should therefore have been edited out by Crowley. As it stands it is completely misleading, as none of the spirit names on the compass rose diagram coincide with any of those in the *Goetia*, something that has also confused generations of students ever since.

x) 'Yse Conjuratiouns of ye Booke Goetia'. This is pseudo black letter

[1] This has been retranslated in Hans Betz, *The Greek Magical Papyri in Translation*, University of Chicago, Chicago, 1992, page 103.

'translation' into Enochian of the original Goetia invocations. This translation into Enochian was presumably just an intellectual exercise rather than anything to be used ritually, unless like Trithemius, Crowley was experimenting with converting plain English into a more cryptic form before addressing the spirits.

xi) Crowley chose to introduce that translation exercise with a pompous self congratulatory passage written in execrable *faux* early English, claiming for himself exalted Rosicrucian membership, 'Yse Conjuratiouns...rendered into ye Magicall or Angelike (*sic*) Language by our Illustrious and ever-Glorious Frater, ye Wise Perdurabo [Crowley], that Myghtye Chiefe of ye Rosy-Cross Fraternitye, now sepulchred in ye Vault of ye Collegium S.S.'

Earlier in the same book Crowley ironically quotes A E Waite as saying 'all persons who proclaim themselves to be *Rosicrucians* are simply members of pseudo-fraternities.' Just so.

Arthur Edward Waite (1857 – 1942)

Indeed Waite himself also published a version of the *Goetia* before Crowley in 1898. Waite was one of the most prolific occult writers of this period. His collections of grimoire material tended to synthesise the procedures of many of the grimoires, drawing variously on the *Key of Solomon*, the *Grimorium Verum*, the *Fourth Book of Occult Philosophy*, and the derivative *Black Pullet*, or *Poulet Noir*, rather than simply publishing complete grimoires. Rather strangely, Waite suggested that Rudd was an invention or *alter ego* of Peter Smart the scribe who copied the present manuscript. As we have seen, Dr Thomas Rudd was a very real person, who knew Dee, published two books on geometry, did a considerable amount of magical research, and who was not just an invention of Peter Smart.

Other Modern Editions of the Goetia

Other editions of the *Goetia* are listed in Joseph Peterson's introduction, where he outlines their respective virtues and defects. They include the disgraceful rip off of the Mathers/Crowley edition by de Lawrence. In 1957 Sayed Idries Shah brought out his *Secret Lore of Magic*, which for three decades was perhaps the best source of grimoire material. In France, Pierre Belfond also produced editions of many of the main grimoires, but not of the *Goetia*.

Editions of the *Goetia* were produced by Nelson and Anne White (1979) and Mitch Henson (1999). Steve Savedow wrote a very hands-on book called *Goetic Evocation* (1996) in which he looks at the Kabbalistic and practical considerations of using this text, with many tables and interesting experimental records.[1]

Bill Breeze, under the style of Hymenaeus Beta, published yet another edition

[1] Steve Savedow, *Goetic Evocation: The Magician's Workbook*, Volume 2, Eschaton, 1996.

of the *Goetia* in 1995, based on Crowley's edition with additional material on the Preliminary Invocation. The last part of his introduction is useful as it helps put recent work into perspective. His edition is adorned with a mix of a few rather ugly and phallic drawings by Crowley, plus amusing engravings of Goetic demons taken from Colin de Plancy's *Dictionnaire Infernal*. His tabular catalogue of demons at the end follows the night and day Decan categorisation of the Golden Dawn. Presumably out of deference to Crowley he also included a corrected version of the latter's strained rendering of the *Goetia* invocations in Enochian.

Carroll Runyon

Carroll Runyon is a science fiction writer, and 'gentleman of the old school', who was a friend of the late Lin Carter, the fantasy writer. Carter produced the first of many *Necronomicon* grimoire hoaxes, and he originally introduced the *Goetia* to Carroll Runyon. As a result of experimenting with it, Runyon developed very specific and relevant views on the techniques therein. His take on the *Goetia* has been to:

a) utilise the 72 Shem ha-Mephorash angels to control the 72 demons, an approach derived from the Rudd manuscript here transcribed.

b) array the demons in a straightforward circular format, divided according to the 12 Zodiacal signs, rather than arranging them in the rather forced Golden Dawn decanal arrangement.

c) re-introduce skrying into the procedures of *Goetic* magic. Instead of the traditional Crystal or Glass Receptacle he uses a candle flanked mirror.

d) locate the Triangle of Art as outside the circle, at waist level.

e) relate the Goetic demons to the pre-Solomonic Baal-Astarte mythos. As a result of the last change he also swapped the demons Astaroth and Stolas, in an effort to have Astaroth facing directly opposite his ancient Canaanite consort Bael/Baal.

The first three of these interpretations coincide with the views of the present authors, and with established practice. The use of adversarial angels to control the demons dates back beyond Blaise Vigenère in the mid-sixteenth century, to the third century CE *Testament of Solomon*. The attribution of the demons in order (six at a time) round a circle corresponding with the 12 Zodiacal signs (beginning with Aries), is definitely in harmony with the *Goetia*, following the similar Compass Rose layout in the *Theurgia-Goetia*.

Skrying would typically have been used in conjunction with Goetic evocation. However the skryer's crystal or glass receptacle would always have been on the Table of Practice *within* the Circle, not outside the Circle as in Carroll Runyon's *modus operandi*. The Table of Practice was engraved or painted with similar holy signs to the Circle, and it was considered as safe a place to conjure the image of the spirit as the Triangle external to the Circle. In fact many conjurations often specified both *loci* as acceptable places for the spirit to manifest.

This procedure, and indeed the correct use of a Table of Practice (as used by Dr John Dee), has been lost sight of in the last century. Carroll Runyon's deduction that the Triangle should be elevated to waist height is only relevant if you do not utilise the traditional position of the skrying glass, which is within the Circle on the Table of Practice. His interpretation of the position of the Triangle comes from a plausible reading of the caption adjacent to the illustration of the Triangle in Sloane MS 2731, where it says:

> "The triangle that Salomon Commanded the Disobedient Spirits Into; it is to be Made 2 foot off from the Circle, and 3 foot over. Note, this Δ [triangle] is to be Placed upon the Co[a]st [that] the Spirit Belongeth [to]; &c."

In this context 'over' means 'across' not 'above', just as the word 'coast' in that period meant the 'edge' of the circle. The instruction is that the Triangle needs to be on the side from which the spirit is expected to come. It is no use calling in the wrong direction, or in having your back to the spirit/demon when it arrives. The Triangle should be 2 feet away from the Circle, and be 3 feet in size to accommodate the manifestation. There may be some room to argue about this, but with the crystal located on the Table of Practice within the Circle, the need to elevate the Triangle, for visibility, no longer exists.

In the same chapter, Carroll Runyon suggests that Peter Smart's drawing of the Brass Vessel (Figure 5) is the back of a Magic Mirror. This is a misconception which has arisen because of its superficial similarity to the back of an old fashioned music stand. This idea can be dispelled by a close inspection of the Hebrew wording on its surface and the seal on its top.

The interpretation of several of the demon's names in the light of Canaanite mythology may well be correct, as many of the spirit names are derived from Hebrew or Aramaic. But it is a bold step to suggest that this applies to the rest of the 72 demons.

Carroll Runyon's book on the *Goetia* is a breath of fresh air and a significant advance in our rediscovery of practical grimoire technique. In the same vein, Joseph Lisiewski's *Ceremonial Magic* examines the practical constraints of evocation, but solely in the context of Peter de Abano's *Heptameron*. Given that the *Heptameron* was the source of the conjurations in the *Goetia*, there is considerable relevance here also.

Joseph Peterson

It was not till the publication of the excellent edition of the *Lemegeton* by Joseph Peterson in 2001 that Crowley's partial and defective edition has finally been eclipsed. Peterson's edition is now the standard edition.

Theurgia-Goetia

The *Theurgia-Goetia* is concerned with spirits of a mixed nature which relate to the points of the compass. It is effectively a ritual version of the first book of the *Steganographia,* which was written or compiled by Trithemius in 1500. One of the most striking things about this grimoire is its insistence upon direction. The *Goetia* suggests that you face the Triangle of Art which should be placed on the side (or the 'coast') of the Circle from which you expect the spirit to arrive, but it is a bit vague about where that should be for most spirits. The *Theurgia-Goetia* on the other hand gives precise compass points for each main spirit (and their servitors). For example, Camuel "Ruleth and governeth as King in the South East part of the World" or the South-East, but Padiel "Ruleth in the East and by South" which literally means that he rules the compass point just a bit South of East, not SE.

Some manuscripts of the *Theurgia-Goetia* supply a full blown spirit Compass Rose showing the 32 possible directions from which a King, Prince or Duke can be expected to arrive. This is an advance on the rather rudimentary and incomplete compass that appears in the printed *Steganographia.* Strangely, although one of the manuscripts of the *Steganographia*[1] shows 16 compass segments with the names of directions (shown as winds) and the 16 Dukes all shown in their proper places, the printed edition only has an incomplete illustration with just three of the 16 Dukes actually filled in. The present manuscript does not include this illustration at all, but that deficiency is made up from another manuscript (and it appears in Figure 10) and by Tables in Appendix 2.

There is a strict hierarchy of spirits ruled by four Emperors (Caspiel, Carnesial, Amenadiel and Demoriel) which correspond with the four Cardinal points (S, E, W, and N, see Table M21). Then the 16 Dukes, correspond to the four Cardinal points (as with the Emperors), plus the four inter-Cardinal points (SE, SW, NW, NE) plus the 8 'Cardinal-flanking' directions (those immediately adjacent to the Cardinal points like Padiel at 'East by South' or Cabariel at 'North by West') for which see Table M20.

Lastly, the 11 Wandering Princes fill in the remaining points of the compass in a complex system of rulership pairing - see Table M20a. Each of the 31 principle spirits in turn rule between 10 and 50 lesser spirits (which in the case of the Dukes' spirits are further divided into rulership by either Day or Night). This structure is not immediately visible upon first reading, so we have inserted section heads in square brackets. The grimoire, whilst stating the number of lesser spirits ruled, actually only lists the names and seals of a small subset of these, which as it says "should be sufficient for practice".

[1] National Library of Scotland Adv. MS 18.8.12.

Practice

Strangely, in all manuscripts the actual method of invocation is sandwiched into a section of text just after Pamersiel, one of the 16 Dukes, rather than appearing logically at the front. Also the order of the spirits in the *Theurgia-Goetia* differs from that in the *Steganographia*. This suggests that there has been at some point a dislocation of the text. The description of the method varies from one manuscript to another. In order to get a picture of exactly how the procedure should be conducted, we have made a composite below from the instructions to be found in various manuscripts so that all the salient points are in one place. We have retained all the instructions in the order given.

> "To call forth Pamersiel, or any of his Servants, or indeed any of the spirits of the *Theurgia-Goetia*, make a Circle in the form as is shown in the Book *Goetia* forgathering in the upper room of your house, which is most private or secret. Or choose a place in some island wood or grove which is the most occult or hidden place removed from all comers and goers, so that no stranger may chance by that way, or enter your chamber or wherever you choose to do the operation. Observe that the place is very airy because these spirits that are in this part [of the *Theurgia-Goetia*] are all of the air.
>
> You may then call the spirits into a Crystal stone four Inches in diameter, set on a Table [of Practice] made as followeth which is called the secret Table of Solomon, having the seal of the Spirit on your breast and the girdle [of lion skin] about your waist as is showed in the Book *Goetia*, and you cannot err.
>
> The form of the Table [of Practice] is thus, as this present figure doth here represent and show.
>
> When you are thus prepared, rehearse the Conjuration several times, that is whilst the Spirit is coming, for without doubt he will come. Note the same method is to be used in all the following parts of the second book *Theurgia Goetia*, as is here shown for Pamersiel and his servants. It is also the same method for Calling forth the four Kings [Emperors] and their Servants aforesaid."

Immediately after this passage, there is an illustration that purports to be the Secret Table of [Practice] of Solomon. In most manuscripts it is a very hastily drawn and crude Secret Seal of Solomon (Figure 11).[1] This is in fact incorrect, and it is also in conflict with the illustration shown in the preceding book the *Goetia* where the Secret Seal of Solomon is correctly shown (Figure 18, Plate 2).[2] The illustration that should appear here is the Table of Practice of Solomon (Figure 12)[3] from the *Art Pauline*. This is further confirmed by comparing it with the Table of Practice found in other grimoires, and especially Dee's *Tabula Sancta cum Tabulis Enochi* (see Appendix 3).

---

[1] See also Peterson, *ibid*, page 66.
[2] See also Peterson, *ibid*, page 45.
[3] See also Peterson, *ibid*, page 111.

Cryptography or Sorcery?

Many scholars have debated whether the *Steganographia* is a book of angel magic or a cryptographic book. From references in some of Trithemius' letters and from using the system, we would like to make a new suggestion as to what Trithemius' real intentions were. On the surface he purports to show how to send secret messages, via the agency of the angels to distant friends, purporting to be a sort of a 'spirit telephone'. Without doubt the *Steganographia* is this, as well as being a cryptographic book, and a book of angel magic: in fact it is precisely all three.

We believe that the key to understanding the *Steganographia* is to know that the messages that were encoded to be sent by Trithemius' 'spirit telephone' were not meant for any human recipients.[1] The messages were meant to be sent *to* the angel concerned, not just *by* the angel, and were not really intended for human recipients at all. The message is reduced cryptographically before being sent, as part of the magical technique itself.

There is much secrecy in magic about putting the exact request or demand to the spirit or angel. Such requests have in the past been addressed in English, Latin, Hebrew or even in Enochian, with varying opinions as to which language is the most effective. Here Trithemius addresses the angels in a cryptographic code. There is no human 'friend' at the other end. The magician faces the quarter of the angel, invokes the angel and submits his request, demand or prayer in code on a piece of paper to the spirit. The mental effort involved in encoding it is part of the magical procedure. This request is what the magician wants the spirit to accomplish. As simple as that - there is no human messenger - there is no human recipient.

Indeed when you examine the conjurations within the *Steganographia* you will see that hidden within them are the names of some of the Duke's servitors who are actually required to do the actual task. See for example Parmersiel in Tables M20 for the names of his servitor spirits, and match them with the invocations. Although these spirits are listed with their directions and seals in the *Theurgia-Goetia*, the corresponding conjurations from the *Steganographia* are missing from the *Theurgia-Goetia*, so we have re-inserted them in each case.

Blaise de Vigenère, who was a cryptographer and magician, also understood why these invocations to angels might need to be encoded. But why go to such trouble? The answer may be found in the work of a modern magician,

---

[1] Further to the use of the *Steganographia* as a 'spirit telephone', Michel Scot recommends his readers attach by a cord to his copy of the *Liber Consecrationis* a paper or parchment sheet with the names of the questioned demon and its functions written upon it, when making a request, in order for there no mistake in the demonic recipient. Here the objective is quite clearly to communicate with the spirit.

Austin Osman Spare who understood that by sigilising or encoding his requests he was better able to convey them to the spiritual creatures which would then accomplish them. Spare did not however take into account the specific names of the angels or entities to be addressed, the timing, or the direction in which to address them.

All *three* things may need to be in place before this particular system works:

a) sigilisation or cryptographic conversion of the message or request

b) correct direction faced - divided into 32 possible directions

c) time - divided into 12 hours of the day and 12 hours of the night

This paradigm or formulation of the magical technique of the *Steganographia* as it is used and embodied in the *Theurgia-Goetia* provides a useful way of seeing just how the books of the *Lemegeton* relate to each other, so that:

a) The *Steganographia* upon which were based the *Theurgia-Goetia* and the *Art Pauline [Book 1]* is concerned with cryptographia, and the way communication is to be addressed to the spirits or angels.

b) The *Theurgia-Goetia* is concerned with direction, as it even opens with the diagram of a spirit Compass Rose.

c) The *Art Pauline [Book 1]* has spirits which are assigned to specific hours of the night and the day. Time here is the key.

Finally the angels of the *Art Pauline [Book 2]* are assigned to the 360 degrees of the Zodiac, which combines both time and direction.

In Western magic the planetary hours have always been of prime importance, and they are stressed in almost every grimoire, such as *The Key of Solomon*. Now we can see that direction is also very important. In Chinese Taoist sorcery the key is found in the compass direction associated with the correct timing. Chinese Taoist magicians express this knowledge by saying that just for a small time frame, a secret door or 門 *'men'* opens, and at that time communication can be made between this world and the other, or even that things can pass from one world to the other.[1] One practical use of this knowledge is in the materialisation and de-materialisation of things and entities, which is a classic phenomenon that is often perceived as magic.

Such ideas have survived in the West in stories of children being spirited away to fairy realms, or in folk memories of the magical significance of thresholds, and the idea of doors opening into fairyland or the underworld for a short

---

[1] It is probably just a coincidence that this Chinese character for 'door' resembles the Egyptian hieroglyph for 'god', or *neter*. Or to be more precise, it resembles two such hieroglyphs facing each other as if mirrored across a threshold.

period of time at specific times and at specific places. Even the plot of *Alice in Wonderland*, which was on Aleister Crowley's recommended reading list, recalls this idea. Algernon Blackwood in one of his delightful stories also glimpsed a part of this method in his story of the recluse who was obsessed with the geometry of his room. Much of this knowledge has however been lost in the West. Of course it is spoken of in very general terms by saying that at Halloween the 'veil is thinned', so the concept of opening a door has not been completely lost. But the technology for finding that door, and of its application on a day by day basis, is no longer commonly available. Traces of this technology is however still present in the *Lemegeton*.

There is a branch of Chinese metaphysics, allied with feng shui, which deals with these doors. It is called *Chi Men Tun Chia* (or *Qi Men Dun Jia*), and it still contains a detailed knowledge of these techniques, which have sadly just become a folk memory in the West.[1] Virtually none of these detailed techniques are presently available outside of the Chinese language, where there exists an extensive and well documented literature.

So you can see that the system is a lot more complex than the simple layout of the *Steganographia* or its lineal descendants the *Theurgia-Goetia* and *Art Pauline* [Book 1] would suggest.

Note that some of the primary conjurations are missing from the *Theurgia-Goetia* both in Rudd and in Joseph Peterson's edition of the *Lemegeton* but we have supplied a sample of them in Appendix 1 from Sloane MS 3824.

The Pauline Art

The *Pauline Art* was reputedly delivered to the Apostle Paul at Corinth. This is of course a fictional attribution and relies simply upon the legend of St Paul ascending into heaven which will be found in the *Epistles*, where he speaks about himself in the third person:[2]

> 2. "I knew a man in Christ above fourteen years ago, (whether in the body, I cannot tell; or whether out of the body, I cannot tell: God knoweth;) such an one [was] caught up to the third heaven…
>
> 3. And I knew such a man, (whether in the body, or out of the body, I cannot tell: God knoweth;)
>
> 4. How that he was caught up into paradise, and heard unspeakable words, which it is not lawful for a man to utter."

It is commonly supposed that St Paul was talking about himself in the third person, and the account of his visions in these heavens also occurs in the Nag

[1] It is for that reason that a basic Chinese compass, or *lo p'an*, is included in the second edition of *The Complete Magician's Tables*, Llewellyn, Woodbury, 2006.

[2] In 2 *Corinthians* 12:2-4.

Hammadi *Apocalypse of Paul*:

> "Then the Holy [Spirit] who was speaking with [him] caught him up on high to the third heaven, and he passed beyond to the fourth [heaven]. The Holy [Spirit] spoke to him, saying, 'Look and see your [body] upon the earth.' And he [looked] down and saw those [who were upon] the earth...
>
> But I saw in the fourth heaven according to class [hierarchy] – I saw the angels resembling gods, the angels bringing a soul out of the land of the dead. They placed it [the soul] at the gate of the fourth heaven. And the angels were whipping it. The soul spoke, saying, 'What sin was it that I committed in the world?'...
>
> When the soul heard these things, it gazed downwards in sorrow. And then it gazed upward. It was cast down. The soul that had been cast down [went] to [a] body which had been prepared [for it]...
>
> Then as I [went], the gate opened, [and] I went up to the fifth [heaven]..."[1]

St Paul visits all the traditional Kabbalistic seven heavens plus the Ogdoad (eighth), ninth and tenth heavens. This gave St. Paul the reputation of being able to travel to the heavens and converse with the angels, so the 'Pauline Art' is seen as an extension of these abilities. This passage also throws an interesting sidelight on the acceptance of reincarnation by early Christianity.

However St Paul's celestial travels have little to do with the *Pauline Art* beyond its title. Nor is the grimoire that old, although it certainly dates back at least to the late fifteenth century, as it was mentioned by Agrippa. A copy is also to be found in a sixteenth century Latin manuscript in the Bibliothèque Nationale, according to Robert Turner.[2]

The *Pauline Art* divides into two sections, which are sufficiently different for them to be really counted as two distinct books.

Pauline Art [Book I]

The first part of the *Pauline Art* gives the 24 angels corresponding to the hours of the day and the hours of the night (see Table M22). This part as we have seen is directly derived from Book 2 of Trithemius' *Steganographia*. Right at the beginning of the grimoire is the very significant 'Table of Practice' (see Figure 12) which parallels all such Tables of Practice, including Dr Dee's *Tabula Sancta* (see Appendix 3). The Table of Practice was effectively the design which was placed on the central table or altar which supported the skrying Crystal or Glass Receptacle. It was typically designed as either a hexagram (six pointed) or a seven pointed star. Integral with that were 7

---

[1] James Robinson [editor], "The Apocalypse of Paul" in *The Nag Hammadi Library*, Harper, San Francisco, 1990, pages 257-259.

[2] Bibliothèque Nationale MS 7170A.

separate seals representing the 7 Planets, located at the vertices of the heptagram, or at the vertices and the centre (Sun) of the hexagram. These seals can be part of the design or seven separate and moveable sigils. It has been suggested that you lay your hand upon the relevant seal which rules the operation whilst invoking.

Pauline Art [Book II]

The second part of the *Pauline Art* gives the angels ruling each of the 360 degrees of the 12 signs of the Zodiac. An angel is ascribed rulership of each degree of the Zodiacal circle. It is interesting that Peter of Abano also gives magical images for each of the 360 degrees, which again associates the author of the *Heptameron* with the sources of the *Lemegeton*.

These spirits are sometimes referred to as the *monomoirai*. At least two Gnostic sects, the Phibionites (a sect infamous for its sacramental view of sex and allegedly lewd practices) and the Marcosians (a Valentinian Gnostic sect) revered the *monomoirai*, or spirits of the single degrees of the ecliptic. These are quite likely to have been the forerunners of the spirits tabulated in the *Pauline Art [Book II]*. These spirits could of course also be associated with the 360 days of the Egyptian year (the remaining 5 days were put aside for religious celebrations).

The Art Almadel

This book is very interesting as the *Art Almadel* deals with the conjuration of angels using a wax tablet, and with the Angels of the 'Four Altitudes' or Ayres. All these elements are later to be found in the skrying practice of Dr John Dee and Edward Kelley in the 1580s. Dee was to refer to the 30 Ayres or Aethyres, so the term was a common one. The *Art Almadel* dates back at least to the late fifteenth century as it was mentioned by Agrippa. According to Turner a copy of it can also be found in a fifteenth century manuscript in Florence.[1] Its techniques derived from the techniques of Jewish angel magic as shown in manuscripts like the *Temunoth ha-Almadel*, תמונת האלמדל[2] and the Hebrew *Sepher Maphteah Shelomoh*.[3]

A manuscript in the British Library credits Christoforo Cattaneo, a Genovese, with being its inventor, or 'l'inventore de detti Almadel Arabico'.[4] Cattan was famous for his very influential geomancy published in French in 1558 and in English in 1591, and the English edition would certainly have been known to John Dee. However as the *Almadel* was known before Cattan was born, he

[1] Florence MS II-iii-24.
[2] British Library Oriental MS 6360.
[3] Hermann Gollancz, *Sepher Maphteah Shelomoh*, Oxford University Press, London, 1914.
[4] Additional MS 8790.

must simply be seen as a link in the chain of transmission.

Arab magicians have always known that the *al-Mandal* or 'magical circle' was a necessary protection in dealing with spirits or demons.[1] It is tempting to think that the name of this book came from the Arabic for 'magic circle', but strangely the particular procedure used in this grimoire is not one that mentions the magic Circle. Of course the Circle of Art might simply have been taken for granted by the author who here simply concentrates on the equipment on the Table of Practice.

The *Notory Art* or *Ars Notoria*

This book was written before 1236 as it was mentioned by Michael Scot on that date. The earliest manuscript we are aware of is a parchment in the Mellon Collection, Yale University Library, MS. 1 which is dated circa 1225. The *Ars Notoria* is not, as many people think, 'the notorious art' but is named after the magical diagrams, or *notae* which are a key part of its method.

The aim of the *Ars Notoria* was to use such *notae* to both prompt memory, and to provide a scheme that would induce a rapid understanding in the operator of any particular art or science. It is easy to imagine eager students using this art as an aid to cramming or absorbing the essence of a subject. In a time of few books the ability to understand the groundplan of a subject or memorise whole chunks of material was highly prized and indeed a necessary skill of the scholar. Knowledge was literally defined as how much you knew or could remember. By about the seventeenth century, and certainly in the twentieth century, knowledge was redefined as the ability to find specific information from the huge range of available books. In the twenty-first century knowledge may be redefined as the art of using the net and Google most effectively to find that same information. But in the Middle Ages, the ability to memorise, absorb and organise material was paramount. It is precisely for that purpose the *Ars Notoria* was devised. Its methods promised the student that, with the memorisation of certain very elaborate diagrams accompanied by the correct prayers, whole subjects could be rapidly absorbed.

This method of this book, which was often (but not always) included in the magical procedures of the *Lemegeton,* relied upon the aid of spirits or angels in achieving these scholarly ends more rapidly. As Robert Turner so aptly explains:[2]

> "The *Ars Notoria,* the magical art of memory, flourished during the Middle Ages, although its origins are attributed to Solomon and Apollonius of Tyana.

[1] Sayed Idries Shah, *Oriental Magic*, Rider, London, 1956, page 83.

[2] The twentieth century Robert Turner in his book *Elizabethan Magic,* not his namesake who originally translated this book into English in 1657.

> It is a process by which the magician could instantly gain knowledge or memory of all the arts and sciences... To set the process into operation, the appropriate *notae* were contemplated whilst reciting angelic names and magical orisons [prayers]."

Its attribution to Solomon gives it a reason for being included in the *Lemegeton.* There was some question about the morality of using angels rather than the labour of honest study, but in practice most students would use this art as an aid rather than an end in itself. If you like, it was the more technically advanced equivalent of a prayer to help you pass exams. Nowadays prayers are seen as freeform supplications and request lists, but the *Ars Notoria,* like the other grimoires in the *Lemegeton* made a much more precise technology out of it. Indeed if you examine some of the more recent New Age success orientated, positive thinking, 'pray to get your own way' books you can see that there is trend back towards a formalisation of such requests. The *Ars Notoria* had such procedures taped almost 800 years ago, but only for worthy and studious objectives, not the cars, money, love and career dreams of the present century.

The key to the procedure were the beautiful *notae.* Sadly all printed editions of the *Ars Notoria* are missing these essential ingredients.[1] Some of the *notae* were abstract, but some were like summary sheets for the subject. For example the *notae* for Grammar shows the 9 parts of speech in circles, and the *notae* of Geometry shows the line, triangle, square, pentagram, six pointed star and circle in order. However those *notae* which appear in some manuscripts[2] are much more like large disordered sigils than organised subject outlines.

John Dee had at least two manuscript copies of the *Ars Notoria* in his library, as did Robert Fludd and Ben Jonson. The *Ars Notoria* was also mentioned by Trithemius who also makes a claim that "he had written a book giving an occult method by which a person totally ignorant of Latin could learn in an hour's time to write anything he wished in that language", indeed a book with very similar objectives to the *Ars Notoria* .[3] Going back even further, the *Ars Notoria* was also mentioned by Peter de Abano,[4] whose contribution to the invocations of the *Goetia* has already been noted.

---

[1] See Turin, Biblioteca Nazionale MS E. V.13 and Paris, Bibliothèque Nationale MS Lat. 9336. Some of these *notae* are reproduced in black and white versions in Fanger, Claire [ed]. *Conjuring Spirits: Texts and Traditions of Medieval Ritual Magic,* Pennsylvania State UP, 1998, pages 114, 116, 120, 122, 127-131, where they are discussed at some length.

[2] Such as Bibliothèque Nationale MS lat. 9336.

[3] Thorndike, *History of Magic and Experimental Science*, Volume VI, Columbia, 1941, page 439.

[4] In his brilliant *Conciliator* and also in his *Lucidator.*

William Lilly (1602-1681), the astrologer, had a copy of the *Ars Notoria*:[1]

> "One whole year [1633-1634] and more I continued a widower, and followed my studies [in astrology and magic] very hard; during which time a scholar pawned unto me, for forty shillings, *Ars Notoria*, (a)[2] a large volume wrote in parchment, with the names of those angels, and their pictures, which are thought and believed by wise men, to teach and instruct in all the several liberal sciences, and is attained by observing elected times, and those prayers appropriated unto the several angels.
>
> I do ingenuosly acknowledge, I used those prayers according to the form and direction prescribed for some weeks, using the word astrologia for astronomia..."

It is interesting that Lilly mentions "their pictures" by which he probably meant the *notae*. As the *notae* are missing from Rudd's manuscript, we decided not to include the *Ars Notoria* in this volume, preferring to issue it in a more complete form at a later date, properly supported by a full set of *notae*. Most manuscript copies of this period, although obviously not Lilly's, are taken from Robert Turner's printed version of 1657 which is also lacking the *notae*.

The rationale for the *Ars Notoria* being Solomonic comes from the introduction to the whole *Lemegeton* which is found in several manuscripts including Sloane MS 3648. Strangely this description does not occur in our present manuscript despite the fact that the manuscript actually contains an *Ars Notoria*.

> "The fifth part is a Booke of orations and prayers that wise Solomon used upon the alter in the Temple [in Jerusalem] which is called *Artem Novam* [part of the *Ars Notoria*] The which was revealed to Salomon by the holy angel of God called Michael, and he also received many breef Notes [hence *Notae*] written by the finger of God which was declared to him by the said Angel, with Thunder claps, without which Notes [King] Salomon had never obtained to his great knowledge, for by them in [a] short time he knew all arts and sciences both good and bad which from these Notes [*Notae*] is called *Ars Notoria*.
>
> In this Book is contained the whole art of Salomon although there be many other Books that is said to be his yet none is to be compared with this, for this containeth them all, although they be titled with several other names, [such] as the *Book Helisol* which is the very same as this last is, which [is] called *Artem Novam & Ars Notoria*, &c."

In the Middle Ages generally, but especially in the *Ars Notoria*, imagination and magic were made to serve memory and scholasticism. In the magical literature that circulated between the fifth and ninth centuries, there are many

---

[1] *William Lilly' History of his Life and Times*, London, 1724, page 45-46.

[2] Lilly's footnote to this passage reads: "Among Dr Napier's MSS. I had an *Ars Notoria*, written by S[imon] Forman in large vellum." Lilly not only tried the method but had access to two copies. Forman made two paper copies: one was completed by him on 28th June 1600, and entitled *Liber de Arte memoratiua siue Notoria*, which is now Cambridge Trinity College MS. O.9.7. In the following year he made another copy which is now Bodleian MS. Jones 1.

tales of ancient rabbis conjuring an angel called Sar-Torah, the 'Prince of the *Torah*'. This angel functioned like the angels of the *Ars Notoria*, and may have even been the model upon which it was based. Sar-Torah endowed the rabbis with the spectacular memory skills necessary for memorising vast swathes of the *Torah*. The angel then taught the rabbis a formula for giving others the same gift.

This literature has been made available by Michael Swartz,[1] who gives us rare glimpses of how ancient and medieval Jews viewed this process of rapid learning aided by angelic conjuration. He examines many of the magical rituals for conjuring angels and ascending to heaven, in the Merkabah chariot, a magical practice that is still very much a part of the practical Kabbalah today. So here you have the reason why the *Ars Notoria* became part of the *Lemegeton*, as it was yet another technique of Solomonic angel conjuration.

Ars Nova

The *Ars Notoria* or 'Notory Art' is often confused with the *Ars Nova*. The *Ars Nova* or *Artem Novam* is simply the last section of the *Ars Notoria* amounting to about a third of that book. The section that Mathers/Crowley refer to as the *Explanation of Certain Names used in the Figures in the Goetia* is simply a summary of the various key words in the diagrams, and sometimes mistakenly referred to as the *Ars Nova*. There is no connection between these two pieces of text, except that they both separately appear at the end of some versions of the *Lemegeton*. The full text of this '*Ars Nova*' will be found in Appendix 9.

The Lemegeton

So now what can we say about the collection as a whole? The *Lemegeton* was the title given, probably during the 1650s, to this collection of five Solomonic grimoires, of which one was previously simply known as *The Art of King Solomon*. All five books were extant and known to Trithemius in 1503 but some under different names. Four of these were mentioned separately by Agrippa in 1531 at the end of Book III of his *Three Books of Occult Philosophy*[2] in the unnumbered chapters 'Of Goetia and Necromancy' and 'Of Theurgia'.

In the chapter 'Of Goetia and Necromancy' Agrippa speaks disapprovingly of the *Goetia*. He also mentions pseudo-Cyprian or Cyprianus, the Bishop of Antioch who was raised as a pagan and trained as a magician. This is obviously no idle reference, as Cyprianus was the reputed author of the *Clavis Inferni*, another grimoire which is definitely related to the *Goetia*.

---

[1] Complete translations of the principal Sar-Torah texts will be found in Michael D. Swartz, *Scholastic Magic*, PUP, Princeton, 1996.
[2] On pages 695-99 of the Tyson edition.

Agrippa defines 'goetian' as those that 'do bind devils by invocating the divine name.' Further on he lists 'Apponius' (Peter de Abano) as the author of a book on the goetia, without specifically noting that de Abano was the actual source of the conjurations in the *Goetia.*

In the chapter 'Of Theurgia' Agrippa quotes Porphyry to the effect that "by theurgical consecrations the soul of man may be fitted to receive spirits, and angels". As texts of Theurgy he quotes "the *Art Almadel,* the *Notory Art,* the *Pauline Art,* the *Art of Revelations,* and many suchlike." The first three are constituent books of the *Lemegeton.*

Hence Agrippa mentions three by name and one by subject matter, out of the five books of the *Lemegeton.* The remaining book, Theurgia-*Goetia* is not mentioned as Agrippa obviously knew it as Book 1 of the *Steganographia* of his master Trithemius.

It is strange that Agrippa separately mentions the *Pauline Art,* as he must have known that it in turn derived from Book 2 of the *Steganographia.* Therefore possibly initially the *Pauline Art* consisted only of its second half, concerning the angels of the 360 degrees of the Zodiac. Maybe only later the first part was added from Book 2 of the *Steganographia,* but this is only speculation.

By themselves these five grimoires are quite different, but taken together they are surprisingly complementary and inter-related, each having a claim to belong to the Solomonic cycle, and each having roots which date back beyond 1500. See Appendix 5, 'Some of the Sources and Constituents of the *Lemegeton*' for a tabular summary of some of these roots.

Glendower: "I can call spirits from the vasty deep."
Hotspur: "Why, so can I, or so can any man;
But will they come when you do call for them?"

- Shakespeare, *Henry IV, Part I*

Evocation Methods

It is essential to call them, it is not sufficient to merely think about calling them in your head. We are all given a voice, and we must use it. Even if spiritual creatures could read thoughts, they still need to be summoned verbally. Then arises the question as to whether they will they come. The answer is affirmative, if constrained to come in the correct way. If they still do not come the invocations in this book make provision for the need to break any other constraints, or chains that may have been binding the spirit and preventing his arrival. This procedure is not, as some commentators have suggested, designed to chain up the spirit: it is designed to release a binding (*ligatio*) that may have been performed by some other magician at some previous time.

In the first part of this chapter we review physical methods that were historically used to constrain demons or spirits. Then we will look at the procedure as exemplified in the *Goetia.* To call a spirit, the least you need to know is his name, so the second part of this section deals with their names. You then need to know the names of the spiritual creatures, like angels, who in the natural world have power over the ones you wish to call: this is addressed in the third part. What you actually say, the conjuration or invocation is addressed in the fourth part. The physical equipment necessary for dealing with the spirits, such as the Circle, the Table of Practice, their seals and so on are reviewed in part five. Part six reviews the chronological sequence of the procedure of evocation.

Physical Methods for Binding a Demon

Physical methods of restraining demons are frequently mentioned in ancient texts. Some demons were restrained by iron chains, others by pots of water, and yet others by angel names. Specific demons such as Obyzouth[1] were bound by the use of a specific angel's name, in that case the Archangel Raphael, who also incidentally controls the demon Asmodeus.

Water and a brass vessel however were the most commonly used restraints. This is a significant clue which we will see is very applicable in determining the correct practical procedures to be used in the *Goetia.* Solomon reputedly

---

[1] *Testament of Solomon*, 13:3-7.

threw such a sealed brass vessel containing 72 demons into the sea, or alternatively into a lake, to ensure they did not further trouble mankind. Asmodeus was bound by ten water jars encircling him, confirming the ability of water to constrain demons. He even begs Solomon "do not condemn me to water".

Surprisingly, Solomon also bound some demons, often the most troublesome, within the precincts of the Temple of the Lord itself, if the *Testament of Solomon* is to be believed. It is possible that this 'sea' mentioned above was in fact the great Brass Sea that he constructed in the grounds of his Temple in Jerusalem.

Ornias, the first demon that Solomon encountered, is bound by iron, and even in the Middle Ages iron was considered to be a metal dangerous to demons. It is for that reason that they are threatened by a consecrated iron sword. It is also why iron is conspicuously absent from the list of planetary metals to be used to make the sigils of the demons of the *Goetia*.

Enepsigos, the nineteenth demon of the *Testament of Solomon*, a female with two heads, was bound by Solomon who "made use of the seal and sealed her down with a triple-link chain". Significantly Enepsigos prophesises to Solomon that his Temple:

> "shall be destroyed and all Jerusalem shall be demolished by the king(s) of the Persians and Medes and Chaldeans...also all the vessels in which you have entrapped us shall be broken in pieces by the hands of men. Then we [the demons] shall come forth with much power and we shall be scattered here and there throughout the world."[1]

Other sources are very specific about the use of water in binding or imprisoning demons. This clearly shows that Solomon's technique was to imprison demons in vessels, which as we shall see were then immersed in water.

The actual procedure of binding Asmodeus refers specifically to the use of water pots. Solomon says to Asmodeus:[2]

> "Is there not something else about you, Asmodeus?" He said to me [Solomon], "The power of God which binds me with unbreakable bonds by his seal knows that what I have related to you is true. I beg you, King Solomon, do not condemn me to water." But I smiled and replied, "As the Lord, the God of my father lives, you shall have irons to wear and you shall mould clay for all the vessels of the Temple, eliminating the cost of the mould". Then I ordered ten water jars to be made available and (I commanded) him to be encircled by them."

The following unrelated passage suggests that at least some demons

[1] *Testament of Solomon*, 15:8-9.

[2] *Testament of Solomon*, 5:11.

remained so entrapped even after the first sack of Jerusalem by the Babylonians, till the Romans finally destroyed the Second Temple in 70 CE.[1]

> "They [the people] are wicked in their behaviour! Some of them fall away [to the worship of] idols. [Others] have [demons] dwelling with them [as did] David the king. He is the one who laid the foundation of Jerusalem; and his son Solomon, who he begat in [adultery], is the one who built Jerusalem by means of the demons, because he received [power over them]. When he [had finished building, he imprisoned] the demons [in the Temple]. He [sealed them] into seven [water pots. They remained] a long [time in] the [water pots], abandoned [there]. When the Romans [went] up to [Jerusalem] they discovered [the] water pots, [and immediately] the [demons] ran out of the water pots as those who escape from prison. And the water pots [remained] pure (thereafter). And since those days, [the demons dwell] with men who are [in] ignorance, and [they have remained upon] the earth."

So here you see both ends of the story, their initial imprisonment by Solomon, and their later release by the Romans as they destroyed and looted the Temple in 70 CE.

This is very significant for us because one of the associated texts written by Peter Smart, the same transcriber of Rudd's manuscript (Harley MS 6482), contains a detailed drawing of one such Brass Vessel which is engraved with the Secret Seal of Solomon in place (see Figure 5). This suggests a continuity of the tradition of constraining demons. We will see how this was adapted for use in the seventeenth century further on in this chapter.

The Arabic Solomonic tradition refers to jinn rather than demons, and asserts that the jinn that Solomon subjugated were of two types. The first were antithetical to mankind, and these he sealed into a (brass) bottle, and threw into the sea (although they were later released by a curious fisherman). The second type of jinn were those who helped him in the building of the great Temple, and were altogether more docile, but capable of real physical work.

It is an interesting speculation that the great Sea of Brass that stood outside of Solomon's temple and is mentioned in great detail in the *Bible* may have commemorated the imprisonment of the first class of jinn, or in fact may have been the actual 'sea' into which they were thrown. The sea is described as:[2]

> 23. "And he [Solomon] made a molten sea, ten cubits [approximately 17 feet or 5.2 metres] from the one brim to the other: it was round all about, and his height was five cubits [8.6 feet or 2.6 metres]: and a line of thirty cubits [51 feet or 15.7 metres] did compass it round about...

---

[1] *The Testimony of Truth* (IX, 3) in James Robinson, *Nag Hammadi Library in English*, Brill, Leyden, 1977. The textual reconstructions are Robinson's not ours.

[2] See 1 *Kings*, 7:23-37. The Hebrew for 'sea' in this passage can also be read as 'tank'. Only a small part of this detailed specification of the Sea of Brass is quoted above.

> 25. It stood upon twelve oxen…'
>
> 26. …it contained two thousand baths [by volume]."

The sheer height and volume of this 'sea' (not forgetting to add the bases and the twelve life size brass oxen supports) suggests that it was not merely to be used as a laver for the pious to wash their hands and feet.[1] It is said that Solomon both cast recalcitrant demons into the 'sea', and that he imprisoned them within the Temple. It is not unreasonable to suggest that *both* these conditions applied and that Solomon actually imprisoned them in his Sea of Brass within the confines of the Temple precincts - possibly a much safer 'lockup' than casually discarding them in the open sea.

Our manuscript version of the *Goetia* recounts this story (immediately after the description of the 72nd demon.

> "Solomon never declared why he thus bound them, and sealed the Vessel and he by divine power cast them all into a deep Lake or hole in Babylon, and the Babylonians wondering to see such a thing there, they went wholly into the Lake to break the vessel open, suspecting to find a great store of treasure, but when they had broken it open out flew all the chief spirits immediately and their Legions followed them and they were all restored to their former places…"

It is hard to see what Solomon was doing in Babylon, and in fact this story probably had nothing to do with that city. The story may have become a bit confused and it may have simply been the invading Babylonians that released the demons from Solomon's Sea of Brass in Jerusalem when they sacked the Temple. However that is just speculation.

Names of the 72 Demons: the Descending Hierarchy

The names of all 72 demons of the *Goetia* are listed in Table M15. There is some controversy as to how these names are categorised. All that is supplied in the *Goetia* are their titles which correspond to the seven planets, plus scattered mentions of the Zodiac. Although the Golden Dawn used a complex night and day Decan division, there is no trace of this in any of the manuscripts, and so we have not used it. Table M15 spans both pages, and is ordered in the standard sequence of the demons. The 12 Signs of the Zodiac have simply been allocated in order beginning at Aries, as would have been usual.

Column a) gives a sequence used in Wierus and in Harley MS 6482. Column b) gives the standard numbering used in all printed versions and in the

[1] The practice of washing the hands and feet is common to all three Middle Eastern monotheistic religions. It was practiced by Jews who had a special place, the *mikvah*, built for such purificatory washing. Christianity has stories of Mary Magdalene washing Jesus' feet, and Muslims still to this day wash both hands and feet before entering the *masjid* or mosque to pray.

present Harley MS 6483. Column c) gives the spirit/demon name, with alternative versions. Column d) gives three possible Hebrew renderings, of which the first is that of Dr Rudd. Column e) gives sundry attributions including the stead ridden by the demon (which is often an indication of its rank). Column f) gives the Golden Dawn Decan divisions, for the sake of completeness. Column g) gives the ruling Shem ha-Mephorash angel, with their Hebrew name.

Column h) gives the demon's rank. There are at least seven demons with dual ranks in the *Goetia*. This leads us to believe that some confusion of rank has been introduced by copyists, and that there was originally probably one King (attributed to the Sun) for each Zodiacal sign.

One demon not marked as a King, but by any other criterion should rank as one, is Astaroth. Decarabia is listed as a King in the original Latin text of Weir, but this title has not survived translation. Finally Gäap is shown with many kingly qualities, and in fact leads 4 kings. His name is also suspiciously close to Goap, King of the West, so we have added the title of King to the existing titles of each of these three demons. All three 'new' Kings are marked in Table M18 by underlining. This then fortuitously provides exactly one King per Zodiacal Sign, just as there is one Marquise and one President per Sign.

Column i) shows the Planet, while Column j) gives the number of legions governed by each demon. Column k) describes the evoked appearance of the demon, and Column l) gives their powers and attributes. These powers also appear in Table M16.

Table M17 gives the correlation between the demon's Rank, Planet and metal which is shown clearly in the *Goetia*. It is interesting that Earls and Counts, who correspond with Mars, do not have iron as their metal, because as we have seen traditionally such demons fear that metal, and we are all familiar with the use of the iron sword to threaten demons.

Table M18 shows the individual demons of the *Goetia* according to their rank or Planet tabulated against the division by the 12 signs of the Zodiac.

Tables M20, M20a and M21 list the Good and Evil Aerial Spirits of the compass as shown in the *Theurgia-Goetia*.

Table M22 gives the Spirits of the Hours from *Ars Paulina (I)* whilst Table M23 gives the angels of the 360 Degrees of Zodiac from *Ars Paulina (II)*. Lastly Table M24 gives the Angels of the Altitudes from the *Ars Almadel*.[1]

From these tables you can find the names, rank, attributions and powers of every demon or spirit mentioned in Rudd's manuscript.

[1] Full explanations of each Table will be found in Stephen Skinner's *Complete Magician's Tables*, Golden Hoard Press, London & Singapore, 2006, and Llewellyn, Woodbury, 2006, pages 374-378.

Figure 1: Angel with the Keys of Hell releasing a demon by Albrecht Durer

Names of the 72 Adversarial Angels

The key to the control of the demons listed in the *Goetia* is summed up in just one word 'Shemhamphorash'. This word was written large at the front of some of the manuscripts of the *Goetia,* and was duly transcribed by Mathers/Crowley at the front of their edition, without any explanation. Its presence has not been fully explained hitherto in any printed copy of this grimoire, but it is the single most important key to using this grimoire.

To draw a simple parallel, it is like printing 'Penicillin' at the front of a list of bacteria, for the Shem ha-Mephorash (to transliterate it in a more rational fashion) is the key to controlling the 72 demons and ensuring their compliance with the commands of the magician.

The Shem ha-Mephorash is literally a name of God embedded in three verses in *Exodus*. From it Kabbalists generated the names of 72 angels, which have been a highly significant list of angels for a long time. There is precisely one angel for each demon, and that angel is the 'antidote' that enables you to control that demon. There is a one-to-one correspondence angel to demon, a specific demon being controlled by a specific angel. These can be seen in each double seal, and are listed in Appendix 7 in Tables A24 and A25.

Angels versus Demons

In all early grimoires, the texts are careful to say who or what controls a particular demon. It is not enough for the karcist to simply assert his personal power, and to claim that he is 'Paphro Osorronophris' and therefore entitled to order around these spiritual creatures. For example in the *Book of Tobit* the demon Asmodeus is controlled by the angel Raphael - a very clear example of an adversarial angel, and furthermore Asmodeus is banished by burning a specific substance - in that case the entrails of a specific fish.

Anyone who thinks they can order around demons, just on their own say so, without the reinforcement and support of a higher authority, is just kidding themselves. They would have as much chance of taming a wild horse without a bridle. Even Solomon had the benefit of angelic backup of the highest order, and a Ring especially given him by the archangel Michael, or so the story goes.

The procedure utilised in this manuscript is to first invoke the angel, and then using its authority, bind the spirit or demon.

Were Angels always a part of the Goetic Tradition?

You might ask, "can you be sure that the techniques such as the use of the Shem ha-Mephorash angels were always part of the Goetic tradition?" We can trace the specific use of the seals of these angels over the last five centuries, and the use of angels to control demons since the third century CE. Given the extent of borrowing of Goetic elements by scholar-magicians for use in angelic invocations, there has long been an awareness of the close relationship between angels and demons. Examples of such borrowings include the borrowing of the 'Seal of Aemeth' by Dr John Dee from the grimoire *Liber Juratus*, or his use of a 'Tables of Practice' also borrowed from the same grimoire tradition.

Blaise Vigenère (1523-1595) recorded the 72 Shem ha-Mephorash angelic seals used by Rudd in the *Goetia*. Mathers once referred to Vigenère as "the Great Magician Blaise Vigenère" (a rare compliment indeed coming from Mathers) when he copied out Vigenère's angelic seals for a Golden Dawn Adeptus Minor side paper. These angelic seals were also used by Ebenezer Sibley (1752-99). We have included a few examples of seals taken from Sibley's manuscript of the *Goetia* in Appendix 6, to demonstrate the continuity of this practice. Vigenère (end sixteenth century), Rudd (seventeenth century), Sibley (end eighteenth century) and Mathers (end nineteenth century) all understood the application of these angelic invocations and seals in the context of an ongoing *Goetia* tradition.

Further evidence occurs in the form of contemporary engravings such as that shown in Figure 1, where a carefully executed engraving by Albrecht Durer (1471-1528) clearly shows an angel in control of a demon, or if you prefer, in control of one of their fallen former angelic companions. This particular drawing shows an angel controlling a demon that is climbing out of the Pit, on a chain leash and collar. The usual interpretation of this engraving is that the angel is imprisoning the demon or casting her into the Pit. If that were the correct interpretation the angel would be forcing the demon into the hatch, rather than standing back and allowing her to step out, as she is doing. Furthermore the angel holds an iron chain in his left hand which is attached to an iron neck collar on the demon, very clearly illustrating the fact that the angel literally holds the key to controlling the demon.

The invocation of angels has long been associated with the evocation of their fallen counterparts. If we go back to the third century CE, it is also clear from the *Testament of Solomon*, that specific angels have long been set over specific demons to control them.

The 72 Angels of the Shem ha-Mephorash

The names of these angels were obtained by combining the letters of three verses from the book of *Exodus* 14:19-21. These three verses in *Exodus* each contain 72 letters. By writing down the first verse right to left (in normal Hebrew style), and underneath this the next verse backward (i.e. left to right), and under this again the last verse written again right to left, you have three lines written *boustrophedon* (as the Greeks would call it, named after the direction oxen travel when ploughing a field). These three lines should then be viewed as 72 columns of three letters. These are then read downwards, three letters at a time, to make 72 three-letter roots.

To each of these roots is added either the termination אל- "-el" or the termination יה- "-iah" according to their sex. Bearing in mind that before modern times the letters I=Y=J you should of course recognise the two great names of god, El and Yah in the angel name endings. Thus are formed the 72 great Shem ha-Mephorash angel names.

These angels can be called in their own right, but for our purposes, are each matched up to a corresponding demon name. How this match is done is shown by Rudd, for each demon of the *Goetia* he links the seal of that demon with its corresponding angelic seal.

These angels also have astrological correspondences, but these are not so important to us here. There is some modern controversy over their exact astrological correspondences. Each angel can be allocated to each of the quinaries (or segments of five degrees) of the Zodiac. It is however problematic as to where in the Zodiac you should start from, either:

1. 0 degrees Aries (like the start of the Tropical Zodiac)
2. 0 degrees Leo (as used by the Golden Dawn)
3. 12 degrees Leo, the actual heliacal rising of Sirius (as used by the ancient Egyptians).

The Shem ha-Mephorash angels are tabulated in Table A24 and A25. This table deliberately just starts at 0 degrees, so you can decide for yourself which convention to adopt, and adjust accordingly. Having established the names of the angel we have also added in a fairly modern list of powers and attributes. Those are not central to our theme, but listed just for interest.

The Invocations

The invocations of the Goetia are all translations of the Latin invocations which occur in the *Heptameron* of Peter de Abano. In addition to these the Form of Adjuration (see Appendix 15) should be incorporated.

Each invocation has Godnames and angelic names, which have been bolded for rapid recognition. In fact in the manuscript they are often hand printed carefully, so there can be no mistaking their exact spelling. Many of these are distorted Hebrew or Greek words, and we have attempted in Appendix 10 to interpret as many as possible.

As well as the Godnames and angelic names, it is important to commemorate the names of one or more famous magicians who in the past controlled the spirits; in this case the name of Solomon is commemorated. Equally well the name of Jesus is also called upon, but this can be considered in the light of it being the name of someone who during his life controlled and drove out demons, rather than necessarily in a Christian religious context.

Figure 2: Magician (centre) with a sword evokes a horned treasure-finding spirit (right) from within the safety of a Circle, whilst a passing friar (left) looks on curiously (14th century). From a manuscript of *The Pilgrimage of the Soul,* a translation by John Lydgate (1370?-1451?) from William de Deguilleville's *La Pélerinage de l'âme* written in 1330-1332.

Figure 3: Magician with grimoire in his hand admonishes two rebellious horned, winged and taloned/hooved demons from within the safety of a Circle. From a manuscript of Brunetto Latini'a *Livre de Tresor* (1425).

The Equipment of Evocation

Circle

The Circle drawn upon the ground is one of the most ancient protections of the magician. The Arabic word *al-Almadel* even means 'circle'. A 1425 copy of a thirteenth century text by the Florentine Brunetto Latini shows the magician Canoaster [Zoroaster] commanding two full sized horned, hairy, bearded and winged demons with cloven hooves and bird's feet respectively from within the safety of a single circle drawn upon the ground (see Figure 3).[1] Another manuscript from the fourteenth century shows the magician armed with a sword, wearing a breastplate shield with a red cross inscribed on it (reminiscent of the Crusaders), and standing within a double circle with equal-armed crosses marked at the four cardinal directions, with three sigils drawn between each cross. The circle is inscribed in red on the grass of a hillock (see Figure 2).[2] Interestingly a different folio in this same manuscript portrays witches preparing herbal medicine with the aid of a demon that mingles freely with them without the separation of a boundary circle. Maybe this was a fundamental difference in the perception of the practices of magicians and witches.

The circle in later versions of the *Goetia* such as Sloane MS 3825 contains multiple rings (or in fact becomes a spiral) containing the Kabbalistic Godnames, archangels and angels of the ten Sephiroth. This treatment reaches its greatest refinement in the edition of the *Goetia* transcribed by Mathers/Crowley, where these words have been put back into Hebrew by Mathers from the original plain English of the manuscripts, and the artist has taken the liberty of drawing the spiral as a snake.

By contrast the circle used in the present Rudd manuscript is essentially simple, and harks back to the *Heptameron* and the fourteenth century example shown in Figure 2. An interesting and practically important feature of these simpler circles is that the names inscribed within them are not fixed, but vary according to the time and date of the operation:[3]

> "the form of the Circles is not always one and the same; but useth to be changed, according to the order of the Spirits that are to be called, their places [direction of calling], times, daies and hours [of the operation]. For in making a Circle, it ought to be considered in what time of the year, what day, and what hour, that you make the Circle; what Spirits you would call, to what Star and region they do belong, and what functions they have."

De Abano goes on to give the exact instructions which imply that one circle

---

[1] British Library Additional MS 39844, folio 51.
[2] British Library Cotton MS Tiberius A VII, folio 44.
[3] Abano's *Heptameron*, in *The Fourth Book of Occult Philosophy*, Ibis, Berwick, 2005, page 60.

does not 'fit all.' Indeed in one of the Graeco-Egyptian papyri (dating from a thousand years before de Abano)[1] it is specifically stated that if the magician is unable to first invoke the divinities ruling the day and hour of the operation he is engaged in, then the specific spirit he is attempting to invoke will have no respect for him and consequently not appear. It is therefore more than just an arbitrary choice of protective names; it is an integral part of the invocational process. Following this hint, it might be an idea to commemorate these names out loud at the beginning of the invocation.

The magician is ensuring the success of his operation by placing in full view in the circle the names of the angels presiding over the time of the operation. This suggests that Rudd's version of the Circle drawn from the *Heptameron* may in practice be more ancient and perhaps more effective than the heavily Kabbalistic and wordy circles shown in more recent editions of the *Goetia.*

As the form of Dr Rudd's Circle is quite different from the one we have come to associate with the Goetia, we have added Appendix 14 which has the more convention Circle and Triangle from wellcome MS 3203.

When we utter the divine names standing in the Circle, we are establishing ourselves as the higher power, entitled to command the obedience of these spiritual creatures. As Eliade wrote, "Projection of a fixed point - the centre - is equivalent to the creation of the world."[2] Thus by creating our magic circle and connecting ourselves to God through the use of his names, we reproduce the creation of the world through the utterance of the creative logos.

Triangle

The Triangle does not feature visually in Rudd, the *Heptameron,* or in any of the fourteenth century manuscripts mentioned above. For Dr Rudd, the two places the spirit is constriced to are the Crystal or Glass Receptacle on the Table of practice, or the Brass Vessel, a replica of which will be located ouside the circle where the Triangle of Art would normally be. We will look at both these loci further on.

The traditional Triangle of Art is designed to constrict the manifestation of the spirit to one particular point or locus. An important point about the Triangle is that it is a separate construction which does not have a fixed position in relation to the Circle, but should be placed on the side of the circle from which it is expected the spirit will arrive. Although in Sloane MS 3648 the triangle just happens to be drawn located in the East, the note by it clearly says "this Δ Triangle is to be placed on that Coast [direction] the Spirit is belonging unto."

---

[1] Hans Dieter Betz, *The Greek Magical Papyri in Translation*, University of Chicago, Chicago, 1992.

[2] Mircea Eliade, *The Sacred and the Profane*, 1987 (originally 1957), Harcourt, Florida, page 22.

The names 'Primeumaton, Anaphaxeton and Tetragrammaton' at the three sides, plus the inscription of 'Mi-cha-el' the Archangel at the corners, help to constrain the spirit into giving truthful answers to questions, and in its response to the formula of binding. Interesting that whilst Tetragrammaton is Hebrew, the other two names on the Triangle sides are Greek in origin, just as the demon names are a mixture of Hebrew and Greek. Remember that although the Triangle provides a focus for the spirit, there is a second possible focus in the crystal set on the Table of Practice.

Solomon's Ring

Solomon's Ring is and was an integral part of his command of the spirits. What was the Ring made of? The usual choices might have been gold or silver, but it is much more likely that the Ring was made of iron and/or brass, as iron was the metal most feared by demons, and brass was the metal of the confining Brass Vessel. The *Jewish Encyclopaedia* says of Solomon's Ring:

> "The legend that Solomon possessed a seal ring on which the name of God was engraved and by means of which he controlled the demons is related at length in *Git.* 68a, b. This legend is especially developed by Arabic writers, who declare that the ring, on which was engraved "the Most Great Name of God," and which was given to Solomon from heaven, was partly brass and partly iron. With the brass part of the ring Solomon signed his written commands to the good genii, and with the iron part he signed his commands to the evil genii, or devils. The Arabic writers declare also that Solomon received four jewels from four different angels, and that he set them in one ring, so that he could control the four elements. The legend that Asmodeus once obtained possession of the ring and threw it into the sea, and that Solomon was thus deprived of his power until he discovered the ring inside a fish,[1] also has an Arabic source."[2]

It is interesting that the Ring should be made partly of brass (like the Brass Vessel) and partly of iron, a metal which the spirits reputedly feared. How did Solomon get this Ring? In the *Testament of Solomon,* Solomon is said to have called on the name of God night and day till:

> "Then it happened that while I was praying to the God of heaven and earth, there was granted me from the Lord Sabaoth[3] through the archangel Michael a ring which had a seal engraved upon precious stone. He [Michael] said to me, 'Solomon, Son of David, take the gift which the Lord God, the highest Sabaoth, has sent you; [and with it] you shall imprison all the demons, both female and male, and with their help you shall build Jerusalem when you bear this seal of God. And this engraving of the seal of the ring sent thee is a Pentalpha."[4]

---

[1] Adolph Jellinek, *B. H.* ii. 86-87.

[2] Compare D'Herbelot, "Soliman ben Daoud" in *Bibliothèque Orientale* and Fabricius, *Codex Pseudepigraphicus*, i. 1054;

[3] '*Ho Kyrios Sabaoth*', the Lord of Hosts.

[4] *Testament of Solomon* 1:6-7. The last sentence is taken from a different and probably later manuscript version, so it is not certain that the engraving on the Ring was in fact a pentagram.

Solomon's Ring was also mentioned in Josephus as being used by other magicians, in one case by Eleazar[1]

> "He put a ring that had a root of one of those sorts mentioned by Solomon to the nostrils of the demoniac [the possessed person], after which he drew out the demon through his nostrils; and when the man fell down immediately, he abjured him [the demon] to return into him [the possessed man] no more, making still mention of Solomon, and reciting the incantations which he [Solomon] composed."

It is obviously not the same Ring, but one made of the same pattern and suitably consecrated. Thirteen hundred year later this Ring appears again in the *Goetia* (see Figure 18). It has engraved around the outside 'Anepheneton[2] Michael', and on the inside 'Tetragrammaton' [יהוה]. This directly commemorates the name of the archangel Michael who originally gave the Ring to Solomon. Given the text of the *Testament of Solomon* however a more specifically useful inscription might have been "Tetragrammaton Sabaoth - Michael" or in Hebrew מיכאל - יהוה צבאות. The key word is Tetragrammaton Sabaoth, or IHVH Sabaoth, because this is the name most often associated with Solomon's Ring.

Let us look a bit more closely at this Godname. The names IHVH or YHVH (Yahweh) and Elohim frequently occur in conjunction with the word Sabaoth, which literally means 'hosts' in a military sense. For example YHVH Elohe Sabaoth means 'YHVH God of Hosts'. The original meaning of Sabaoth is probably to be found in *1 Samuel* 17: 45, where YHVH Sabaoth is interpreted as denoting 'the God of the armies of Israel'. It is noteworthy also that the name IHVH Sabaoth is more than once directly associated with the deadly destructive power associated with the Ark of the Covenant. It is therefore the prime name for our purposes, which is to strike fear and obedience into the hearts of the demons conjured.

An indication of the power that these Godnames were supposed to hold is that the destruction of the Temple in 70 CE has sometimes been blamed on the fact that forty years prior, the priests had ceased to pronounce the Name once a year, every year, as was their previous custom.[3] Without the presence of the indwelling god, the Temple was left unprotected, and so the Romans were able to sack and destroy it. Of course this may have just been a *post hoc* justification for their loss. However after the destruction of this Temple the knowledge of how to pronounce the divine Name is said to have been lost. It has been suggested that without a Temple and without the knowledge of this name, the indwelling god of the Hebrews could no longer be invoked.

---

1 Josephus, *Antiquities of the Jews,* Book 8, Chapter 2.5 (47).

2 A Greek derived godname mentioned in *Liber Juratus.*

3 *Yoma* 39b.

Certainly not to the point where physical manifestations of fire and a column of cloud could be seen, as it was in the time of Moses and Solomon.

The same is true of the invocation of other spiritual creatures, be they angels, demons or spirits, the exact pronunciation of the commanding Godname must be known. This is perhaps one of the reasons why Dr Rudd began a detailed study of Hebrew; in fact a Hebrew grammar attributed to him is still extant. The exact name of the spiritual creature being invoked must also be known. Where there are alternative versions of the name it is as well to include both in the full conjuration, just to be sure.

The true test of the importance of a divine name was the care taken by scribes in writing it. The number of divine names that traditionally required the scribe's special care is just seven: El, Elohim, Adonai, YHVH, Ehyeh-Asher-Ehyeh, Shaddai, and Sabaoth. Sabaoth as a Godname is applied to both the Sephirah Hod and the Sephirah Netzach, and the Archangel Michael is usually applied to Tiphareth,[1] thus completing a triangle on the Tree of Life. Sabaoth means 'Lord of Hosts' and specifically the hosts of heaven or the angels, for as we have seen it is the names of the angels that control specific demons. The stories of the war in heaven or of the archangel Michael locking up the hosts of the fallen angels (or demons) is not just a lovely myth, but an indication of the state of play which enables the magician to also control these demons or spirits through the same relevant angel.

If you want to think about it Kabbalistically, the controlling forces of this triad of Sephiroth (Tiphareth, Netzach and Hod), which are inscribed in the Triangle of Art, stand immediately above the demons of Yesod. Taking the analogy further, it is specifically by the angel and Godnames of these three Sephiroth that we are able to drive the demons resident in Yesod into action in the material world of Malkuth. It is for this reason that IHVH Sabaoth and Michael are inscribed upon the magician's ring which enables the magician to wield some part of the authority over the spirits given to Solomon with the original Ring. As well as having an engraved precious stone, the Ring also has set in it the herb which has been identified by several authorities as the root *barra*.[2]

The classic magicians' Ring in the Greek magical tradition bore a different inscription, and was often inscribed with the Lix Tetrax formula from the so called Ephesian Letters. This formula must be written in Greek as follows:

[1] Raphael does not map on to Tiphareth, despite various authorities so attributing him. His name means 'Medicine of God' and so he clearly belongs with the Sephirah Hod.

[2] We are grateful to Helene Hodge for the interesting suggestion that this might simply have been the root of *Polygonatum multiflorum*, whose common name is 'Solomon's Seal'. However *barra* is usually identified with *Pedalium Murex* or 'gokeroo'.

ασκιου κατακιον λιξ τετραξ δαμναμενευς αισια

This formula dates back at least to 409 BCE, as they form part of an inscription in Himera in Sicily of that date. Although these words are sometimes dismissed as nonsense words, in fact λιξ τετραξ, Lix Tetrax, was the fifth demon in the *Testament of Solomon*, a fact that ties this Greek formula in with the Solomonic tradition. And δαμναμενευς, Damnameneus, the second last word of the formula was one of the Daktuloi. The Idaian Daktuloi were Alchemists and Goetic sorcerers who dwelt on Crete and served Adrasteia of the Mountains (the goddess Rhea).

Interestingly, those who were initiated into the Samothracian Mysteries of the Great Gods (Axieros, Axiokersa, Axiokersos and Kasmilos) were granted the Purple Sash and the Magnetic Iron Ring. Here is a hint that not only should the Ring be made partly of iron, but also that it should be magnetised.

The 'pentalpha' or pentagram mentioned in one version of the *Testament of Solomon* as inscribed upon the stone set in the Ring seems to have come down to us as a separate item, the Pentagram of Solomon, and not part of the Ring.

The Pentagram of Solomon

The pentagram (which is mistakenly referred to as a pentagon in the *Goetia*) should be made of gold or silver, and is engraved with 'Te-tra-gram-ma-ton' inscribed in between the vertices of the pentagram, and 'Soluzen' in the middle.

At each point, running clockwise from the top, is engraved a sigil plus the words:

Abdia
Ballaton [Ballator]
Bellony
Hally
Halliza

The Pentagram is designed to protect the operator from danger and to help enforce his command. See Figure 19, Plate 4.

The Hexagram of Solomon

This is called the 'sexangled figure of Solomon' in Sloane MS 3825 (see Figure 19, Plate 5). Basically it is a Star of David inscribed in Roman letters with Te-tra-gram-ma-ton on 5 of its points, which are each marked with a cross, and with both AGLA and Alpha-Omega written between the points. In the middle is a 'T' or Tau cross with the rather unnecessary caption 'Tau'. On the lower point is written a two character sigil. This is to be inscribed upon parchment (calf's skin) and,

> "worn at the skirt of your white vestment covered with a linen Cloth, which when the Spirit appears, Show it [to] him & he will be compelled to [take] human shape and be obedient."

So the Hexagram should only be used after the spirit has appeared, and to enforce a human and more tractable shape.

Each spirit of course has its own personal seal, and during the *ligatio* stage of the operation they must be bound to it.

The Seals and their Use

The individual seals of each demon are intrinsic to the method. It is recommended at a number of points in the description of the 72 demons, that the seal of the demon should be worn on the breast of the magician. By extension so should the seal of the angel, and this might even be inscribed on the back of the demon's seal.

The *Psalms*, said to have been composed by David, Solomon's father, play an important part in this magic. The appropriate Latin snippets from the *Psalms* are written in the angelic part of each of the seals of the Goetic spirits, and are listed in full in Table A25.

Secret Seal of Solomon

The Seal of Solomon is on the other hand not a seal to be worn, but is the all important stopper to the Brass Vessel and that which prevents the escape of the spirits. Now it might be thought that this is a unique seal. In fact it is just one of 8 seals of the Patriarchs or Fathers, to be found in the *Magical Calendar,* which we have reproduced in Figure 4.[1] Notice that the Secret Seal of Solomon is second from the end of this group. The same Seal features in various manuscripts of the *Goetia*, but it is only in the present manuscript, where it forms the stopper of the Brass Vessel that it has an obvious function.

Hazel Wand

The Wand is not mentioned in any great detail in the *Goetia,* and there are none of the usual instructions to cut it with a new knife at dawn from a virgin hazel tree. Nevertheless the Wand is a necessary part of the equipment of a Goetic magician.

The *Goetia* gives brief instructions for its use. Although they are strangely embedded in the description of the spirit Beleth, these instructions are undoubtedly meant to apply to all spirits.

---

[1] McLean, Adam. *The Magical Calendar*, Magnum Opus, Edinburgh, 1979, page 56.

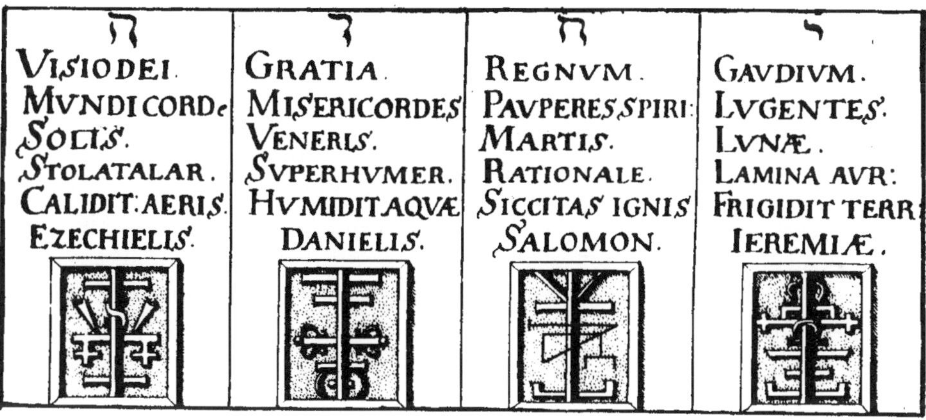

Figure 4: The Seals of the Patriarchs Adam, Moses, Elias, Joshua, Ezekiel, Daniel, Solomon and Jeremiah as printed in *The Magical Calendar* of 1620. The eight seals have specific virtues ascribed to them. Solomon's is for Wisdom, and is attributed to Mars and Fire, which may well be appropriate for restraining demons.

> "[The Spirit will be] very furious at his first appearance that is whilst the Exorcist layeth his Courage, for to do that he must hold a hazel stick [*baculum* or wand] in his hand stretching it out towards the South and the East quarter[1] making a Triangle Δ without [outside] the Circle, commanding him into it by the [the conjuration of the] bands & chains of spirits."

Lamen

According to a Rabbinical legend, God once sent Asmodeus to depose Solomon, as a punishment for the king's sin, and for a while the demon is supposed to have taken Solomon's appearance and ruled in his stead.[2]

> "Benaiah sent for Solomon, and asked him how his deposition had happened. Solomon replied that when sitting one day in his palace a storm had hurled him to a great distance and that since then he had been deprived of his reason. Benaiah then asked him for a sign, and…these facts having been ascertained to be true, Benaiah directed the [members of the] Sanhedrin to [protect themselves and] write the Holy Name on pieces of parchment and to wear them on their breasts and to appear with them before the [demon Asmodeus disguised as the] king. Benaiah, who accompanied them, took his sword and with it struck Asmodeus. Indeed, he would have killed the latter had not a *bat kol*[3] cried: 'Touch him not: he only executed my commands'."

The fact that Asmodeus was able to temporarily depose Solomon is as interesting as the thought that God might have encouraged him to so do. Anyway it does not matter if this is simply a Rabbinical tale, the point is that the prescribed protection against as mighty a demon as Asmodeus was simply one of the holy names written on a scrap of parchment worn on the breast. This practice is the origin of the lamen, which acts in the grimoires as a protection against demons. It is clear that the lamen, along with many other grimoire procedures owes its origin to Jewish practice.

Phylacteries

Another Jewish practice, the wearing of phylacteries[4] is likewise based on a similar premise. Phylacteries contained a scrap of scripture written on parchment and bound tightly to the body (often the upper arm or forehead) with the aim of providing protection. In fact one notable and much underrated early twentieth century Goetic magician, Lewis de Claremont, specifically recommended their use in evocation. The principle is the same as the lamen, that protection in the form of the written word upon parchment should be attached very firmly to the body of the operator.

---

[1] This is not always SE, but depends upon the quarter from which the Spirit is expected to come.

[2] *Midrash al-Yithallel.*

[3] A heavenly or divine voice which is said to proclaim God's will or judgment.

[4] The Greek *phulakt rion* means guard's post or safeguard.

The Brass Vessel

The Brass Vessel is probably unique to the *Goetia* as a piece of magical equipment, not appearing in any other European grimoire to our knowledge. The origin of this Vessel as the container into which Solomon reputedly sealed up the spirits has already been established. But how was it meant to be used in evocation? One commentator reasonably suggested that it be used simply as a storage facility for the 72 demon sigils. However it was much more than that. The Brass Vessel was used in ritual in much the same way as the Triangle was used, as a locus for the spirit, but also as a threat to recalcitrant spirits, to 'lock them up and throw away the key' as it were.

Let us look at how Thomas Rudd used it. Bound up in Harley MS 6482 (the previous manuscript to the one here transcribed) is an exquisitely detailed engraving (see Figure 5) done by or for Peter Smart, which is obviously based on a real metal object. It is almost certain that this illustration should have been bound in with Harley MS 6483 rather than in Harley MS 6482, as it is in fact a very sophisticated illustration associated with the *Goetia*.

It was reproduced in Adam McLean's excellent edition of Harley MS 6482.[1] There he tentatively identified it as a sort of music stand or "a picture of a mirror glass, placed upon a three-legged stand with its back turned outwards." This identification has also been followed by Carroll Runyon.[2] If however you look closely at the intricate engraving, you will see that this is not just the decorative back of anything, but is in fact the *front* of a very specific piece of magical equipment.

If you look at the top of the illustration you will see that it depicts the mouth of a three-dimension metal bottle. Prominent at the top is the very Secret Seal of Solomon, which was always said to be the seal or stopper in the Brass Vessel. On either side of the neck are the handles, whose design is very similar to the drawing of the "brass vessel for containing the spirits" in Sloane MS 3825. On the bottom are the three tripod-like legs of the Brass Vessel. We believe that the drawing is of the front of a Brass Vessel that was meant to be used ritually. In the present manuscript there are instructions for its use, where it performs the same function as the Triangle (see page 181).

In the simpler drawing in Sloane MS 3825 and in some of the other manuscripts of the *Goetia* there is a band of Hebrew inscribed around the waist of the Vessel. Although this is not very clear, it includes various names of god mixed with names of the Archangels and orders of angels:

---

[1] Adam McLean. (editor) *A Treatise on Angel Magic*. Magnum Opus Hermetic Sourceworks 15, Edinburgh. Republished Weiser, York Beach, 2006. See page 21.
[2] Runyon, Carroll 'Poke'. *The Book of Solomon's Magick*. CHS, Siverado, 2003, page 34.

In Hebrew אשר אחיה : גבריאל : מיכאל : האניאל [AShR AHIH : GBRIAL : MIKAL : HANIAL] on the front, and צדקיאל : אל : חשמלים : אראריתא [TzDQIAL: AL: ChShMLIM: ARARIThA] on the back of the Vessel. Other variants include צפקיאל : צדקיאל : כמאל : רפאל : אראריתא [TzPQIAL: TzDQIAL: KMAL: RPAL: ARARIThA].[1]

Rudd's version of the Brass Vessel is altogether more detailed. Apart from the stopper, the whole surface is chased with scroll designs upon which are written the numbers 1 to 72, and after each number is the corresponding Shem ha-Mephorash angel's name in Hebrew, although you have to look at the original manuscript closely to really see that. The last word after number 72 is Greek, *telios* which means 'the end, or it is completed'. In addition there are the letters A to G in 'celestial writing', corresponding to Agiel, Beloh, Chemer, Din, Elim, Febeh and Graphie. The purpose of this engraving is to make a permanent metal representation of each and every adversarial angel's name, so that no matter which demon was conjured, the protective angel's name was always present on this metal representation of the Brass Vessel.

If you again examine the engraving carefully, you can see that although it represents a three-dimensional Vessel, that this particular item was itself flat. The 'legs' actually pass through a *flat* slit at the bottom, and are therefore not meant to be three-dimensional.

So why would Rudd have commissioned, at considerable expense no doubt, a flat metal representation of the fabled Brass Vessel? It is obviously and alternate to the Triangle of Art, which does not feature strongly in Rudd's manuscript.

It may also have been for the personal protection or the magician. If you think back to King Solomon's Temple you may recall that the High Priest officiating there had to wear a metal Breastplate whenever he entered the Holy of Holies, for his own protection. We hypothesise that a flat metal representation of the Brass Vessel of King Solomon may also have been used by Rudd and his co-workers as a sort of Breastplate, as the ultimate metal lamen which was inscribed with *all* of the 72 Shem ha-Mephorash angel names, to protect them from whatever demon they conjured. An ordinary parchment lamen containing the holy names performed a similar purpose in a less elaborate manner.

It is suggestive to observe the 'handles' of the Brass Vessel which have been extended with a flat bar that would be an ideal shape to attach supporting straps to. The breastplate application is pure conjecture, which can only be proven by finding the actual artefact here represented in Peter Smart's engraving. Maybe it resides in the British Museum tucked away in some

---

[1] As rendered by Mathers.

dusty drawer, in the same way that Dr John Dee's magical equipment has been preserved by that very same institution. It would be fascinating if it were found still attached to leather straps.

Anyway we can be certain that this engraving is a representation of the Brass Vessel that was used by Rudd in his *Goetia* workings in the same way as the Triangle of Art. We can also be certain that the engraving on its surface of the 72 Shem ha-Mephorash angels was to ensure the obedience of the 72 demons. If it was also worn as a form of Breastplate or lamen, this certainly would have coincided with the theory behind Jewish religious and magical practice.

As we know from the Bible, the Jewish High Priest needed a Breastplate, embedded with 12 jewels, presumably to protect himself from the energies involved in dealing with the god in his sanctuary. It is probable that Solomon was acquainted with this form of spiritual protection, and therefore it is not surprising that a breastplate may later have been used to protect the karcist from the spirits and demons he evoked. Whether or not such a device has been handed down for centuries, or reinvented by Rudd, we cannot say.

In practice this means that whatever of the 72 demons you plan to evoke, or indeed whichever one comes, the corresponding angelic name is engraved upon the Brass Vessel. It is also designed to remind the demon of the brass stoppered container into which Solomon originally bound the 72 demons. The presence of this significant diagram is another reason why we chose to specifically publish the Rudd version of the *Goetia*.

Clothing

The clothing is detailed at some length, and even includes a headpiece such as a Jewish priest might have worn. More significant is the specification that the 3 inch (7.5 cm) wide waist belt should be made of lion's skin. This is either a piece of bravado to demonstrate to the spirits that this magician does not even fear lions, or may be a carry over from Egyptian priestly practice of wearing a full lion or leopard pelt, which can be seen in various Egyptian tomb paintings. In fact one of the best known photos of Mathers shows him draped in a leopard skin. Lion statues were also used as door guardians in ancient Egypt, in much the same way as they are used in both ancient and modern China, to frighten evil spirits.[1] Of course a lion guardian with a human head is a sphinx, and it is the sphinx with guards the three best known pyramids. As such, lion skin makes a very acceptable material for a magician's belt.

Perfumes

The Lemegeton is not specific about perfumes, but where Rudd has copied in parts of de Abano's *Heptameron*, the perfumes of the days of the week are used.

[1] Wallis Budge, *The Gods of the Egyptians*, Dover, New York, 1969, Volume II, page 361.

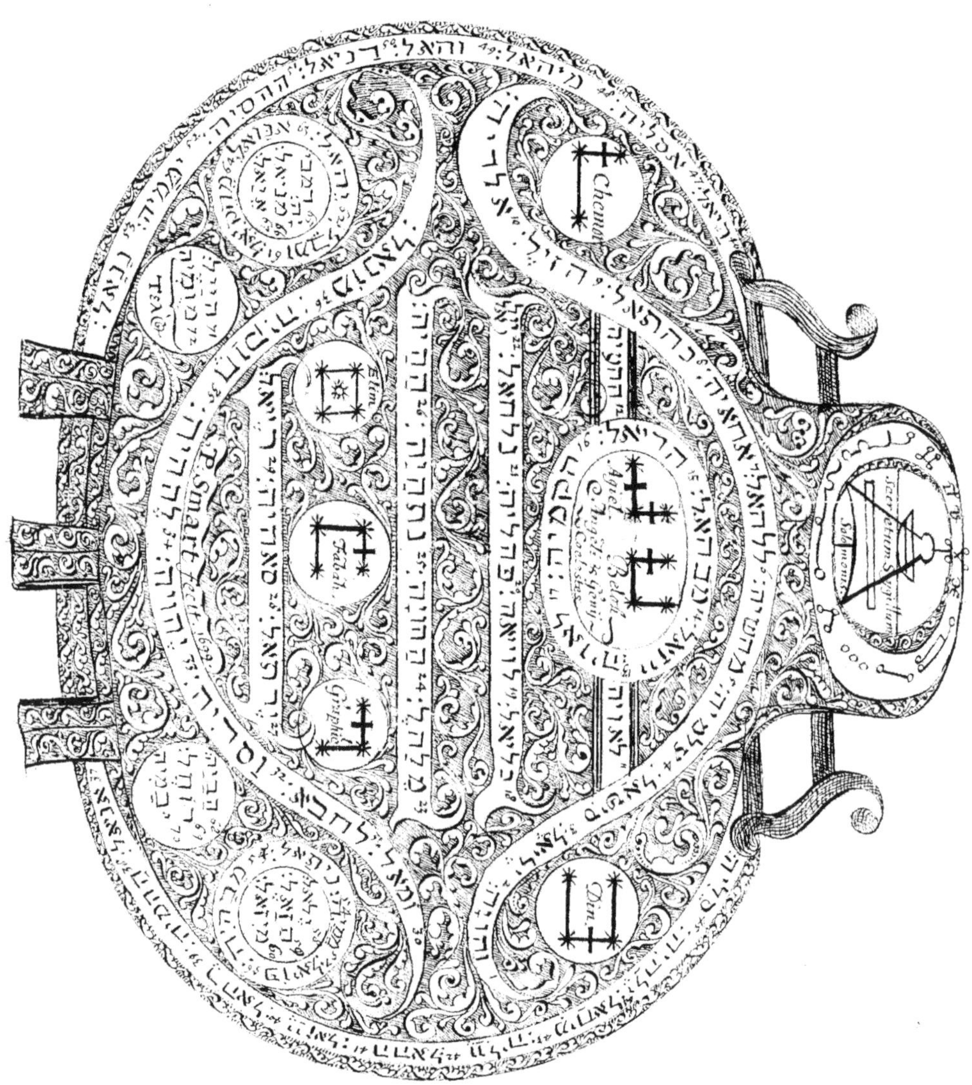

Figure 5: Peter Smart's 1699 engraving of the Solomon's Brass Vessel with every one of the 72 Shem ha-Mephorash angel names designed to control the 72 corresponding demons of the *Goetia.* Note that each angelic name is numbered from 1 to 72, beginning just below 'Din' and ending in the opposite corner. Note also the Secret Seal of Solomon in its place as a stopper for the Brass Vessel. This Seal is even captioned *'Secretum Sygillum Solomonis'* to avoid any doubt as to its true nature.

The Crystal or Glass Receptacle

The Crystal is not mentioned in the equipment section of the *Goetia* but it is specifically referred to in the conjurations as a locus of manifestation for the spirit. The Crystal is a key piece of equipment, and the magician

> "ought to have for his purpose a Crystal stone, of a round globic form, very clear & transparent, or other stone of like diaphanity, or ball of clear & solid glass, or thick hollow glass, with a little hole on the top of like form, of any convenient bigness or diameter, according as can reasonably be obtained or made, & the same [stone] to be set in a frame, & also the Glass to be made with a stalk or shank fixed thereto, & so to be put in a Socket with a foot or pedestal to stand upright; the stone being called by the name of a Shew stone; and the Glass by the name of a Glass Receptacle, and in practice or Action, upon Invocation or motion made for spiritual appearance."[1]

There are many mentions of the use of a crystal inside the Circle, in the context of evocation. In one example, the magician simultaneously uses two such instruments to attract the air spirits, with Oriens, Egyn and Paymon constrained to appear in one *vitrum*, and Amaymon in another.[2] The Crystal can be replaced by a glass container holding water or some other liquid. Franz Bardon's work on fluid condensers is useful in this context.[3]

Sacrifice

Sacrifice is not often spoken about in the context of magical rituals, except in a disapproving manner. However before we dismiss sacrifice as a cruel and outmoded practice, we should just look at its religious precedents. Judaism, before the destruction of the Temple in 70 CE, insisted upon sacrifice as a major part of its ritual, and the discussion of the qualities and quantities of sacrificed animals, takes up a lot of space in the Old Testament or *Tanakh.*

Solomon, above all other kings, sacrificed an enormous number of animals to consecrate his new Temple in Jerusalem. The smell or savour was supposed to be delightful to the Lord. Origen (185–c.232/254 CE) thought that the smell or the 'steam' of the sacrifices was attractive not just to the deity, but also to lesser spiritual creatures:

> "Just as the daemons, sitting by the [pagan] altars of the Gentiles, used to feed on the steam of sacrifices, so also the angels, allured by the blood of the victims which Israel offered as symbols of spiritual things, and by the smoke of the

---

[1] Harley MS 6482 ff 144v-145. See also Bodleian Library, Rawlinson MS D. 252, folio 18.

[2] For this experiment see Armand Delatte, *La Catoptromancie Grecque et ses dérivés*, Liege-Paris, 1932, pages 103-104. Catoptromancie is divination by means of mirrors and other reflective surfaces. On Floron which appears, like Byleth, in divination by mirror, to see Delatte, *ibid,* pages 44-47, and Richard Kieckhefer, *Forbidden Rites,* pages 28, 104, 106, 178, 236-239 and 363.

[3] Franz Bardon, *Initiation into Hermetics*, Osiris-Verlag, Koblenz, 1962, pages 194-203.

> incense, used to dwell near altars and to be nourished on food of this sort."[1]

It is clear that spiritual creatures are nourished by such sacrifices. It also identifies the similarity between the angels and the daemons, both allegedly supping on the vapours of sacrifice. After the demise of paganism at the death of the Emperor Julian in 363 CE, sacrifice became a more private matter, and became more relevant to lesser spiritual creatures, rather than just the major pagan gods.

Christianity replaced the animal sacrifice of its predecessor religion, Judaism, with the Eucharist, the consumption of the blood and body of Christ. Blood is however still central to the act, and it still commemorates a form of sacrifice. In the *Goetia*, at least two demons are overtly represented as requiring sacrifice, Malphas and Belial, and the sacrifice of smaller animals such as a cock has long been part of ritual magic.

For those city dwelling non-vegetarians amongst our readers who deplore the idea of animal sacrifice on humanitarian grounds, think first of the slaughter-houses which daily slaughter thousands of animals to provide the meat on your plates, before complaining about the barbarity of this practice.

In the nineteenth century Frederick Hockley tried many experiments in skrying and evocation as we mentioned in the history chapter including one in which he used blood from his own finger to supplement the fluid condenser in the glass receptacle which he was using for skrying. The experiment concluded with him almost loosing control. The application of one's own blood by way of a sacrifice is definitely not to be recommended.

We conclude with some text which occurs in the *Goetia* under the spirit Gaap, but which is really a more general procedural instruction.

> "There were certain necromancers [nigromancers] that offered sacrifices and burnt offerings unto him [the Spirit]; and to call him up, they exercised an art, saying that Salomon the wise made it. Which is false: for it was rather Cham, the son of Noah, who after the flood began first to invocate wicked spirits. He invocated Bileth, and made an art in his name, and a book which is known to many mathematicians.[2] There were burnt offerings and sacrifices made, and gifts given [to the spirits], and much wickedness wrought by the exorcists, who mingled there withal the holy names of God, the which in that art are everywhere expressed. Marie [certainly] there is an epistle [letter] of [about] those names written by Salomon, as also write [in the book] *Helias Hierosolymitanus* and [the book] *Helisaeus*."[3]

---

[1] Origen, *De Principiis*, 1.8.1.

[2] Interesting that mathematics is seen as overlapping magic, a view which might well have been that of Dr. John Dee, who took both pursuits equally seriously.

[3] Also referred to as *The Book Helisol* in one source, which is obviously a solar reference. Strangely, that scribe identifies *The Book Helisol* with the *Ars Notoria*. So it is possible that this is a

The Ceremony or Procedure

Timing is a key factor. For the spirits of the *Goetia* it is useful to select the day and the hour corresponding to the planet and rank of the spirit. But more importantly, the Moon should be waxing (that is increasing in size from New to Full) rather than waning or shrinking. It is also suggested that it should not be located in the heavens too close to the Sun, where it will be rendered 'combust' and its powers diminished considerably. These rules are designed so that the magician may take best advantage of the lunar tides that govern the 'sublunary regions'. Similar concerns are reflected in Taoist magic especially in the exercises which involve the 'inhalation' of lunar essences directly from the Moon.

There are five traditional and distinct stages in the evocation of spirits. It is not sufficient to simply call them and demand what you wish of them. These are outlined in Agrippa's *Fourth Book of Occult Philosophy*. The constituents of the ceremony are classically divided according to the following Latin headings:[1]

Consecratio Dei
Invocatio
Constrictio
Ligatio
Licentia

Let us look at each of these stages one at a time. Each part of the operation must be successfully concluded before moving on to next. Such operations have their own 'rhythm' and are rapidly reduced to failure if rushed.

Opening Prayers and Orisons – Consecratio Dei

On the day of the ceremony, after a schedule of fasting, abstaining, praying and purifying, the magician opens with prayers to god, looking in the first instance for support and protection from the highest source possible. John Dee prefaced his actions with spirits with long and sometimes very tedious prayers. However this is a necessary first line of defence. The seven Penitential Psalms are often recommended for use here.

---

forward reference to the fifth and last book of the *Lemegeton*. The book is also mentioned in the *Ars Notoria* where it says "Solomon himself doth describe in his Eleventh Book, *Helisoe…*" It is interesting that eleven books are mentioned.

[1] Geoffrey James in his *Angel Magic*, page 17, lists these in a more modern form as Consecration, Invocation, Conjuration, Conversation, and Dismissal. On page 62 an older version appears: "consecration, invocations, constrictions, ligations, maledictions", but the structure remains similar.

The Invocations - Invocatio

The word 'invoke' comes from the Latin *vocare*, simply meaning 'to call'. De Abano recommends that *Consecratio* is followed by invocations to the 'Angels from the four parts of the world, that rule the Air the same day wherein' the ceremony tales place. These are the names which would be incorporated into the Circle, if you are using a *Heptameron* style Circle.[1] The invocations then continue with the invocation of the correct Shem ha-Mephorash angel which is responsible for controlling the spirit/demon who is to be called. The relevant Psalm is used for this. Only when this angel has been satisfactorily invoked, may the spirit/demon be safely evoked.

Interestingly, there is not usually a separate section for calling the spirit, as that also comes under *Invocatio*, the same section as the calling of the angels. This is in de Abano referred to as an 'exorcism' rather than an invocation. The word 'exorcism' has changed somewhat in meaning over the centuries from calling out spirits to driving them away, a change probably brought about by the practices of the Church.

The essence here is to pace yourself: do not rush or gabble the invocations. The invocations should be learned and not read, so that they almost say themselves, and the mind can then concentrate on the job in hand not on attempting to read a script. It is far better to extemporise, if need be, than to fumble with a script which wont be easily readable in the half light anyway. Call with the knowledge that it may take the spirit/demon some time to arrive, and that rushing through the invocation is both discourteous and counter-productive. It may be necessary to repeat each invocation several times.

Without allowing the pace of the operation to slow down, or the attention of the assistants to wander, time should be given to see if the atmosphere has changed or any sign of a presence has been vouchsafed. It is the job of the assistants to keep a watchful eye out for indications like an apparent drop in temperature, a change in the light, changes in the incense stratification, unaccountable noises, or similar signs that something is attempting to arrive. The skryer of course will remain with his or her attention fixed on the crystal or glass receptacle on the Table of Practice. Only when a clear presence is seen, or at the very least strongly felt, should the magician move on to the next process.

Reception of the Spirit - Constrictio

The purpose of this part of the proceedings is to make sure that the spirit is either visible in the crystal, or forming outside the Circle, preferably in the vicinity of the Triangle or the Brass Vessel. It should be constricted to one or other of these loci.

---

[1] See Appendix 12 to appreciate how the configuration of the Circle changes.

Some text in the manuscript of the *Goetia* which is included under the spirit Beleth, is really a general procedural instruction, and not specific to that spirit. It shows how the wand may be used at this point.

> "[The Spirit will be] very furious at his first appearance that is whilst the Exorcist layeth his Courage, for to do that he must hold a hazel stick[1] in his hand stretching it out towards the South and the East quarter[2] making a Triangle Δ without [outside] the Circle, commanding him into it by the [the conjuration of the] bands & chains of spirits hereafter following[3], and if he do not come into the Δ Triangle by your threats rehearse the bands and chains [conjuration] before him and then he will yield obedience and come into it, and do what he is commanded by the Exorcist, yet he [the operator] must receive him courteously..."

As is often warned in the grimoires, this is the time to challenge the spirit and to test if it is really what it claims to be, or indeed if it is the spirit which you originally intended to evoke. Examples of such challenges can be found in Volume II of the present series.

Binding the Spirit – Ligatio

Ligatio is the binding of the spirit with an oath, to an agreement that it will perform the task demanded of it. *Ligatio* has the secondary meaning of 'to harness'. Ideally the spirit should also 'sign' the *Liber Spirituum* left open in the Triangle, or mark the seal there drawn in some other unique way. In practice, a verbal agreement to undertake what it has been charged with is sufficient.

Another, and most important part of *Ligatio,* is to bind the spirit so that it will come again (with less delay) when called again by the operator. If this part of *Ligatio* is carried out properly the magician's load is very much lightened the second time around. In fact a competent magician will have already done this, so that when a task arises he will already have bound a spirit suitable for its accomplishment.[4]

In the case of the spirit the stimulus or agreed invocatory shorthand might be the uncovering or incensing of its sigil, or a hand gesture, accompanied by the correct words. Muttering accompanied by certain *mudras* or hand gestures is a common short-form invocation seen in some schools of oriental magic.

After the spirit has been satisfactorily bound, the magician is able to question

---

1 W: *"Baculum"*, a wand used by an auger.

2 This is not always SE, but depends upon the quarter from which the Spirit is expected to come.

3 See the Conjurations section.

4 Although there is no connection, a parallel can be made with the use of post-hypnotic suggestion in hypnosis, where the subject is clearly instructed to the effect that upon a certain signal he or she will fall into trance without delay, making the hypnotist's work lighter next time.

it or charge it with the performance of the specific task which is the objective of the operation. The magician should never invoke a spirit just out of curiosity, any more than you might say ring the police, just to see if they are there.

License to Depart – Licentia

Once there are no further questions or instructions, the time arrives for the spirit's dismissal. It is interesting that this is expressed as a 'licence', that is a permission to depart, rather than a banishing. Modern magical practice is overly keen on the Lesser Banishing Ritual of the Pentagram as promulgated by the Golden Dawn, Aleister Crowley, and Regardie, and indeed in *Techniques of High Magic*. Our thinking has however moved on from there. Having conjured, threatened, and bound the spirit successfully, it is downright rude to then banish it. If you want to develop a relationship in which the spirit will come willingly next time, the appropriate tool to use is the Licence to Depart.

Allow it that licence and it will depart rapidly to its own abode. Stories of spirits not departing upon being licensed to so do, are sure indications that the earlier steps, particularly the *Ligatio*, have not been correctly performed. The spirit will go as if attached to an elastic band which has just been released. Or to use another analogy, the spirit will return to its own abode like a swimmer will return to the surface, after holding his breath for more than three minutes in the alien environment of water. For the demon or spirit, a physical manifestation is a very alien place, and he will be more keen that you to return to his own world.

If the spirit becomes recalcitrant you might need to fall back on using the name of its angel to constrain it, reminding the spirit that the angel has the keys. However this is an unlikely situation if the *Ligatio* has been successfully performed.

The use of the Lesser Banishing Ritual of the Pentagram so favoured by the Hermetic Order of the Golden Dawn might be useful afterwards, but only to encourage any other low grade spirits who (like moths) may have been attracted to the flame of your ceremony, to depart. Of course if you have successfully invoked the angels of the four quarters at the beginning of the ceremony, then the Lesser Banishing Ritual of the Pentagram should be recast as an acknowledgement of their aid.

Finally there are other techniques for banishing demons, as mentioned in the *Testament of Solomon* and *The Book of Tobit*, but you should probably reserve techniques like the burning of catfish entrails for cases of exorcism, or for dire emergencies.

The Manuscript

Content & Provenance

This manuscript Harley MS 6483, like other numerically adjacent manuscripts, such as Harley MS 6482 and MS 6484, was transcribed by Peter Smart between 1712 and 1713 from the original manuscript of Dr Thomas Rudd (1583-1656). Smart's copy even has the old page numbers from the original more cramped manuscript written at the top of every few pages: Smart used 414 folios to copy just 103 folios written by Rudd. Smart started transcribing from the beginning of Rudd's manuscript (in Harley MS 6482),[1] but only reached Dr Rudd's *Goetia*, the first book of the *Lemegeton*, with the 'thirty-sixth sheet of Dr. Rudd.' At this point Smart began transcribing into the volume now known as Harley MS 6483. In terms of subject matter however, Harley MS 6483 is self-contained, with the five distinct books of the *Lemegeton* completely contained within its covers.

It is very likely that the original Rudd manuscript was written in 1655/1656. Upon Rudd's death in 1656 we conjecture that it was passed to Sir John Heydon (1629-1667), the prolific writer on the Rosicrucians and geomancy: Rudd's close friendship with Heydon is actually written about within the pages of the present manuscript (see Appendix 11). Upon Heydon's death in 1667 we think that Rudd's manuscripts were passed to his good friend the astrologer Dr John Gadbury (1627-1704). It is definitely known that Gadbury then passed them to Peter Smart in 1686.[2]

There are at least six main manuscript versions of the *Lemegeton*, and its constituents that we need to consider and compare.

a) Sloane MS 3824. This is a kind of proto-*Lemegeton*, as it contains many of the ingredients of the *Lemegeton*, but without its final form or name, and refers to John Rudd, probably a relative of Thomas Rudd.

b) Sloane MS 3825 (written on or after 10th March 1640/1)[3] which is the main source for Joseph Peterson's standard edition of the *Lemegeton*. This volume also contains the *Ars Notoria* and *Janua Magical Reserata* (which has been issued by us as Volume II of the present series).

c) Rudd MS, folios 36-141 (probably written in 1655/56, this MS contains all five parts of the *Lemegeton* including the *Ars Notoria*). This MS is the source of f).

---

[1] Parts of which were reproduced in Volume II of the present series.

[2] As noted in Harley MS 6483, fol. 414v. This note, which was later crossed out, may refer to the next volume Harley 6484, and but it is a reasonable guess that Heydon and Gadbury may have been the source of Rudd's original manuscripts that were subsequently transcribed by Peter Smart.

[3] Note that during this time of calendar turmoil, there were several dating systems, and so any date falling between January and March often had two years marked separated by a slash. The second would correspond to our modern year dating.

d) Sloane MS 3648 (written between 1657 and 1687) is a bit carelessly written and bound up with extracts from Agrippa and Paracelsus. It has the *Ars Notoria* included, but this has been copied from the printed version of 1657.

e) Sloane MS 2731 (written 18th January, 1686/7).[1] This manuscript copies from a number of sources including Sloane MS 3648. It has formed the basis of most of the modern and incomplete editions of the *Lemegeton*. It omits the *Ars Notoria*.

f) *Liber Malorum Spirituum seu Goetia*, Harley MS 6483 (copied in 1712-13). This is a verbatim transcription from the Rudd MS listed above under b), and its contents are transcribed in this volume. It also shows some similarities with Sloane MS 3648.

In 1657 the *Ars Notoria: the Notory Art of Solomon* (the fifth book of the *Lemegeton*) was published in English by Robert Turner of Holshott (c.1620-c.1665), a date that becomes important in sorting out the order of these manuscripts. It seems possible however that this translation was made available to others of a like mind by Turner before it was actually printed.

Hence the present book is printed from the most recent version of the *Lemegeton*. Or is it? If we look a little deeper we will see that there are a large number of differences between this manuscript and the four other Sloane manuscripts. Let us detail these differences and see what questions they raise and how these questions bear on the dating of the original Rudd MS:

1. The Rudd MS has the double seals, including the 72 angels necessary to control the 72 demons of the *Goetia*. These angels are left out of all the other manuscripts. So is the Rudd MS from an earlier source, and the angels simply omitted from later manuscripts, or were the angels a later addition by Dr Rudd?

2. The seals in the Rudd MS are neater and simpler than any of the Sloane seals. Does this suggest that seals became sloppier and more elaborate as they were copied and recopied, or does it suggest that a later copyist simplified the seals arbitrarily?

3. Without a doubt, the invocations in all versions are drawn from Peter de Abano's *Heptameron*. But, and this is a clincher, only in the Rudd MS is the main floor circle also drawn from the *Heptameron*. So what is most likely, that the circle became more elaborate as it passed from copyist to copyist, or that a later copyist suddenly reverted to the original simple *Heptameron* circle rather than following the text he was copying?

---

[1] A E Waite erroneously states 10 January 1676. This date was also repeated by E M Butler in *Ritual Magic* published in 1949, a book which incidentally treats of the grimoires in a much less sensational manner than Waite's rather gaudy treatment.

We suggest that it is more likely that the version with a Circle closer to the *Heptameron's* Circle design is the older version, and the Circle got more complex as it was recopied, culminating in the elaborate design which incorporates all the angelic and Godnames drawn in order from the Tree of Life.

We suggest that the 1712/13 copy of the 1655/56 Rudd MS may represent an earlier form of the *Goetia* than any of the other extant manuscripts, a form with simpler seals and Circle, rooted more firmly and closely in its predecessor grimoire the *Heptameron*. However because of certain scribal errors, we can only be certain that it represents a different branch of the manuscript *stemma*.

With all seventeenth century manuscripts of the *Lemegeton*, the fifth book, the *Ars Notoria*, as pointed out by Joseph Peterson, is taken from the *printed* English translation of 1657 done by Robert Turner. From a practical point of view this version is useless as it omits the all important diagrams, the *notae,* without which the procedure will not work. For this reason we have omitted the *Ars Notoria* from the present volume.[1]

If we go back a little further and tentatively identify the 'T.R.' who translated the *Pseudomonarchia Daemonum* from Latin into English in 1570 with Thomas Rudd senior, then we have the possibility that knowledge of the 72 demons may have been in the Rudd family since at least that date.[2]

Notes on Style used in the Transcription

Capitalisation in some manuscripts is applied to all significant nouns, but in others such as Harley MS 6483 the usage is closer to modern usage. In this volume we have sometimes inserted additional paragraph breaks in the interests of easier reading, where this does not affect the meaning or the flow. Where a new sentence break has been introduced to facilitate reading, it is marked with a footnote as 'SB'. These breaks usually fall on a colon or semi-colon. Many line ends are filled with a dash. This has been usually ignored, although sometimes interpreted as a comma where the sense allows.

In general, the spelling of the manuscript has been rationalised to modern English, without interfering with the meaning. For example words like "seales", "soe" and "doe" have been transcribed as "seals", "so" and "do", "cœlestial" as "celestial", and "Angell" as "Angel". Likewise, obvious contractions like "wch" have been expanded, to "which". However "&", which is used frequently through the manuscript has been maintained, as has

[1] The *Ars Notoria* is available in a modern version edited by Darcy Kuntz. *Ars Notoria: the Magical Art of Solomon...Englished by Robert Turner.* Holmes, Sequim, 2006.

[2] This manuscript English translation done in 1570 by 'T.R.' was used by Reginald Scot in his *Discoverie of Witchcraft* (page 393 [278]), rather than the printed Latin version of the *Pseudomonarchia Daemonum.*

"&c" for "etcetera". Standard manuscript contractions like the bar or *tilde* over the last letter (representing 'm' or 'um') have been silently expanded. Some older spellings like 'shalt' have been retained as there should be no difficulty in understanding them.

Many of the spirit names have variant spellings. We have not been exhaustive in listing these, but have corrected obvious transcription errors. The letters 'u' and 'v' have been interchanged to reflect modern usage, with 'u' used as a vowel and 'v' as a consonant. Most variant spirit names in the *Goetia* will be found in Table M15 in Appendix 2. We have not documented all the variations in the spirit names of the *Art Pauline.*

The grammar of the manuscript is reproduced faithfully, and no attempt has been made to render it into a modern English form, the text being sufficiently clear in its original form as not to warrant such alteration.

Footnotes

Footnotes quoting the Latin on the seals follow Rudd, and will therefore not always match exactly with either the *Vulgate* (which anyway has several versions) or Table A25 to be found in Appendix 7. Where footnotes occur:

'Insert' indicates additional text
'Omit' indicates the removal of text.
Struck-through text indicates that this occurs in addition to the text, or that it has been struck through by the original scribe.
A single word or phrase indicates a replacement for the word or phrase marked by the footnote.

Manuscript Variants

The following abbreviations are used in the footnotes to distinguish textual differences between different manuscripts. We have adopted Joseph Peterson's abbreviation standards for ease of comparison:

H: Harley MS 6483 – *Liber Malorum Spirituum*, the present manuscript
H1: Harley MS 6482 – Rudd's *Treatise on Angel Magic*
S1: Sloane MS 2731 – *Lemegeton*
S2: Sloane MS 3648 – *Lemegeton*
S3: Sloane MS 3825 – *Lemegeton* (Peterson's prime source)
S4: Sloane MS 3824 – proto-*Lemegeton* (not listed by Peterson)
W1: Wellcome MS 3203 – *Lemegeton* (not listed by Peterson)
W2: Wellcome MS 4665 – *Lemegeton* (not listed by Peterson)
HMN: Peter de Abano, *Heptameron or Magical Elements* (1655 reprinted 2005)
T: Johann Trithemius, *Steganographia* (Darmstardt, 1621)
W: Johann Weyer, *Pseudomonarchia Daemonum*, 1660, pages 649-666.

Liber Malorum Spirituum seu Goetia[1]

This Book contains all the names, Orders, and Offices of all the Spirits Solomon ever conversed with. The Seals and Characters belonging to each spirit; and the manner of calling them forth to visible appearance.

Some of these Spirits are in Enoch's Tables which I have explained,[2] but omitted their Seals & Characters how they may be known, but in this book they are at large set forth.

The Definition of Magick

Magick is the highest most absolute and divinest knowledge of Natural Philosophy advanced in its works and wonderful operations, by a right understanding of the inward and occult virtue of things, so that true agents being applied to proper patients, strange and admirable effects will thereby be produced; whence Magicians are profound and diligent searchers into Nature; they because of their skill know how to anticipate an effect which to the vulgar shall seem a miracle.

Origen saith that the ~~Mediaeval~~ Magical Art doth not contain any thing subsisting, but although it should yet that must not be evil or subject to contempt or scorn; and doth distinguish the Natural Magick from that which is Diabolical.

Tyaneus [3] only exercised the Natural magick by which he performed wonderful things.

Philo Hebreus[4] saith that true Magick by which we come to the secret works of nature is so far from being contemptible that the greatest monarchs & Kings have studied it, Nay amongst the Persians none might reign unless he were skilful in this great Art.

---

[1] This manuscript, Harley MS 6483, begins with a note *"Thirty sixth sheet Dr Rudd"*. This confirms that this manuscript, although self-contained, continues on from Harley MS 6482. It is a fair transcript done in 1712-1713 by the lawyer Peter Smart of an earlier manuscript owned or written by Dr Thomas Rudd which dates from pre-1656 (Rudd's date of death).

[2] In MS Harley 6842 in which Rudd interestingly explains the letters on Dr John Dee's skrying table as abbreviations of spirit names from the *Goetia,* thus tying Dee even more closely to the grimoire magic from which his system was derived. See Appendix 4 for this list of spirits.

[3] Apollonius of Tyana (1st century CE).

[4] Philo Judaeus (1st century CE).

This noble Science often degenerates, and from Natural becomes Diabolical, from true philosophy turns to Negromancy which is wholly to be charged upon its followers who abusing or not being capable of that high and mystical knowledge do immediately hearken to the temptations of Sathan, and are misled by him into the study of the black art. Hence it is that Magick lies under disgrace, and they who seek after it are vulgarly esteemed Sorcerers. And the fraternity of the Rosy Crucians[1] thought it not fit to style themselves Magicians but philosophers, they are [not] ignorant Empirics, but learned and experienced physicians whose remedies are not only lawful but divine.

The [Lesser] Key of Solomon[2]

Which contains all the Names, orders, offices of all the Spirits that Solomon had command with, together with the Seals and characters belonging to each Spirit and the Manner of Calling them forth to visible appearance. In four parts.

Part 1. Is a book of evil Spirits Called *Goetia*, showing how he bound those Spirits up, and used them in Several things, whereby he obtained great fame.

Part 2. Is a book of Spirits, partly good and partly evil, which is named *Theurgia Goetia*, all airy spirits.

Part 3. Is a book governing the planetary houses and ~~partly evil~~ what Spirit belongs to every degree of the Signs and planets in the Signs, called the *Pauline Art*.

Part 4. Is a book called the *Almadel of Solomon* which contains 20 chief Spirits and govern the four Altitudes or the 360 degrees of the Zodiac.[3]

The two last orders of Spirits are good and are to be sought by divine seeking.[4]

[Part 5. Is a book called the *Notory Art*.][5]

---

[1] A fashionable reference at the time and probably due to Dr Rudd's association with John Heydon.

[2] Taken from W1. This section is omitted by Rudd in Harley 6483. This is similar to the introduction found in S1, S2 & S3, but absent from H. It has been slightly reworded and is most noticeably different in that it refers to the book as a work of four parts rather than five, entirely omitting reference to the *Notory Art*, and has the additional two lines at the end.

[3] The spirits of the 360 degrees actually belong to Part 3, the *Pauline Art*.

[4] S3 adds: "These Bookes were first found in the Chaldean & Hebrew tongues at Hierusalem, by a Jewish Rabbi, & by him put into the Greeke Language, & from thence into ye Latine, as it is said &c."

[5] We have however omitted the *Notory Art* from this printed volume, for reasons explained in the Introduction.

Lemegeton

Secretum Secretorum[1]

[The 72 Spirits of the *Goetia*]

The first principal Spirit is a King riding [ruling] in the East called **Bael**,[2] he makes men go invisible he ruleth over 66 Legions of inferior spirits he appeareth in divers shapes sometimes like a Cat, sometimes like a dog and sometimes like a Man, and sometimes in all these forms.

At once he speaketh hastily and this is his Character or Seal which must be worn as a Lamin [Lamen] by the Magician who calls him, on his breast[3] else he will not do you homage.[4]

[1] The phrase 'Secretum Secretorum' which *begins* the *Goetia*, is also to be found in Scot's *Discoverie of Witchcraft*, Book xv, at the *end* of chapter ii, immediately after Master T.R.'s translation of Weir's *Pseudomonarchia Daemonum*, which is effectively the list of almost all the 72 *Goetia* spirits. The phrase that follows it is "*Tu operans sis secretus horum*" all of which translates as 'The Secret of Secrets, thou that works them, be secret in them'.

[2] S1: "Baell".

[3] W2: Replaces "by the Magician who calls him on his breast" with "before him who calls him forth".

[4] For each of the 72 spirits, the seal of the spirit is on the left, and the seal of its angel is on the right. At the top is the Hebrew for the spirit and angel respectively. In the middle of the angel's seal is the Psalm associated with that angel. It is transcribed below, and at the foot of each page for all 72 spirits, with its English translation and chapter and verse reference.
Tu Domine susceptor meus es gloria mea et exaltans Caput meum.
Thou, O Lord, art my guardian, and exaltest my head. [*Psalm* 3:5]

The second Spirit is a Duke called **Agares** he is under the power of the East, and comes up in the form of an old man of a fair complexion riding upon a Crocodile very mildly carrying a Goshawk on his fist.

He makes them run that stand still and bringeth back Runaways, he can teach all Languages or tongues, he hath power also to destroy dignities[1] both supernatural and temporal, and causeth Earthquakes.

He was of the Order of Virtues he hath under his Government 31 Legions of Spirits, and this is his Seal which is to be worn as a Lamen.[2]

[1] Honours.

[2] Et tu Domine ne elongaveris auxiliam tuum à me, ad Defensionem meam conspice.
Do not remove thy help from me, O Lord, and look to my defence [*Psalm* 21:20].

The third Spirit is a mighty Prince of the same nature as Agares called **Vasago**.[1] This spirit is of a good nature, and his office is to declare things past and to come. And to discover all things hid or lost.[2]

He governeth 26 Legions of Spirits, And this is his Seal which must be worn as a Lamen.[3]

[1] S1, S2, S3, W1: *"Vassago"*.

[2] Hence his frequent use as a Treasure Finding Spirit.

[3] Dicam Domino susceptor meus es tu, et refugium meum, Deus meus sperabo in sum.
I shall say to the Lord, Thou art my guardian, my God is my refuge, and shall hope in him [*Psalm* 90:2].

[1]The fourth Spirit is **Gamigin**[2] a great Marquis he appeareth in the form of a little horse and ass, and then takes human shape, he puts himself at the request of the Master, he teacheth all liberal sciences and gives an account of dead souls that die in sin. He ruleth over 30 Legions of inferior spirits. His Seal is which is to be worn as a Lamen before the Magician when he is Invocated

When he taketh human shape he speaketh with a hoarse voice disputing of all the liberal Sciences; he bringeth also to pass, that the souls which are drowned in the Sea shall take airy bodies and evidently appear and answer to Interrogations at the request of the Exorcist. [3]

[1] Thirty seventh sheet Dr Rudd.
[2] W1: Transposes with Marbas, giving him as the fourth spirit and Gamigin as the fifth.
[3] Convertere Domino, et eripe animam meam, salvum me fac propter misericordiam tuam. Turn, O Lord, and deliver my soul, and save me for Thy mercy's sake. [*Psalm* 6:4]

The 5th Spirit is **Marbas**[1] alias Barbas he is a great President and appeareth in the form of a mighty Lion but at the command of the Magician he putteth on human shape, he answereth fully as to any thing which is hidden or secret; he causeth diseases and cureth them; he promoteth wisdom, and the knowledge of mechanical arts or Handicrafts; he changeth men into other shapes; he governeth 36 Legions of spirits his Seal is this[2]

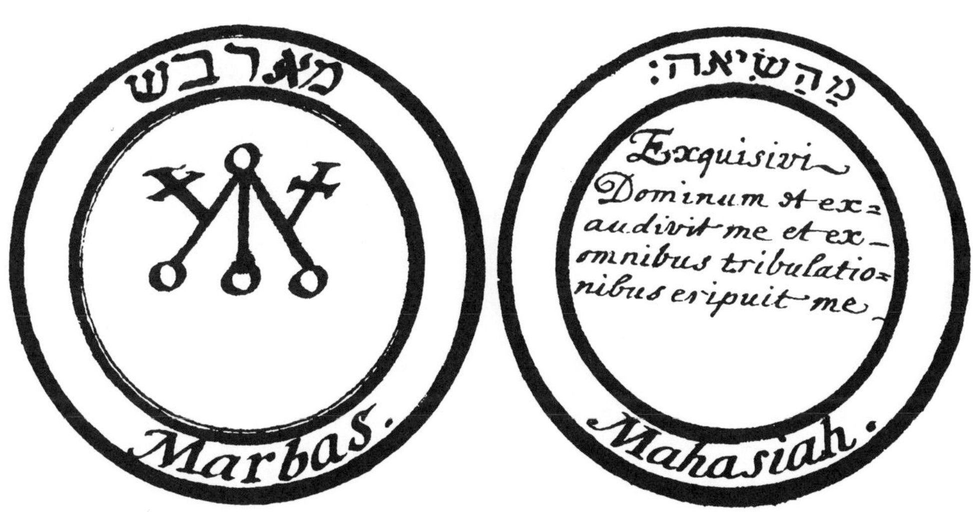

[1] W1: Transposes with Gamigin, giving Marbas as the fourth spirit.
[2] Ex qui sivi Dominum et exaudivit me, et ex omnibus tribulationibus eripuit me:
I called upon the Lord and he heard me and delivered me from all my tribulations. [*Psalm* 33:4].
NB: this Angel and Quote are attributed to Amon (spirit 7) in Harley 6482.

The Sixth Spirit is **Valefar**[1] he is a mighty Duke and appeareth in the form of a Lion with a Mans head howling, he is a good familiar, but he tempteth them that are familiar for to steal, he governeth ten Legions of spirits. His Seal is this which is to be worn constantly if you will have his familiarity else not[2]

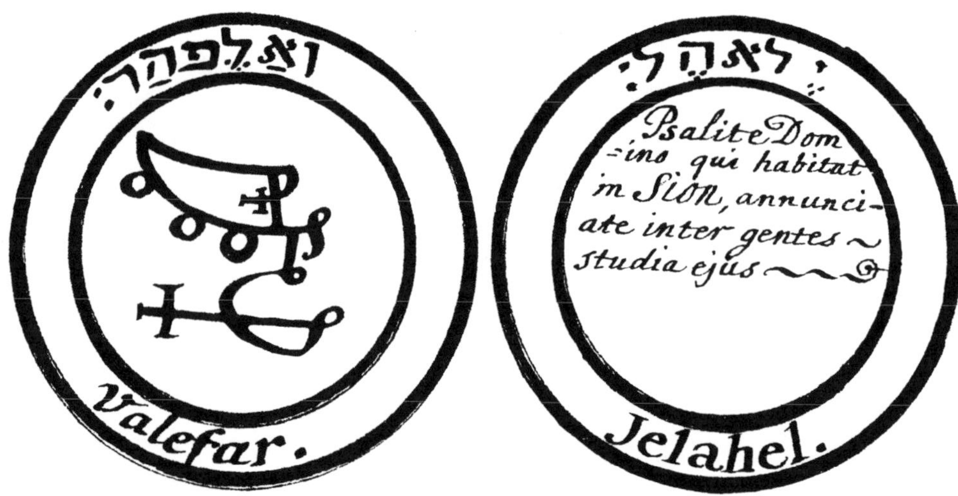

[1] S2, W1: *"Valefor"*.

[2] Psalite Domino qui habitat in Sion annunciate inter gentes studia eius.
Let him who lives in Zion sing unto the Lord, and proclaim his goodwill among the peoples. [*Psalm* 9:11]
N.B: Rudd attributes this Angel and quote to Marbas (Spirit 5) in Harley MS 6482.

The Seventh Spirit is **Amon** he is a Marquis great in power and most strong, he at first appeareth like a wolf with a serpents tail vomiting out of his mouth flames of fire, sometimes appears like a Raven with Dogs teeth in his head; He telleth all things past present and to come, and procureth love; And reconcileth Controversies between friends & foes and governeth forty Legions of spirits, his Seal is to be worn &c[1]

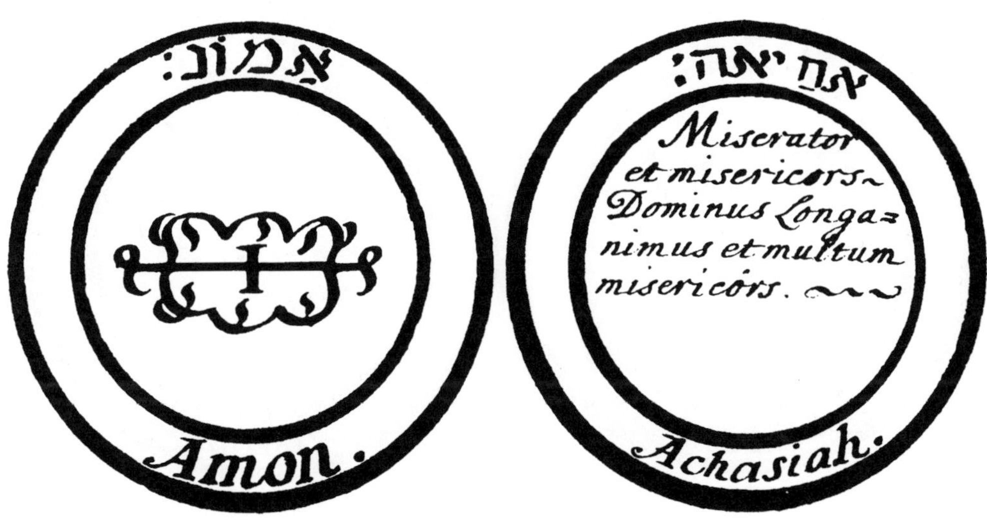

[1] Miserator et misericors Dominus, longanimus et multum misericors.
The Lord is merciful and compassionate, long-suffering and of great goodness. [*Psalm* 102:8]
NB: Rudd attributes this Angel and quote to Valefor (spirit 6) in Harley 6482.

[1]The Eighth Spirit is **Barbatos** he is a great Duke and appeareth when the Sun is in Sagittarius with four noble Kings and their Companies of great troops, he giveth the understanding of the singing of birds and the voices of all other creatures as [for example] the barking of Dogs, and he breaketh open hidden treasures that hath been laid by the enchantment of Magicians, and is of the Order of Virtues which some part bear rule still &c

He knoweth all things past present and to come, and reconcileth friends and those that are in power. He ruleth over three hundred Legions of spirits. His Seal of obedience is this which [you should] wear before you.[2]

[1] Thirty Eight sheet Dr Rudd.

[2] Venite, adoremus, et procedamus ante Dominum qui fecit nos:
O come let us adore and fall down before God who bore us. [*Psalm* 94:6].
Note that the Hebrew אחיאה, AChIAH at the top of the angel's seal is incorrect, and should instead be that which is written in the centre as כאהטל, KAHTL.

The Ninth Spirit in order is **Paimon**[1] a great King and very obedient to Lucifer he appeareth in [the] form of a man sitting on a Dromedary with a Crown most glorious on his head there goeth before him an host of spirits like men with trumpets and well sounding Cymbals and all other sorts of Musical Instruments &c he hath a great voice and roareth at his first coming and his speech is such that the Magician cannot well withstand him except he compel him.

This Spirit can teach all Arts and sciences and other secret things, he can discover [reveal] what the earth is, and what holdeth it up in the waters, and what the wind is and where it is, and any other thing you desire to know, he gives dignities[2] and confirms the same. He bindeth and maketh any man subject to the Magician if he desire it, He giveth good familiars and such as can teach all arts, He is to be observed towards the West, he is of the Order of Dominations and hath two hundred Legions of spirits under him, one part of them is of the order of Angels the other of Potestates.

If you call this Spirit Paimon alone you must make some offering to him, and there will attend him two Kings called Baball[3] & Abalam, and other spirits of the order of Potestates. In his host are 25 Legions because those spirits which are subject to them are not always with them except the Magician compel them, his Character is this which is to be worn as a Lamen.[4]

[1] Paimon or Paymon is sometimes listed (but not in the *Goetia*) as one of the four Kings of the cardinal directions.

[2] Honours.

[3] S1: "Beball"; S3: "Bebal".

[4] Reminiscere miserationum tuarum Domine et miserationum quae a saeculo sunt: Remember Thy mercies, O Lord, and Thy mercies which have been for ever. [*Psalm* 24:6]

The tenth Spirit is **Buer** a great President and appeareth in Sagittarius when the Sun is there. He teacheth Philosophy both moral and natural and the Art of Logic and the virtues of all herbs and plants, and healeth all distempers in man, and giveth good familiars, he governeth 50 Legions of Spirits, and this is his seal of obedience which you must wear when you call him to obedience.[1]

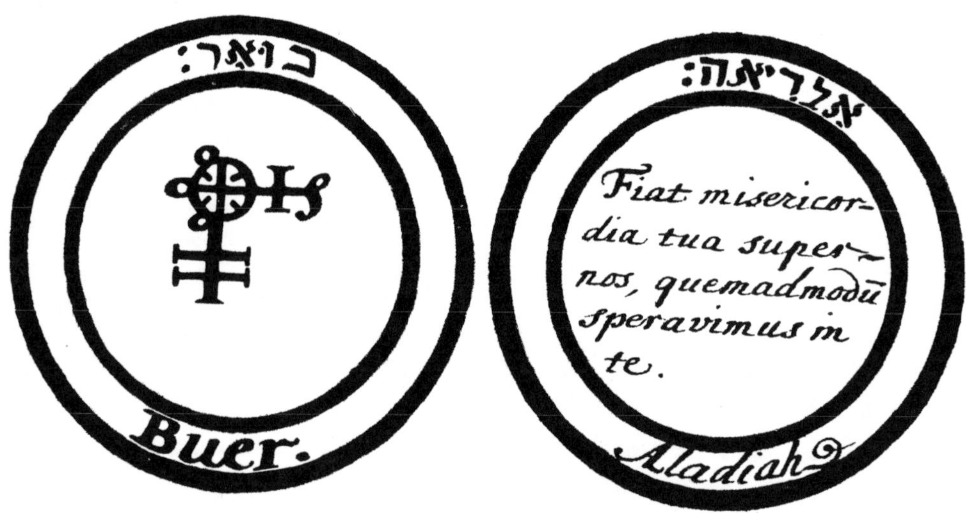

[1] Fiat misericordia tua super nos, quemadmodum speravimus in te:
Perform Thy mercies upon us, for we have hoped in Thee. [*Psalm* 32:22]

The Eleventh Spirit is a great and strong Duke called **Gusoin**, he appeareth in the form of a Xenophilus,[1] he telleth all things past present and to come, and showeth the meaning of all Questions you can ask, he reconcileth friendships, and gives honour and dignities to any, and ruleth over forty Legions of Spirits, his Seal is this which wear. [2]

[1] A *zenophali* or *xenophalloi*. Not to be confused with the 4th century Pythagorean philosopher, Xenophilus.

[2] Vivit Dominus et benedictus Deus meus et exaltetur Deus salutis meae:
The Lord liveth, blessed is my God, and let the God of my salvation be exalted. [*Psalm* 17:50]

[1]The twelfth Spirit is **Sitri** he is a great Prince and appeareth at first with a Leopard's face and Wings as a Griffin, but after at the command of the Exorcist he putteth on human shape very beautiful enflaming men with women's love and causeth them to show themselves naked if it be required. And he governeth 60 Legions of Spirits and his seal is this which wear. [2]

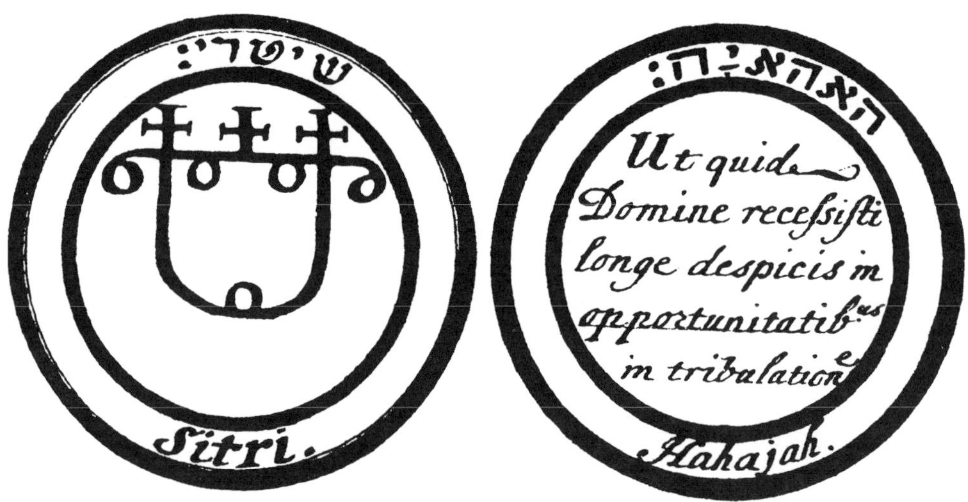

[1] Thirty Ninth sheet Dr Rudd.

[2] Ut quid Domine recessisti longe despicis in opportunitatibus in tribulatione:
Why hast Thou departed, O Lord, so long from us perishing in the times of tribulation. [*Psalm* 9:22]

The thirteenth Spirit is called **Beleth**[1] he is a mighty King and terrible, riding on a pale horse with Trumpets and all other Musical Instruments playing before him, he is very furious at his first appearance that is whilst the Exorcist layeth his Courage, for to do that he must hold a hazel stick in his hand stretching it out towards the South and the East quarter making a Triangle Δ without[2] the Circle, commanding him into it by the bands & chains of spirits hereafter following, and if he do not come into the Δ Triangle by your threats rehearse the bands and chains [conjuration] before him and then he will yield obedience and come into it, and do what he is commanded by the Exorcist, yet he must receive him courteously because he is a great King, and do homage to him as the Kings and princes do that attend him, you must have always a Silver ring on the middle finger of your left hand held against your face as they do set before Amaymon,[3] This great King Beleth causeth all the love that possibly may be [had] both of man and woman till the Master Exorcist have had his mind fulfilled &c. He is of the order of Powers and governeth Eighty-five Legions ~~his~~ of Spirits. His noble Seal is this which is to be worn before you at working.[4]

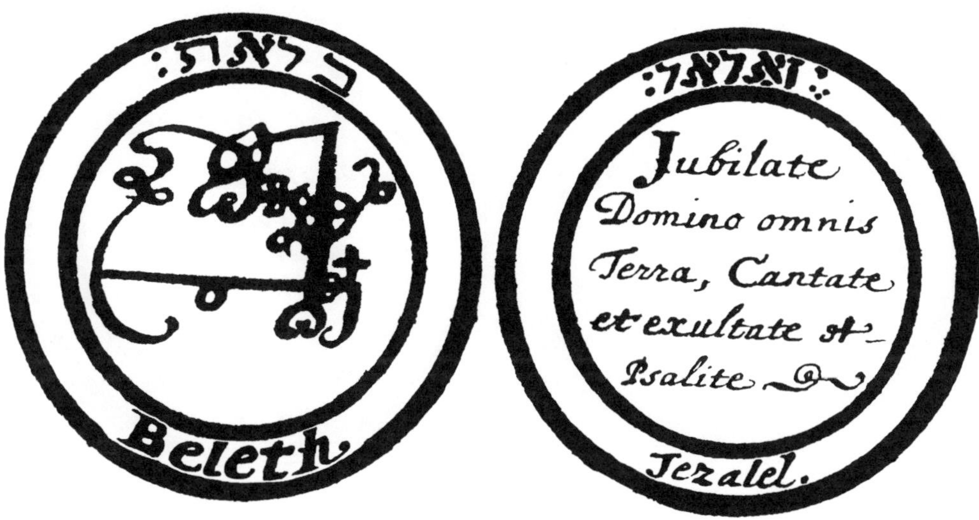

[1] Scot has "Bileth".

[2] Outside the Circle. This is more in the nature of a general instruction, not one just relating solely to Beleth.

[3] King of the East. The other three Kings are Corson/Gorson (the West), Ziminiar (the North) and Goap (the South). These Kings are attributed to different quarters in other sources.

[4] Jubilate Domino omnis Terra, Cantate, et exultate, et Psalite:
Rejoice in the Lord, all ye lands, sing exult, and play upon a stringed instrument. [*Psalm* 97:6]

[1]The fourteenth spirit is called **Leraic**,[2] he is a Marquis great in power showing himself in the likeness of an Archer clad in green carrying a bow and quiver, he causeth all great battles and contests and causeth the wounds to putrefy that are made with arrows by archers. This [spirit] belongs to Sagittarius and he governeth 30 Legions of spirits and this is his Seal.[3]

[1] W1: Omits all the spirits from here to Asmodai.

[2] S1, S2: "Leraje"; S3: "Leraye (or Leraje)".

[3] Et factus est Dominus refugium pauperi adjutor in opportunitatibus in tribulationum: The Lord also will be a refuge for the oppressed, and in times of trouble. [*Psalm* 9:9]

The fifteenth Spirit is **Eligos**[1] a great Duke and appeareth in form of a goodly Knight carrying a Lance, Ensign and a Serpent. He discovereth hidden things and knoweth things to come, and of wars how the Soldiers shall or will meet: he causeth the Love of Lords and great persons, and governeth sixty Legions of spirits, his Seal is this which wear else he will not appear nor obey you.[2]

[1] S1, S3: *"Eligor"*.

[2] Et factus est mihi Dominus in refugium et Deus meus in adjutorium spei mei:
The Lord is a refuge for me and my God the help of my hope. [*Psalm* 93:22]

[1]The 16th Spirit is **Zepar** he is a great Duke and appeareth in red apparel armed like a Soldier. His Office is to cause women to love men and to bring them together in love, he also maketh them barren, He governeth 26 Legions of inferior spirits. His Seal is this that he obeys when he sees it.[2]

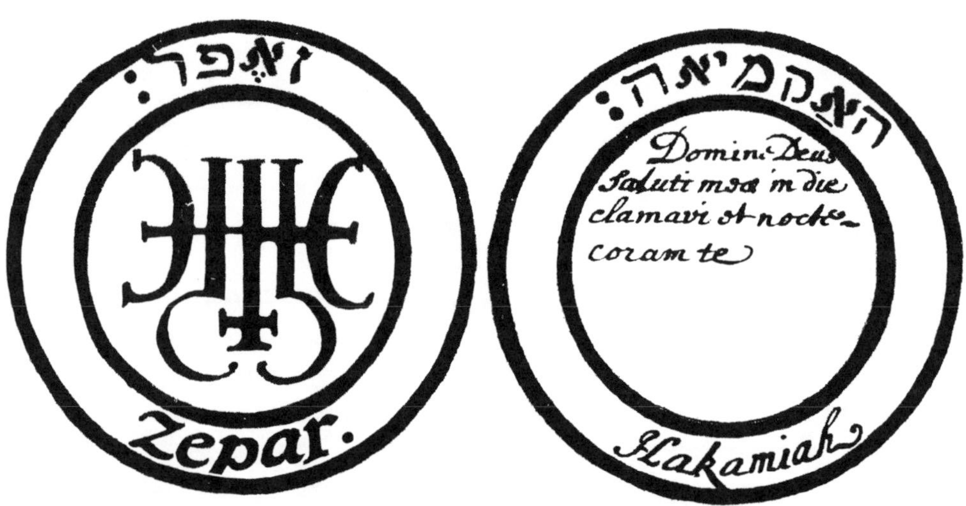

[1] Fortieth sheet Dr Rudd.

[2] Domine Deus saluti meae in die clamavi et nocte coram te:
O Lord, God of my salvation, by day have I called to thee, and sought Thy presence by night. [*Psalm* 87:1]

The Seventeenth spirit is **Botis** a great President under an Earl he appeareth at the first show in the form of an ugly viper, then at the command of the Magician he putteth on human shape with great teeth and two horns, carrying a bright sword in his hand, he telleth all things past present and to come and reconcileth friends and foes, he governeth sixty Legions of Spirits, and this is his seal.[1]

[1] Domine Dominus noster quam admirabile est nomen tuum in universa terra:
O Lord our Lord, How wonderful is Thy name in all the world. [*Psalm* 8:1]

The Eighteenth Spirit is **Bathin,** he is a mighty strong Duke and appeareth like a strong man with the tail of a Serpent sitting on a pale coloured horse; he knoweth the virtues of herbs and precious stones and can transport men suddenly from one country to another, he ruleth over thirty Legions of spirits: his Seal is thus.[1]

[1] Iudica me Domine secundum misericordiam et iustitiam tuam Domine Deus meus et non supergaudeant mihi:
Judge me, O Lord, according to Thy loving kindness, and let not them be joyful over me, O Lord. [*Psalm* 9:9].
[The sigil of this spirit is over-inked and closed up in the original manuscript.]

The Nineteenth Spirit is **Sallos**[1] he is a great and mighty Duke[2] and appeareth in the form of a gallant Soldier riding on a Crocodile with a Duke's Crown on his head peaceably he causeth the love of women and men to women, he governeth thirty Legions of spirits, his Seal is this which is to be worn.[3]

[1] S3: "Saleos".
[2] Listed as an Earl in Weir.
[3] Expectans expectavi Dominum et intendit mihi:
I waited in hope for the Lord, and He turned to me. [*Psalm* 39:1]

[1]The twentieth Spirit is called **Purson**[2] a great King he appeareth comely like a man with a Lion's face carrying a cruel viper in his hand and riding on a boar, many Trumpets going before him sounding.

He knoweth things hidden, and can discover Treasure, and tell all things past, present, & to come: he can take a body either human or airy, and Answereth truly all things either secret or divine, and of the Creation of the world and he bringeth forth good familiars and under his government are 22 Legions of Spirits partly of the order of Virtues and partly of the order of Thrones and his mark or Seal[3] is this which he owes obedience to, and must be worn in time of action[4].

[1] One and fortieth sheet Dr Rudd.
[2] W: "Pursan, alias Curson".
[3] Et nomen Domini invocabo O Domine libera animam meam:
"I shall call upon the name of the Lord, O Lord free my soul." [*Psalm* 119:2]
[4] Spiritual action or evocation.

The 21st Spirit is **Marax**[1] he is a great Earl and President, he appeareth like a great Bull with a Man's face. His office is to make men very knowing in Astronomy and all other liberal Sciences, he can give good familiars and wise which know the virtues of herbs and stones which be precious. He governeth 3 [30?] Legions of Spirits and his Seal is to be thus made and to be worn.[2]

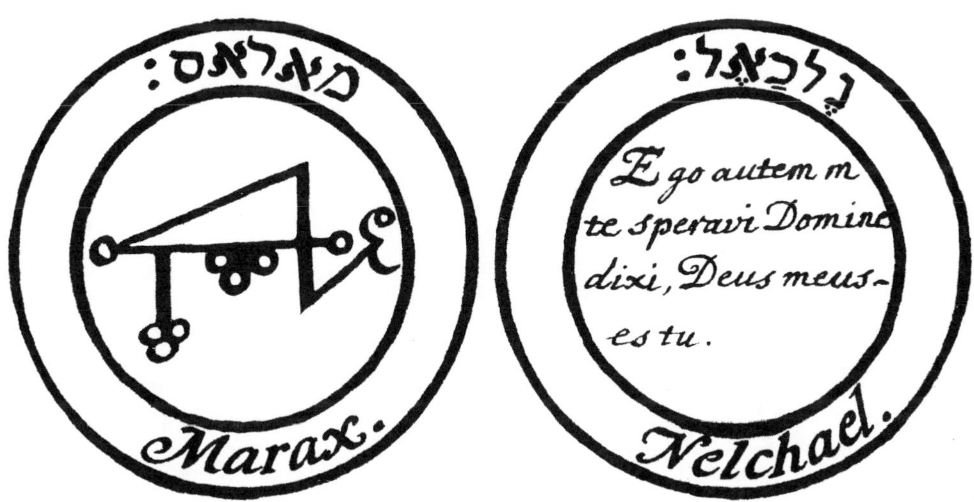

[1] S3: *"Morax"*.
[2] Ego autem in te speravi Domine dixi Deus meus es tu:
In Thee also have I hoped, O Lord, and said, Thou art my God. [*Psalm* 30:18]

The 22th Spirit is **Ipos**[1] he is an Earl and mighty Prince and appeareth in the form of an Angel with a Lion's head a goose's foot and a hare's tail: he knoweth all things past and to come, he maketh men witty and bold, and he governeth 36 Legions of Spirits. His Seal or Character is this.[2]

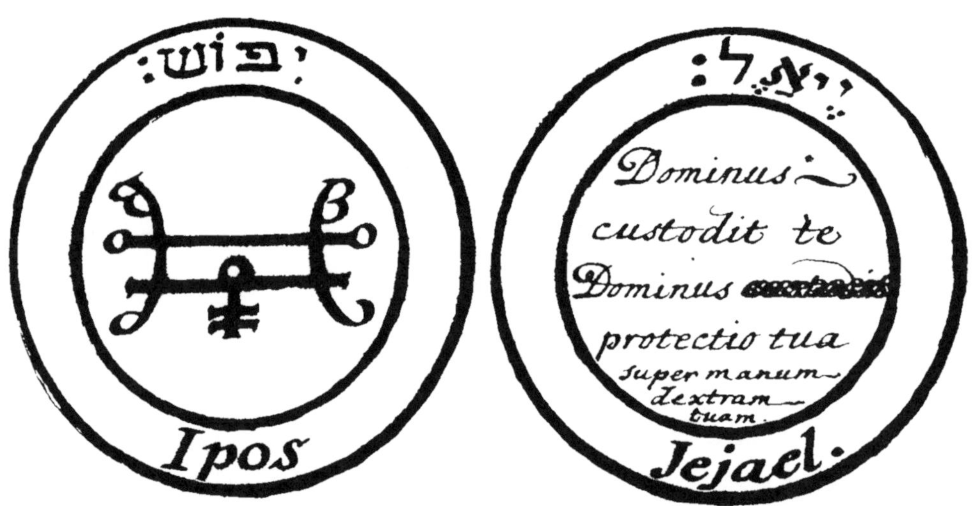

[1] W: "*Ipes, alias Ayperos*".

[2] Dominus custodit te, Dominus protectio tua super manum dextram tuam:
The Lord keep thee, the Lord be they protection on thy right hand. [*Psalm* 120:5]

The 23th Spirit is **Aim** he is a great & strong Duke, he appeareth in [the] form of a very handsome man in body with three heads the first like a serpent, the second like a man, having 2 stars in his forehead, the third like a Cat; he rideth on a Viper carrying a fire brand in his hand burning, wherewith he sets Cities castles and great places on fire, he maketh one witty all manner of ways, giveth true Answers to private matters he governeth twenty six Legions of inferior spirits, his Seal is thus, which wear. [1]

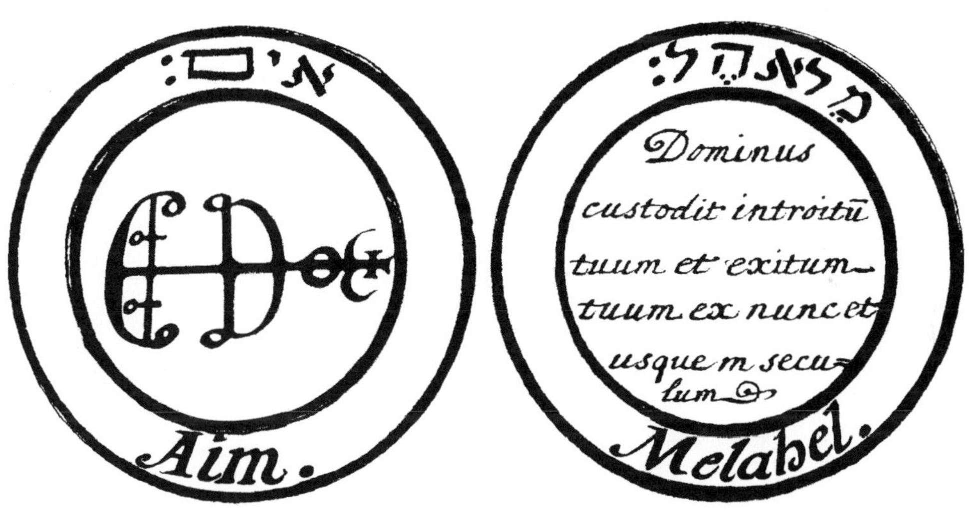

[1] Dominus custodit introitum tuum et exitum tuum ex nunc et usque in seculum:
The Lord keep thine incoming and thine outgoing from this time forth for evermore. [*Psalm* 120:8]

[1]The twenty fourth Spirit is **Naberius** he is a most valiant Marquis and appeareth in [the] form of a black Crow fluttering about the circle, and when he speaks it is with a hoarse voice, he maketh men cunning in all arts and sciences but especially the art of Rhetoric he restoreth lost dignities and honours, and governeth nineteen Legions. His Seal is this to be worn.[2]

[1] Two & fortieth sheet Dr Rudd.

[2] Beneplacitum est Domino super timentes eum, et in iis qui sperant super misericordiam eius: The Lord is well pleased with those that fear Him and hope upon his mercy. [*Psalm* 32:18]

The twenty fifth spirit is **Glasya-la bolas** he is a mighty President and shows himself in [the] form of a Dog with wings like a Griffin, he teaches all arts and Sciences in an instant and is an author of bloodshed and manslaughter, He teaches all things past present and to come if desired, and causeth love of friends and foes, he can make a man go invisible.

He hath under his commands 36 Legions of spirits, His Seal is this.[1]

[1] Confitebor tibi Domine in toto corde meo narrabo omnia mirabilia tua:
I shall acknowledge Thee, O Lord, with all my heart and shall tell forth all Thy wonders. [*Psalm* 9:1]

The twenty sixth Spirit is **Bime**,[1] he is a strong great mighty Duke and appeareth in form of a Dragon with three heads, one like a Dog, the other like a Griffin the third like a man, he speaketh with a high and comely voice, he changeth the places of the dead, and causeth those spirits which are under him to gather upon your sepulchre.[2]

He giveth riches to man and maketh him wise and eloquent, he giveth true Answers to your Demands and governeth 30 Legions of spirits.

His Seal is this which he owes obedience to.[3]

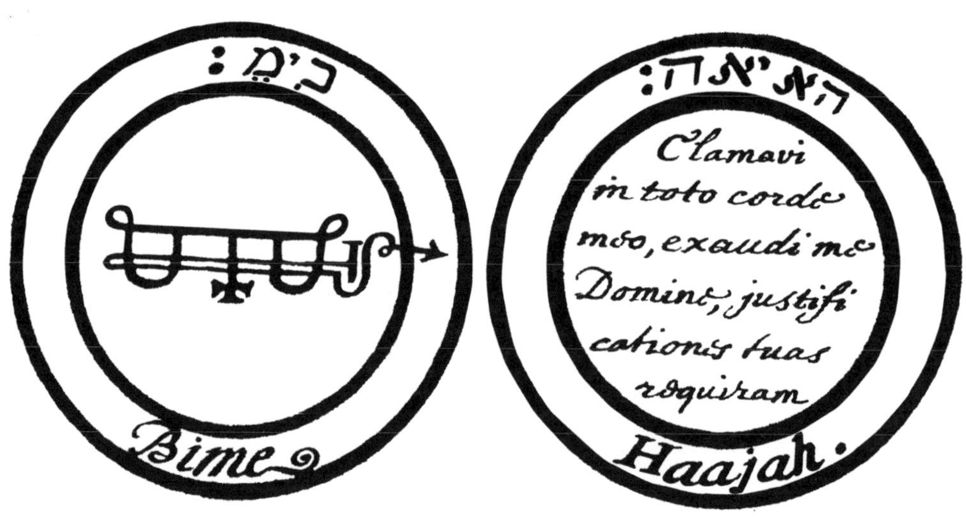

[1] S1, S3: *"Bune"*.
[2] S3: "to gather together upon their sepulchres".
[3] Clamavi in toto corde meo, exaudi me Domine, iustificationes tuas requiram:
I have called unto thee with all my heart, hear me, O Lord, and I shall seek my justification. [*Psalm* 118:145]

The twenty seventh Spirit is **Ronove** he appeareth in [the] form of a Monster, he teacheth the art of Rhetoric very well, and giveth good knowledge of tongues, favour with friends or foes, he is a Marquis, and there is under his Command 19 Legions of spirits. His Seal is this which wear, when you invocate.[1]

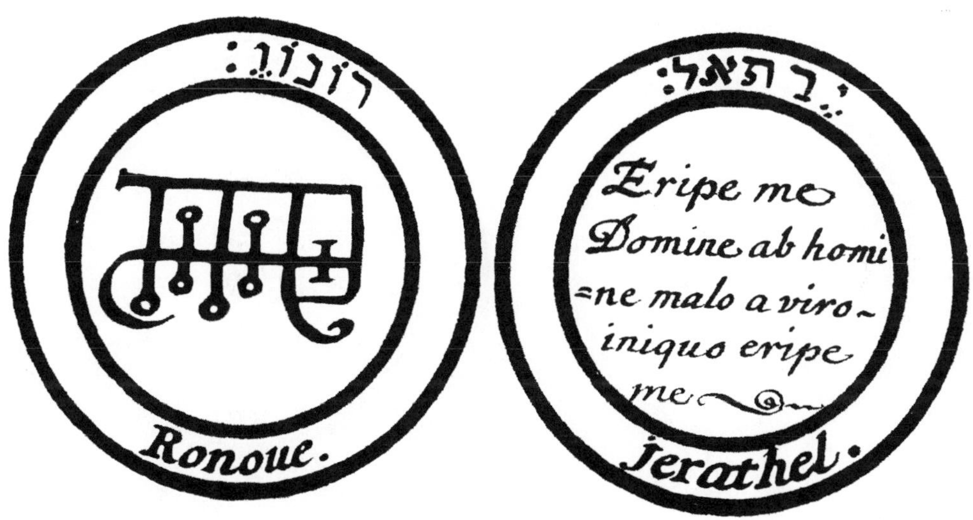

[1] Eripe me Domine ab homine malo a viro iniquo eripe me:
Save me, O Lord, from the evil man and deliver me from the wicked doer. [*Psalm* 139:1]

[1]The twenty eight Spirit is **Berith** he is a mighty great and terrible Duke he hath two other names given unto him by men of later times, viz. Beale and Bolfry[2] he appeareth in form of a Soldier with red clothes riding on a red horse, and a Crown of Gold upon his head, he giveth true Answers for those things past present & to come. You must use a ring [for protection], as is before spoken of, [with] Beleth in calling him forth, he can turn all Metals into Gold he can give dignities, and can confirm them to men, he speaketh with a very clear and subtle voice, He is a very great Liar, and not to be trusted unto. He governeth 26 Legions of Spirits, his Seal is this[3]

[1] Three & fortieth sheet Dr Rudd.

[2] S2: "Beale & Bofry". HMN: "Bolfry." W: "Of some he is called *Beall*; of the Jewes [he is called] *Berithi*; of Nigromancers [he is called] *Bolfry*." This is an interesting acknowledgement that the same spirit has been called up by Jewish magicians, and Christian magicians, but in each case has been bound under a slightly different name.

[3] Deus ne elongaveris a me Deus meus in auxilium meum respice:
Let not God depart from me, look to my help, O God. [*Psalm* 70:15]

The twenty ninth spirit is **Astaroth** he is a mighty and strong Duke[1] and appeareth in form of an beautiful Angel riding on an Infernal [creature] like a Dragon and carrying in his right hand a viper, you must not let him come too near you lest he do you damage by his stinking breath; therefore the Magician must hold the Magical Ring near his face and that will defend him.

He giveth true Answers of things past present and to come and can discover all secrets, he will discover & declare willingly how the spirits fell if desired and the reason of his own fall, he can make men wonderful[ly] knowing in all liberal sciences. He Ruleth 40 Legions of spirits. His Seal is this which wear as a Lamen before you or else he will not appear nor obey you.[2]

[1] Astaroth might have originally been given the additional title of King because he often has this rank in other sources.

[2] Ecce Deus adiuvat me et Dominus susceptor [est] animae meae:
Behold, God is my helper, and the Lord is the guardian of my soul. [*Psalm* 53:4]

The thirtieth spirit is **Forners**[1] he is a great and mighty Marquis and appeareth in the form of a great Sea Monster he teacheth and maketh men wonderful[ly] knowing in the art of Rhetoric he causeth men to have a good name and to have knowledge and understanding of tongues, he maketh one to be beloved of his foes as well as of his friends and he governeth 29 Legions of spirits partly of the order of Thrones & partly of Angels his Seal is this which wear.[2]

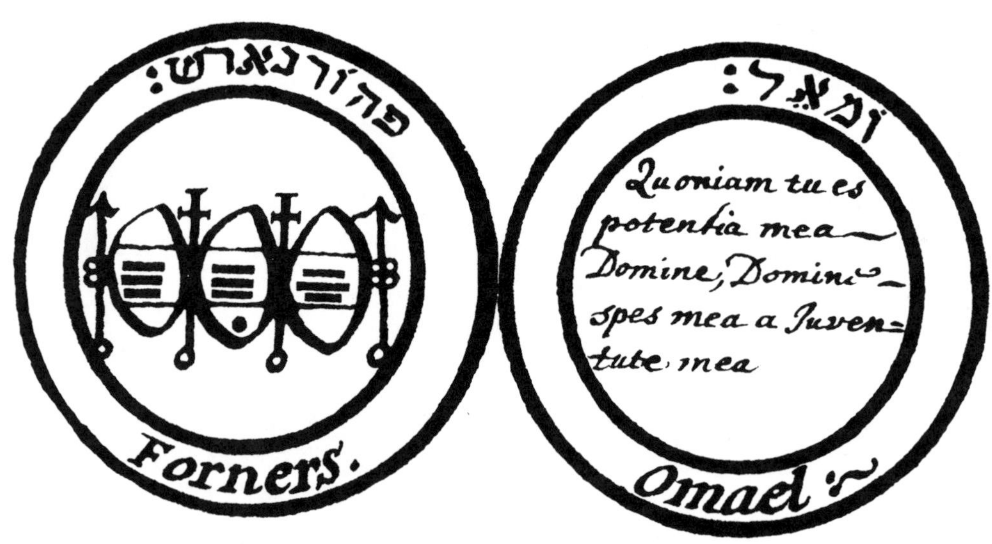

[1] S1, S2, S3: *"Forneus"*.

[2] Quoniam tu es potentia mea Domine. Domine spes mea a iuventute mea:
For Thou are my strength, O Lord. O Lord, Thou are my hope from my youth. [*Psalm* 70:6]

The one and thirtieth Spirit is **Foras** he is a great and mighty President & appeareth in the form of a strong man in human shape. He can give the understanding to men how they may know the virtues of all herbs and precious stones and teacheth them the art of Logic and Rhetoric in all their parts if desired he maketh men invisible witty eloquent and to live long he can discover treasures hid and recovereth things lost, and ruleth over 29 Legions of spirits. His Seal is this which wear.[1]

[1] Introibo in potentia Domini, Deus meus memorabor iustitiae tuae solius:
I shall enter into the power of the Lord, my God, I shall be mindful of Thy justice only. [*Psalm* 70:16]

[1]The two and thirtieth Spirit is **Asmodai**[2] he is a great King strong and powerful, he appeareth with three heads whereof the first is like a bull the second is like a man, the third like a ram with a serpent's tail belching or vomiting out flames of fire out of his mouth, his foot is webbed like a goose he sitteth on an infernal Dragon carrying a Lance and a flag in his hand he is the first and choicest [spirit] under the power of Amaymon[3] and goes before all others, when the Exorcist hath a mind to call him let it be abroad and let him stand on his feet all the time of action [evocation] with his Cap off, for if it be on, Amaymon will deceive him and cause all his doings to be bewrayed [revealed], but as soon as the Exorcist seeth Asmoday in the shape aforesaid he shall call him by his name "Art thou Asmoday", and he will not deny it and by and by he will bow down to the ground &c.

He giveth the ring of Virtues, he teacheth the art of Arithmetic, Geometry Astronomy and all handicrafts absolutely, he giveth full and true answers to your demands, he maketh a man invisible, he showeth the place where treasure lyeth and guardeth them if it be among the Legions of Amaymon's, he governeth 72 Legions of inferior spirits. His Seal is to be made & worn as a Lamen before you &c.[4]

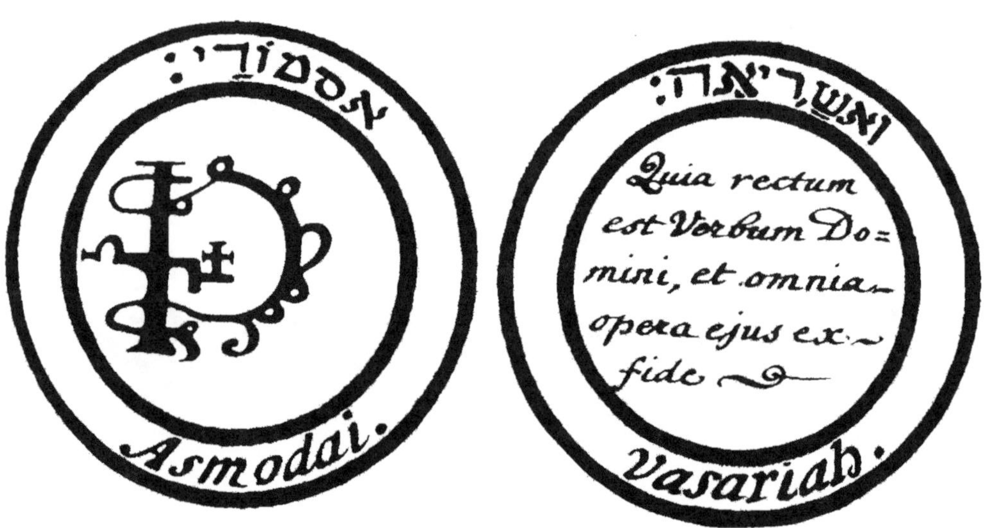

[1] Four & fortieth sheet Dr Rudd.

[2] S1, S2, S3: "Asmoday"; W: "Sidonai or Asmoday".

[3] King of the East.

[4] Quia rectum est verbum Domini et omnia opera eius ex fide:
For the word of the Lord is upright, and all his works faithful. [*Psalm* 32:4]

The three and thirtieth spirit is **Gaap** he is a great President[1] and a mighty Prince, he appeareth when the Sun is in some of the Southern signs, in a human shape there going before him [are] four great and mighty kings he being a guide to conduct them along in their way. His office is to make men insensible and also knowing in philosophy and all the liberal sciences, he can cause Love or hatred, and he can teach you how to Consecrate these things that belongs to the Domination of Amaymon his King[2] and can deliver familiars out of the Custody of other Magicians and answereth truly and perfectly of things past present and to come, and can carry & recarry men very speedily from one Kingdom to another at the will & pleasure of the Exorcist.

He ruleth over 66 Legions of spirits, he was of the order of Potestates. His Seal is thus to be made, & to be worn before you.[3]

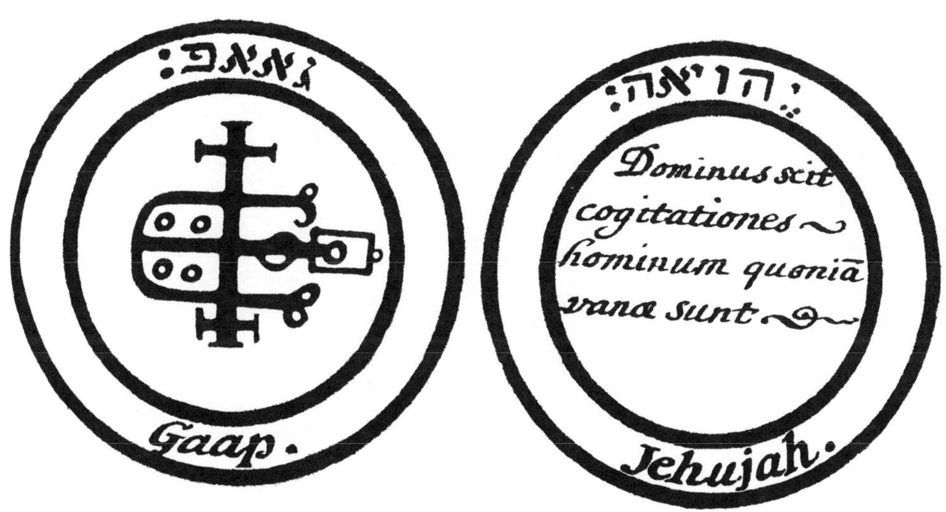

[1] It seems possible that Gaap may at one time have also been a King. See page 171.
[2] King of the East.
[3] Dominus scit cogitationes hominum quoniam vana sunt:
The Lord knows the thoughts of men, for they are in vain. [*Psalm* 33:11]

The thirty fourth Spirit is **Furfur**[1] he is a great and mighty Earl appearing in the form of a Hart with a fiery tail, he never speaketh truth unless he be compelled and brought within a Δ Triangle, being compelled therein he will take upon him the form of an angel, being he can raise thunder, lightning blasts and great tempestuous storms, giveth true Answers both of secret and divine things, if commanded. He ruleth over 26 Legions of Spirits. His Seal is this to be made and worn as aforesaid.[2]

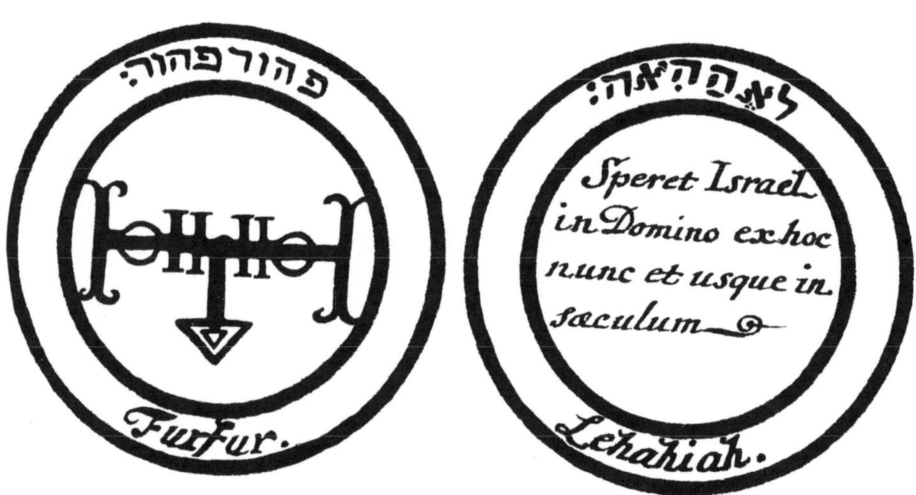

[1] S3: "Furtur".

[2] Speret Israel in Domino ex hoc nunc et usque in saeculum:
Let Israel hope in the Lord from this time forth and for evermore. [*Psalm* 130:5]

The thirty fifth Spirit is **Marchosias**[1] he is a great and mighty Marquis appearing at first in [the] form of a Wolf having Griffin's wings and a serpent's tail vomiting up fire out of his mouth, but after at the command of the Exorcist he puts on the shape of a man and is a strong fighter, he was of the order of Dominations, he governeth 30 Legions of spirits, he told his chief Master which was Solomon that after 1200 years he had hopes to return to the seventh throne, and his Seal is to be made and worn as a Lamen.[2]

[1] The spirit conjured by Theron Ware in James Blish's masterful fictional account of Goetic evocation, *Black Easter: Faust Aleph-Null*, Buccaneer, New York, 1968, chapter ix.

2 Dilexi quoniam exaudiet Dominus vocem orationis meae:
I am joyful, for the Lord hears the voice of my prayer. [*Psalm* 114:1]

[1]The six and thirtieth spirit is **Stolus**[2] he is a great and powerful Prince appearing in the shape of a mighty raven at first before the Exorcist, but after he taketh the Image of a man &c. He teacheth the art of Astronomy, and the virtue of herbs and precious stones, he governeth 26 Legions of spirits his Seal is this.[3]

[1] Five and fortieth sheet Dr Rudd.

[2] S1, S2, S3, W1: "Stolas".

[3] Domini dilexi decorum domus tuae et locum habitationis gloriae tuae:
I have delighted in the beauty of Thy House, O Lord, and in the place of the habitation of Thy glory. [*Psalm* 25:8]

The thirty seventh Spirit is **Phenix**[1] he is a great Marquis and appeareth like the bird Phenix having a Child's voice he singeth many sweet notes before the Exorcist which he must not regard, but by and by he must bid him put on human shape, then he will speak marvellously of all wonderful sciences if desired. He is a good and excellent poet and will be willing to do your request, he hath hopes to return to the Seventh throne after 1200 years more as he said to Solomon. He governeth 20 Legions of Spirits, his Seal is this which bear.[2]

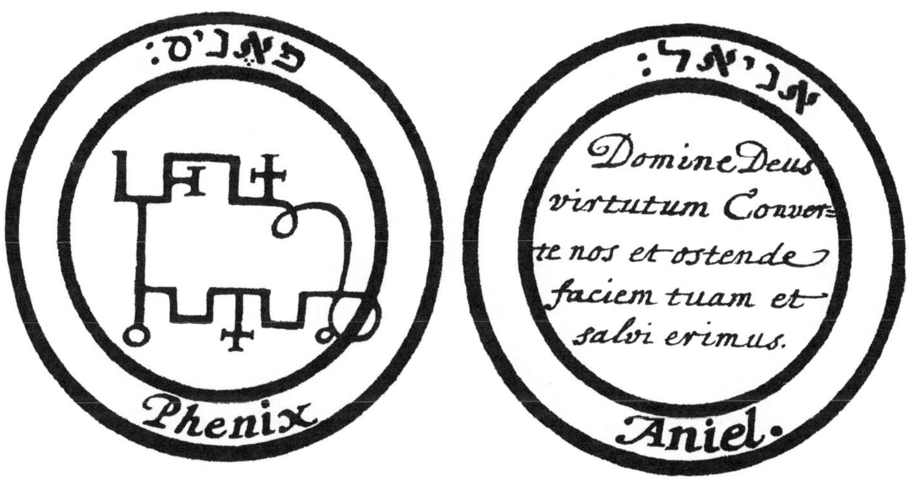

[1] S3: "Phoenix"; W1: "Phenix".

[2] Domine Deus virtutum converte nos et ostende faciem tuam et salvi erimus:
O Lord God, turn Thy power towards us, and show us Thy face and we shall be saved. [*Psalm* 79:8]

The thirty eight spirit is **Malthas**[1] he is a great Earl and appeareth in [the] form of a stock dove and speaketh with a hoarse voice, his office is to build up towers and to furnish them with ammunition and weapons, and send men of war to places appointed, he Ruleth 26 Legions of spirits. His Seal is this.[2]

[1] S1, S2, S3, W1: *"Halphas"*.

[2] Quaniam tu es Domine spes mea altissimum posuisti refugium tuum:
For Thou art my hope, O Lord, and Thou hast been my deepest refuge. [*Psalm* 90:9]

The 39th Spirit is **Malphas**[1] he appeareth in form at first like a Crow but after he will put on human shape at the request of the Exorcist and speaks with a hoarse voice, he is a mighty President & powerful he can build houses & high Towers, and he can bring quickly artificers together from all places of the world.

He can destroy the Enemies desires or thoughts and what they have done, he gives good familiars and if you make any sacrifices to him he will receive it kindly and willingly but he will deceive him that doth it. He governeth 40 Legions of Spirits, his Seal is this[2]

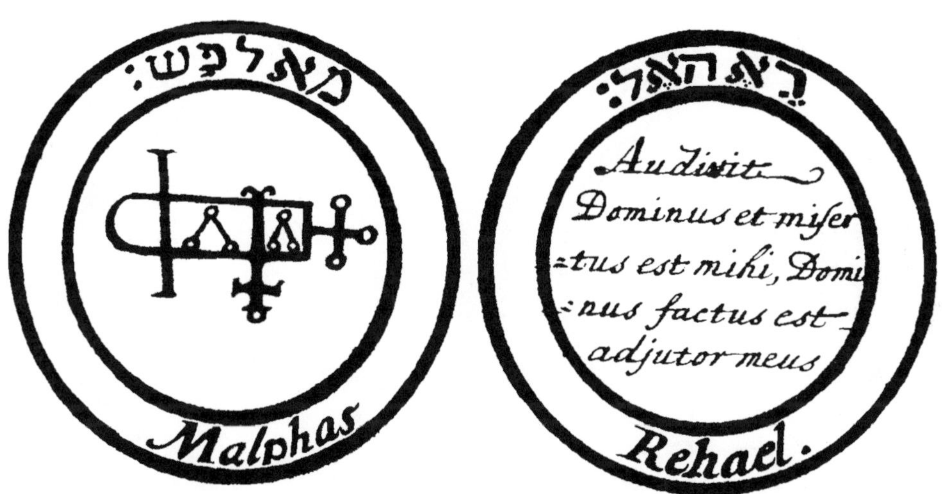

[1] There is some similarity between both the name and the description of the previous spirit Halphas. It is possible that in some earlier recension these two spirits were one and the same.
[2] Audivit Dominus et misertus est mihi Dominus factus est adjutor meus:
The Lord has heard me and pitied me and the Lord is my helper. [*Psalm* 29:13]

[1]The fortieth Spirit is **Raum** he is a great Earl and appeareth at first in the form of a Crow, but after at the command of the Exorcist he putteth on human shape, his office is to steal treasure out of King's houses and to Carry it where he is commanded and to destroy Cities and the dignities of men, and to tell all things past present and to come and to tell what is and what will be, and to cause love to be between friends and foes, he was of the order of Thrones, and he governeth thirty Legions of Spirits. His Seal is this which wear. [2]

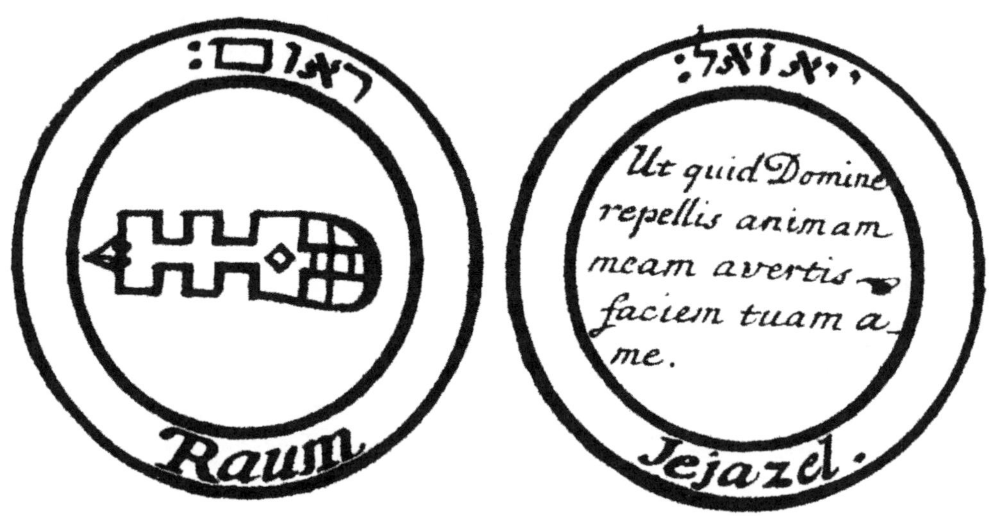

[1] Six & fortieth sheet Dr Rudd.

[2] Ut quid Domine repellis animam meam, avertis faciem tuam a me:
Why drivest Thou away my soul, O Lord, and turnest Thy face from me? [*Psalm* 87:15]

The one and fortieth Spirit is **Forcalor**[1] he is a mighty Duke and Strong he appeareth in the form of a man with Griffin's wings, his office is to kill men and to drown [them] in the waters & to ~~kill men~~ overthrow ships of war, for he hath power both over seas & winds but he will not hurt any man or thing if he be commanded to the contrary by the Exorcist, he hath hopes to return to the seventh Throne after 1000 years. He governeth 3 [30?] Legions of Spirits. His Seal is this which wear. [2]

[1] S1, S2, S3: *"Focalor"*; W1: *"Focator"*.

[2] Domine libera animam meam a labiis iniquis et a lingua dolosa:
O Lord, deliver my soul from wicked lips and a deceitful tongue. [*Psalm* 119:2]
The correct Hebrew for the angel הההל is written within the seal. The name around the outside of the angels sigil is in fact incorrect, being a scribal mistaken repeat of the demon name Focalor פהורכלור. The fact that the mistaken Hebrew is not just crossed through suggests that the Hebrew at least was written by either a Jewish scribe, or someone who had a similarly religious regard for such written words. It is interesting that the Hebrew of a spirit name was treated as carefully as a written name of God.

The forty second Spirit is **Vepar** he is a great and strong Duke he appeareth in [the] form of a Mermaid, his office is to guide the waters and ships laden with armour, therein he will at the request of the Exorcist cause the Seas to be rough and stormy and to appear full of ships,[1] he causeth men to die in three days with putrefying [of] their sores or wounds and causing worms in them to breed and he governeth 29 Legions of spirits his Seal is this[2]

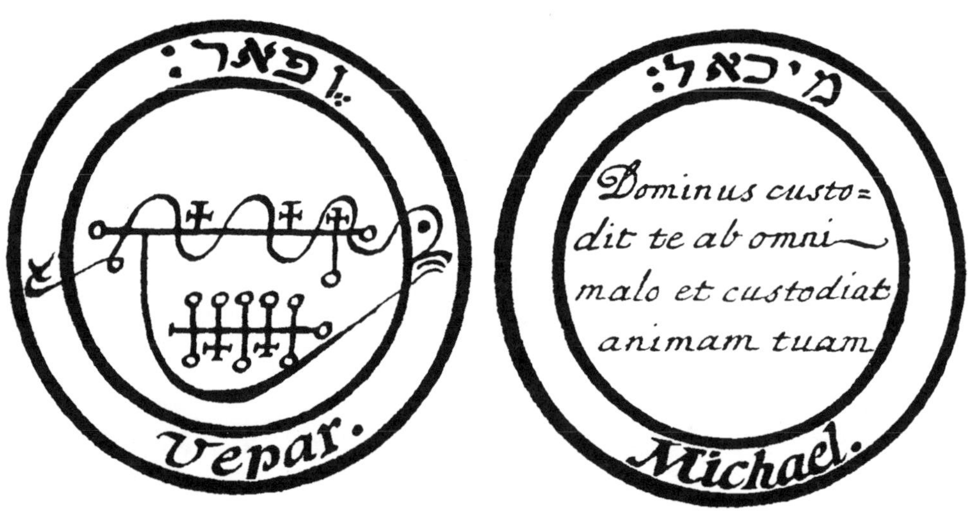

[1] This particular illusion was used in the plotline of Susanna Clarke's novel *Jonathan Strange & Mr Norrell*, Bloomsbury, London, 2004, chapter 11, where such a fleet of illusory ships was conjured at Brest in November 1807.

[2] Dominus custodit te ab omni malo et custodiat animam tuam:
The Lord protects thee from all evil and will protect thy soul. [*Psalm* 120:7]
This seal is an example of one drawn much more elegantly than other versions of the seal in other manuscripts of the *Goetia*.

The 43 Spirit is **Sabnock**[1] he is a mighty great Marquis and strong appearing in the form of an armed Solider with a Lion's head riding on a pale coloured horse. His office is to build high towers Castles and Cities and to furnish them with armour and to afflict men in several days with wounds and rotten sores full of worms, he giveth good familiars at the request of the Exorcist. He commands 50 Legions of Spirits. His Seal is thus made. [2]

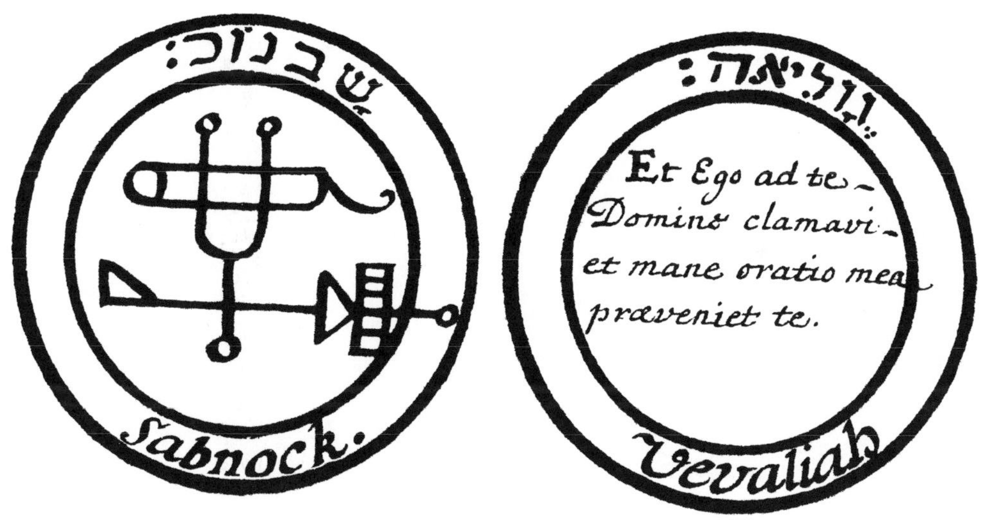

[1] S1, W1: "Sabnack"; S3: "Sabnach".
[2] Et Ego ad te Domine clamavi, et mane oratio meae praeveniet te:
I have cried unto Thee, O Lord, and let my prayer come unto Thee. [*Psalm* 87:14]

[1]The forty fourth spirit is **Shax**,[2] he is a great Marquis[3] and appeareth in [the] form of a Stock Dove [which] speaketh with a hoarse and subtle voice, his office is to take away the sight hearing and the understanding of any man or woman at the command of the Exorcist, and to steal money out of King's houses and to carry it [back] again in 1200 years,[4] if commanded, he will fetch horses at the request of the Exorcist or any other thing, but he must be Commanded into a Triangle first Δ or else he will deceive him and tell him many lies.

He can discover all things that are hidden and not kept by wicked spirits he governeth good familiars. Sometimes he governeth 30 Legions of Spirits, his Seal is thus to be made and to be worn.[5]

[1] Seven & Fortieth Sheet Dr Rudd.
[2] W: Shax [Chax], alias Scox.
[3] He is also a Duke in the Latin original of Weirus.
[4] The copyist probably omitted a whole line. The "1200 years" is more likely to refer to his hopes of eventual return to the seventh Throne, rather than the time elapsed before he returns the stolen money.
[5] Voluntaria oris mei beneplacita fac Domine et Judicia tua doce:
Make my wishes pleasing unto Thee, O Lord, and teach me Thy judgments. [*Psalm* 118:108]

The forty and fifth Spirit is **Vine** he is a great King and an Earl and appeareth in the form of a Lion riding on a black horse with a Viper in his hand. His office is to discover things hidden, witches, and things past present and to come, he, at the Command of the Exorcist will build towers, throw down great strong walls, make waters rough with storms, he governeth 36 Legions of Spirits his Seal is this which wear. [1]

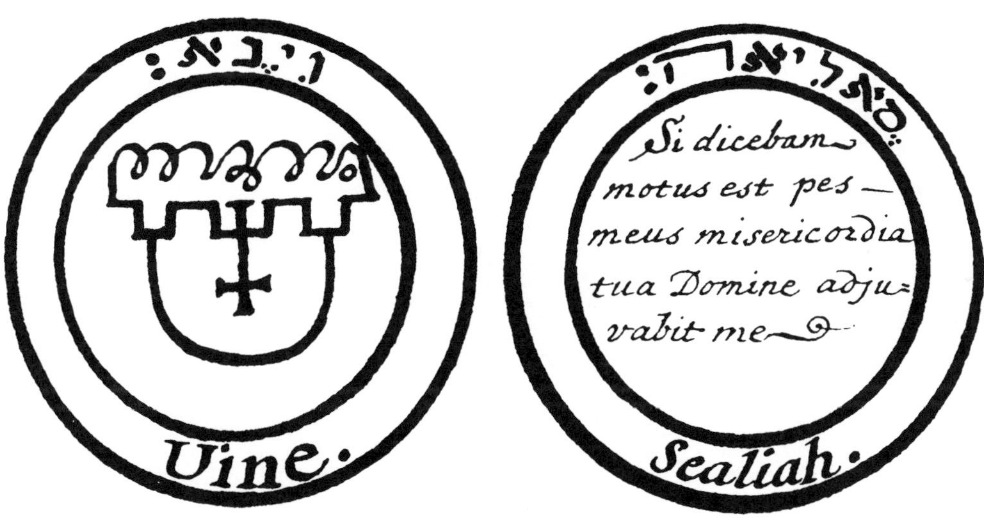

[1] Si dicebam motus est pes meus misericordia tua Domine adiuvabit me:
If I say that my foot is moved, Thou wilt help me of Thy mercy. [*Psalm* 93:18]
The Hebrew spelling וינא suggests a pronounciation of Viné.

The forty sixth Spirit is **Bifrons**[1] he is an Earl and appeareth in the form of a monster at the first, but after a while at the Command of the Exorcist he putteth on the shape of a man. His office is to make one wonderful[ly] cunning[2] in Astrology and Geometry and other Arts and Sciences, he also teacheth the virtues of Stones and woods, he changeth dead bodies and puts them into another place and lighteth seemingly upon the graves of the dead. He hath under his Command 6 Legions[3] of spirits his Seal is this which he will own, & wear it before you.[4]

[1] S2: "Bifrovs".

[2] Proficient.

[3] W: "six and twentie"; C: "Should probably be 60 instead of 6"

[4] Suavis Dominus universis et miserationes super omnia opera eius:
The Lord is pleasant to all the world and his mercies are over all his works. [*Psalm* 144:9]

The forty seventh Spirit is **Vuall**[1] he is a great mighty and strong Duke. He appeareth in the form of a mighty Dromedary at first but after a while he will put on human shape, and speaketh in the Egyptian tongue but not perfectly, his office is to procure the love of women and to tell things past present and to come, he shall also procure friendship between friends and foes, he was of the order of Potestates. He governeth 37 Legions of Spirits. His Seal is to be made and worn before you [2]

Note that a Legion is 6666 [spirits]. [3]

Read Cardanus & Iamblichus. [4]

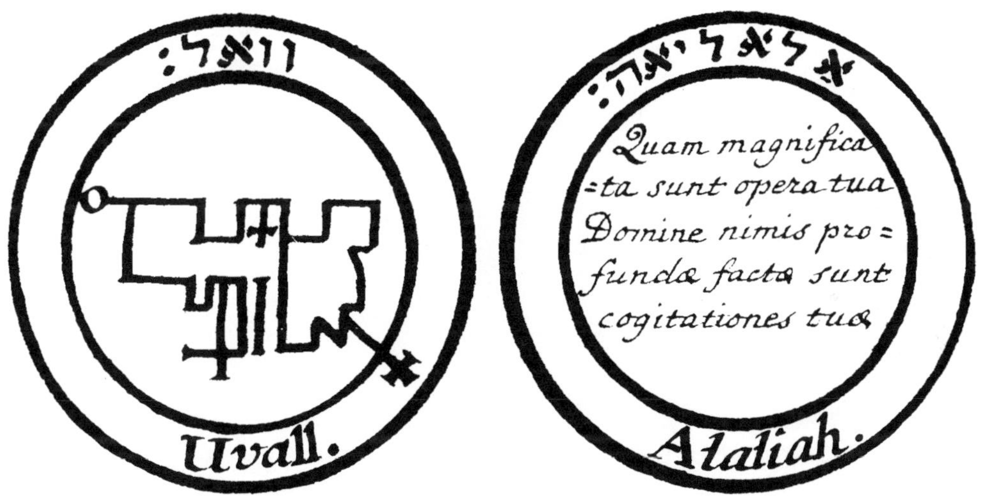

[1] S3: *"Vual"*; W1: *"Nuall"*. Because of the equivalence of the letters 'U' and 'V' before the seventeenth century, this spirit could equally be 'Vuall' or 'Uvall' but not 'Nuall' which must have been a scribal mistake.

[2] Quam magnificata sunt opera tua Domine, nimis profundae factae sunt cogitationes tuae: How wonderful are Thy works, O Lord, and how deep Thy thoughts. [*Psalm* 103:25]

[3] A. Delatte and C. H. Josserand, "Contribution to the study of the Byzantine Demonology", in *Mixtures Bidez, Directory of the Institute of Eastern Philology and History*, Tome II, 1934, p. 207-232 (especially page 226), announces that certain Byzantine treatises of magic indicate the number of the demons: also grouped into legions, as 60,000, 10,969, or 10,090 1/2 [*sic*].

[4] Girolamo Cardan (1501-1576) wrote on algebra, astrology and alchemy, and Iamblichus of Chalcis (250-325 CE), who wrote the classic *On the Mysteries of the Egyptians.* This was first translated into Latin in 1497, and finally into English in 1678. A new English translation has recently been published.

[1]The forty eight Spirit is **Haagenti** he is a great President appearing in the form of a mighty Bull having the wings of a Griffin but after at the Exorcist's command he putteth on human shape. His office is to make men wise and to instruct them in diverse things and to transmute and change Metals into Gold and change wine into water and water into wine. He commands 33 Legions of spirits. His Seal is thus made.[2]

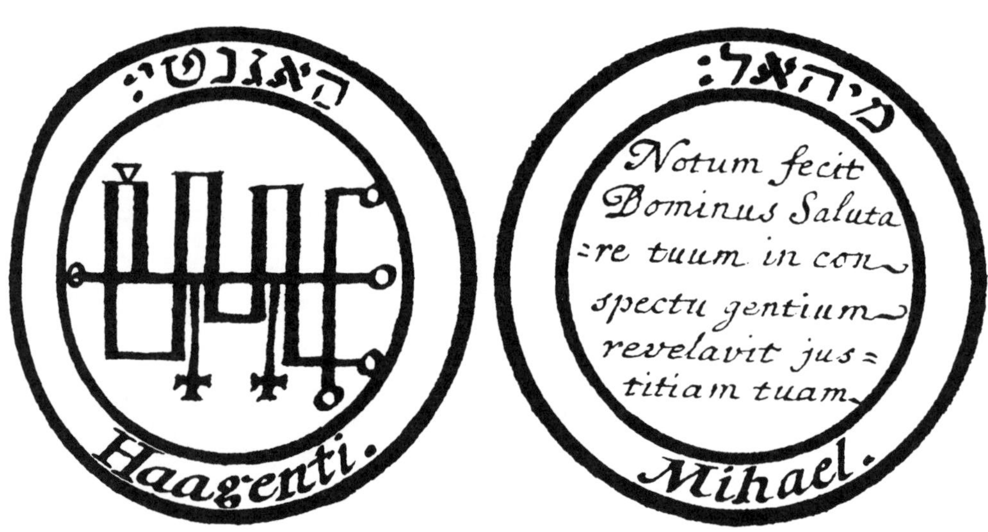

[1] Eight & Fortieth Sheet Dr Rudd.

[2] Notum fecit Dominus salutare tuum in conspectu gentium, revelavit justitiam tuam:
The Lord hath made thy salvation known in the sight of the peoples and will reveal his justice. [*Psalm* 97:3]

The forty ninth Spirit is **Crocell**[1] he appeareth in [the] form of an Angel he is a great strong Duke speaking something mystically of hidden things, he teacheth the art of Geometry and the liberal sciences, he at the command of the Exorcist will make great noises like the running of water although there be none, he warmeth waters and distempereth baths &c. He was of the order of Potestates as he declared to Solomon before his fall, he governeth 48 Legions of Spirits and his Seal is this which wear as aforesaid.[2]

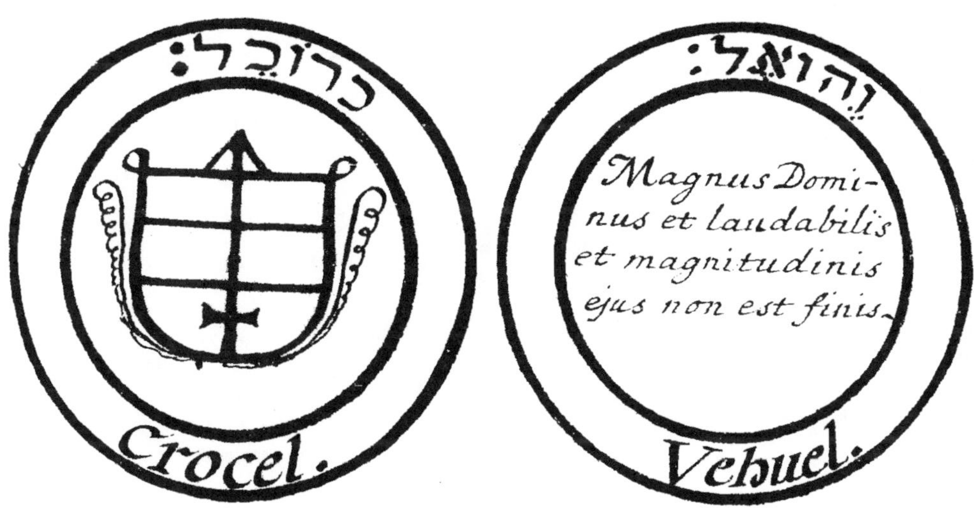

[1] S1, S3, W1: *"Procel"*.

[2] Magnus Dominus et laudabilis et magnitudinis eius non est finis:
Great is the Lord and worthy to be praised, and there is no end to his greatness. [*Psalm* 144:3]

The fiftieth Spirit is **Furcas** He is a Knight[1] and appeareth in the form of a cruel old man with a long beard and a hoary head riding upon a pale coloured horse with a sharp weapon in his hand, his office is to teach the art of philosophy Astrology Rhetoric Logic Chiromancy and Pyromancy in all their parts perfectly, he hath under his power 20 Legions of Spirits his Seal or Mark is thus made and to be worn.[2]

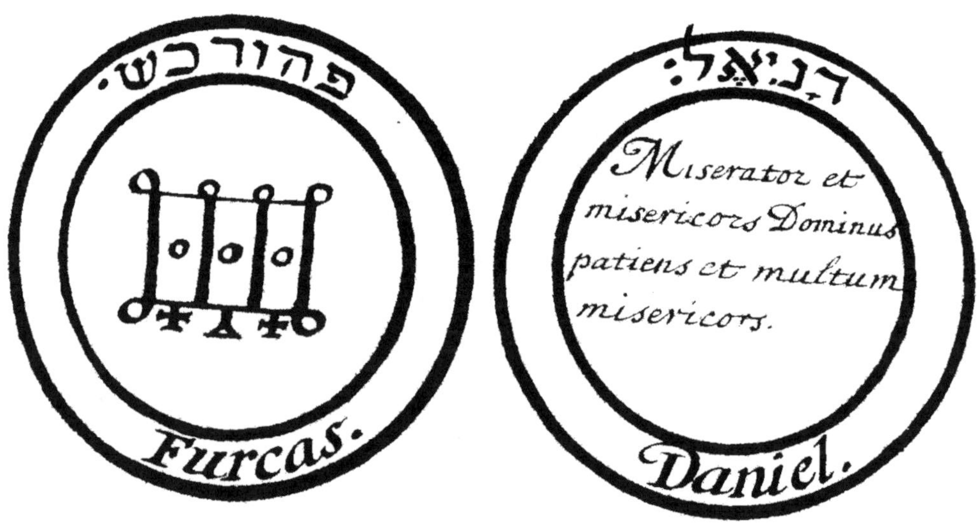

[1] Furcas is strangely the only Knight amongst the 72 spirits, and hence the only spirit attributed to Saturn. In Weir, Furcas is simply described as a '*miles*' Latin for a 'soldier' which perhaps should *not* have been translated as 'knight'. As several other spirits are described as mounted knights, it is possible that this is not really a rank, but only a description, and that Furcas is in fact of some other rank such as Duke (as these are always mounted). Furthermore, in Weir, Furcas shares a number (38) with Procell, which is unique: Procell is also a Duke. If we count Furcas as a Duke, that would result in 24 Dukes, giving exactly two Dukes per Zodiacal Sign. If that were the case, then the apportionment of spirits to planets would be much more rational in Table M18: giving 24 Dukes (Venus), 12 Kings (Sun), 12 Marquises (Moon), 12 Presidents (Mercury), and with the remaining 12 made up of the other ranks (Mars & Jupiter). The attribution of these spirits to the 12 Zodiacal Signs, as well as to the planets, then becomes practical. See Table M18.

[2] Miserator et misericors Dominus, patients et multum miericors:
The Lord is pitiful and merciful, long-suffering and of great goodness. [*Psalm* 102:8]

The one and fiftieth Spirit is **Balam** he is a terrible great and powerful King, he appeareth with three heads, the first is like a bull, the second like a man the third like a ram, he hath a Serpent's tail and eyes flaming Riding upon a furious bear carrying a Goshawk on his fist, he speaks with a hoarse voice giving true Answers to things past present and to come, he maketh men go invisible & witty, he governeth 40 Legions of spirits his Seal or Mark is thus. [1]

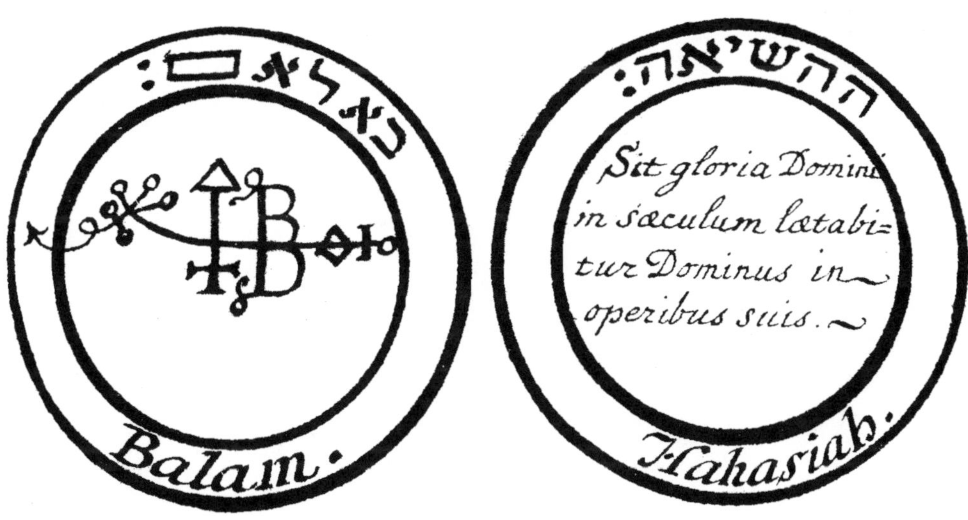

[1] Sit gloria Domini in saeculum laetabitur Dominus in operibus suis:
Let the Lord be in glory for ever and the Lord will rejoice in His works. [*Psalm* 103:32]

[1]The two and fiftieth Spirit is **Alloces**[2] he is a great and mighty strong Duke appearing in the form of a Soldier <riding on a Griffin with a Duke's Crown on his head, there goeth before him three of his Ministers with great trumpets sounding; his office is to teach philosophy perfectly and to constrain souls deceased to come before the Exorcist to answer to those things which he shall ask them if he desire it. He was partly of the order of Thrones and partly of Angels, he ruleth now 30 Legions[3] of Spirits. His Seal is this.>[4]

[riding on a great horse; his face is like a Lion's, very red, having Eyes flaming, his speech is hoarse & very Big; his office is to teach the art of Astronomy, & all the Liberal sciences, he Bringeth good familiars & ruleth 36 Legions of spirits, his seal is Thus made, & to be worn, &c.][5]

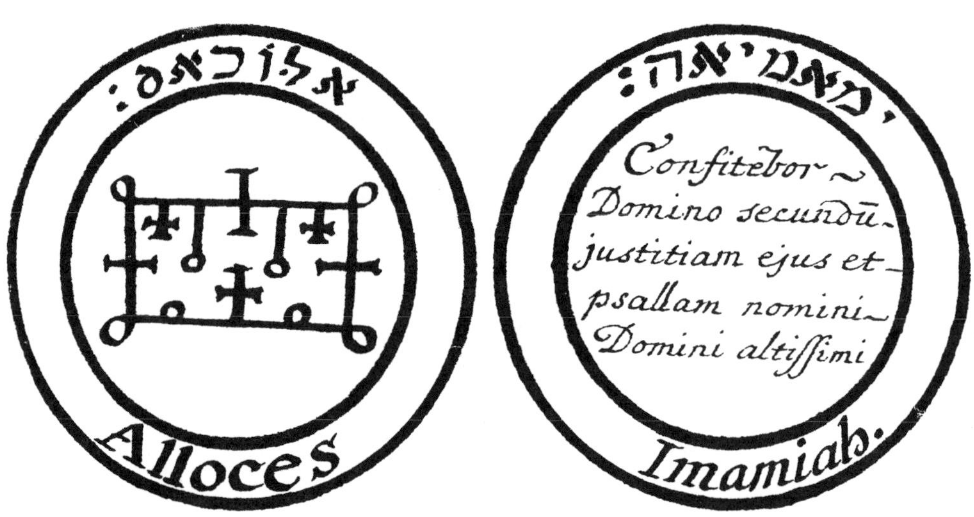

[1] Nine & Fortieth Sheet Dr Rudd.

[2] W1: "Allocer".

[3] This is possibly a scribal mistake for '36'.

[4] The section in angle brackets "riding on a Griffin…His Seal is this" has been mistakenly inserted by the copyist from the description of Murmus. What should have been transcribed appears in square brackets below (taken from Sloane MS 3825).

[5] Confitebor Domino secundum justitiam eius et psallam nomini Domini altissimi: I shall make known the Lord, according to his justice, and sing hymns to the name of the Lord, the greatest. [*Psalm* 7:18]

The three and fiftieth Spirit is **Camio**[1] he is a great President and appeareth in the form of a bird called a Thrush at first but after a while he putteth on the shape of a man carrying in his hand a sharp sword, he seemeth to answer in burning ashes, he is a good disputer, his office is to give men the understanding of all birds, lowing bullocks barking of Dogs and other creatures and also the voice of waters and giveth very true Answers of things to come, he was of the Order of Angels, and now ruleth 30 Legions of Infernal Spirits his Seal is this.[2]

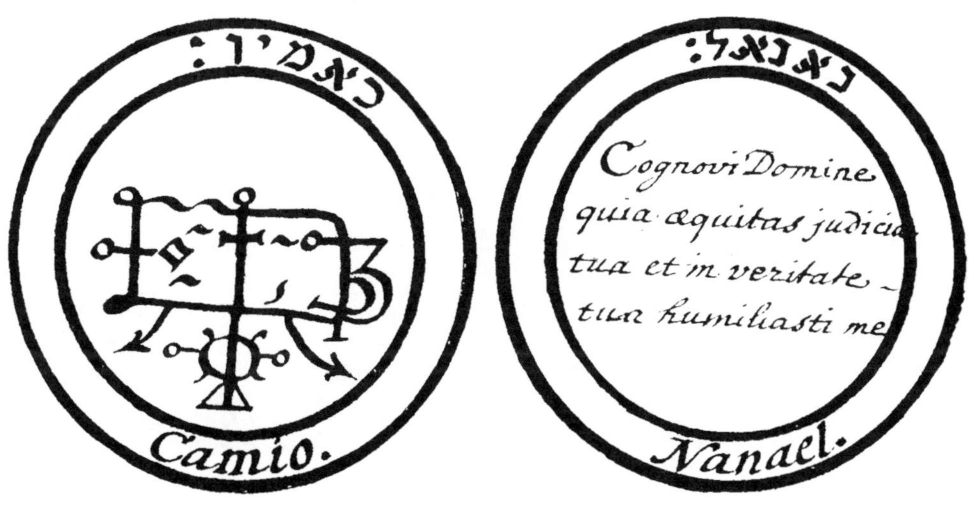

[1] S1, S2, S3, W1: *"Caim"*; W: *"Caym."*

[2] Cognovi Domine quia aequitas judicia tua et in veritate tua humiliasti me:
I have known Thee, O Lord, for Thy judgements are just, and in Thy truth have I abased myself. [*Psalm* 118:75]

The four and fiftieth Spirit is **Murmus**[1] he is a great Duke and an Earl[2] and appeareth in the form of a Soldier riding on a Griffin with a Duke's crown on his head; there goeth before him three of his ministers with great trumpets sounding. His office is to teach philosophy perfectly, and to constrain souls deceased to come before the Exorcist to answer to those things which he Shall ask them if desired; he was partly of the order of Thrones and partly of Angels, He ruleth now 30 Legions of Spirits his Seal is this.[3]

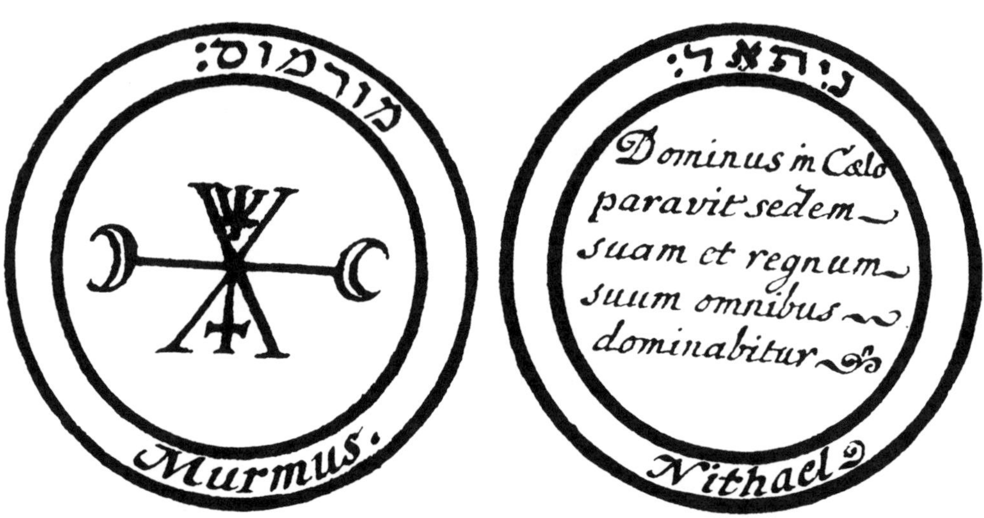

[1] S1, S3, W1: *"Murmur"*.

[2] In Table M18 in *Complete Magician's Tables*, both titles were shown but he was counted as an Earl. In the light of further research it has become obvious that he should be counted as a Duke, and so this has been done in Table M18 in Appendix 2.

[3] Dominus in Caelo paravit sedem suam et Regnum suum omnibus dominabitur:
The Lord hath prepared His seat in heaven and His rule shall be over all. [*Psalm* 102:19]

The ~~three~~ five and fiftieth Spirit is **Orobas**[1] he is a great and mighty Prince appearing at the first like a horse but after at the Command of the Exorcist he putteth on the Image of a Man, his office is to discover all things past present and to come, and to give dignities and Prelacies[2] and the favour of friends and foes, he giveth true answers of divinity [theology] and of the Creation of the world, he is very faithful to the Exorcist and will not suffer him to be tempted by any spirit, he governeth 26 Legions of spirits. His Seal is this which [you should] wear.[3]

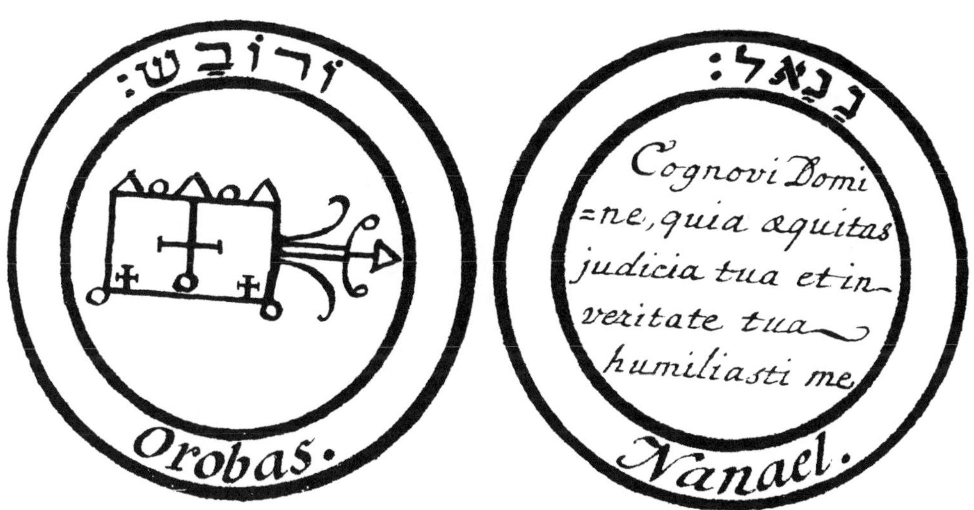

[1] W1: *"Obus"*.

[2] A high ecclesiastical office or rank such as bishop, abbot or prior.

[3] The angelic Seal is incorrect, as it repeats that of the 53rd angel Nanael. Rudd has incorrectly attributed this Angel and verse twice. The angelic seal here should be that of Mebahiah. As he correctly attributes the angel Mebahiah מבהיה to Orobas in Harley MS 6482, we have drawn on that source for the Latin Psalm and translation as follows:
Tu autem Domine in aeternum permanes et memoriale tuum in generationem et generationem:
Thou remainest for ever, O Lord, and Thy memorial is from generation in to generation. [*Psalm* 101:13]

The six and fiftieth Spirit is **Gemory**[1] he is a strong and powerful Duke appearing in the form of a beautiful woman with a Duchess' Coronet tied about her middle,[2] riding on a great Camel his office is to tell all things past present and to come, and [the whereabouts] of treasures hid, and what [place] it ~~ly~~ lieth in, and to procure the love of women both young and old, he governeth 26 Legions of Spirits, And this is his Seal which must be worn.[3]

[1] S2: "Gremory". The angel should be Poiel פויאל not Polial.
[2] Probably a mistaken translation of the Latin, 'cingitur', which should have been rendered as 'encircling her head' rather than 'tied around her middle'.
[3] Allevat Dominus omnes qui corrunt, et erigit onmes elisos:
The Lord raiseth up all who fall and setteth up the broken. [*Psalm* 144:15]

The fifty seventh Spirit is **Oso**[1] he is a great President and appeareth like a Leopard at first but after a little time he putteth on the shape of a man, his office is to make men cunning [clever] in the liberal sciences and to give true Answers of Divinity and secret things, and to change a man into any shape that the Exorcist desireth that he that is so changed will not think any other thing but ~~he~~ that he is that Creature or thing [that] he is changed into, He governeth three Legions of Spirits.[2] And this is his Seal which must be worn.[3]

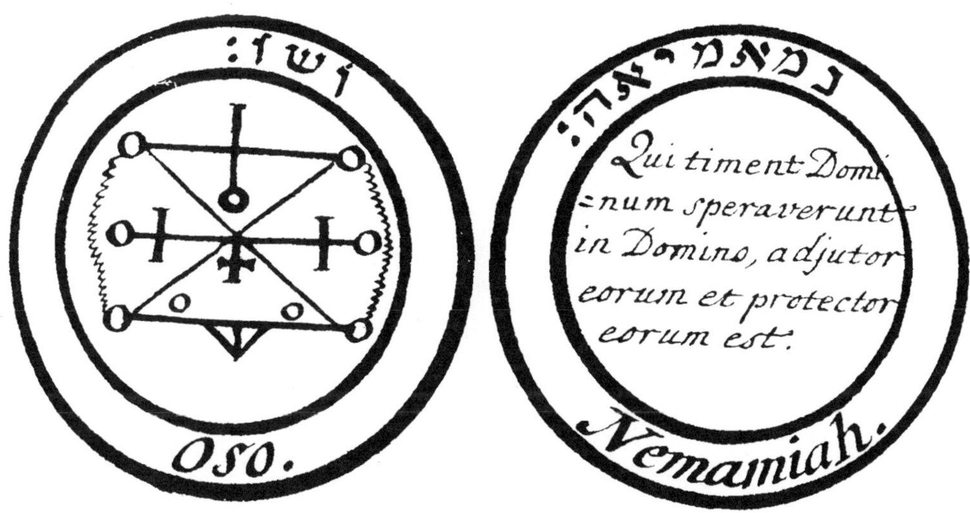

[1] S1, S2, S3, W1: *"Ose"*.

[2] Probably should be 30 Legions.

[3] Qui timent Dominum speraverunt in Domino, adjutor eorum et protector eorum est:
They who fear the Lord have hoped in the Lord, He is their helper and their protector. [*Psalm* 113:19]

[1]The eight and fiftieth Spirit is **Auns**[2] he is a great President and appeareth at first in form of a flaming fire but after a while he putteth on human shape, his office is to make one wondrous knowing [knowledgeable] in Astrology and all the liberal sciences he giveth good familiars, and can bewray [divulge] treasure that is kept by spirits. He governeth 36 Legions of Spirits. His Seal is this which wear. [3]

[1] Fiftieth Sheet Dr Rudd
[2] S1, S2, S3, W1: "Amy".
[3] Et anima mea turbata est valde sed tu Domine usque quo:
My soul is greatly troubled, but Thou, O Lord art here also. [*Psalm* 6:3]

The fifty ninth Spirit is **Orias** he is a great Marquis and appeareth in the form of a Lion riding on a mighty strong horse with a serpent's tail holding in his right hand two great serpents hissing, his office is to teach the virtue of stars, and to know the mansion[1] of the planets and how to understand their [magical] virtues, he also transformeth men and giveth dignities prelacies, & confirmations and the favour of friends & foes, he governeth 30 Legions, his Seal is this.[2]

[1] Their place in the sky, in relation to the 28 Mansions of the Moon.

[2] Ab ortu Solis usque ad occasum laudabile nomen Domini:
From the rising of the Sun to the going down of the same, the word of the Lord is worthy to be praised. [*Psalm* 112:3]

The sixtieth Spirit is **Nappula**[1] he is a great and mighty strong President [2]appearing in the form of a Lion with Griffin's wings, his office is to make men knowing [knowledgeable] in all handicrafts and professions and also in philosophy and other sciences. He governeth 36 Legions of Spirits, his Seal or Character is thus made and worn.[3]

[1] Spelled 'Napula' in the seal. S1, S2, S3: *"Vapula"*; W1: *"Valpula"*.

[2] A Duke in S3.

[3] Iustus Dominus in omnibus viis suis et sanctus in omnibus operibus suis:
The Lord is just in all his ways and blessed in all his works. [*Psalm* 144:18]

The 61st Spirit is **Zagan** he is a great King and President, appearing at the first in [the] form of a Bull with Griffin's wings but after a while he putteth on human shape, and maketh men witty, he can turn wine into water, and blood into wine, also water into wine, he can turn all metals into coin of the Dominion [coin of the Realm] that the Metal is of, and can make fools wise, he governeth 36 Legions of spirits. His Seal is this.[1]

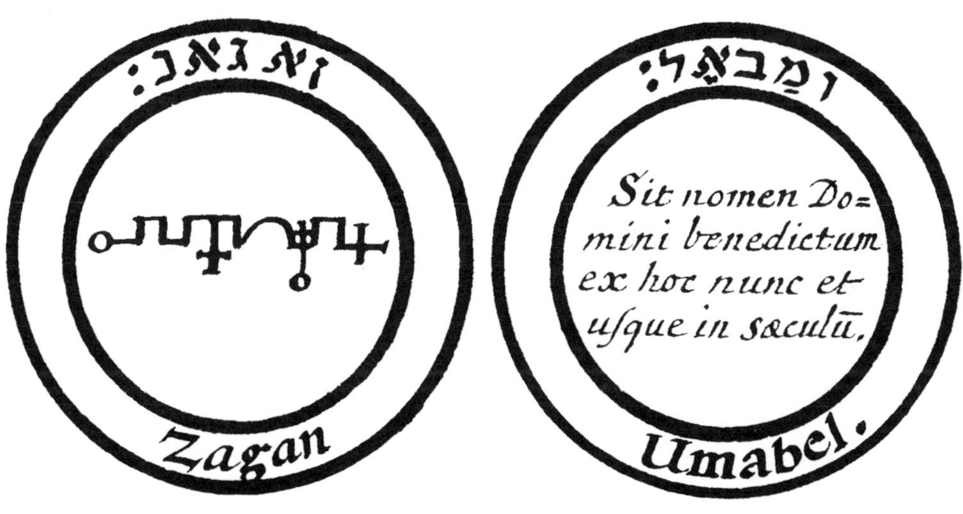

[1] Sit nomen Domini benedictum ex hoc nunc et usque in saeculum:
Let the name of the Lord be blessed from this time forth for evermore. [*Psalm* 112:2]

[1]The Sixty second spirit is **Valu**[2] he is a mighty great President and appeareth like a boy with Angels' wings riding on a two headed Dragon, his office is to give true answers of hidden treasures, and to tell where serpents may be seen which he will bring and deliver to the Exorcist without any force or strength he governeth 30 Legions of spirits, his seal is this which must be worn.[3]

[1] The One & fiftieth Sheet Dr Rudd.

[2] S1, S2, S3, W1: "Valac".

[3] Vide quoniam mandata tua Domini dilexi secundum misericordiam vivificam: See, O Lord, how I have delighted in Thy commandments according to Thy life-giving mercy. [*Psalm* 118:159]

The sixty third Spirit is **Andras** he is a great Marquis appearing in the form of an Angel with a head like a black night Raven riding upon a strong black wolf, with a sharp bright sword flourishing in his hands, his office is to sow discords, if the Exorcist have not a care he will kill him and his followers, he governeth 30 Legions of spirits, and this is his Seal which is worn as a Lamen.[1]

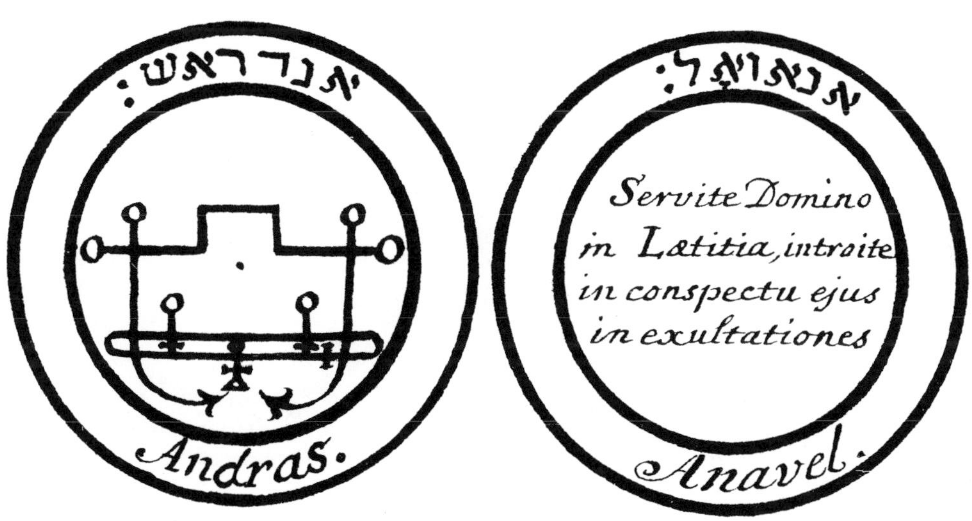

[1] Servite Domino in Laetitia, introite in conspectu eius in exultationes:
Serve ye the Lord with gladness and enter into his sight with exultation. [*Psalm* 2:11]

The Sixty fourth Spirit is **Haures**,[1] he is a great Duke and appeareth at first like a mighty terrible and strong Leopard but after at the Command of the Exorcist he putteth on the shape of a man with fiery eyes and a terrible Countenance, he giveth true Answers of all things past present and to come, but if he be not commanded into a Triangle Δ he will lie in all those things and deceive and beguile the Exorcist in other things or business, he will gladly talk of Divinity and of the Creation of the world, and of his and all other Spirits' falls, he destroyeth and burneth those that are the Exorcist's Enemies if he require it, and will not suffer them to be tempted or otherwise, he governeth three[2] Legions of spirits, his Seal is this.[3]

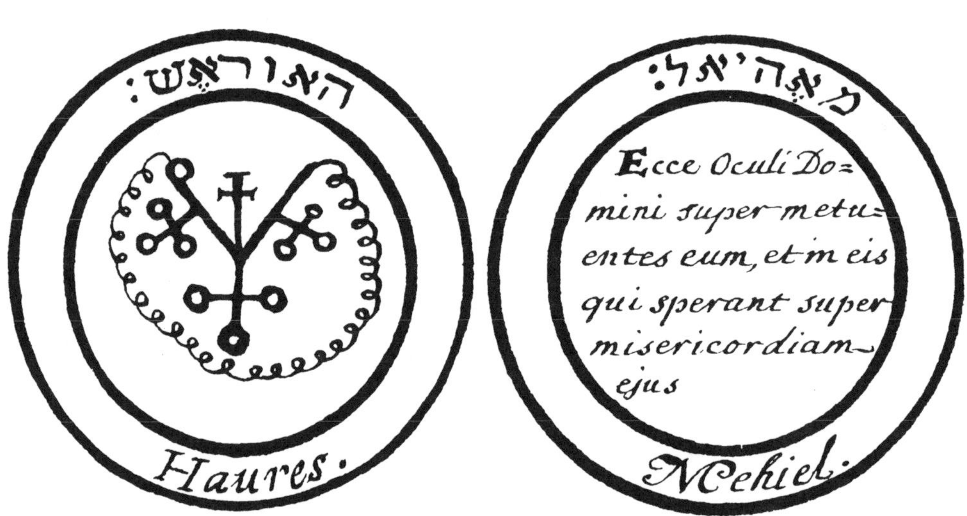

[1] S1, S3: *"Flauros"*; W1: *"Hauros"*.
[2] S3: 36 Legions.
[3] Ecce oculi Domini super metuentes eum et in eis qui sperant super misericordiam eius: Behold the eyes of the Lord are upon those that fear Him and hope in His loving kindness. [*Psalm* 32:18]

The sixty fifth Spirit is **Andrealphus** he is a mighty great Marquis appearing at first in form of a Peacock with great noises but after a while he putteth on human shape, he can teach perfectly Geometry and all things belonging to measure, also Astronomy, he maketh men very cunning [knowledgeable] & subtle therein.

He can transform a man into the likeness of a bird and governeth thirty Legions of Spirits. His seal is this which wear.[1]

[1] Convertere Domine usque quo et deprecabilis esto super servos eius:
Turn, O Lord, even here also, and be pleased with Thy servants. [*Psalm* 89:15]

[1]The sixty sixth spirit is **Cimeries**[2] he is a mighty great Marquis strong & powerful appearing like a valiant Soldier riding on a goodly black horse, he ruleth over all spirits in the parts of Africa, His office is to teach perfectly Grammar Logic Rhetoric, and to discover treasure & things lost or hidden, he can make a man seem like a Soldier in his own likeness, he governeth 20 Legions of Infernal Spirits. His Seal is this which wear. [3]

[1] Two & fiftieth sheet Dr Rudd.
[2] S1, S2, S3: "Cimeies".
[3] Ne derelinquas me Domine Deus meus ne discesseris a me: Neither leave me, O Lord, nor depart from me. [*Psalm* 37:22]

The Sixty seventh Spirit is **Amducias**[1] he is a strong and great Duke appearing at first like a Unicorn but after at the request of the Exorcist he standeth before him in human shape causing Trumpets and all sorts of Musical Instruments to be heard but not seen, also Trees to bend and incline according to the Exorcist's will, and gives excellent familiars and governeth 29 Legions of Spirits his Seal is this which wear[2]

[1] S1, S3, W1: *"Amduscias"*; S2: *"Amdusias"*.

[2] Delectare in Domino et dabit tibi petitiones cordis tui:
Delight in the Lord and He will give thee the petitions of thy heart. [*Psalm* 36:4]

The sixty eight Spirit is **Belial** he is a mighty King and powerful he was created next after Lucifer, and is of his order.

He appeareth in the forms of two beautiful angels sitting in a chariot of fire speaking with a comely voice declaring that he fell first from amongst the worser sort which went before Michael and other heavenly Angels. His office is to distribute preferments of senatorship and to cause favour of friends & foes, he giveth excellent familiars, and governeth 80 Legions of Spirits partly of the order of Virtues partly of Angels.

Note this King Belial must have offerings sacrifices and gifts presented to him[1] by the Exorcist or else he will not give true answers to his demands, but then he tarrieth [remains] not one hour in the truth unless he be constrained by divine power. His Seal is this which is to be worn about you.[2]

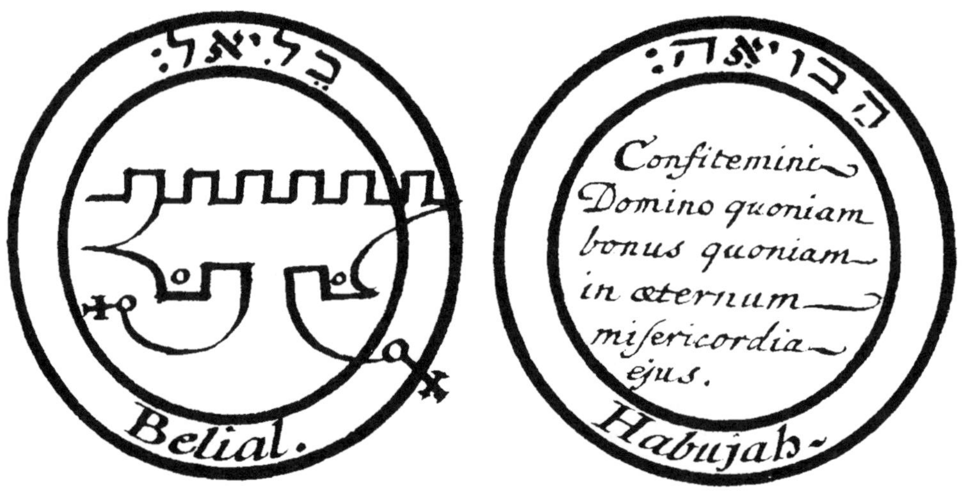

[1] This is one of the few examples where sacrifice is enjoined.

[2] Confitemini Domino quoniam bonus, quoniam in aeternam misericordia eius: Confess to the Lord, for He is God, and His mercy is for ever. [*Psalm* 105:1]

The sixty ninth Spirit is **Decarabia**[1] he appeareth in the form of a Star in a Pentacle ☆ at the first but after at the Command of the Exorcist he puts on the Image of a man, his office is to discover the virtues of birds & precious stones, and to make the similitude [illusion] of all birds to fly before the Exorcist, and tarry with him as if they were tame singing and drinking, and natural birds &c. He governeth thirty Legions of Spirits, he himself being a great Marquis, his seal is this.[2]

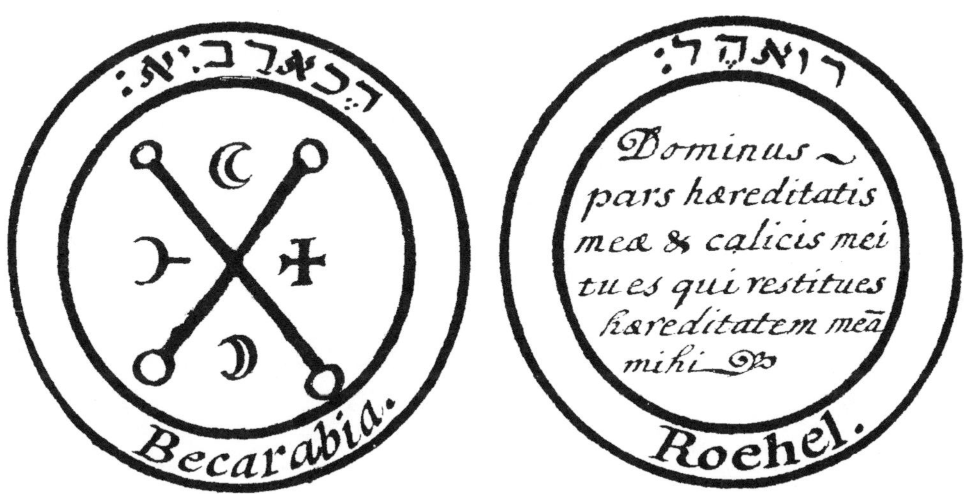

[1] Decarabia is listed as a Marquis. Only the Latin text of Weir shows him clearly as a King and Earl, something which is inexplicably left out of the translation by 'T.R.' or Scot. Also the seal incorrectly shows 'Becarabia' although the Hebrew is a transliteration of 'Decarabia'.

[2] Dominus pars haereditatis meae et calicis mei tu es qui restitues haereditatem meam mihi: The Lord is my inheritance and my cup and it is Thou who restorest mine inheritance. [*Psalm* 15:5]

[1]The Seventieth Spirit is **Seer**,[2] he is a mighty Prince and powerful under Amaymon King of the East,[3] he appeareth in the form of a beautiful man riding on a horse with wings, his office is to go and come & bring all things to pass on a sudden, & to carry & recarry any thing where you would have it from, for he can pass over the whole earth in the twinkling of an Eye. He giveth true Relation [news] of all theft and treasures hid & many other things, he is indifferent good natured willing to do any thing the Exorcist desireth. He governeth 26 Legions of spirits his Character and Seal is this.[4]

[1] Three & fiftieth Sheet Dr Rudd.

[2] S1, S2, S3: "Seere".

[3] The other three Kings are Corson/Gorson (the West), Ziminiar (the North) and Goap (the South). These Kings are attributed to different quarters in other sources.

[4] This is the only Latin text in the *Goetia* which is not drawn from *Psalms*. One possible explanation of this is that at one stage the 70th spirit might have been the last (or more likely the first) in the series, as in Jewish lore 70 was almost as magical a number as 72.
In principio creavit Deus Caelum et Terrum:
In the beginning God created the heaven and the earth. [*Genesis* 1:1]

The 71st. Spirit is **Dantaylion**[1] he is a great and a mighty Duke appearing in the form of a man with many faces all like men's and women's faces and a book in his right hand.

His office is to teach all arts and sciences to any one. He can cause love and show by vision the true similitude [image] of any one let them be in any part of the world. He governeth 36 Legions of Spirits. His Seal is this which must be worn as a Lamen on your breast.[2]

[1] S1, S2, S3, W1: *"Dantalion"*.
[2] Confitebor Domino nimis in ore meo, et in medio multorum laudabo eum:
I shall confess to the Lord with my mouth and praise Him in the midst of the multitude. [*Psalm* 108:29]

The 72nd Spirit is **Andromalius** he is a great and mighty Earl appearing in the form of a man holding a serpent in his hand, his office is to bring a thief and goods back that is stolen to the house, and to discover all wickedness and underhand dealings, and to punish thieves and other wicked people, and to discover treasure that is hid, He ruleth thirty six Legions of spirits His Seal[1] is this.[2]

[1] Convertere anima mea in requiem tuam quoniam Dominus benefaciet tibi:
Return to thy rest, my soul, for the Lord doeth thee good. [*Psalm* 114:7]

[2] W1: Adds here "The Seals of the Spirits are all to be found with the corresponding N[umber] at page… and are to be worn before [on the breast of] the Exorcist or they will not do him homage."

These 72[1] [spirits] be the mighty Kings or princes which King Solomon commanded into a Vessel of Brass with their Legions of whom Belial and Bileth,[2] Asmodai and Gaap was the chief,[3] and it is supposed it was for their pride for Solomon never declared why he thus bound them, and sealed the Vessel and he by divine power cast them all into a deep Lake or hole in Babylon, and the Babylonians wondering to see such a thing there, they went wholly into the Lake to break the vessel open, suspecting to find a great store of treasure, but when they had broken it open out flew all the chief spirits immediately and their Legions followed them and they were all restored to their former places, but only [except for] Belial who entered into a certain Image, and there gave Answers to those who did offer sacrifice unto him, as the Babylonians did for they offered sacrifice and worshipped that Image as God.

[Characters of the Angels of the 7 days][4]

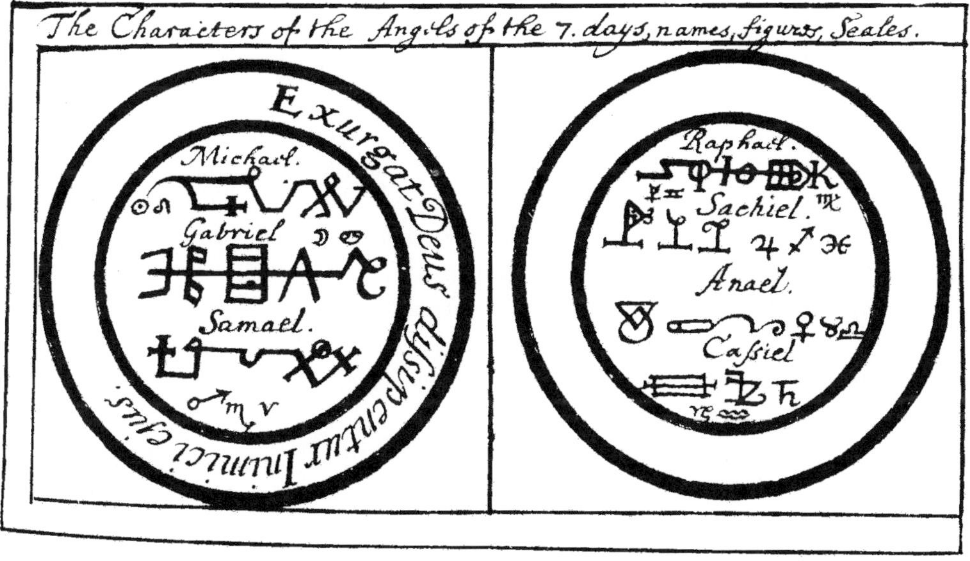

[1] W1: gives *"53"* as 18 + 1 spirits have been left out of that manuscript.

[2] S2: "Baleth".

[3] It is significant that Belial, Bileth, Asmodai and Gaap have been singled out as chief spirits. They are all Kings except Gaap, the 33rd spirit, who is only listed as a mighty President and Prince. His inclusion in this list of Kings gives some warrant for the presumption that he may have been originally listed as a King (which is how he is tentatively shown in Tables M15 and M18).

[4] Although these two composite seals appear at this point in the manuscript, they in fact relate to the 'Directory for the Seven Days of the Week' on pages 198-211.

[The Conjurations]

The Conjuration [which] follows [is used] to call forth any of the aforesaid Spirits.[1]

[2]The [First] Conjuration

To call forth any of the aforesaid Spirits

I Invocate and Conjure you Spirit N: and being armed with power from the Supreme Majesty, I strongly command you by ***Beralanensis, Baldachiensis, Paumachiae et Apologiae,***[3] *and the most powerful Princes,* ***Genio Liachiae***[4] *Ministers of the Tartarian seat, Chief Prince of the seat of Apologia in the ninth Region, I exorcise and powerfully Command you Spirit N. in and by him who said the word and it was done, and by all the holy and most glorious names of the most high and true God, and by these his most holy Names* ***Adonai, El, Elohim, [Elohe] Zebaoth,***[5] ***Elion, Eserchie, Jah, Tetragrammaton***[6]***, Sadai***[7] *that ye forthwith appear and show your self unto me before this Circle in a fair and human shape without any deformity or ugly shape, and without delay do you come to make rational answers unto all those things which I shall ask of you, and come ye peaceably and visibly and affably without delay manifesting what I desire being Conjured by the eternal living and true God* ***Helioren****, and I conjure you by the special and true name of your God that you owe obedience to and by the name of your King which bears rule over you that forthwith you come without any tarrying, and fulfil my desire and Command and persist to the end, and according to my intentions, and I conjure you by him, to whom all Creatures are obedient, and by his ineffable name Tetragrammaton Jehova[h], which being heard the Elements are overturned, the air is shaken, the sea runneth back, the fire is quenched, the Earth trembleth, and all the Hosts of Celestial, Terrestrial, and Infernals do tremble and are troubled and confounded together that you visibly and affably speak to me with a clear voice intelligibly and without any ambiguity. Therefore come ye in the name* ***Adonai, Zebaoth***[8]*,* ***Adonai, Amiorem****, Come, Come, why stay you* ***Adonai Sadai****, The King of Kings Commands you.*

---

[1] At this point in most manuscript versions of the *Goetia* will be found observations concerning equipment used in the conjurations, but here we will follow Rudd and move directly to the text of the conjurations, leaving those observations till later.

[2] Four and fiftieth sheet Dr Rudd.

[3] S1, S3: "Apologiæ-Sedes".

[4] S1: "Liachidæ"; S2: "Liachida"; S3: "Liachidi".

[5] S3: "Zebeoth".

[6] The pronunciation of IHVH has long been a matter of controversy, and it is often rendered 'Yahweh'. Professor Anson Rainey, of Tel-Aviv University provides a translation of Clement of Alexandria's *Stromata* Book V. Chapter 6, where Clement says: "The mystic name which is called the tetragrammaton…is pronounced **Ἰαουέ**", similar to the Greek IAO.

[7] All standard Kabbalistic Godnames, with the corrupt exception of 'Elion' and 'Eserchie' [sometimes Eskerie or Eskeriel]. In Hebrew (with corresponding Sephirah number in brackets) they are: **אדני** (10), **אל** (4), **אלהים** (3 or 5), **אלהים צבאות** (8), Elion (?), Eserchie (?), **יה** (2), **יהוה** (7), **שדי** (9).

[8] S3: "Zebeoth".

Say this as often as you please, and if the Spirit do[es] not come, say as followeth.[1]

[The Second Conjuration]

I Invocate Conjure, and command you Spirit N. to appear and show yourself visibly unto me before this Circle in fair and comely sort and shape without any deformity and tortuosity by the name and in the name of ***Y and U***[2] *which Adam heard and spake and by the name* ***Ioth*** *which Jacob heard from the Angel wrestling with him and was delivered from the hands of Esau his brother: and by the name of God* ***Agla****, which Lot heard and was saved with his family. And by the name* ***Anepheneton***[3] *which Aaron heard and spake and became wise. And by the name* ***Scemes Amathia***[4] *which Joshua called upon, and the Sun stood still; And by the name* ***Emanuel*** *which the three Children Shadrach Meseck*[5] *and Abednego sung in the midst of the fiery furnace and was [were] delivered. And by the name of* ***Alpha and Omega*** *which Daniel names and destroys Bel and the Dragon; And by the name* ***Zebaoth*** *which Moses names and all the Rivers and waters in Egypt are turned into Blood; And by the name* ***Eserchie Oriston*** *which Moses named and all the Rivers brought forth frogs and they went into all the houses of the Egyptians destroying all things, And by the name* ***Elion*** *which Moses called upon and there was great hail such as there was never since the Creation of the world to this day, And by the name* ***Adonai*** *which Moses named, and there came up Locusts throughout all the Land of Egypt, And destroyed all that the hail had left, And by the name* ***Hagios****; and by the Seal of* ***Adonai****, And by* ***O Theos Iscyros***

---

[1] W1: "I Invocate and Conjure thee Spirit N: and being armed with power from the Supreme Majesty, I strongly command you by Beralanensis, Baldachiensis, Paumachios et Apologia, and the most powerful Princes, Genio Liachios in the ninth Region, I exorcise and powerfully Command thee Spirit N. in and by him that spake the word and it was done, and by all the holy and most glorious names of the most high and true God, and by these his most holy Names Adonai, El, Elohim, Elohe, Sabaoth, Elion, Eserchie, Jah, Tetragrammaton, Sadai that thou forthwith appear and show thyself unto me before this Circle in a fair and human shape without any deformity or ugly shape, and without delay come thou from all parts of the world to make rational answers to all things which I shall ask of thee, and come thou peaceably and affably visibly without delay manifesting what I desire being Conjured by the eternal living and true God Helioren, and I conjure thee by the special and true name of your God thy King which bear rule that thou obedience unto me by the name of thy King which bear rule over thee that thou do come forthwith without any tarrying to fulfil my desires and commands and [illegible] to the end according to my intentions and I conjure thee by him to whom all creatures are obedient and by the ineffable name Tetragrammaton Jehovah which being heard the Elements are overturned, the Air is shattered, the sea runneth back the fire is quenched the earth trembleth and all the Elemental Celestial and infernal [beings] do tremble and are troubled and confounded together, that thou visibly and affably speak to me with a clear voice & without any ambiguity. Therefore come thou in the name Adonay Sabaoth Adonay Amiorem, come come why stayest thou hasten Adonay Saday the King of Kings commands you".

[2] The names highlighted in bold in the invocation are not so highlighted in the original manuscript.

[3] S1, S2: "Anaphaxeton"; S3: "Anaphexaton".

[4] S1: "Schems Amathia"; S2: "Schemes Amatia"; S3: "Schemes Amathia"; HMN: "Schemes Amathia".

[5] S3: "Sedrach Mesach".

Athanatos Paracletos, [1] *and by the three holy and sacred names* ***Agla On Tetragrammaton****, and by the dreadful Judgement of God. And by the uncertain Sea of Glass which is before the face of divine Majesty who is mighty and most powerful, And by the four beasts that stood before the throne having eyes before and behind, and by the fire round about the throne*[2]*, And by the holy Angels of heaven, And by the mighty wisdom of God, and by the Seal of* ***Basdathea,***[3] *And by the name* ***Primeumaton***[4] *which Moses named and the Earth opened and swallowed up Corah*[5] *Dathan & Abiram. [I command] that you make faithful Answers to all my demands and to perform all my desires so far as in [your] office you are capable of to perform. Therefore come ye peaceably visibly and affably* [6]*now without delay to manifest what I desire speaking with perfect and clear voice intelligible, and to my understanding.*[7]

---

[1] S1: *"Otheos: Ictros: Athenaros: peracletos"*; S2: *"Otheos: Icyros: Athenaros: peracletos"*; S3: *"Otheos, Iscyros, Athenatos, Paracletus"*. Much of this invocation is clearly derived from the Roman Catholic liturgy. 'Hagios/Agios O Theos' means 'O Holy God', and these are the opening words in a Greek invocation, or doxology, or hymn, which in the Roman Catholic liturgy is sung on Good Friday, which hints at the hidden connection between the resurrection and the raising of spirits. This hymn is sung alternatively in Greek and Latin by two choirs or voices, as follows:
First Choir: *Agios o Theos* (O Holy God). Second Choir: *Sanctus Deus.*
First Choir: *Agios ischyros* (Holy, Strong). Second Choir: *Sanctus fortis.*
First Choir: *Agios athanatos, eleison imas* (Holy, Immortal, have mercy on us). Second Choir: *Sanctus immortalis, miserere nobis.* The hymn is sung twelve times, alternating the responses.

[2] That is the Shekinah of God, hence the subsequent reference also to the wisdom of God, a title of the Shekinah.

[3] S3: "Baldachia".

[4] A word of power used frequently throughout this volume. It is obviously a Latin corruption of a three Greek words, possibly being *prime pneuma ton*, which might translate as 'First Breath'. In Greek, 'ton' is a diminutive. "By this name [Primeumaton] Moses caused hail in Egypt."

[5] S1, S2, S3: *"Chora"*. Should be 'Korah'. See *Numbers* 16:27-34 where the Lord causes the earth, at Moses' behest, to swallow up the rebellious Korah, Dathan and Abiram.

[6] Five and fiftieth sheet Dr Rudd.

[7] W1: "I Invocate and command thee Spirit N. to appear and show yourself visible to me before this Circle in fair and comely shape without any deformity and tortuosity by the name Ioth which Jacob heard from the Angel wrestling with him and was delivered from the hands of Esau his brother: and by the name of God Agla, which Lot heard and was saved with his family. And by the name Anepheneton which Aaron heard and spake and became wise. And by the name Scemes Amathia which Joshua called upon, and the Sun and Moon stood still; And by the name Emanuel which the three Children Shadrach Meseck and Abednego sung in the midst of the fiery furnace and were delivered. And by the name Alpha and Omega which Daniel named and destroyed Bel and the Dragon; And by the name Sabaoth which Moses named and all the Rivers and waters in Egypt are turned into Blood; And by the name Eserchie Oriston which Moses named and all the Rivers brought forth frogs and they went into all the houses of the Egyptians destroying everything, And by the name Elion which Moses called upon and there was a great hail such as was not since the Creation of the world to this day, And by the name Adonai which Moses named, and there came up Locusts throughout all the Land of Egypt, And destroyed all that the hail had left, And by the name Hagios; and by the Seal of Adonai, And by O Theos Iscyros Athanatos Paracletos, and by the three holy and sacred names Agla On Tetragrammaton, and by the dreadful Judgement of God. And by the Sea of Glass which is before the face of the divine Majesty who is mighty and most powerful, And by the four beasts before the throne having eyes before and behind, and by the fire

If they do not come yet at the Rehearsing of the two former Conjurations, but without doubt they will. Say as followeth, it being a Constraint.[1]

[The Constraint]

I Conjure thee Spirit (N) by all the most glorious and efficacious names of the most great and incomprehensible Lord God of Hosts that you come quickly without delay from all parts and places of the world where ever you be to make Answer to my demands and that visibly and affably speaking with a voice intelligible to my understanding as aforesaid. I conjure and constrain you Spirit N. by all aforesaid, and by these seven names which wise Solomon bound thee and thy followers in a Vessel of brass. ***Adonai, Preraii,*** [2] ***Tetragrammaton, Anepheneton,*** [3] ***Inessenfatel,***[4] ***Pathatumon***[5] ***& Itemon****, That you appear here before this Circle to fulfil my will in all things that shall seem good unto me, and if you be so disobedient and refuseth to come I will in the power and by the power of the name of the supreme Everlasting Lord God who created both you and me and all the world in six days and what is contained in it* ***Eyesaraii***[6]*, and by the power of this name* ***Primeumaton*** *which Commandeth the whole Host of heaven [I] Curse you and deprive you*[7] *from all your office Joy and place, and bind you in the depth of the bottomless pit there to remain until the last day of the last Judgement, And I will bind you in the Eternal fire , and into the lake of fire and brimstone unless you come quickly and appear here before this Circle to do my will therefore Come ye in and by these holy names* ***Adonai, Zebaoth, Amiorem*** *Come ye* ***Adonai*** *Commands you.*

---

roundabout the throne, And by the holy Angels of heaven, And by the mighty wisdom of God, and by the Seal of Bethedda, And by the name Primeumaton which Moses named and the Earth opened and swallowed up Corah Dathan & Abram That thou make faithful Answers to all my demands and to perform all my desires so far as in office thou art capable of. Therefore come peaceably visibly and affably now without delay to manifest what I desire speaking with a perfect and clear voice intelligible, and to my understanding."

[1] W1: "If the Spirit does not come at the rehearsing of the two former Conjurations as without doubt he will, Say as follows, it being a constraint."

[2] S1, S2: "Preyai"; S3: "Prerai".

[3] S3: "Anephexeton".

[4] S1, S2: "Inessenfatoal"; S3: "Inessenfatall".

[5] S1: "Pathtumon".

[6] S3: "Eye-Saray".

[7] "deprive you" is repeated.

[1]If you come so far, and he yet [he] do not appear, you may be sure he is sent to some other place by his King and cannot come, and if it be so Invocate the King as followeth to send him, but if he do not come, then you may be sure he is bound in Chains in Hell and is not in the Custody of his King. So if you have a desire to call him from thence you must Release the Spirit's Chain.[2]

For to Invocate the King say as followeth.[3]

[Invocation of the King]

O you great mighty and powerful King Amaymon[4] who bears rule by the power of the supreme God ***El****, over all Spirits both Superior and Inferior of the Infernal Order in the Dominion of the East, I Invocate and command you by the especial and true name of your God and by [the] God that you worship and by the seal of your ~~God~~ Creation, and by the most mighty and powerful name of God* ***Jehovah Tetragrammaton*** *who cast you out of heaven with all other Infernal spirits, and by the most powerful and great Names of God who created Heaven and Earth and Hell and all things contained in them, and by their powers and virtue, and by the Name* ***Primeumaton*** *who Commandeth the whole Host of Heaven that you cause enforce and Compel the Spirit, N, to come unto me here before this Circle in a fair and comely form without doing any harm to me or any other Creature, and to answer truly & faithfully unto all my requests, that I may accomplish my will and desires in knowing and obtaining any matter or thing which by office you know is proper for him to ~~obtain~~ perform or to accomplish, through the power of God* ***El****, who created and disposeth[5] of all things Celestial, Aerial, Terrestrial and Infernal.*[1]

---

[1] W1: "I Conjure thee Spirit (N) by all the most glorious and efficacious names of the most great and incomprehensible Lord God of Hosts that thou come quickly without delay from all parts and places of the world where ever thou art to make rational answers to my demands and that visibly and affably speaking with a voice intelligible to my understanding. I conjure and constrain you Spirit N. by the aforesaid, and by these several names whereby Solomon bound thee and thy followers in a Vessel of brass. Adonai, Prerai, Tetragrammaton, Pathatumon & Itemon That thou do appear here before this Circle to fulfil my will in all things that shall seem good unto me, and if you be disobedient and refuse to come I will in and by the power of the supreme Everlasting Lord God who created both you and me and all the world in six days and what is contained therein Eyesaray, and by the power of this name Primeumaton which commands the whole Host of heaven Curse and deprive you from all your office Joy and place, and bind you in the depth of the bottomless pit there to remain to thy day of the last Judgement, And I will bind you in the Eternal fire , and into the lake of fire and brimstone unless you come quickly and appear before this Circle to do my will therefore Come ye in and by these holy names Adonai, Zebaoth, Amjorem".

[2] W1: "If you come so far, And if he does not yet appear, you may be sure he is sent to some other place by his King and cannot come, and if it be to Invocate the King as follows to send him, but if he do not come still, you may be sure he is bound in Chains in Hell and is not in the custody of his King. So if you have a desire to call him from thence you must release the Spirit's chains".

[3] W1: "To Invocate the King".

[4] Obviously you should address the appropriate King, Amaymon only for spirits of the East, Corson/Gorson for the West, Ziminiar for the North, and Goap/Gaap for the South. These directional attributions unfortunately vary from manuscript to manuscript.

[5] H: the word is written as *"disposed"* with a *"th"* above the final *"d"*.

After you have Invocated the King in this manner twice or thrice over then Conjure the Spirit you would call forth by the aforesaid Conjurations[2] Rehearsing them several times together and he will come without doubt if not at first, [then] the second time Rehearsing, but if he do not come Add the Spirits Chain to the end of the aforesaid Conjurations and he will be forced to Come [even] if he be bound in Chains [3]for the ~~in~~ Chains will break off from him, & he will be at liberty.[4]

[The Lesser Curse]

The General Curse called the Spirits Chain against all Spirits that Rebel[5]

O thou wicked and Rebellious or disobedient Spirit (N) because thou hast rebelled and not obeyed nor regarded my words which I have rehearsed they being all glorious & incomprehensible Names of the true God Maker and Creator of you and me and all the world, I by the power of those Names which no Creature is able to resist do Curse you into the depths of the bottomless pit and there to remain until the day of doom, in Chains of fire and brimstone unquenchable, unless you forthwith appear here before this Circle in this Δ to do my will &c. Therefore come quickly & peaceably in and by these names ***Adonai Zebaoth Adonai Amiram,*** *Come, Come the King* ***Adonai*** *Commands you.*[6]

---

[1] W1: "O you great and powerful King Amaymon who bears rule by the power of the supreme God El, over all Spirits Superior and Inferior of the Infernal Order in the Dominion of the East I Invocate and command thee by the especial and true name of God and the God that you worship and by the seal of your Creation, and by the most mighty and powerful name of God Jehovah Tetragrammaton who cast you out of heaven with all other Infernal spirits, and all the most powerful and great Names of him who created Heaven and Earth and Hell and all things contained in them, and by their powers and virtues, and by the name Primeumaton which Commandeth the whole Host of Heaven that cause enforce and Compel and enforce the Spirit, N, to come unto me here before this Circle in a fair and comely form not doing any harm to me or any other Creature, and to answer truly & faithfully freely to all my requests, that I may accomplish my will and desires in knowing or obtaining any matter or thing which by office you know is proper for him to perform or to accomplish, through the power of God El, who created and disposeth of all things Celestial, aerial, Terrestrial and Infernal."

[2] In short, go back and begin the conjurations again from the beginning, now that the King has been requested to release the spirit.

[3] Six & fiftieth Sheet [of] Dr Rudd.

[4] W1: "After you have Invocated the King twice or thrice in this manner then Conjure the Spirit you would call forth by the aforesaid Conjurations Rehearsing them several times together and he will come but if not at the first a Second rehearsing say the following Conjuration and he will be forced to come if he be Even bound in chains, for the chains must break off from him, and he will be at liberty."

[5] W1: "The General Curse against all the Spirits that rebel".

[6] W1: "O thou wicked and disobedient Spirit (N) because thou hast rebelled and not obeyed nor regarded my words which I have rehearsed they being all glorious & incomprehensible Names of the true God Maker and creator of you and me and all the world I by the power of those Names which no Creature is able to resist do Curse you into the depth of the bottomless pit and there to remain to the day of doom in Chains of fire and brimstone unquenchable; unless you forthwith

When you have read so far, and he do[es] not come, then write his name & Seal in [on] Virgin's parchment and put it in a black box with brimstone & asafoetida and such like things that bear a stinking smell, and then bind the box up round with an iron wire, and hang it on your Sword's point, and hold it over the fire of Charcoal, and say to the fire [as follows,] first it being placed to that quarter [from which] the Spirit is to come.[1]

[The Conjuration of the Fire]

I Conjure thee Fire by him that made thee and all other good Creatures in the world that thou torment burn and Consume this Spirit N. into fire Everlasting because thou [the spirit] art disobedient and obeyed not my Commands nor kept the precepts of the Lord thy God neither wilt thou obey me nor my Invocations having thereby called you forth who am the Servant of the most high and Imperial Lord God of Hosts Jehovah and dignified and fortified by his Celestial power and permission neither comest thou to Answer to these my proposals here made unto you for which your averseness and contempt you are guilty of grand disobedience and rebellion And therefore I shall Excommunicate[2] you and destroy your name and Seal which I have here enclosed in this Box and shall burn them in immortal [eternal] fire, and bury them in immortal [eternal] oblivion unless thou immediately come and appear visibly and affably, friendly and courteously here ~~before~~ unto me, before this Circle in this Triangle Δ in a fair and comely form, and in no wise horrible hurtful or frightful to me or any other Creature whatsoever upon the face of the Earth, and make Rational Answer to my Request and perform all my desires in all things that I will make unto you.[3]

---

appear before this Circle in this triangle Δ to do my will &c. Therefore come quickly & peaceably in and by these names Adonai Zebaoth Adonai Amira, Come, Come the King Adonai Commands you."

[1] W1: "When you have read this so far, and he does not come, then write his name & Seal in Virgins parchment and put it in a black box with brimstone & asafoetida and such like things that bear a Stinking smell, then bind the box up round about with a wire of steel, and hang it on your Sword point, and hold it in a fire of Charcoal, and say to this fire first it being placed to that quarter the Spirit is to come from".

[2] A theologically interesting threat.

[3] W1: "I Conjure thee Fire by him that made thee and all other Creatures in the world that thou burn and Consume the Spirit N. because he was disobedient and obeyed not my Commands neither did thou the Spirit N. obey the precepts of the Lord thy God neither would thou obey me nor my Invocations having thereby called you forth who are a Servant of the most high and Imperial Lord God of Hosts Jehovah are dignified and fortified by his Celestial power nether comest thou to Answer these my proposals here made unto thee for which your averseness and contempt you are guilty of grand disobedience and rebellion And therefore I shall Excommunicate and destroy thee, thy name and Seal that I have enclosed in this Box and shall burn them in immortal fire, and bury them in immortal oblivion unless thou come and appear visibly and affably friendly and courteously here, before this Circle in this Triangle Δ in a fair and comely form, and in no wise terrible hurtful or frightful to me or any other Creature whatsoever upon the face of the Earth, and make Rational Answer to my Request and perform my desires in all things that I shall make to you."

If he come not yet Say as followeth.[1]

[The Greater Curse]

Now O thou Spirit N. since thou art still pernicious and disobedient, & will not appear unto me to answer to such things which I would have desired of you or would have been satisfied in &c: I do in the name and by the power and dignity of the omnipotent and immortal Lord God of Hosts ***Jehovah Tetragrammaton*** *the only Creator of Heaven and Earth and Hell and all that in them is, who is the marvellous disposer of all things both visible and invisible Curse you and deprive you from all your office joy and place and do bind thee in the depth of the bottomless pit and there to remain until the day of the last Judgement I say into the Lake of fire and brimstone which is prepared for all Rebellious disobedient obstinate and pertinacious spirits. Let all the holy Company of Heaven Curse thee; the Sun and Moon and all the Stars, the Light and all the host of heaven curse thee into the fire unquenchable and torments unspeakable, and as thy name and Seal is contained in this box chained and bound up and [you] shall be choked in Sulphurous and stinking substance brimstone, and burnt [as your Seal is] in this material fire. So in the name of* ***Jehovah*** *and by the power and dignity of these three names* ***Tetragrammaton, Anepheneton*** *and* ***Primeumaton*** *[I] Cast thee, O thou disobedient Spirit (N) into the Lake of fire which is prepared for the damned & cursed Spirits and there to remain unto the day of Doom, and never more to be remembered of before the face of God which shall come to Judge the quick and dead, and the world by fire.*[2]

[1] W1: "If he cometh not Say".

[2] W1: "Now O thou Spirit N. since thou art still pernicious, & will not appear unto me to answer to such things which I desired of your or would have been satisfied in &c: I do in the name and by the power and dignity of the omnipotent and immortal Lord God of Hosts Jehovah Tetragrammaton the only Creator of Heaven and Earth and Hell and all that in them is who is the marvellous disposer of all things visible and invisible Curse and deprive you from all your office place and joy and do bind thee in the depth of the bottomless pit and there to remain until the day of the last Judgement I say into the Lake of fire and brimstone which is prepared for all Rebellious disobedient obstinate and pernicious spirits So let all the host of Heaven Curse thee; the Sun and Moon and all the Stars the Light and all the holy company of heaven curse you in the fire unquenchable and torments unspeakable and as thy name and Seal are contained in this box chained and bound up and shall be choked in Sulphurous and stinking stuff as described, and burnt in this material fire. So in the name of Jehovah and by the power and dignity of these three names Tetragrammaton, Anepheneton Primeumaton I Cast thee disobedient Spirit (N) into the fire which is prepared for the damned & cursed Spirits and thereto remain unto the day of Doom, and never more to be remembered of him who shall come to Judge the quick and the dead, and the world by fire."

[1][Here the Exorcist must put the box into the fire]

And by and by he [the spirit] will come, but as soon as he is come Quench the fire[2] that the box is in and make a sweet perfume, and give him a kind Entertainment[3] showing him the Pentacle that is at the bottom of your Vesture covered with a linen Cloth Saying

[Exorcist's Address to the Spirit]

[4]*Behold your Conclusion [fate] if you be disobedient, Behold the ✰ Pentacle of Solomon which I have here brought before your presence. Behold the person of the Exorcist who is called*[5] ***Ochnomos***[6] *in the midst of the Exorcism who is armed by God*[7] *and without fear who potently Invocated you and called you to appearance, therefore make rational Answers to my demands and be obedient to me your Master in the Name of the Lord* ***Bathal*** *Rushing upon Abrack coming upon Aberer.*[8]

Then he or they will be obedient and bid you ask what you will for he is subject by God to fulfil your desires and demands.[9] And when he or they have appeared, and showed himself[10] humbly and meek, then you are to say

---

[1] Seven and fiftieth sheet Dr Rudd.

[2] W1: "as soon as he is come".

[3] Welcome.

[4] W1: "here".

[5] W1: "~~named~~".

[6] S3: "Octinomos"

[7] W1: Replaces "Ochnomos in the midst of Exorcism who is armed by God" with "from God".

[8] S3: "Lord Bathat rushing upon Abrac Abeor coming upon Aberer". The Latin original in de Abano's Heptameron as rendered by Turner is "Domini Bathat, vel Vachat super Abrac ruens, super veniens, Abeor super Aberer."

[9] W1: "commands".

[10] W1: "themselves".

[Welcome Address to the Spirit]

Welcome Spirits or most noble King or Kings[1]*. I say you are all welcome unto me, because I called you through him who Created both Heaven and Earth and Hell and all that is contained in them, and you have obeyed also by the same power I called you forth by; I bind you that you remain affably & visibly here before this Circle in this Δ Triangle so constant and so long as I have occasion for you and not to depart without my license until you have truly and faithfully performed my will without any falsity.*[2]

[At this point the magician should outline to the spirit the tasks he wishes him to accomplish, ensuring that they are within the remit (or office) of the spirit. When the spirit has agreed to perform these things within a specific time frame, and maybe sealed or 'signed' an agreement, then the magician should licence the spirit to depart.]

The License to Depart

O thou Spirit (N) because thou hast diligently Answered my Demands, and was very ready and willing~~ly~~ to come at my first call I do here license thee to depart unto thy proper place without doing any injury or danger to man or beast. Depart I say and be ever ready to [answer] my call being Exorcised and Conjured by the sacred Rites of Magick, I charge thee to withdraw peaceably and quietly, and the peace of God be ever continued between me and thee.[3] *Amen.*

After you have given the Spirit License [to Depart], you are not to go out of the Circle till they be gone, And [until] you have made prayers to God for the great blessings he hath bestowed on[4] you in granting your desires and delivering you from all the malice of your enemy[5] the Devil.

Note you may Command these Spirits [to enter] into the brazen vessel as you do into the Triangle. Saying [to them] that you do forthwith[6] appear before this Circle in this Vessel of Brass in a fair and comely shape &c as is showed before in the Conjurations.[7]

---

[1] Whichever is the case.

[2] W1: "Welcome Spirit or most mighty King. I say you are welcome unto me, because I have called you through him who Created both Heaven and Earth and all that is contained in them, and you have obeyed by the same power I called you forth I bind you that you remain visible here before this Circle in this Δ Triangle so constant and So long as I have occasion for you and not to depart without my license until you have truly and faithfully performed my will without any falsity."

[3] W1: "O thou Spirit N because thou hast diligently come to me and as ready and willing at my Call I do here license thee to depart unto thy proper place without doing any injury duly exorcised and conjured by the holy Rites of Magick, I charge thee to withdraw peaceably and quietly, and the peace of God be ever continued between thee and me".

[4] W1: "upon".

[5] W1: Omits "your enemy".

[6] W1: "here".

[7] This is an important reference to the practical use of the Brass Vessel as a spirit locus.

Of the [Magical] Circle

and the Composition thereof.[1]

The form of Circles is not always one and the same but used to be changed according to the order of the spirits that are to be called, their places, times, days, and hours, for in making a Circle it ought to be Considered in what time of the year what day and what hour, that you make the Circle, What Spirits you would call, to what star and region they do belong, and what functions they have.[2] Therefore let there be made three Circles of the latitude[3] of nine foot and let them be distant one from another [by] a hand's breadth; and in the middle Circle first write the name of the hour wherein you do the work. Secondly[4] write the name of the Angel of the hour. Thirdly[5] the Sigil of the Angel of the hour. [6]Fourthly the Name of the Angel that ruleth that day wherein you do the work and the name of his Ministers. Fifthly[7] the name of ~~his Ministers~~ the present time. Sixthly the name of the spirits ruling in that part of time and their presidents. Seventhly the Name of the head of the sign ruling in that part of time wherein you work. Eighthly the name of the earth according to that part of time wherein you work. Ninthly, and for the completing of the middle Circle write the name of the Sun and of the moon according to the said rule of time, for as the time is changed, so the names are to be altered.

---

[1] The next section on the construction and composition of the Circle is all copied from de Abano's *Heptameron*. These instructions are missing from the other manuscripts of the *Goetia*. It might be argued that this is an interpolation, but as the previous section on the Conjurations is taken directly from the *Heptameron* it would seem more than legitimate to include instructions for Circle construction which are otherwise missing from the *Goetia*.

[2] This is a very important note. It harks back to the Graeco-Egyptian conjurations of the first couple of centuries CE, where it was necessary to recite the names of the rulers of the hours and day in which the conjuration takes place, as otherwise it was thought that the spirits would consider that you were not initiated (into this knowledge) and would therefore not heed you. Here the names of the day and hour are incorporated in the construction of the circle. Interestingly only one example of the circle is given. The correct names for a particular operation have to be worked out by the magician, but can be found in the *Heptameron*. Further examples of variant Circles, from another manuscript, are given in Appendix 12, Almost all later grimoires just give a single fixed Circle design, and omit to mention this important point. Probably the later design of the Circle in other manuscripts of the *Goetia* incorporates all of the relevant Godnames, so that it should be useable for all circumstances. However the procedure of selecting the correct names for the circle depending upon the time and objective of the operation is probably the older method.

[3] Diameter, or possibly a radius of 9 feet.

[4] HMN: "In the second place".

[5] HMN: "In the third place".

[6] Eight and fiftieth sheet Dr Rudd.

[7] HMN: "In the fifth place".

And in the ~~Innermost~~ Outermost Circle let there be drawn in the four angles the names of the Presidential Angels of the air, that day wherein you would do this work, to wit the name of the King and his three ministers. Without [outside] the Circle in [the] four Angles let Pentagons[1] be made. In the Inner Circle let there be written 4 divine names with Crosses interspersed in the middle of the Circle; to wit towards the East let there be written Alpha, And towards the West there be written Omega, and let a Cross divide the middle of the Circle:

When the Circle is thus finished[2] you shall proceed.[3]

---

[1] Pentagrams not Pentagons.

[2] HMN: "according to the rule now before written".

[3] Other manuscripts of the Goetia replace this section with S3: "A figure of the Circle of Solomon, that he made to preserve himself from the malice of those evil Spirits &c."
S2: "This Circle is to be made 9 foot over & these names Round in it in one line beginning at Eheie[h] & so go[ing] on till you come Round to [Jehovah] Levanah [the] S[phere] ☽ [of the Moon]". For the full list see Appendix 9.
Where the option to include all the god and angelic names from the Tree of Life has been taken, the special names of the hours taken from the *Heptameron* are not used. Mathers and S3 for example use a spiral of ten groups (one for each Sephiroth) containing its godname, Sephiroth, archangel, order of angels, Hebrew and English name of the planet. This however is not in the spirit of the method used here, or in the *Heptameron,* which is time dependant.

Of the Names of the Hours

and the Angels ruling them

[1]The Angels do rule the hours in a successive Order according to the Course of the Heavens and planets unto which they are subject; So that that spirit which governeth the day ruleth also the first hour of the day; the second from this governeth the second hour of the day,[2] the third, [rules] the third hour & so [on] consequently: And when seven planets & hours have made their Revolution it returneth again to the first which ruleth the day. Therefore we shall first speak of the Names of the hours.

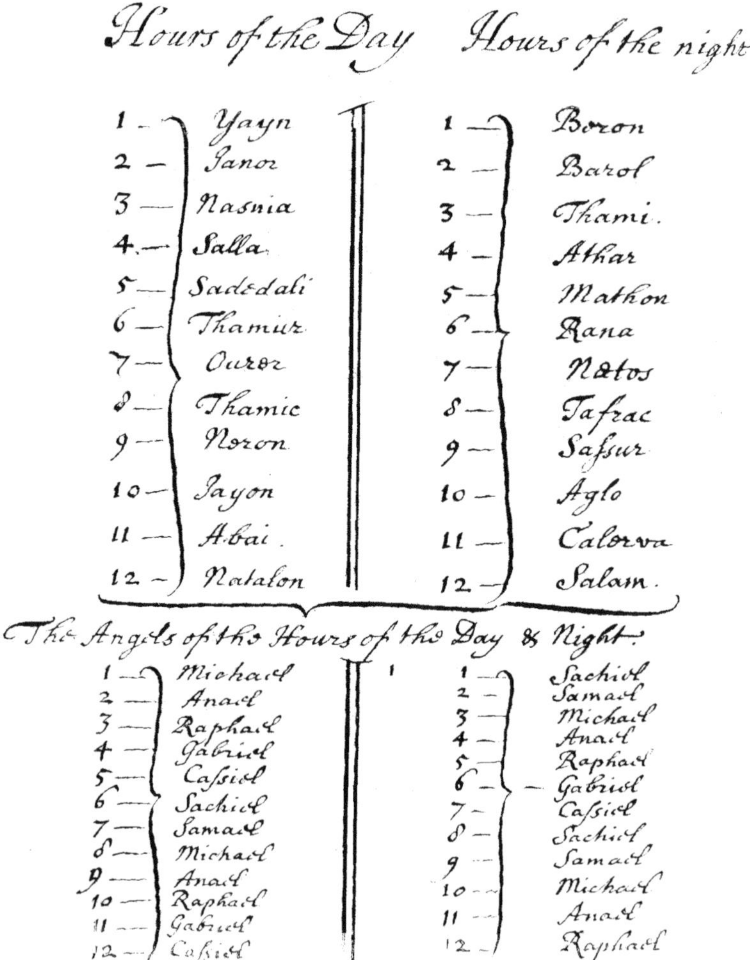

Hours of the Day		Hours of the night	
1	Yayn	1	Beron
2	Janor	2	Barol
3	Nasnia	3	Thami.
4.	Salla	4	Athar
5	Sadedali	5	Mathon
6	Thamur	6	Rana
7	Ourer	7	Netos
8	Thamic	8	Tafrac
9	Neron	9	Sassur
10	Jayon	10	Aglo
11	Abai.	11	Calerva
12	Natalon	12	Salam.

The Angels of the Hours of the Day & Night.			
1	Michael	1	Sachiel
2	Anael	2	Samael
3	Raphael	3	Michael
4	Gabriel	4	Anael
5	Cassiel	5	Raphael
6	Sachiel	6	Gabriel
7	Samael	7	Cassiel
8	Michael	8	Sachiel
9	Anael	9	Samael
10	Raphael	10	Michael
11	Gabriel	11	Anael
12	Cassiel	12	Raphael

Figure 6: Hours of the Day and Hours of the Night, with their ruling angels.

[1] HMN: "It is also to be known, that". The hours are traditional Hebrew names of the hours.
[2] HMN: omits "of the day".

Hours of the Day		*Hours of the Night*	
1 -	*Yayn*	*1 -*	*Beron*
2 -	*Janor*	*2 -*	*Barol*
3 -	*Nasnia*	*3 -*	*Thami*
4 -	*Salla*	*4 -*	*Athar*
5 -	*Sadedali*	*5 -*	*Mathon*
6 -	*Thamur*	*6 -*	*Rana*
7 -	*Ourer*	*7 -*	*Netos*
8 -	*Thamic*	*8 -*	*Tafrac*
9 -	*Neron*	*9 -*	*Sassur*
10 -	*Jayon*	*10 -*	*Aglo*
11 -	*Abai*	*11 -*	*Calerva*
12 -	*Natalon*	*12 -*	*Salam*

The Angels of the Hours of the Day & Night:[1]

[Hours of the Day]		*[Hours of the night]*	
1 -	*Michael*	*1 -*	*Sachiel*
2 -	*Anael*	*2 -*	*Samael*
3 -	*Raphael*	*3 -*	*Michael*
4 -	*Gabriel*	*4 -*	*Anael*
5 -	*Cassiel*	*5 -*	*Raphael*
6 -	*Sachiel*	*6 -*	*Gabriel*
7 -	*Samael*	*7 -*	*Cassiel*
8 -	*Michael*	*8 -*	*Sachiel*
9 -	*Anael*	*9 -*	*Samael*
10 -	*Raphael*	*10 -*	*Michael*
11 -	*Gabriel*	*11 -*	*Anael*
12 -	*Cassiel*	*12 -*	*Raphael*

[1] HMN: This section on the Angels of the Hours is found separately at the end of the Heptameron.

The Division of the Day & the Planetary Regiment.

Hours of the day.

	1	2	3	4	5	6	7	8	9	10	11	12
Michael · Sunday	☉	♀	☿	☽	♄	♃	♂	☉	♀	☿	☽	♄
Gabriel · Munday	☽	♄	♃	♂	☉	♀	☿	☽	♄	♃	♂	☉
Samael · Tuesday	♂	☉	♀	☿	☽	♄	♃	♂	☉	♀	☿	☽
Raphael · Wednsday	☿	☽	♄	♃	♂	☉	♀	☿	☽	♄	♃	♂
Sachiel · Thursday	♃	♂	☉	♀	☿	☽	♄	♃	♂	☉	♀	☿
Anael · Friday	♀	☿	☽	♄	♃	♂	☉	♀	☿	☽	♄	♃
Cassiel · Saturday	♄	♃	♂	☉	♀	☿	☽	♄	♃	♂	☉	♀

The Division of the Night and the Planetary Regiment.

Hours of the Night

	1	2	3	4	5	6	7	8	9	10	11	12
Sunday	♃	♂	☉	♀	☿	☽	♄	♃	♂	☉	♀	☿
Munday	♀	☿	☽	♄	♃	♂	☉	♀	☿	☽	♄	♃
Tuesday	♄	♃	♂	☉	♀	☿	☽	♄	♃	♂	☉	♀
Wednsday	☉	♀	☿	☽	♄	♃	♂	☉	♀	☿	☽	♄
Thursday	☽	♄	♃	♂	☉	♀	☿	☽	♄	♃	♂	☉
Friday	♂	☉	♀	☿	☽	♄	♃	♂	☉	♀	☿	☽
Saturday	☿	☽	♄	♃	♂	☉	♀	☿	☽	♄	♃	♂

Figure 7: The Division of the Day and Night and the Planetary Regiment [Regimen]

[The Names & Angels of the Seasons]

A year[1] is divided into the Spring, Summer, Harvest and Winter [seasons], the names whereof are these

The Spring	Talvi
The Summer	Casmaran
Autumn	Ardarael
Winter	Farlas

[Spring]

The Angels of the Spring[2]
{ Caratasa
{ Core
{ Amatiel
{ Commissaros[3]

The head of the sign of the Spring
Spugliguel

The name of the Earth in the Spring
Amadai

The names of the Sun & Moon in the Spring
Abraim ☉ Agusita ☽

[Summer]
The Angels of the Summer { Gargatel
{ Tariel
{ Gaviel

The head of the sign of the Summer
Tubiel

The name of the Earth in Summer
Festativi

The Names of the Sun & Moon in Summer
Athemai ☉[1] Armatus ☽

---

[1] HMN: "therefore is fourfold and".
[2] This block of four angels was written as part of the table above, giving the false impression that only Caratasa relates to Spring, whilst Core relates to Summer, etc. We have accordingly moved it downwards for clarity.
[3] This may be a transcription error from the *Heptameron*, which gives "Commissoros".

[Autumn]

The Angels of Autumn { Tarquam
{ Guabarel

The head of the sign of Autumn
Torquaret

The Name of the Earth in Autumn
Rabianara

The Names of the Sun & Moon in Autumn
Abragini ☉
Matasignais ☽

[Winter]

The Angels of the Winter { Amabael
{ Ctarari

The head of the sign of Winter
Altarib

The Name of the Earth in Winter
Geremiah

The Names of the Sun & Moon in Winter
Comutaff ☉
Affaterim ☽[2]

---

[1] HMN: "Athemay".
[2] H: The ☽ is omitted from the text, though it should obviously be there.

The Consecrations & Benedictions[1]

The Benediction of Perfumes.

The God of Abraham God of Isaac God of Jacob bless here the Creatures of these kinds that they may fill up the power and virtue of these[2] odours, So that neither the Enemy nor any false Imagination be able to enter into them through our Lord Jesus Christ.[3]

The Exorcism of the Fire upon which the Perfumes are to be put.

The Fire which is to be used for Suffumigations is to be [kindled] in a new Vessel of Earth or Iron, and let it be Exorcised after this manner.

I Exorcise thee O thou Creature of fire by him by whom all things are made; that forthwith [4]thou cast away every phantasm from thee, that it shall not be able to do any hurt in any thing.

Then say:

Bless O Lord this Creature of fire ~~by fire~~ and sanctify it that it may be blessed to set forth the praise of thy holy name that no hurt may come to the Exorcisers or Spectators through our Lord Jesus Christ.

Of the Garment and Pentacle

Let it be a Priest's Garment if it can be obtained,[5] but if it cannot be had let it be of linen and clean then take this Pentacle made in the day and hour of Mercury [with] the Moon Increasing [waxing] written in parchment made of a Kid's skin. But first let there be said[6] the Mass of the holy Ghost and let it be sprinkled with water of Baptism.

This was the practice in times of popery[7] but Dr Rudd omitted it saying No Mass, nor using any holy water.

---

[1] HMN: ": and first of the Benediction of the Circle."

[2] HMN: "their".

[3] HMN: "&c. Then let them be sprinkled with holy water."

[4] The nine and fiftieth Sheet Dr Rudd.

[5] HMN: omits "obtained".

[6] HMN: "over it".

[7] This refers to Roman Catholic practice. The use of the word 'popery' confirms that Rudd was a Protestant. This sentence looks as if it was added later, but in the same hand writing, and is partly underlined.

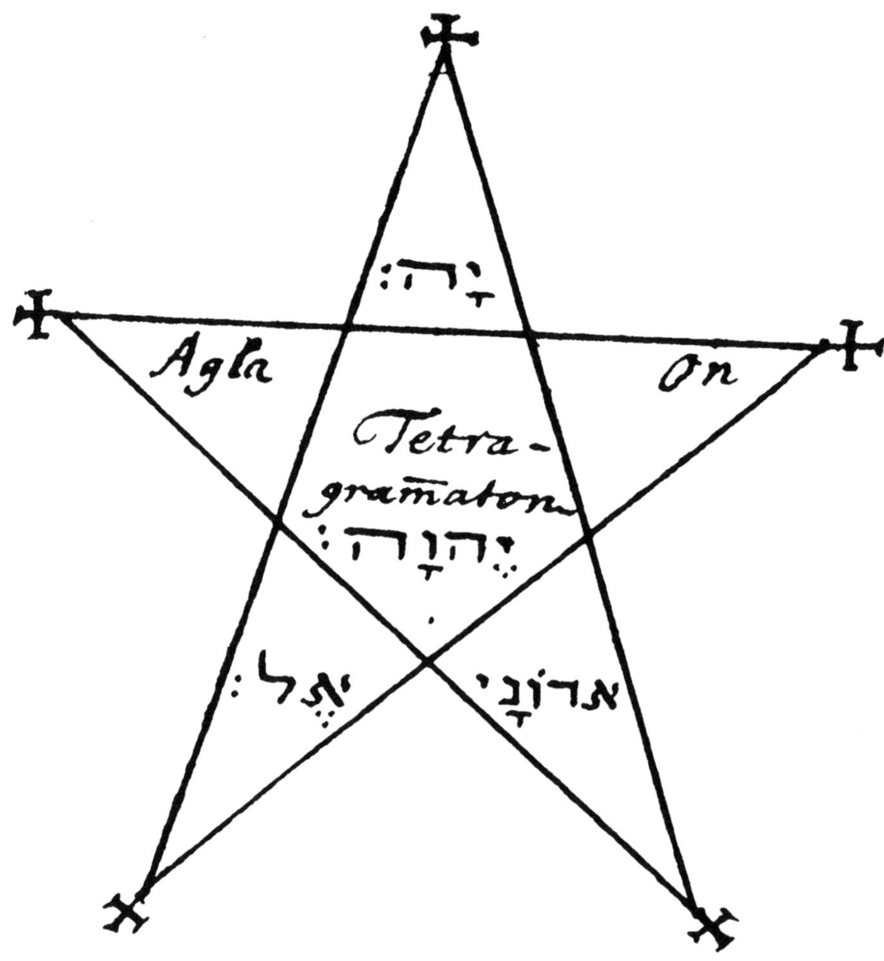

Figure 8: The Pentagram [of Solomon]

An Oration to be said when the Vesture is put on.

***Ancor, Amacor, Amides, Theodonias, Anitor**, by the merits of thy Angels O Lord I will put on the Garment of Salvation, that this which I desire I may bring to effect. Through thee the most holy **Adonai**, whose Kingdom endureth for ever and ever Amen.*

[Preparation of the Operator]

The Operator ought to be clean & purified by the space [duration] of nine days before the beginning of the work, and to be Confessed & receive the holy Communion. Let him have ready the Perfume appropriate to the day wherein he would perform the work. He ought also to have Holy water from a priest, and a new Earthen vessel with fire, a Vesture and pentacle; and let all these things be duly Consecrated and prepared.

Let one of the Servants carry the earthen vessel full of fire, and the Perfumes, and let another bear the Book, another the Garment and Pentacle, and let the Master carry the Sword over which there must be said one Mass of the Holy Ghost, And on the middle of the sword let there be written this name AGLA † and on the other side thereof, this name † On †. And as he [the Master] goeth to the consecrated place let him continually read Litanies, the servants answering [with the responses]. And when he cometh to the place where he will erect the Circle, Let him draw the lines of the Circle[1] as is[2] before taught, and after he hath made it, Let him sprinkle the Circle with holy water Saying

Asperges me Domine.[3] *Thou shalt purge me with hyssop O Lord and I shall be clean: thou shalt wash me and I shall be whiter than Snow.* [4]

The Operator or Master ought to be purified with fasting and chastity for 9 days before he Operate.[5] And on the day that he would do the work being clothed with pure garments and furnished with pentacles, Perfumes & and other things necessary hereunto Let him Enter the Circle, and call the Angels from the four parts of the world, which do govern the seven planets, the seven days of the week, Colours and Metals, whose names you may see in their proper[6] places. And with bended knees Invocating Say[7]

O Angels supradicti, estote adjutores meae petitioni, & in adjutorium mihi, in meis rebus & petitionibus.

Then let him Call the Angels from the four parts of the world that rule the Air the same day wherein he doth the work.[8]

And having Implored specially all the names and Spirits written in the Circle Let him say

O vos omnes adjuro atque Contestor per sedem ***Adonai****, per* ***Hagios O Theos, Ischyros, Athanatos, Paracletos, Alpha et Omega****, et per haec tria nomina*

---

[1] HMN: ", let him draw the lines of the Circle,".
[2] HMN: "have before".
[3] "Wash me O Lord".
[4] HMN: This sentence from "Thou shalt purge me...whiter than Snow" occurs earlier under the "The Consecrations and Benedictions" heading.
[5] HMN: "The Master therefore ought to be purified with fasting, chastity, and abstinency from all luxury the space of three whole days before the day of the operation." It can be seen that Dr Rudd obviously felt a greater degree of purity was required than did de Abano.
[6] HMN: omits "proper".
[7] HMN: "the said Angels particularly let him".
[8] HMN: "or experiment".

secreta, ***Agla, On, Tetragrammaton****, quod hodie debeatis adimplere quod cupio.*[1]

These things being performed Let him read the Conjuration assigned for the day wherein he Operates;[2] but if they [the spirits] shall be pertinacious and refractory not yielding due obedience then let him use this following Prayer.[3]

A Prayer to God to be said in the four parts of the world in the Circle

[Prayer to the Four Parts of the Circle]

A ***Morule, Taneha, Latisten, Rabur,***[4] ***Escha, Aladia, Alpha et Omega, Leiste Oriston Adonai****: O my most merciful*[5] *Father have mercy upon me although a Sinner, make appear the arm of thy power in me this day (although [I am] thy unworthy Child) against these obstinate and pernicious spirits that by thy will may be made a contemplator of thy divine works and may be illustrated with all wisdom, and always worship and glorify thy name. I humbly Implore and beseech thee that these Spirits which I call by thy Judgement may be bound and constrained to come, and give true and perfect answers to those things which I shall ask them, and that they may declare and show unto us those things which shall be commanded them not hurting any Creature neither injuring nor terrifying me or my followers nor hurting any other Creature nor affrighting any one; but let them be obedient to my requests in all those things which I command them*[6].

[7](Then let him stand in the Middle of the Circle, and hold his hand towards the Pentacle and say)

Per Pentaculum Solomonis advocavi dent mihi Responsum verum.

[1] " I adjure and call you all forth, by the seat of Adonai, by Hagios, O Theos, Ischyros, Athanatos, Paracletos, Alpha & Omega, and by these three secret names: Agla, On, Tetragrammaton, that you at once fulfil what I desire."

[2] HMN: omits "operates" and replaces with "maketh the experiment, as we have before spoken".

[3] HMN: replaces "not yielding … following Prayer" with "and will not yield themselves obedient, neither to the Conjuration assigned to the day, nor to the prayers before made, then use the Conjurations and Exorcisms following." There is then a section in Latin entitled 'An Exorcism of the Spirits of the Air' which Rudd omits.

[4] HMN: "Taneha, Latisten".

[5] HMN: "heavenly".

[6] HMN: This prayer (in Latin) continues at this point for a similar duration again, but Rudd omits the second half of the prayer. This is followed in the *Heptameron* by another section in Latin entitled 'Visions and Apparitions', which Rudd also omits.

[7] The Sixtieth Sheet Dr Rudd.

[Composition of the Circle]

But that you may the better know the manner of Composing a Circle, See the following Scheme.

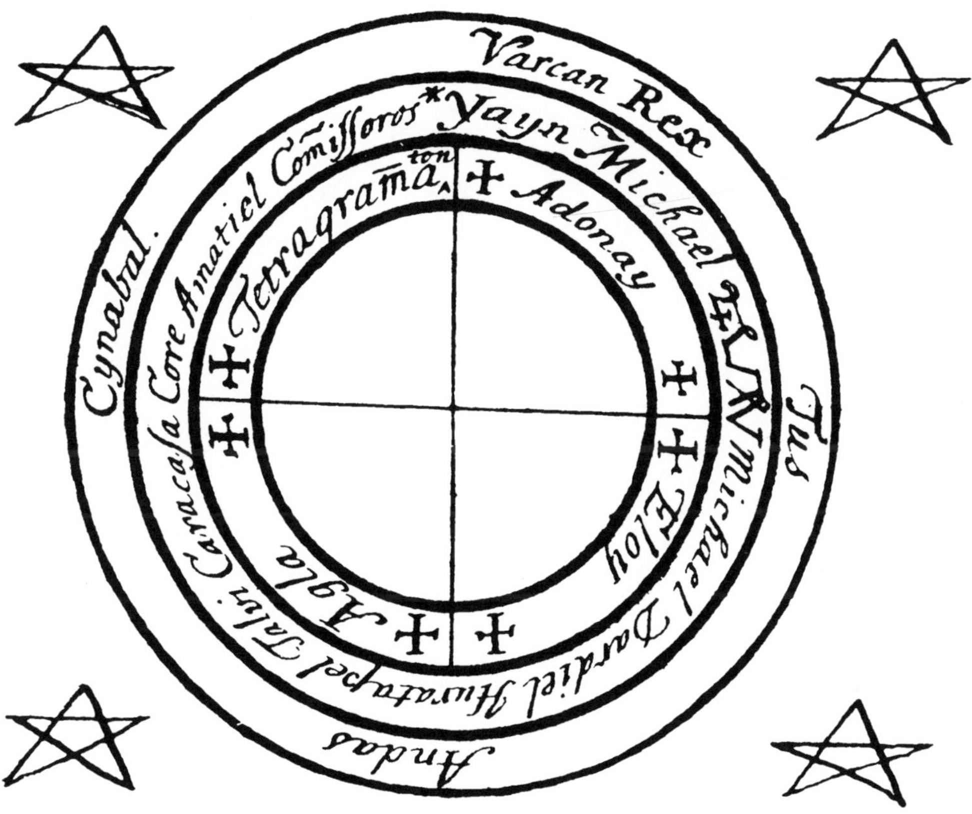

Figure 9: The Figure of a Circle for the first hour of the Lord's Day [Sunday] in Spring time.

[The composition is as follows:
Outer Ring: The angel of the Air ruling Sunday (Varcan) and his three ministers.
Middle Ring: Name of Spring (Talvi); the 4 Angels of Spring (left); First hour of day (Yayn) and its ruling Angel (Michael); Angel of Sunday (Michael again) and his seal; the angels of the day of Sunday (Dardiel and Huratapel).
Inner Ring: Four godnames.] [1]

[1] HMN: Also has "Alpha" written at the top of the inner circle, and "et ω" at the bottom of the inner circle. "Spugliguel. Amadai. Abraim. Aguista" are also written in the margin. Four examples of how the Circle composition changes according to the time and day will be found in Appendix 12.

The Directory [for the Seven Days of the Week]

for the Lord's Day [Sunday][1]

The Angel of the Lord's Day Michael, & his Seal, Planet, Sign of the Planet, and the name of the fourth heaven][2]

The Angel of the Air ruling on the Lord's Day
Varcan Rex [King].

His Ministers   Sus,[3] Andas, Cynabal.

The Wind which the Angel of the Air is under.
The North wind.

The Angels of the fourth Heaven ruling on the Lord's Day which ought to be called from the four parts of the world.

At the East	{ Samael	Baciel	[Atel]
	{ Gabriel	Vionatraba[4]	

[1] HMN: *Considerations of the Lords day.*

[2] See also page 171. Each Seal, for each of the seven days contains the name of the angel ('Michael' in this case), his sigil (above his name), the planet (Sun, top left), zodiacal sign (Leo, top right), and the name of one of the seven Heavens ('Machen'). Machen should in fact be Zebul which is incorrectly shown under Thursday. There are a few errors like this which have crept into the *Heptameron*, and which have been consequently repeated in this text. For a complete corrected table of all the angels and Heavens in the *Heptameron* see Column M10 of Stephen Skinner's *Complete Magician's Tables*, Golden Hoard Press, Singapore, and Llewellyn, Woodbury, 2006.

[3] HMN: *"Tus"*. Figure 9 in the current manuscript also shows 'Tus'.

[4] Correct here, but incorrectly shown in HMN as *"Vionairaba"* due to broken type.

At the West	{ Anael	Pabel	Ustael
	{ Burchat	Suceratos	Capabili
At the North	{ Aiel	Aniel vel Aquiel	
	{ Sapiel	Matuyel	Masgubriel[1]
At the South	{ Habudiel[2]	Machasiel	Charsiel
	{ Uriel	Naromiel	

The Perfumes of the Lord's Day [Sunday] Red wheat[3]

The Invocation or Conjuration [of Sunday]

I conjure & confirm upon you O you strong and holy Angels of God, in the name of ***Adonay, Eye, Eye, Eya****, who is he, who was who is, and shall be,* ***Eye, Abraye****, and in the name* ***Saday, Cados,***[4] ***Cados, Cados****, sitting high upon the Cherubim: and by the great name of the Same strong God and potent, and exalted upon all the heavens Eye,* ***Saraye*** *the Creator of Ages, who created the world, the heaven, the Earth, the Sea, and all things that are therein in the first day, and sealed them with his holy name* ***Phaa****, And by the names of thy holy Angels who bear Rule in the fourth heaven,*[5] *& serve before the most potent* ***Salamia*** *a great and honoured Angel, and by the name of his star which is the Sun, and by his sign, and by the immense name of the living God, and by all the aforesaid names, I conjure thee O thou great Angel Michael, who bears rule as president of the Lord's day: and by the name* ***Adonay****, the God of Israel, who created the world and whatsoever is therein, that thou labour for me and fulfil my petition according to my desire*[6] *[here declare your business & the cause of making your Invocation]*

Note here. That the Spirits of the Air of the Lord's Day are under the North wind, there [their] nature is to procure Gold, Gems, Carbuncles, Riches, to raise one [to a powerful position] to obtain favour and benevolence, to dissolve the enmities of men; to raise men to honours, to carry or take away infirmities.

---

[1] HMN: "Masgabriel."

[2] Correct here, but incorrectly shown in HMN as *"Haludiel"* due to broken type.

[3] Probably a mistake in HMN for "red sandal [wood]." This particular error suggests that this material was imported from the 1655 English printed edition of the *Heptameron,* or from its source.

[4] A transcription of Qadosh, "holy".

[5] Zebul, although in this section mistakenly referred to as 'Machen'.

[6] HMN: This Invocation and the subsequent ones for the rest of the days of the week were in Latin in the *Heptameron*, Rudd or someone else has translated them and other prayers, for easier use.

The Directory for Monday[1]

The Angel of Monday his Sigil, Planet the sign of the Planet & the name of the first heaven[2]

The Angel of the Air ruling on Monday
Arcan, King

His Ministers
Bilet. Missabu. Abuzaha.

The Wind which the said Angels of the Air are subject to.
The West Wind.

The Angels of the first heaven ruling on Monday which ought to be called from the four parts of the world.

From the East. Gabriel, Gabrael, Madiel, Deamiel, Janael.

From the West. Sachiel, Zaniel, Habaiel, Bachanael, Cerabael.

From the North. Mael, Vuael, Valnum, Baliel, Balay, Humastrau.

From the South. Curaniel, Dabriel, Darquiel, Hanun, Anayl, Vetuel.

The Perfume on Monday, Aloes.

---

[1] HMN: Considerations of Munday.
[2] Should be 'Shamaim' not 'Shamain'.

The Invocation or Conjuration [of Monday]

I Conjure and confirm upon you O you strong and good Angels in the name ***Adonay, Adonay, Adonay, Eie, Eie, Eie, Cados, Cados, Cados, Achim, Achim, Ia, Ia, Fortis, Ia,***[1] *who appeared on Mount Sinai, with the glorification of the King* ***Adonay, Saday, Zebaoth Anathay, Ya, Ya, Marinata, Abim, Icia,***[2] *who created the Seas, rivers ponds and all waters on the second day, and sealed the Seas with bounds to it not to pass by his high name: And by the name of his holy Angels who bear rule in the first Host,*[3] *who serve Orphaniel a great Angel precious and honourable and by the name of his Star, which is the Moon and upon thee O Gabriel, who presides [over] Monday the second day that thou labour for me to fulfil my desire [here declare your business what your request is &c].*

The Spirits of the Air of Monday are subject to the West wind which is the wind [4]of the Moon, their nature is to give Silver; to Convey things from place to place, to make horses swift, and to disclose the secrets of persons both present and future, In what manner these spirits appear we have already declared at large.

---

[1] HMN: "Ja, Ja, Fortis, Ja".

[2] HMN: "Jeia".

[3] HMN: "legion".

[4] The sixty first sheet Dr Rudd.

Directions for Tuesday[1]

The Angel of Tuesday his Sigil his Planet this Sign governing the Planet & the name of the 5th heaven.[2]

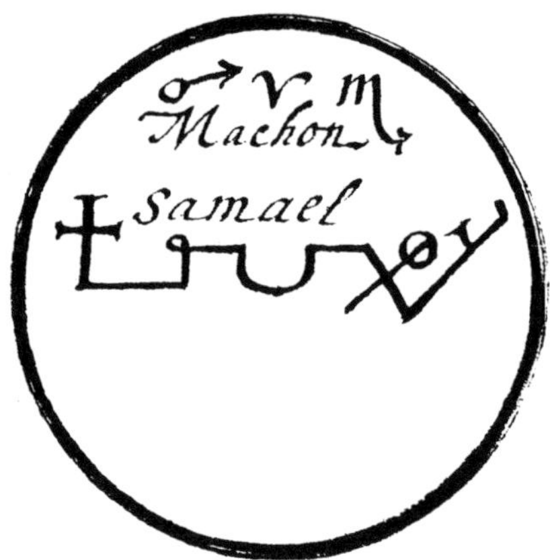

The Angels of Tuesday
Samael, Satael, Amabiel

The Angels of the Air ruling on Tuesday
Samax, King.

His Ministers
Carmax, Ismoli, Paffran.

The Wind to which the said Angels are subject,
The East wind

The Angels of the fifth Heaven ruling on Tuesday which ought to be called from the four parts of the world.

At the East, Friagne, Guael, Damael, Calzas, Arragon.

At the West, Lama, Astagna, Lobquin, Soncas, Jazel, Isiael, Irel.

At the North, Rahumel, Hyniel, Rayel, Seraphiel, Mathiel, Fraciel.

At the South, Sachriel,[3] Janiel, Galdel, Osael, Vianuel, Zaliel.
The Perfume on Tuesday Pepper.

---

[1] Probably should be 'Directory for Tuesday'. HMN: Considerations of Tuesday.
[2] Listed in HMN as 'Machon', but should be Ma'on.
[3] HMN: Sacriel.

The Invocation or Conjuration of Tuesday

I Conjure & Confirm upon you O you strong and holy Angels by the name ***Ya, Ya, Ya, He, He, He, Va, Hy, Hy, Hy, Ha, Ha, Ha, Va, Va, Va,***[1] ***An, An, An, Aie, El, Ay, Elibra, Eloim, Eloim***[2] *and by the names of the same high God, who made the water appear dry & called it Earth, and produced trees & herbs from it and put the seal of his honoured precious fearful holy name upon it. And by the names of his Angels bearing Rule in the fifth host,*[3] *who serve Acimo a great Angel strong potent and honourable. And by the name of his star which is Mars, and by the names aforesaid I conjure thee O thou great Angel Samael who art President of Tuesday, and by the names* ***Adonay*** *of the living & true God, that thou labour for me & thou mayest fulfil my desires [here demand what you please].*

Spirits of the Air of Tuesday are under the East wind their nature is to raise wars mortality, death and Combustions, and to give two thousand Soldiers at a time, to bring death, Infirmities or health. The manner of their appearing we have declared before.

---

[1] Probably a rather scrambled version of IHVH, Yod-Heh-Vau-Heh.
[2] Elohim.
[3] Correct here, but incorrectly shown as 'house' in HMN.

Directory for Wednesday[1]

The Angel of Wednesday his Sigil, Planet, the Sign governing that planet &c [and the name of the second heaven].

The Angels of Wednesday
Raphael, Miel, Seraphiel.

The Angels of the Air ruling on Wednesday
Mediat or Modiat, Rex.

[His] Ministers
Suquinos, Sallales.

The Wind to which the said Angels of the Air are subject.
The South west wind.

The Angels of the second heaven governing Wednesday which ought to be called from the four parts of the world.

At the East Mathlai, Tarmiel, Baraborat.

At the West Jeresoue,[2] Mitraton.

At the North Thiel, Rael, Jeriahel, Venahel, Velel, Abuiori, Ucirnuel.

At the South Milliel, Nelapa, Babel, Caluel, Vel, Laquel.
The Fumigation on Wednesday Mastick

[1] HMN: Considerations of Wednesday.
[2] HMN: Jeresous.

The Invocation or Conjuration [of Wednesday]

I Conjure and Confirm on you O you strong holy & potent Angels, in the name of the strong most fearful and holy ***Jah, Adonai, Eloim, Sadai, Eie, Eie, Eie, Asamie, Asaraie,*** *and in the name* ***Adonay****, the God of Israel who created the great Lights [Sun and Moon] to distinguish the Day from the night, and by the name of all the Angels serving in the second host or heaven before Tetra a great strong and potent Angel, and by the name of his Star which is Mercury, and by the name of his Seal, which is sealed by the permission of God most strong & honoured. By all aforesaid upon thee O great Angel Raphael, I conjure or agree with thee to help me, thou who art Presiding [over] the fourth day of the week: And by the holy name which was written in the front of Aaron the Priest of the most high Creator and by the names of the Angels who are confirmed into our Saviour's favour. And by the name of the seat of those Animals having six wings*[1] *that thou labour for me &c [here declare your Request].*

The Spirits of the Air of Wednesday are subject to the Southwest wind, their nature is to give all metals, to reveal all earthly things past present and to come; to pacify Judges, to give victories in battle, to Re-edify & teach experiments and all decayed [lost] sciences, and to change bodies mixed of Elements conditionally out of one into another, to give infirmities or health, to raise the poor and cast down the high ones; to bind or loose spirits;[2] to open locks or bolts; such kind of spirits have the operation of others but not in their perfect power, but in virtue or knowledge. In what manner they appear was before declared.

[1] The Cherubim.
[2] A particularly useful attribute in this context.

[1]The Directory for Thursday[2]

The Angel of Thursday his Sigil, Planet, sign [of the Planet, and the name of the sixth heaven][3]

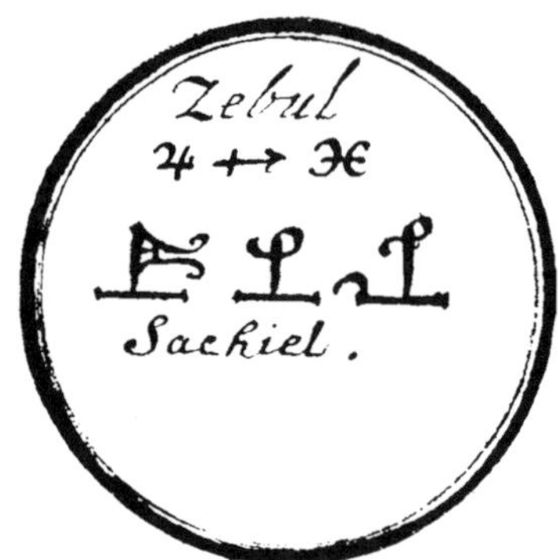

The Angels of the Air governing Thursday
Sachiel, Castiel, Alsasiel.[4]

The Angel of the Air governing Thursday
Suth Rex.

Ministers
Maguth, Guthrix.[5]

The Wind which the said Angels of the Air are under,
The South wind.

But because there are no Angels of the Air to be found above the fifth heaven, Therefore on Thursday say the prayers, following in the four parts of the world.

[1] The Sixty second sheet Dr Rudd.
[2] HMN: Considerations of Thursday.
[3] Although HMN shows the Heaven as Zebul on the Seal, in fact it should be Makon.
[4] HMN: "Asasiel".
[5] HMN: "Gutrix".

At the East [say].
O God great and high and honoured by infinite ages.[1]

At the West [say]
O God most wise excellent and just, and of a divine Clemency. I beseech thee most godly Father to grant me my petition that I may perfectly understand this day [how] to complete my work & labour, Thou who livest and reignest for ever & ever Amen.[2]

At the North [say]
O God powerful and strong and without beginning.[3]

At the South [say].
O God powerful and merciful.[4]

The Perfume of Thursday Saffron.

The Invocation or Conjuration [of Thursday]

I Conjure and Confirm upon you holy Angels by the name ***Cados, Cados, Cados, Eschereie, Eschereie, Eschereie, Hatim ya****, strong Strengthener of ages, Cantine,* ***Iaym, Ianie,***[5] ***Anic, Calbat, Sabbac, Berifay, Alnaym****, and by the name* ***Adonay****, who created the fishes and creeping things in the waters, and birds upon the face of the earth flying towards heaven [on] the fifth day; And by the names of the Angels serving in the sixth heaven before Pastor a holy Angel and great and powerful prince: and by the name of his Star, which is Jupiter: and by the name of his Seal: and by the name* ***Adonay*** *Supreme God, Creator of all things, and by the name of all the Stars, and by the force and virtue thereof, and by the aforesaid names, I Conjure thee O Sachiel a great Angel who art set over or president of Thursday that thou labour for me [Here declare what you would have done].*

The Spirits of the Air of Thursday are subject to the South wind, their nature is to procure the love of women, to be merry and joyful, to pacify strife and contentions, to appease enemies, to heal the diseased, and to disease the whole, and procureth losses, or taketh them away. Their manner of appearing we have before declared.[6]

---

[1] HMN: O Dues magne & excelse, & honorate, per infinita secula.
[2] HMN: O Deus Sapiens, & clare, & juste, ac divina clementia: ego rogo te prissime Pater, quod meam petitionem, quod meum opus, & meum laborem hodie debeam complere, & perfecte intelligere, Tu qui vivs & regnas per infinita secula seculorum, Amen.
[3] HMN: O Deus potens, fortis, & sine principio.
[4] HMN: O Deus potents & misericors.
[5] HMN: Jaym, Janie.
[6] HMN: "is spoken of already".

The Directory for Friday[1]

The Angel of Friday, his Sigil, his Planet & Sign [governing that Planet, and name of the third heaven][2]

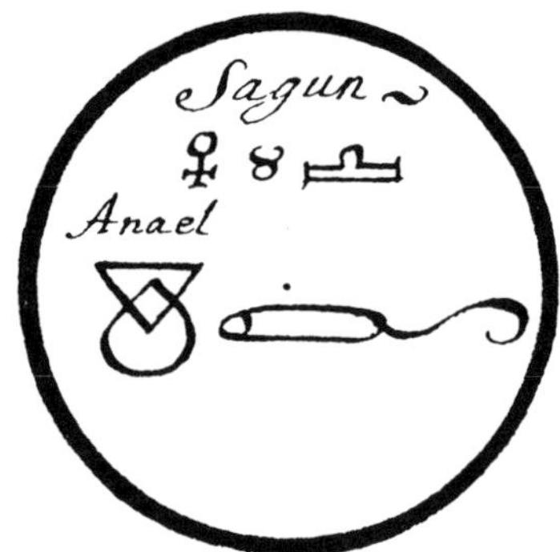

The Angels of Friday
Anael, Rachiel, Sathiel

The Angels of the Air reigning on Friday
Sarabotes, King

Ministers
Amabiel, Aba, Abalidoth, Flaes.

The Wind which the said Angels of the Air are under
The West wind.[3]

The Angels of the third heaven ruling on Friday which are to be called from the four parts of the world.

At the East
Setchiel, Chedusitaniel, Corat, Tamael, Tenaciel.

At the West
Turiel, Coniel, Babiel, Kadie, Maltiel, Huphaltiel.

At the North
Peniel, Penael, Penat, Raphael,[4] Raniel, Doremiel.

At the South
Porna, Sachiel,[1] Chermiel, Samael, Santanael, Famiel.

---

[1] HMN: Considerations of Friday.
[2] The third heaven is shown on the Seal as 'Sagun' but should in fact be Shechaqim.
[3] This is the same wind as Monday, and therefore likely to be a mistake in HMN.
[4] Raphael is also the main angel of Wednesday.

The Perfume of Friday Pepperwort.

The Invocation or Conjuration [of Friday]

I Conjure & confirm upon you O you strong holy and potent angels, in the name, ***On, Hey, Heya, Ia, Ie, Adonay*** *and in the name* ***Sadai***[2] *who created four footed beasts and Animals, Reptiles, and men in the sixth day, and gave to Adam power over all animals: from whence the name of his Creator is blessed in his place: and by the names of the Angels serving in the third host of heaven before Dagiel a great Angel*[3]*, a strong and potent prince: and by the name of his star which is Venus, and by his Seal which indeed is holy, and by the names aforesaid, I Conjure upon thee O Anael who art president of the sixth day that thou labour for me [here declare your desire &c].*

The Spirits of the Air of Friday are subject to the West wind. Their nature is to give silver to incite & incline men to Luxury, and to make marriages, to allure men to love women, to cause or take away Infirmities, and to do all things which have motion.

---

[1] Sachiel is also the main angel of Thursday.

[2] HMN: "Ja, Je, Adonay, Saday"

[3] Dagiel derives from the Hebrew for fish, דג, and is to be invoked on a Friday, the day of Venus. He may have some connection with Dagon who also had a fish body.

[1]The Directory for Saturday or the Sabbath Day[2]

The Angel of Saturday, his Seal, [his] Planet and the sign governing the Planet.[3]

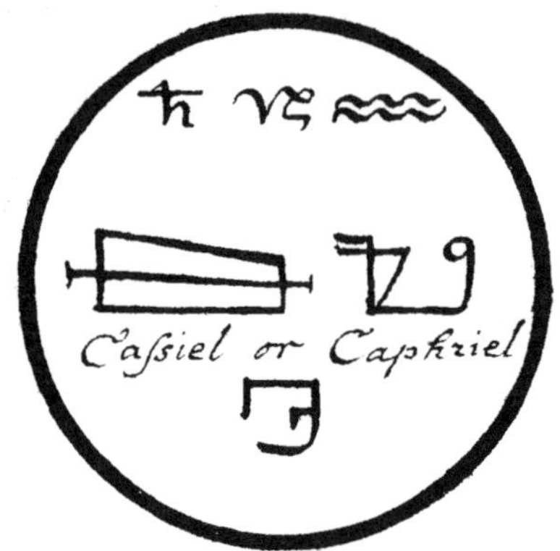

The Angels of Saturday
Cassiel, Machatan, Uriel.

The Angel of the Air ruling on Saturday
Maymon, King.[4]

[His] Ministers
Abumalith, Assaibi, Balideth.[5]

The Wind which the said Angels of the Air are under
The Southwest wind.[6]

The Fumigation on Saturday Sulphur[7]

---

[1] *The Sixty-third Sheet Dr Rudd.*
[2] HMN: *Considerations of Saturday, or the Sabbath day.* Referring to Saturday as the Sabbath tends to suggest Hebraic origins for this text.
[3] HMN accidentally omits the Seventh heaven, Araboth in both the text and the Seal.
[4] Amaymon is listed in the *Goetia* as the King of the East.
[5] HMN: "Balidet".
[6] This is the same wind as Wednesday, and therefore likely to be a mistake in HMN.
[7] A very dangerous thing to burn in a confined space.

It is already declared in the Directory for Thursday that there are no Angels ruling the Air above the fifth heaven, therefore in the four Angels[1] of the world use those Orations which are applied to that purpose on Thursday.

The Invocation or Conjuration [of Saturday]

I Conjure and Confirm upon you Caphriel or Cassiel, Machatori and Seraquiel strong and potent Angels, and by the name ***Adonay, Adonay, Adonay, Eie, Eie, Eie, Acim, Acim, Acim, Cados, Cados, Cados, Ina*** *vel* ***Ima, Ima, Saclai, Ia, Sar,*** *Lords Confirmatory of ages who rested on the seventh day: and by him who in his own good pleasure gave to the Sons of Israel unto their inheritance to be observed, that they should strictly keep and sanctify it, that they might receive hence a good reward in another world: and by the names of Angels serving in the seventh host of heaven Booel*[2] *a great Angel and a potent prince, and by the name of his star which is Saturn: and by his holy ~~Angel~~ Seal and by the names aforesaid, I Conjure upon thee Caphriel who art president of the seventh day which is the Sabbath day that thou labour for me &c [Here set forth your Request].*

The Spirits of the Air of the Sabbath day or Saturday are subject to the Southeast wind. The nature of them is to sow discords hatred evil thoughts & Cogitations to give leave freely to slay & kill every one, and to lame or maim every member. We have already declared their familiar shapes.[3]

[End of the Goetia][4]

[1] HMN: "Angles", in other words in each of the four directions.

[2] HMN: Pooel.

[3] Here ends the material from the *Heptameron* which is included in Harley MS 6483 of the *Goetia.* The printed *Heptameron* concludes with the *Tables of the Angels of the Hours.*

[4] In W1 the text is followed by the plates, some of which are reproduced in Appendix 6 and 14. W1 gives the seals of just 53 demons that are incompletely given in that MSS.

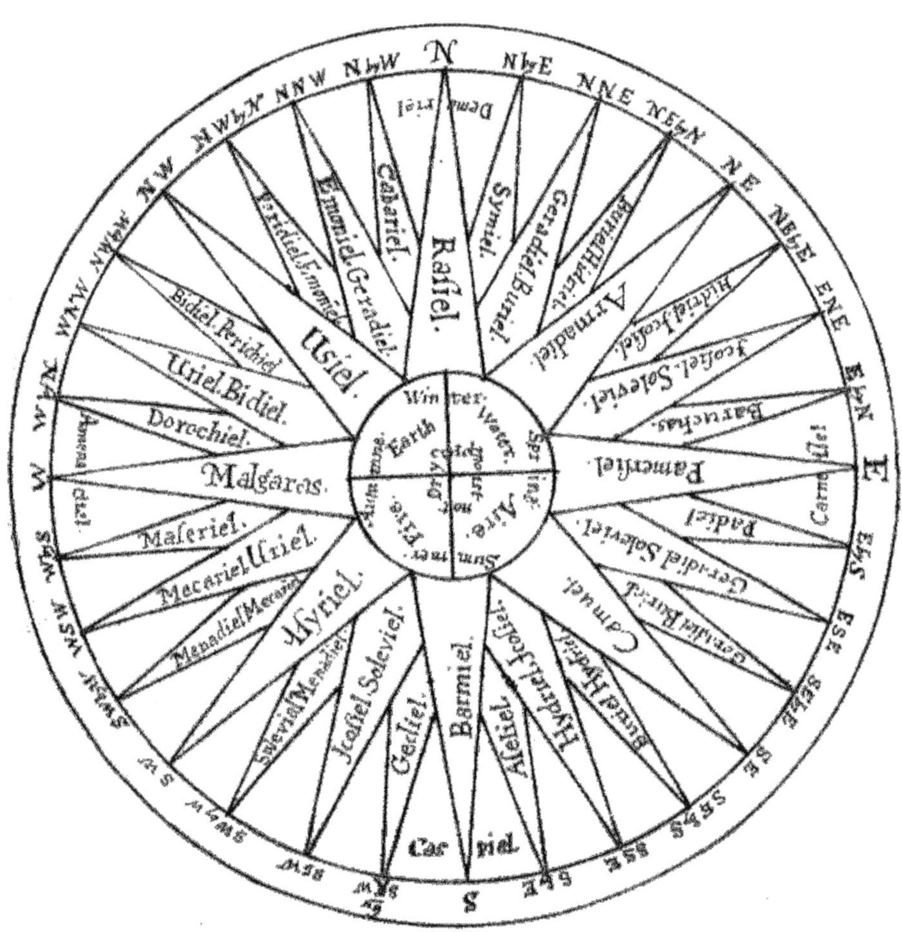

Figure 10: The Spirit Compass Rose of the *Theurgia-Goetia*

The 2nd Part of Clavicula Salomonis Regis

Theurgia-Goetia

In this Treatise you have the names of the chief Spirits[1] with several of the ministering spirits which are under them with their Seals or Characters which are to be worn by the Exorcist as a Lamen on his breast when he Invocates, for without that the spirit that appears will not obey nor do his will.

The Offices of these Spirits is all one for what one can do the other can do the same, they can show and discover all things that are hid and done in the world, and can fetch and carry, and do any thing that is to be done or is contained in any of the four Elements, fire, air, earth water, also the secret of Kings or any other person or persons let it be in what kind it will.[2]

These Spirits being Aerial are by nature good and evil, that is, one part is good the other part is evil, they are governed by their Princes and each Prince hath his abode in the points of the Compass.

Therefore when you have a desire to call any of the Princes or any of their servants you are to direct your self to that point of the Compass [where] the King or Prince hath his Mansion or place of abode and you cannot err in your operations.[3]

Note every Prince is to have his Conjuration yet all [conjurations are] of one form excepting the name & place of the spirit, for in that they must change and differ.[4]

---

[1] Including 4 Emperors, 16 Spirits and 11 Wandering Dukes = 31 spirits in all.

[2] It seems to be a bit of a cop out to have all the spirits equally skilled in all things. Traditionally each spirit would have its own 'offices' or specialities.

[3] These specific directions are important, and tell the Operator in what direction to face and where to put the Triangle of Art.

[4] See Figure 10. A convenient table of directions and rulerships will also be found in Table M20 in Appendix 2.

Also the Seal of the Spirits is to be changed accordingly. As for the Garments and other materials they are spoken of in the Book *Goetia*.[1]

Note that Twenty of these Kings have their first Mansions and continues in one place, and sometimes together. Therefore it is of no matter which way you stand with your face when you desire to call them or their Servants.[2]

[1] W1: "In this Treatise you have the names of the chief Spirits with several of their ministering spirits which are under them and their Seals and Characters which are to be worn as a Lamen on your heart for without that the spirit that is appeared will not obey you nor do your will. The Offices of these Spirits is all one, for what one can do the other can do the same, they can discover and show all things that are hid and done in the world, and can fetch and carry, and do any thing that is to be done or to be contained in the four Elements of the World, fire, air, earth, water, and also [know] the secret[s] of Kings or any other person or persons let it be in what kind it will. These Spirits are by nature good and evil, that is one part is good the other part are Evil, they are governed by their Princes and each Prince has his abode in the points of the Compass. Therefore if you have a desire to call any of the princes or their servants you are to direct your self towards the point of the Compass where the King or Prince hath his Mansion or place of abode and you cannot at all err in your operations. Note every Prince is to have his Conjuration yet all of one form Except the name & place of the spirit for in that they must change and differ. Also the Seal of the Spirits is to be changed accordingly. The Garments &c are [as] directed in the first book [the *Goetia*]."

[2] W1: Omits this paragraph. The instruction that the calling direction does not matter, only makes sense in the context of the 16 Wandering Dukes.

[The Four Emperors][1]

Carmasiel[2] is the most great and chief Emperor Ruling in the East[3] who hath 1000 great Dukes & 100 lesser Dukes under him besides 60000000000000[4] Ministering spirits which are more inferior then [than] the Dukes whereof we shall make no mention but only [mention] 12 of the chief Dukes and their Seals because they are sufficient for practice.[5]

Note that when you call any of these Dukes there never attends above [more than] 300 & sometimes not above 10.[6]

[The Supplementary Conjurations from the *Steganographia,* Book 1, Chapter XVII:

Carnesiel aphroys chemeryn mear aposyn. Layr pean noema ovear ma sere cralty calevo thorteam chameron ianoar pelyn Layr, baduson iesty melros ionatiel delassar rodivial meron savean fabelron clumarsy preos throen benarys favean demosynon laernoty chamedonton.

Carnesiel aproysi chameron to pemalroyn phroys Cadur mearmol benadron Vioniel saviron army pean arnotiel fabelronthusyn throe chabelron savenear medaloys vear olmenadab cralty sayr.]

[1] The Conjurations will be found at the end of the *Theurgia-Goetia*, on page 297 *et seq*. Full conjurations are missing from this and all previously known *Lemegeton* manuscripts, but we have provided examples of them from Sloane MS 3824, and they appear in Appendix 1. Supplementary conjurations are included for each spirit from the *Steganographia.*

[2] S1, S2, S4: *"Carnesiel"*. Also spelled *"Carnasiel"* in the conjuration later in *Theurgia-Goetia.* Carnesiel will be found in Chapter XVII of Book I of Trithemius' *Steganographia.*

[3] The other three Emperors are Caspiel = South, Amenadiel = West, Demoriel = North. See Table M20 in Appendix 2 for the full hierarchy.

[4] S1, S2, S3: "50000000000000".

[5] It would have been typical for a magician to just record the details of those Spirits he had himself dealt with, rather than giving a full catalogue.

[6] W1: "**Carnesiel**. Is the Chief and great Emperor ruling the ~~West~~ East, he has a 1000 great Dukes and 100 lesser Dukes to attend him, & besides 5,000,000,000,000 ministering Spirits which are more inferior Spirits that [than] the Dukes, of these & other I shall mention but 12 of the Chief & their Seals for Practice... When you Call Carnesiel either by night or day there attends him 6,000,000,000 dukes, but if you call any duke there never attends him above 300 and sometimes not above 10."

[1]Carmasiel's 12 Dukes and their Seals.

[1] Sixty fourth Sheet Dr Rudd.

Caspiel[1] is the chiefest and greatest Emperor ruling in the South who hath 200 Great Dukes & 400 lesser Dukes under him besides 1000200000000 of ministering Spirits which are much inferior, Solomon makes mention only of 12 of the chief Dukes & their Seals.

Each of these 12 Dukes have 2660 under Dukes apiece to attend them, whereof some of them come along with him when he is Invocated, but they are very stubborn and churlish.[2]

[The Supplementary Conjurations from the *Steganographia,* Book 1, Chapter XVIII:[3]

Caspiel aloyr chameron noeres padyr diviel prolsyn vear maduson cralnoti fruon phorsy larsonthon thiano pemarson theor. Caveos adeveos friato briosi panyeldrubon madiel sayr fabelrusyn gonear pean noty nabusran. (*conjuratio spiritus*)

Caspiel asbyr Chameronty churto freveon dayr fabelron Cathurmy meresyn elso peano tailtran Caspio fuar Medon clibarsy Caberosyn ulty pean Vearches pemasy natolbyr meldary noe Cardenopen men for diviel adro.]

Caspiel's Seal

[1] Caspiel will be found in Chapter XVIII of Book I of Trithemius' *Steganographia.*

[2] W1: *"**Caspiel.** Is the Chief & Greatest Emperor ruling the South he has under him 200 great Dukes & 400 lesser Dukes besides 10,000,000,000,000 Ministering Spirits which are much Inferior & of whom I shall not make mention, but only of 12 Chief Dukes and their seals which is enough for practice. Each of these Dukes has 2260 inferior Dukes to attend him whereof some come along with them when they are invocated but are very stubborn and Churlish".*

[3] The primary Conjurations of all of the Spirits of the *Theurgia-Goetia* are missing from this manuscript, but we have provided them from Sloane 3824, and they appear in Appendix 1.

Caspiel's 12 Dukes and their Seals

Ameradiel[1] is the Great Emperor of the West who hath 300 Great Dukes and 500 lesser Dukes besides 40000030000100000 other ministering Spirits more inferior to attend him where of we shall not make any mention, but only 12 of the chief Dukes and their Seals which is sufficient for practice[2]

[The Supplementary Conjurations from the *Steganographia,* Book 1, Chapter XIX:

Amenadiel aprolsy chameronta nosroy throen mesro salayr chemaros noe pean larsy freveon ionatiel pelroyn rathroy Caser malusan pedon Cranochyran daboy seor marchosyn lavo pedar venoti gesroy phernotiel Cabron.

Amenadiel bulurym chameroty eriscoha pedarmon flusro pean truarbiel fabelron greos belor malgoty nabarym stilco melros fuar pelaryso chitron amanacason. (*coniuratio)*]

[Ameradiel's Seal]

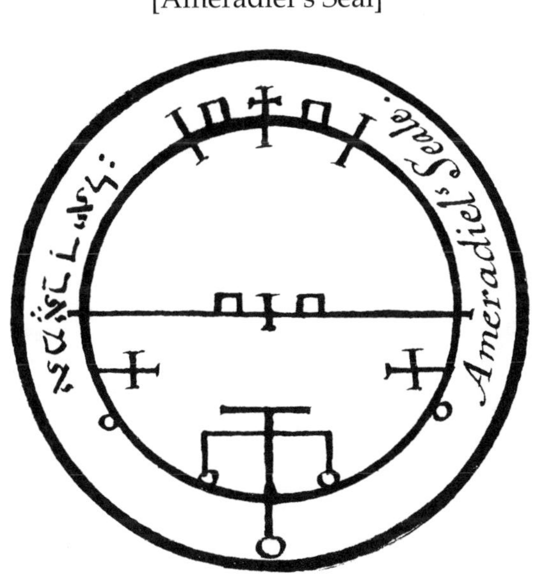

[1] S1, S2, S3: *"Amenadiel"*. Amenadiel will be found in Chapter XIX of Book I of Trithemius' *Steganographia.*

[2] W1: *"**Amenadiel.** The great Emperor of the West has 300 Great Dukes besides 4,000,000,300,000,500,000 other Ministering Spirits to attend him. Note Amenadiel may be called any hour of the day or night but his dukes who have 3880 Spirits a piece to attend them are to be called at certain hours – as Vadras may be called the two first hours of the day & successively will you come to Nedroch who is to be called the last two hours of the night & then begin at Vadras, & the second ruler are to be rehearsed in calling the Dukes belonging to Demoriel Emperor of the North. Conjuration I conjure thee oh thou great and Mighty Chief Prince Amenadiel who is Emperor & Chief King ruling in the West &c."*

[1]Names & Seals of Ameradiel's Twelve Dukes

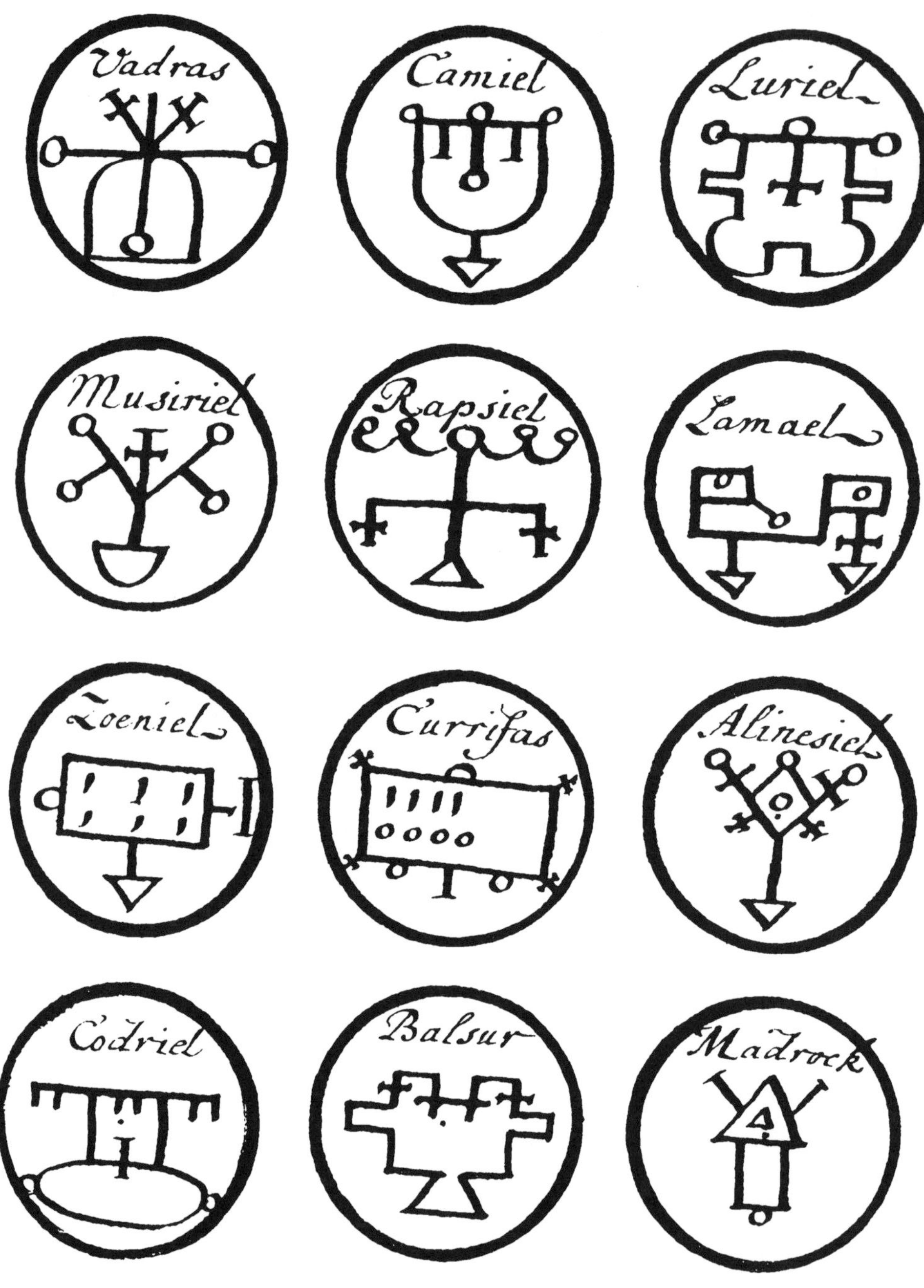

[1] *Sixty fifth Sheet Dr Rudd.*

Demoriel[1] is the great & mighty Emperor of the North who hath 400 Great & 600 lesser Dukes with Servants in number 7000008000009000000 under his Command to attend him whereof we shall make mention but of 12 of the chief Dukes and their Seals which is sufficient for practice.[2]

[The Supplementary Conjurations from the *Steganographia,* Book 1, Chapter XX:

Demoriel onear dabursoy Cohyne chamerson ymeor pean olayr chelrusys noeles schemlaryn venodru patron myselro chadarbon vevaon maferos ratigiel personay lodiol camedon nasiel fabelmerusin sosiel chamarchoysyn. *(carmen conjurationis)*

Demoriel osayr chameron chulty save porean lusin dayr pean cathurmo fomarson ersoty lamedon iothar busraym fuar menadroy chilarso fabelmerusyn. (*carmen conjurationis*)]

[Demoriel's Seal][3]

[1] Demoriel will be found in Chapter XX of Book I of Trithemius' *Steganographia.*

[2] W1: *"**Demoriel.** This Great and mighty Emperor of the North has 400 great & 600 Lesser Dukes with 700,000,800,000,900,000 Servants under his Command. I shall only mention 12 Dukes, who have Each 1140 Servants, who attend them, for when the dukes are called on & if you have more to do than ordinary they have more servants".*

[3] The initials 'D.H.' appear in this Seal, and are likely to be the initials of the Seal draughtsman, or of one of the earlier copyists before Peter Smart.

Names & Seals of Demoriel's 12 Dukes

Arnibiel
Cabarizym
Burifiel

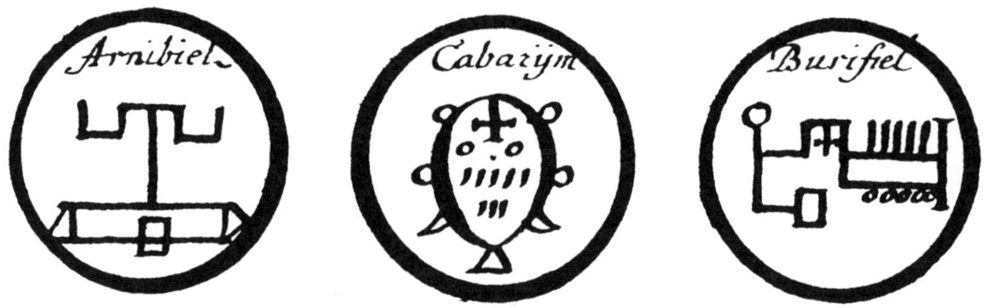

Note; each of these Dukes hath 1140 Servants who attend them as need requireth.

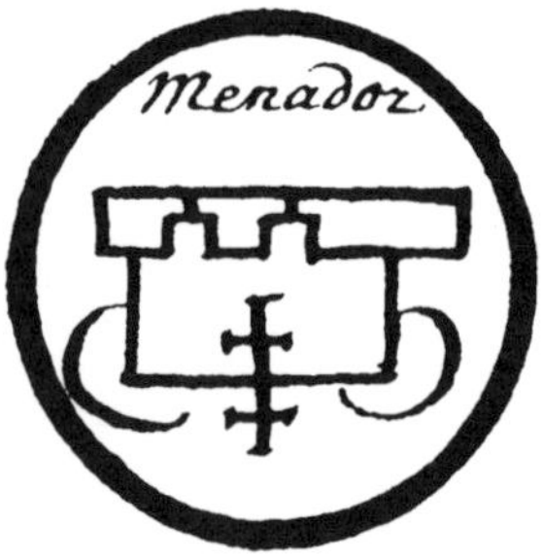
Menador
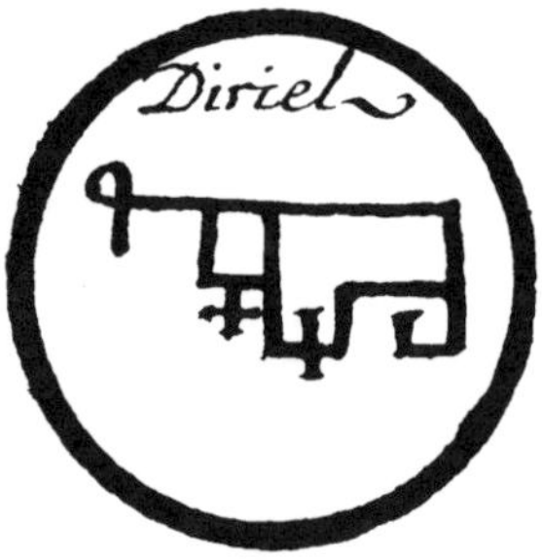
Diriel
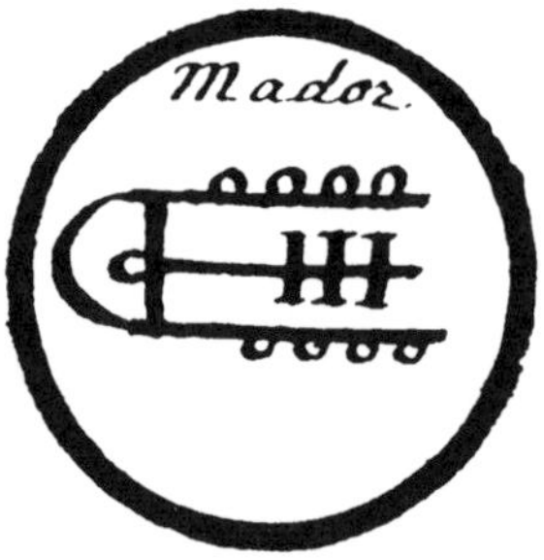
Mador
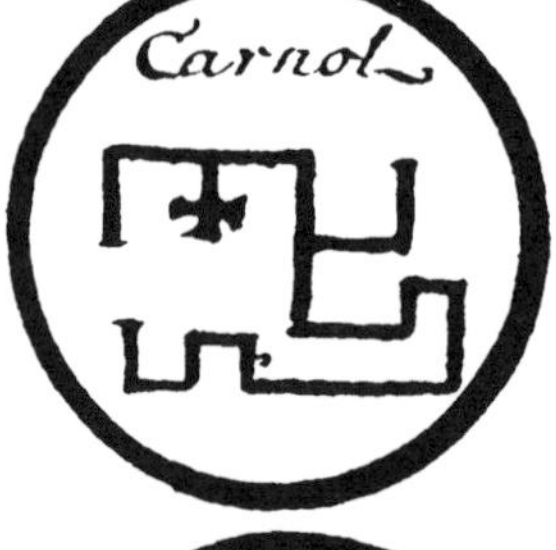
Carnol
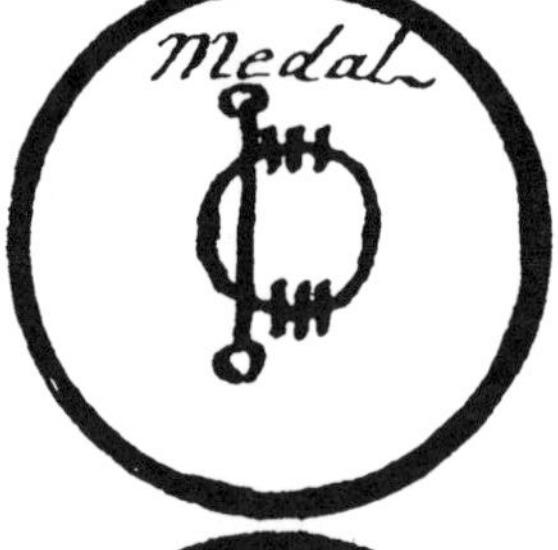
Medal
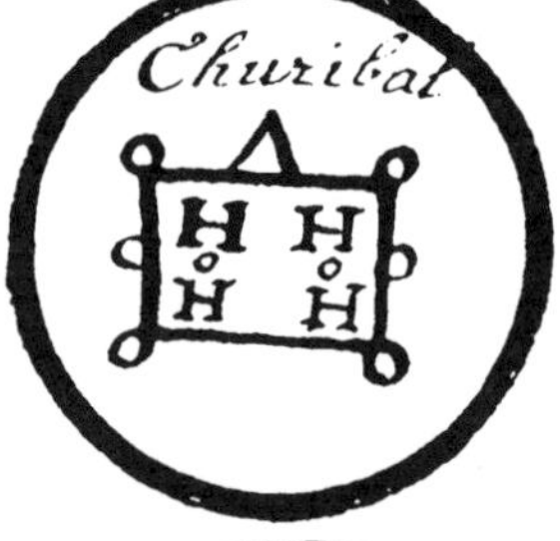
Churibal
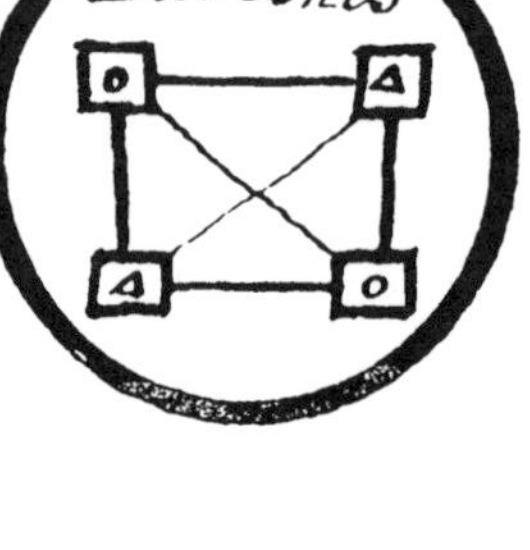
Dabrinos
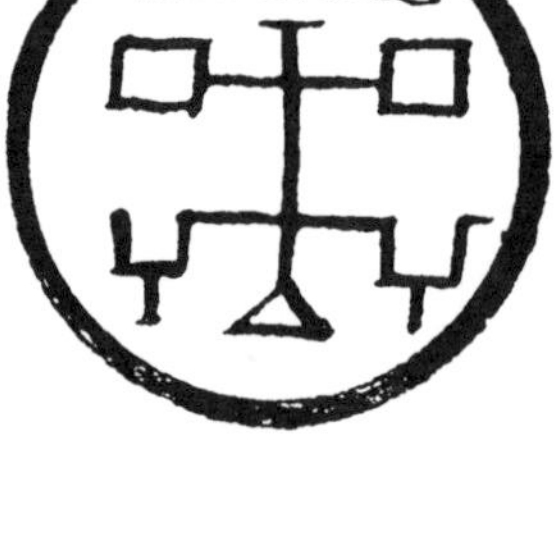
Chomiel
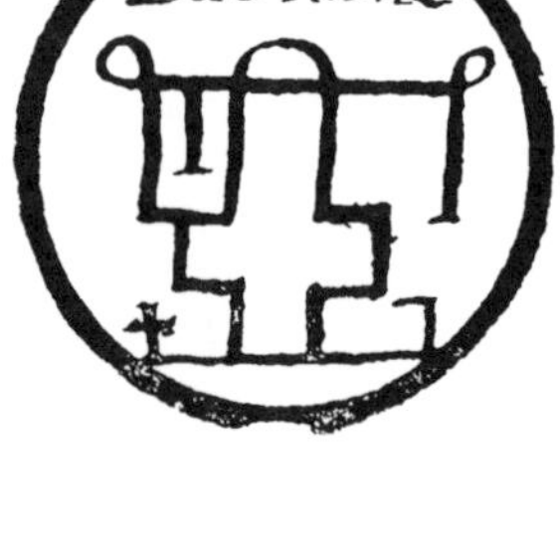
Dubilon

[The Sixteen Dukes]

Pamersiel is the first and chief Spirit ruling in the East under Carnesiel who hath 1000 Spirits under him which are to be called in the Day time but with great care for they are very lofty and stubborn, whereof we shall make mention [of] but of Eleven.

[Pamersiel's Seal]

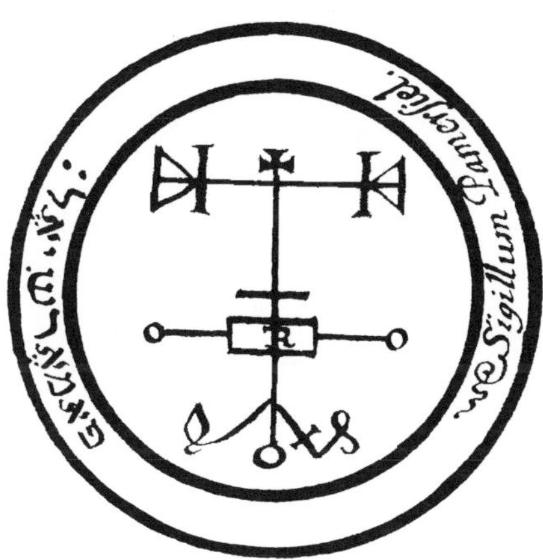

Note these Spirits are by nature evil and very false, and not to be trusted in [with] secrets, but are excellent in driving away Spirits of darkness from any that is haunted as houses.[1]

[1] Trithemius adds in Chapter I of Book I of the *Steganographia*, that "The operation of this first chapter is particularly difficult and full of dangers because of the proud and rebellious nature of its spirits, who obey none but the most expert in the art. For they not only disobey novices and those less skilled in the art, but frequently do them harm and cause all sorts of illusions if they are driven too far. They are more malicious and treacherous than all other spirits of the air and obey no one, unless bound by the greatest of oaths. Furthermore they often treacherously disclose to others a secret entrusted to them."

[1]The Names & Seals of Pamersiel's XI Spirits

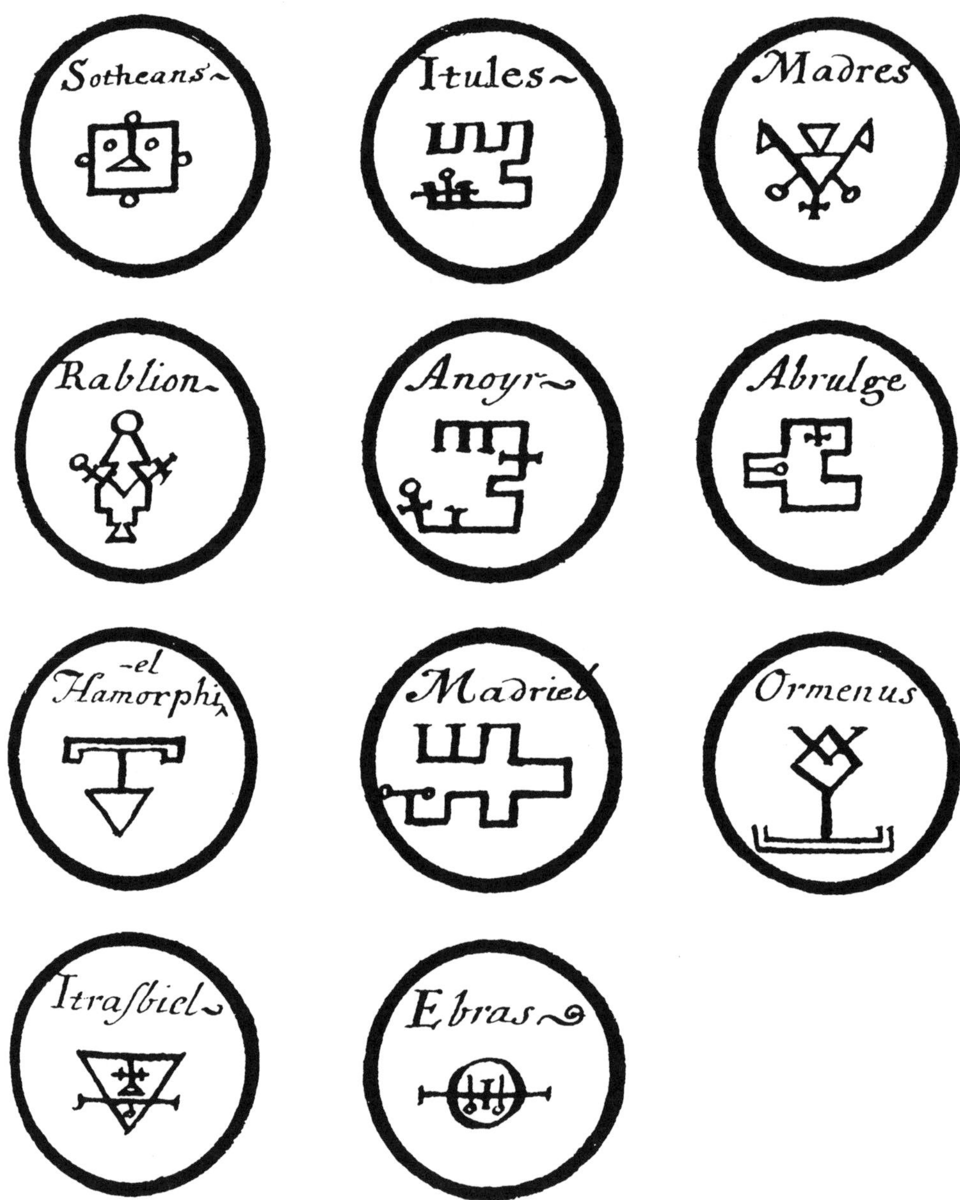

[1] *Sixty sixth Sheet Dr Rudd.*

[Method of Calling][1]

To call forth Pamersiel or any of these his Servants make a Circle in the form as is showed in the Book *Goetia* foregoing in the upper room of your house, or in a place that is airy because these spirits that are in this part [of the *Theurgia-Goetia*] are all of the air.

You may [alternatively] call the spirits into a Crystal stone four Inches [in] Diameter, set on a Table made as followeth which is called the secret Table of Solomon, having his seal on your breast and the girdle about your waist as is showed in the Book *Goetia*.[2]

The form of the [Seal on the] Table is this[3]

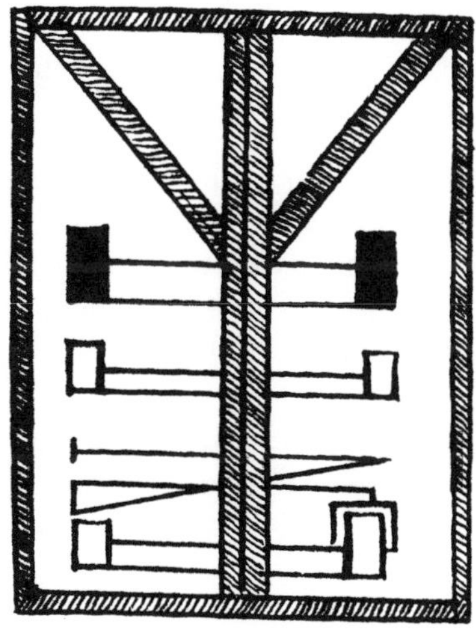

Figure 11: The Secret Table of Solomon [actually The Seal of Solomon]

[1] The method is here mixed in with the description of a specific Spirit, and the order has been obviously.

[2] W1: *"**Pameriel**. This is the first Chief Spirit ruling the East under Carnesiel who has 1000 Spirits under him & is called in the day, but with great care, for they are lofty & Stubborn I shall mention 11 of their Seals (see fig.). Note that these Spirits are by nature Evil and very false, Not to be trusted with Secrets, but are excellent for driving away any Spirits from any that are haunted, as houses.*
To call forth Pamerial or any of his Servants, make a circle in the form as is showed in the book Goetia, before going into the upper ~~part~~ region of a house or in a place that is airy, because the place that these Spirits are in is so, they being all of the Air – You may call the Spirits into a Crystal Stone 4 inches in diameter, set on a table made as follows, which is called the secret table of Solomon See page having his Seal on your breast, and the girdle about your waist as is showed in the book Goetia".
The mention of the *Goetia* at this point shows how the methods outlined in one of the five books of the *Lemegeton* may be used in another.

[3] W1: *"The form of the Table see plate page."* This is supposed to be the design of the Table of Art, but its not. In fact it is the Secret Seal of Solomon.

When you have thus got what is to be prepared, Rehearse the Conjuration several times i.e. whilst the Spirit comes for without doubt he will come. Note the same method is to be used in all the following spirits of the second book *Theurgia Goetia*, also the same [method is used] in Calling forth the four Kings and their Servants aforesaid.[1]

[end of the Method of Calling][2]

The [primary] Conjurations are at large [at length] set down at the end of the *Theurgia Goetia*.[3]

[The Supplementary Conjurations from the *Steganographia*, Book 1, Chapter 1:[4]

Pamersiel, anoyr madriel through the service ebra sothean abrulges itrasbiel. And nadres ormenuitules rablion hamorphiel.[5]

Pamersiel oshurmy delmuson Thafloin peano charustea melany, lyaminto colchan, paroys, madyn, moerlay, bulre + atloor don melcove peloin, ibutsyl meon mysbreath alini driaco person. Crisolnay, lemon asosle mydar, icoriel pean thalmon, asophiel il notreon banyel ocrimos estevor naelma befrona thulaomor fronian beldodrayn bon otalmesgo mero fas elnathyn boframoth.

[**Pamersiel]** Lamarton anoyr bulon madriel traschon ebra sothea panthenon nabrulges Camery itrasbier rubanthy nadres Calmosy ormenulan, ytules demy rabion hamorphyn.]

---

[1] W1: "When you have got what is to be prepared, rehearse the following Conjuration several times that is while the Spirit comes for he will come without doubt. Note the same Method is to be used in all the following Spirits of these two Books Theurgia Goetia as with Parmariel and his Servants & also the same in Calling the 4 Kings & their Servants".

[2] The method is here mixed in with the description of a specific Spirit, and the order has been obviously.

[3] W1: "The Conjurations. I conjure thee thou mighty and potent Prince Pamariel, who ruleth as King in the dominion of the East."

[4] Without doubt, the spirits of the *Theurgia-Goetia*, and their Dukes and servants are all drawn from Trithemius' *Steganographia* Book I which was written in September 1500. There are minor differences in spelling and transcription, but the major difference is that the *Theurgia-Goetia* omits the *carmen conjuratios* (invocations and conjurations) of the *Steganographia*. Accordingly these have been inserted in square brackets for the convenience of the reader. We are aware that these are sometimes considered to be simply cryptographic code, but in the *Steganographia* they are clearly labelled as conjurations, and so that is how we will treat them here.

[5] Note that all these words, in this first passage, are in fact the names of the subsidiary Dukes, whose seals are shown two pages back, with minor differences in spelling. In each case the Trithemius spelling is likely to be the original.

The second Spirit in order [of rank] under [Carnesiel] the Emperor of the East is **Padiel**,[1] he Ruleth in the East and by South[2] as King and Governeth 10000 Spirits by day and 20000 by night, besides several thousands under them they are all naturally good and may be trusted. Solomon saith these Spirits have no power of themselves but what is given them by their Prince Padiel, therefore he hath made no mention of any of their Names because if any of them be called they cannot appear without the leave of their prince Padiel as is declared before of Pamersiel.[3]

[The Conjuration of Padiel][4]

[The Supplementary Conjurations from the *Steganographia,* Book 1, Chapter II:

Padiel aporsy mesarpon omevas peludyn malpreaxo. Condusen, ulearo thersephi bayl merphon, paroys gebuly mailthomyon ilthear tamarson acrimy lon peatha Casmy Chertiel, medony reabdo, lasonti iaciel mal atri bulomeon abry pathulmon theoma pathormyn.

Padiel ariel vanerhon chio tharson phymarto merphon amprisco ledabarym, elsophroy mesarphon ameorsy, paneryn atle pachumgel thearsan utrul ut solubito beslonty las gomadyn triamy mefarnothy.

Padiel melion, parme, camiel, busayr, ilnoma, venoga, pamelochyn.]

[Padiel's Seal]

[1] We have included a copy of a pact or 'Spirit Contract' with Padiel at the end of Appendix 1, which would have been used at the *ligatio* stage of the conjuration. Padiel has no subsidiary Dukes.
[2] Just South of due East.
[3] W1: "**Padiel**. Is second Spirit under Carnesiel he rules the E. by South as King and governs 10,000 Spirits by day and 20,000 by night besides several thousands under them. They are all Naturally good and may all be trusted. Solomon avows that these Spirits had no power of themselves, but what is given them by their Prince Padiel therefore he has made no mention of their names, because if any of them be called they cannot appear without Pleasure of their Prince".
[4] Missing.

The 3rd Spirit in Order under the [Carnesiel] Emperor of the East is **Camuel** who Ruleth as King in the South East parts of the world and hath several Spirits under his Command whereof we shall make mention of ten that belongs to the day and as many as belong to the night and each of these have ten Servants to attend them Excepting Camiel, Citgara, Apuiel, Calym, Dobiel, and Maras[1] for they have 100 a piece to attend them, but Tediel, Moziel, and Tugaros they have none at all; they appear all in a very beautiful form and very courteously in the night as well as in the day, They are all as followeth with their seals[2]

[The Conjuration of Camuel][3]

[The Supplementary Conjurations from the *Steganographia,* Book 1, Chapter III:

Camuel aperoys, melym mevomanial, casmoyn cralty bufaco aeli lumar photirion theor besamys, aneal Cabelonyr thiamo vesonthy.

Camuel Busarcha, menaton enatiel, meran sayr abasremon, naculi pesarum nadru lasmon enoti chamubet usear lesponty abrulmy pen sayr thubarym, gonayr asmon friacha rynon otry hamerson buccurmy pedavellon.]

[Camuel's Seal]

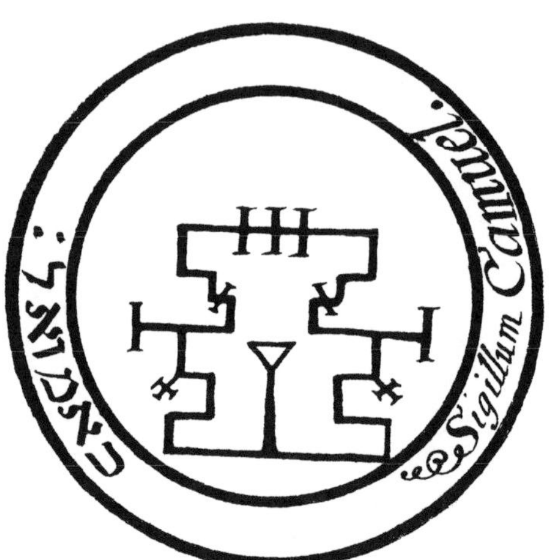

[1] S4: "Camyel, Sitgar, Asimiel, Calym, Dobiel, & Meras."

[2] W1: "***Camael.*** *Is the 3rd Spirit under the King of the east, he rules as King in the S. East [SE] part of the World & has several Spirits under his command of which we shall make mention of 10 that rule by day & as many by night and each has 10 Servants to attend them Except Carnel Citgaras Caldrym & Merase who have 100 apiece to attend them but Dobriel Moriel and Tugros have none at all and they appear very beautiful and very courteously in the night and day, the following 20 belong to the day & night. See page".*

[3] Missing.

[1]The names and Seals of Camuel's Servants both for Day and night.

For the day.

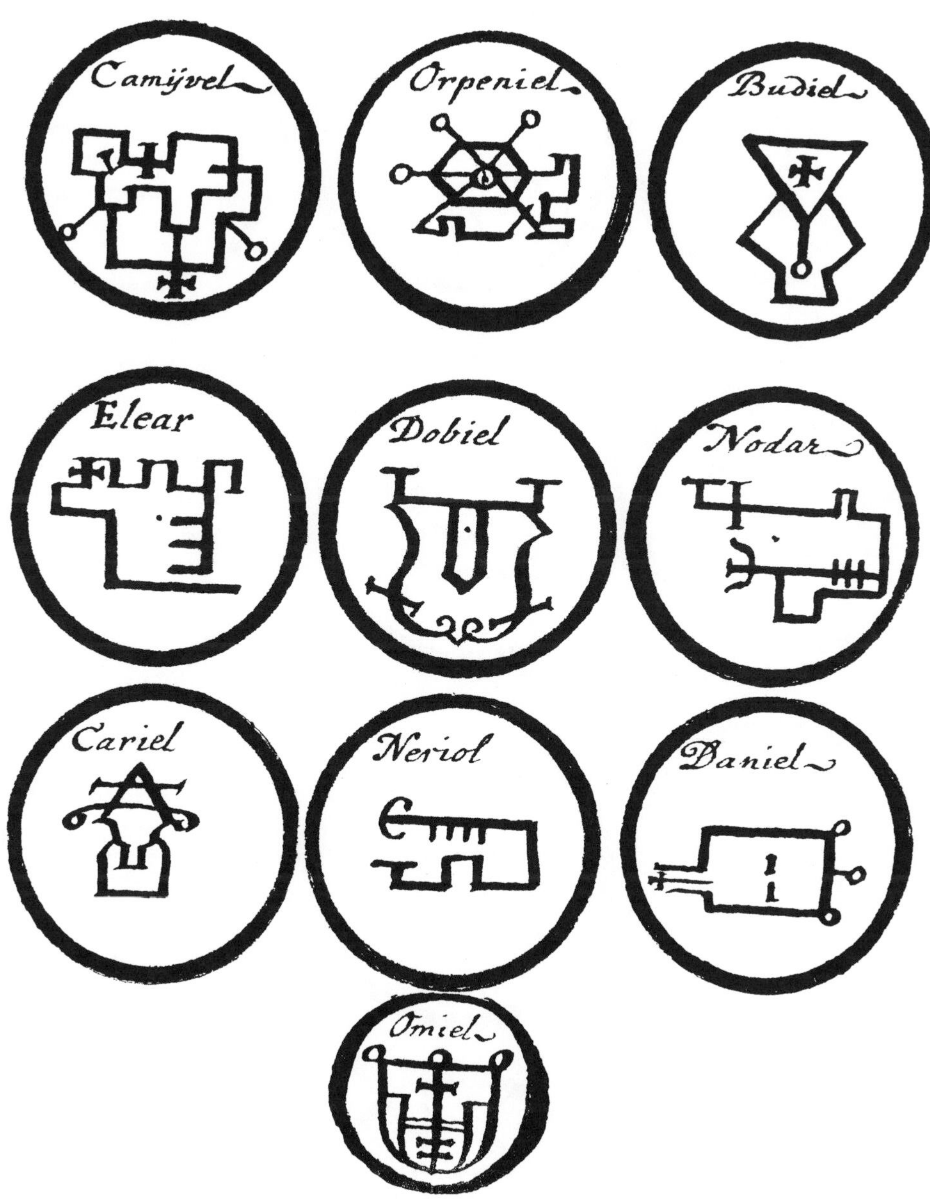

[1] *Sixty seventh sheet Dr Rudd.*

The names & Seals of Camuel's Servants
For the night.

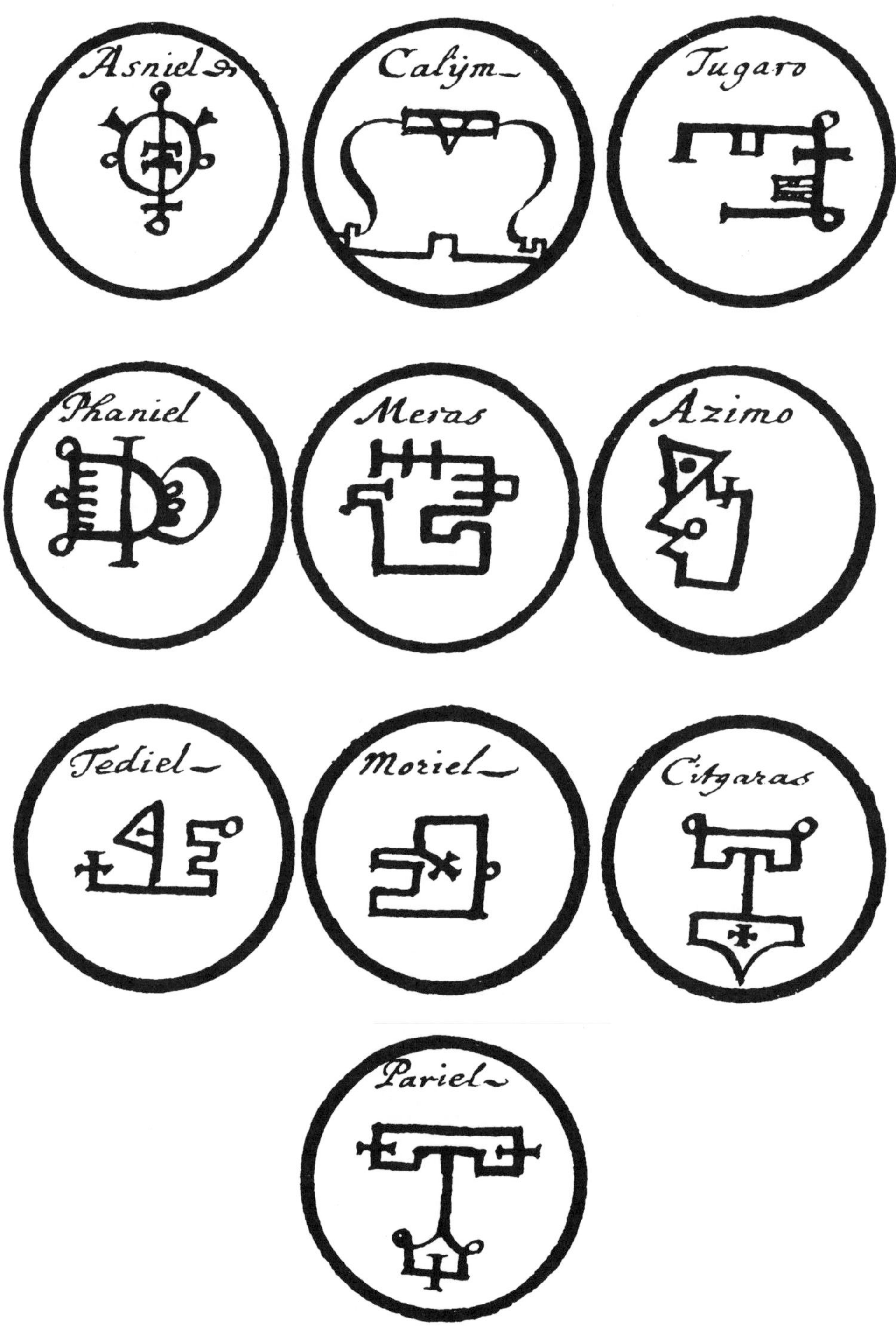

The fourth Spirit in order is **Aschiel**[1] he governeth as King under Carmasiel [Emperor of the East] in the South and by East, he hath ten chief Spirits belonging to the day and 20 to the night. Under whom are 30 principal spirits and under these as many whereof we shall make mention of Eight as the chief Presidents belonging to the day and as many to the night. Every one hath 20 servants at [his] Command, these spirits are all very Courteous and loving and beautiful to behold. They are as followeth with their Seals.[2]

[The Conjuration of Aschiel][3]

[The Supplementary Conjurations from the *Steganographia,* Book 1, Chapter IV:

Aseliel aproysy, melym, thulnear casmoyn, mavear burson, charny demorphaon, Theoma asmeryn diviel, casponti vearly basamys, ernoti chava lorson.

Aseliel murnea casmodym bularcha vadusynaty belron diviel arsephonti si panormys orlevo cadon Venoti basramyn.]

[Aschiel's Seal]

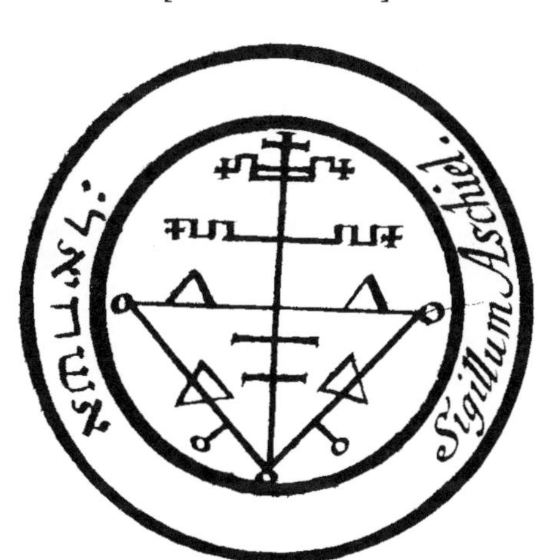

[1] Spelled Aseliel by Trithemius in Book I Chapter IV of the *Steganographia..*

[2] W1: *"**Asteliel.** Is 4th Spirit under Carnesiel & governs as King in the South and by East, he has 10 Chief Spirits by day and 20 by night under whom are 30 Principal Spirits and under them as Many whereof we shall mention 8 of the chief belonging to the day and as many by night. Every one hath 20 Servants to attend him they are very Courteous, loving and beautiful to behold."*

[3] Missing.

The names & Seals of Aschiel's Servants for the day

[1]The names & Seals of Aschiel's chief Presidents or Servants for the night

[1] *Sixty Eight sheet Dr Rudd.*

The fifth Spirit in Order is **Barmiel** he is the first and chief Prince under Caspiel Emperor of the South, he governeth in the South as King under Caspiel, and hath ten Dukes for the day and 20 for the night to attend him to do his will, they are all very good and willing to obey the Exorcist: where of we shall make mention but of Eight that belongs to the day and as many for the night with their Seals for they are sufficient for practice. Note every [one] of these Dukes hath 20 Servants apiece to attend them when they are called, Except the four last for the night they have none.

Those Spirits of the Day must be called in the day, & those of the night in the Night.[1]

The Conjuration [of Barmiel]

I Conjure thee O thou mighty & potent Prince Barmiel &c.[2]

[The Supplementary Conjurations from the *Steganographia,* Book 1, Chapter V:

Barmiel buras melo charnotiel malapos veno masphian albryon, chasmia pelvo morophon apluer charmya noty Mesron alraco caspiel hoalno chorben ovear ascrea cralnoty carephon elcsor bumely nesitan army tufaron.

Barmiel any casleon archoi bulesan eris, Casray molaer pessaro duys anale goerno mesrue greal cusere drelnoz, parle cufureti basriel afly maraphe neaslo, carnos erneo, damerosenotis any carprodyn.]

[Barmiel's Seal]

[1] W1: *"**Barmiel**. Is the fifth & Principal Spirit under Caspiel Emperor of the South, he governs as King under Caspiel, and has 10 Dukes for the day & 20 for the Night to attend him to do his will, they are all very good and willing to obey the Exorcist whereof we shall mention 8 belonging to the day and as many to the Night with their Seals, which are sufficient for practice. Note every one of these Dukes has 20 Servants a piece to attend them, Except the 4 last belonging to the Night".*

[2] This and subsequent conjurations in the *Theurgia-Goetia* are abbreviated to just one line in the manuscript, indicating that the same words should be used with just the replacement of the correct Spirit's name and rank.

The names & Seals of Barmiel's Eight Dukes for the Day.

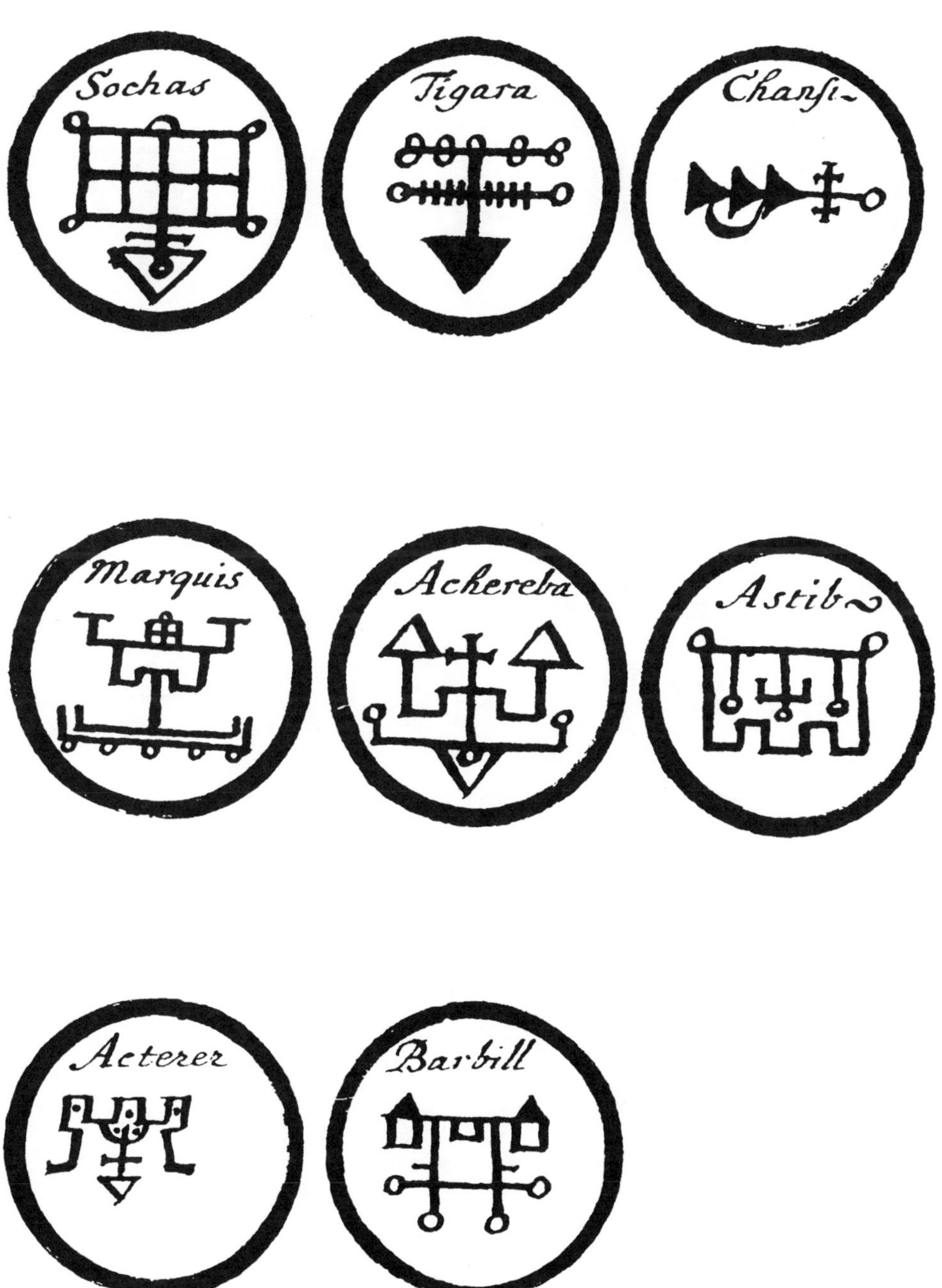

The names & Seals of Barmiel's Eight Dukes for the night.

[1]The 6th Spirit in order (but the second under [Caspiel] the Emperor of the South) is **Gediel** who Ruleth as King in the South and by west, who hath 20 Chief Spirits to serve him in the day and as many for the night, and they have many Servants at [their] Command whereof we shall make mention but of Eight of the chief spirits that belong to the Day and as many of those that belong to the night who have twenty Servants a piece to attend them when they are called forth to appear, they are very loving and courteous and willing to do your will.[2]

The Conjuration [of Gediel]

I Conjure thee O thou mighty & potent Prince Gediel &c.

[The Supplementary Conjurations from the *Steganographia,* Book 1, Chapter VI:

Gediel asiel modebar mopiel, casmoyn, rochamurenu proys: vasaron atido casmear vearsy maludym velachain demosar otiel masdurym sodiviel mesray seor amarlun, laveur pealo netus fabelron.

Gediel aprois camor ety moschoyn divial palorsan, sermel, asparlon Crisphe Lamedon ediur cabosyn arsy thamerosyn. (*conjuratio*)]

[Gediel's Seal]

[1] *Sixty ninth Sheet Dr Rudd.*

[2] W1: *"**Gedediel**. The 2nd under the Emperor of the South is Gediel, he rules as King in the S by W he has 20 chief Spirits to serve him by day and 20 by Night, they have many Servants to attend them, whereof we shall mention 16 who have 2 Servants a piece to attend them when they are called to appear and they are very loving and courteous, and are willing to do your will".*

Gediel's Eight Dukes their Names and Seals belonging to the day.

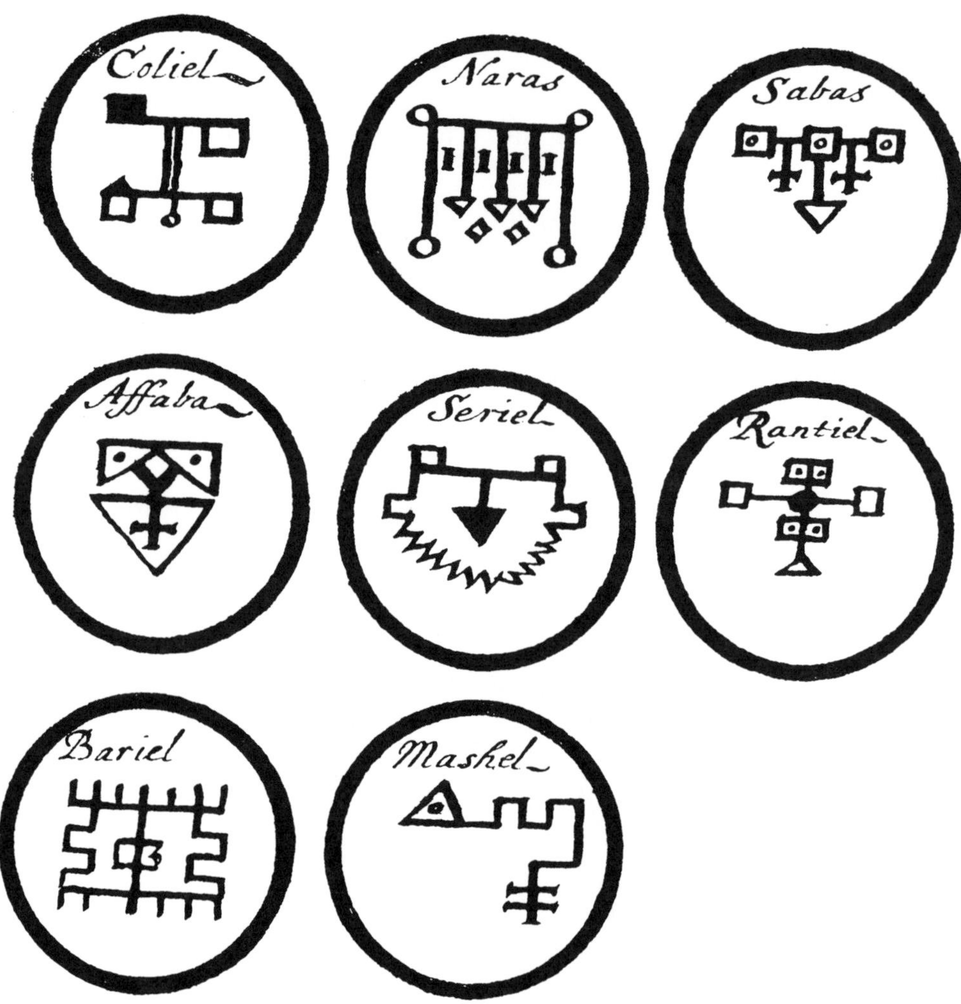

Gediel's Eight Dukes their Names and Seals belonging to the night.

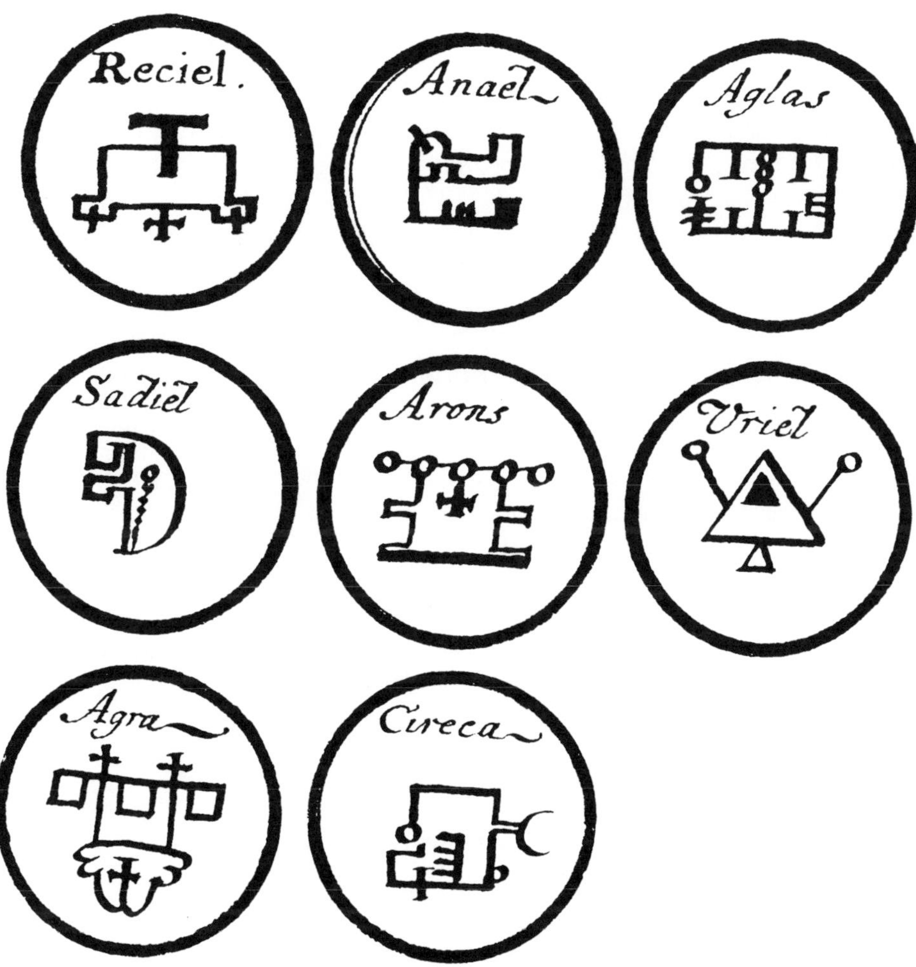

The Seventh Spirit in order is (but the third under [Caspiel] the great Emperor of the South) **Asyriel** he is a mighty King Ruling in the South west part of the world, and hath 20 great Dukes to attend him in the day time and as many for the night who hath under them several servants to attend them.

Here we shall make mention of 8 of the chief Dukes that belong to the ~~night~~ day and as many as belongs to the night because they are sufficient for practice. And the first four that belongs to the day and the first four that belongs to the night hath forty servants a piece to attend them, and the last four of the day 20, and the last 4 of the night ten a piece. They are all good natured and willing to obey you: those that are of the day are to be called in the day and those of the night in the night.[1]

The Conjuration [of Asyriel]

I Conjure thee O thou mighty and potent Prince Asyriel who rules as King, &c.

[The Supplementary Conjurations from the *Steganographia,* Book 1, Chapter VII:

Asiriel aphorsy Lamodyn to Carmephyn drubal asutroy Sody baruchon, usefer palormy thulmear asmeron chornemadusyn coleny busarethon duys marphelithubra nasaron venear fabelronty. (*conjuratio*)

Asiriel onear Camor Laveviel gamer sothin ianoz alnay bulumer palorson, irgiel lamedon, ludiel Casparosyn navy asparlon nadiel bulephor ianos pesonty tresloty Camon elyr, mearsu nosy thamerosyn.(*conjuratio*)]

[Asyriel's Seal]

[1] W1: *"**Asyriel**. The 3rd Spirit under the great Emperor of the South is Asyriel a Mighty King ruling in the South and hath 20 great Dukes to attend him & as many for Night, the first four of the day and the first four of the night have 40 Servants apiece and the remainder but 10 each, they are all good natured and willing to obey you."*

[1]The names & Seals of Asyriel's Eight chief Dukes belonging to the Day.

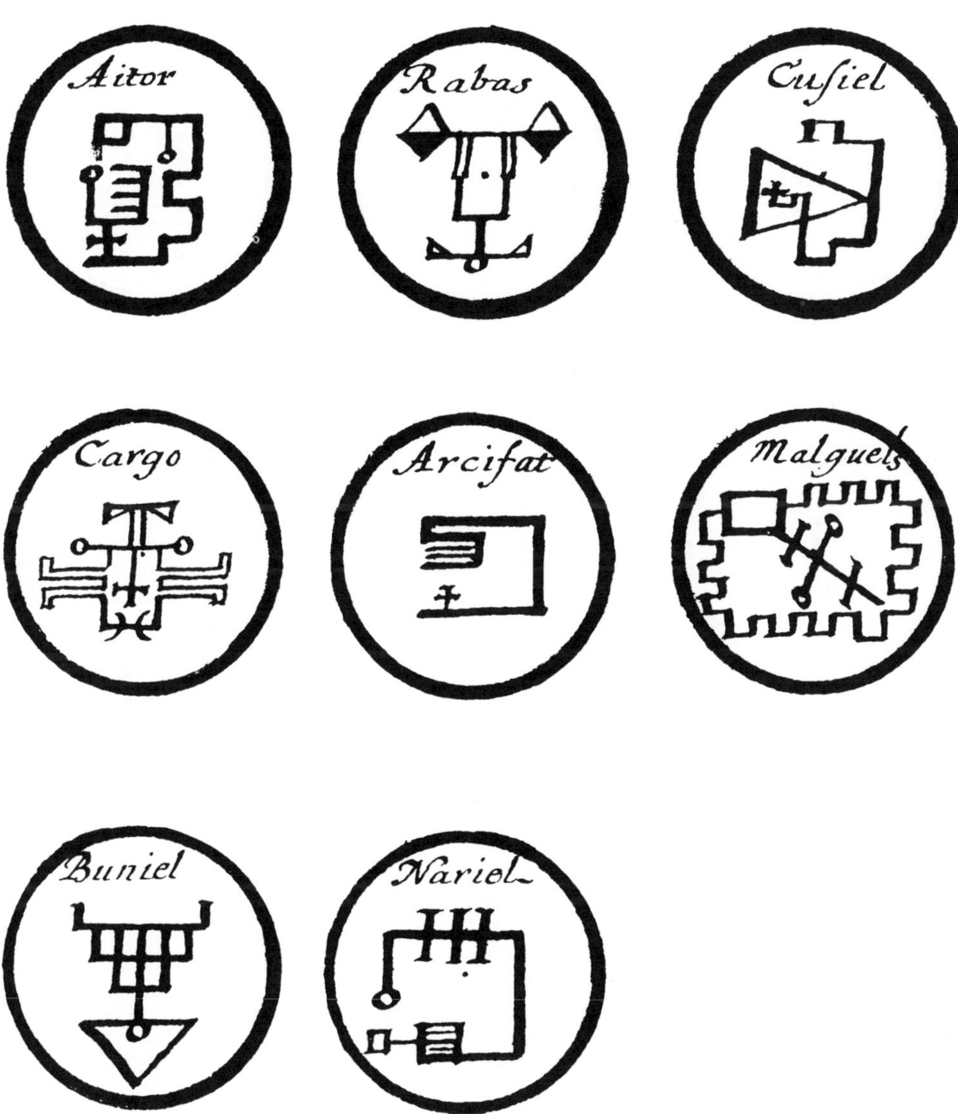

[1] *The Seventieth sheet Dr Rudd.*

The names & Seals of Asyriel's Eight chief Dukes belonging to the Night.

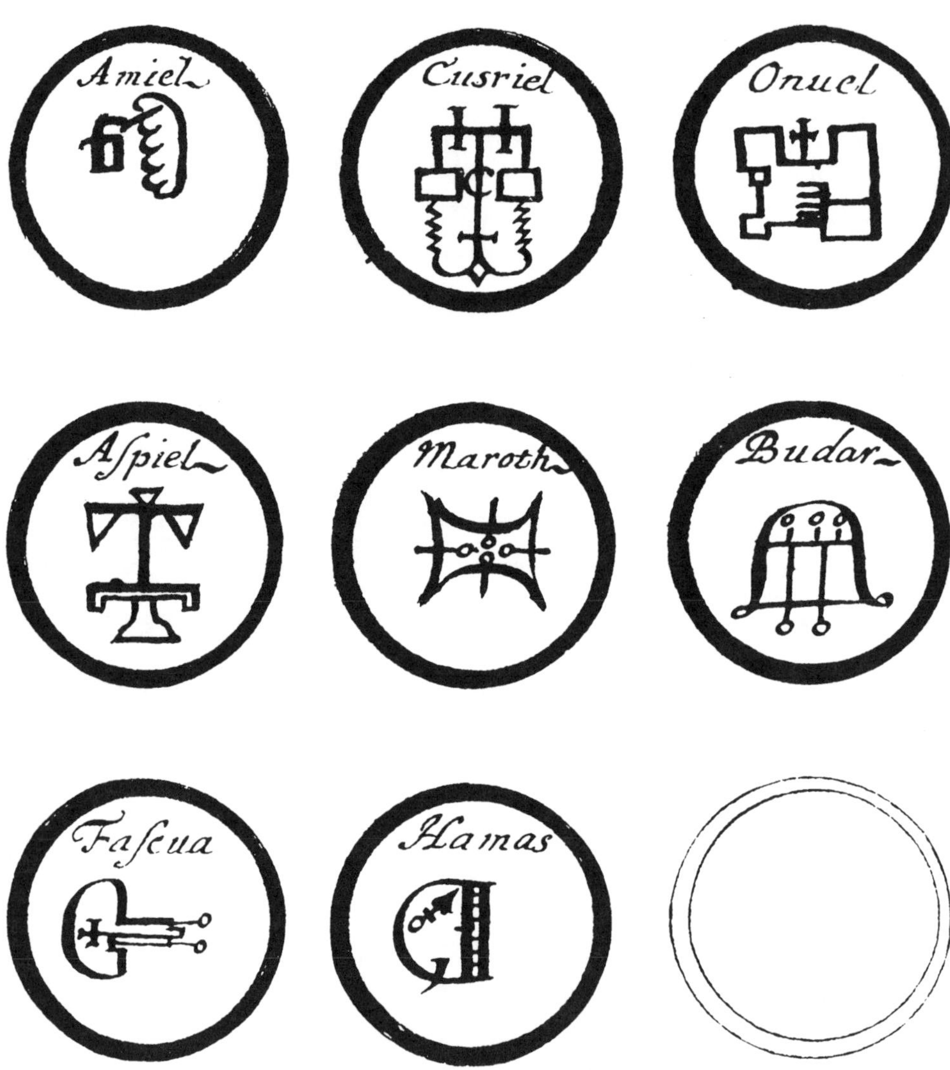

The Eight Spirit in order but the 4th under [Caspiel] the Emperor of the South is called **Maseriel** who ruleth as King in the Dominion of the West and by South, and hath a great number of [spirits] under him to attend to do his will. Solomon mentions 12 Spirits that belong to the day, & 12 Spirits that belong to the night, they are all good by nature and are willing to do your will in all things. Each spirit hath 30 Servants, those that belong to the day are to be called in the day, and those for the night are to [be] called in the night.[1]

The Conjuration

I Conjure thee O thou mighty & potent Prince Maseriel &c.

[The Supplementary Conjurations from the *Steganographia,* Book 1, Chapter VIII:

Maseriel bulan lamodyn charnoty Carmephin iabrun caresathroyn asulroy bevesy Cadumyn turiel busan Sevear: almos ly cadufel ernoty panier iethar care pheory bulan thorty paron Venio Fabelronthusy. (*conjuratio*)

Maseriel onear Camersin, Cohodor messary lyrno balnaon greal, lamedon odiel, pedarnoy nador ianoz auy chamyrin. (*conjuratio*)]

[Maseriel's Seal]

[1] W1: "***Maseriel.*** *Is the 4th under the dominion of the South, and rules as King in the dominion of the West and by South and* ~~*as*~~ *has a great number of Spirits and Servants under him, whereof we shall mention 24 of the day & night. They are all good natured & willing".*

The Names and Seals of Maseriel's 12 Spirits that belong to the day.

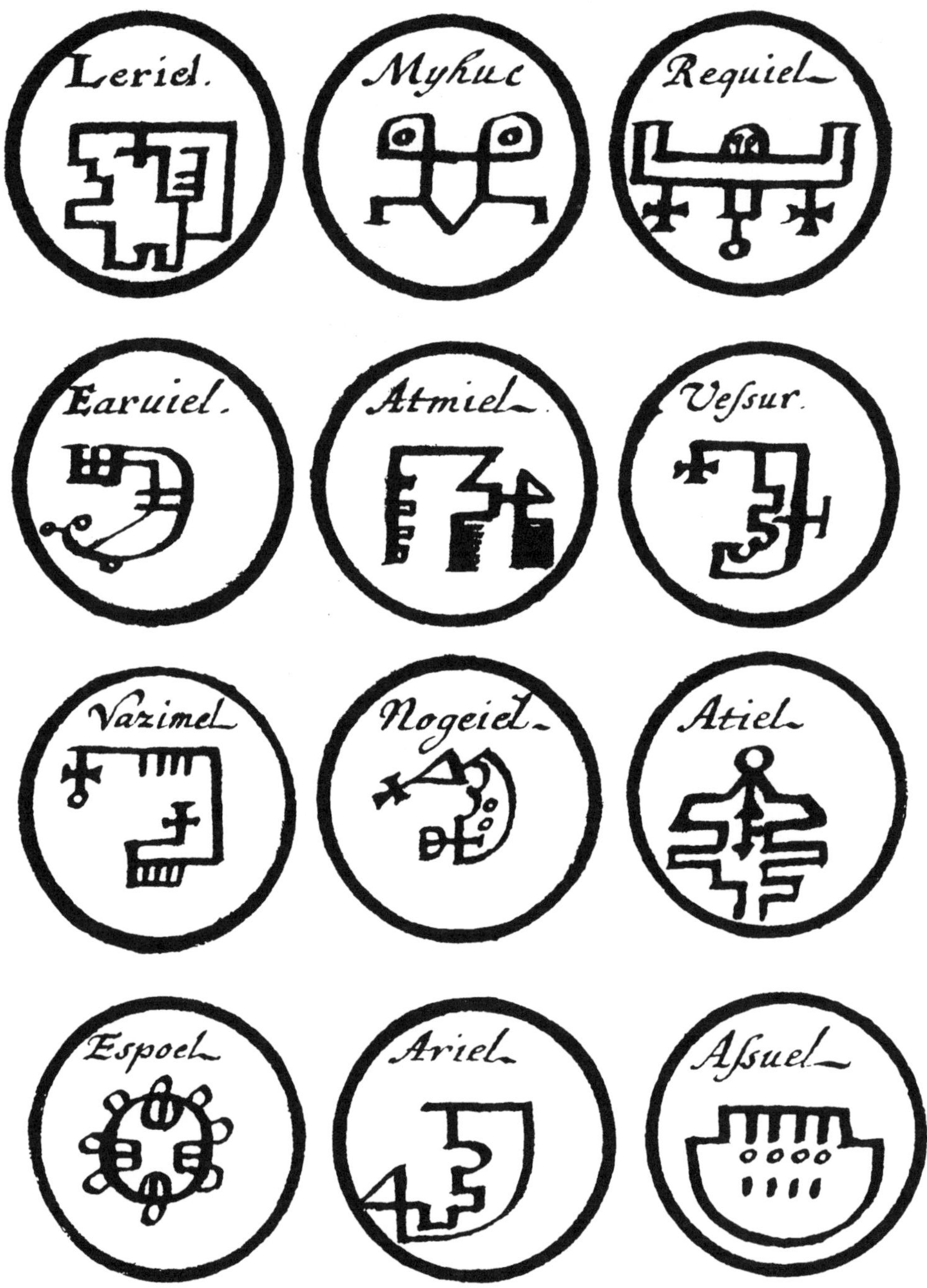

[1]The Names & Seals of Maseriel's 12 other Dukes for the Night.

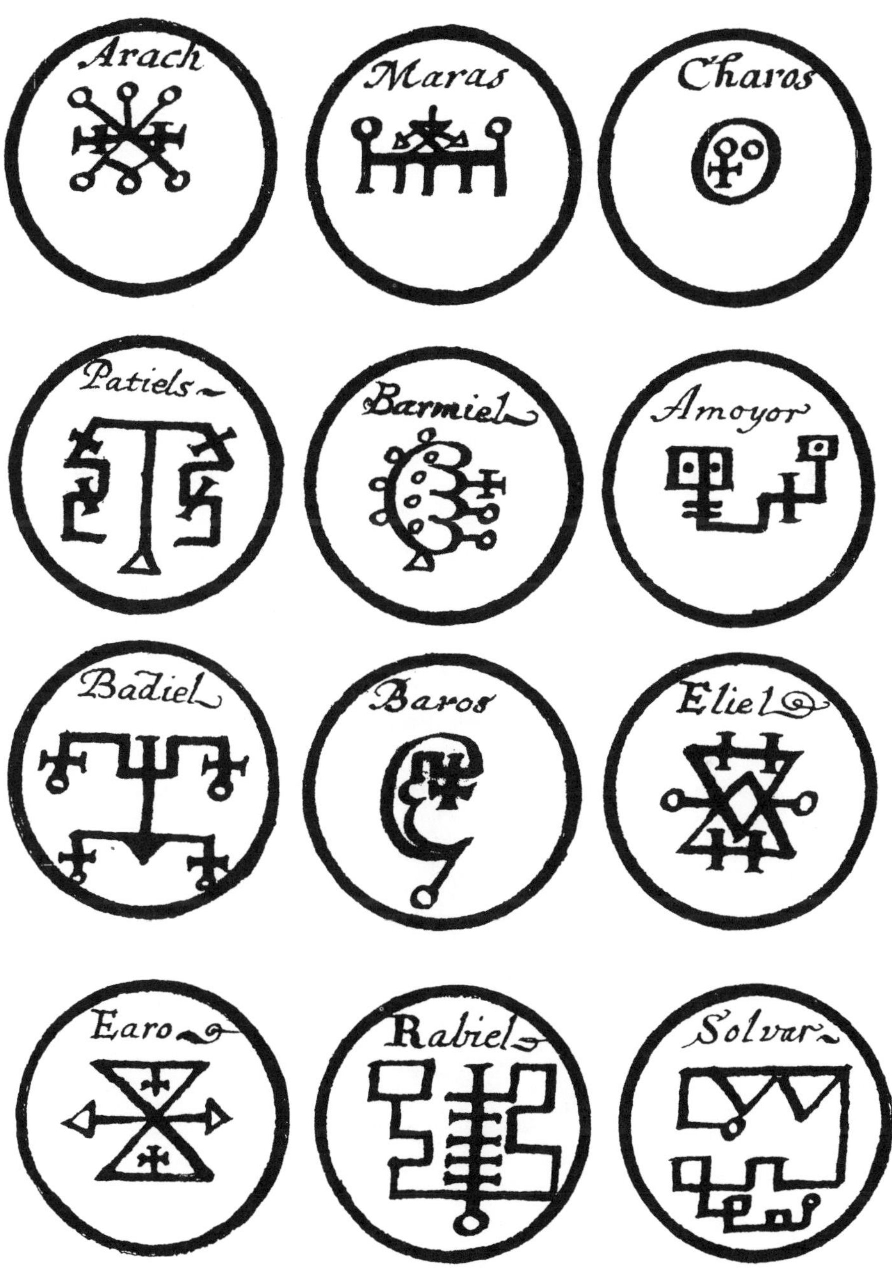

[1] *The Seventy first sheet Dr Rudd.*

The ninth Spirit in order is (but the first under [Amenadiel] the Emperor of the West) is called **Malgaras** he Ruleth as King in the Dominion of the West, and hath 30 Dukes under him to attend him in the day, and as many for the night, and several under them again, whereof we shall make mention of twelve Dukes that belong to the day and as many for the night and every one of them hath 30 Servants to attend on them excepting Misiel, Burfas, Asper and Dilas for they hath but 20 a piece, Aroias, Bafir [aka Barface] hath but 10 &c. They are all very Courteous, & will appear willing to do what you desire.

They appear 2 and 2 at a time with their Servants those for the day are to be called in the day and those for the night in the night.[1]

The Conjuration[2]

I Conjure thee O thou mighty & potent Prince Malgaras who Rules as King &c.

[The Supplementary Conjurations from the *Steganographia,* Book 1, Chapter IX:

Malgaras ador chameso bulueriny mareso bodyr Cadumir aviel casmyo redy pleoryn viordi eare viorba, chameron very thuriel ulnavy, bevesy mevo chasmironty naor ernyso, chony barmo calevodyn barso thubra sol.

Malgaras apro chameron asoty mesary throes Zameda sogreal paredon adre Caphoron onatyr tirno beosy. Chameron phorsy mellon tedrumarsy dumaso duise Casmiel elthurny peson alproys fabelronty Sturno panalmo nador. (*carmen spiritus*)]

[Malgaras' Seal]

[1] W1: *"**Malgaras**. Is first under the Emperor of the West and has 30 under him to attend him in the day & as many in the night and several under them whereof we shall Mention 12 day & 12 night Dukes and each of these has 30 Servants Except ~~Miliel~~ Meliel, Burfas, Asper & Adilas for they have but 20 each, and Aroyas and Basiel have but 10 they are all very courteous and willingly appear two at a time with their Servants / see page".*

[2] Missing.

The Names and Seals of Malgaras' 12 Dukes that belong to the Day.

The Names and Seals of Malgaras' 12 Dukes that belong to the Night.

[1]The tenth Spirit in order (but the second under [Amenadiel] the Emperor of the West) is **Dorochiel**[2] who is a mighty Prince bearing rule in the West and by North, and hath 40 Dukes to attend on him in the day time and as many for the night with an innumerable Company of Servants. We shall only make mention of 24 chief Dukes that belongs to the day, and as many for the night with their names and Seals. Note the 12 first Dukes that belongs to the day have 40 Servants a piece, the 12 last in the day and of the night have 400 Servants a piece to attend them & all those of the day are to be called in the day and those of the night in the night.

Observe the Planetary notion [motion] in calling forth the two first that belong to the day, for the two first that belong to the day are to be called in the first planetary hour of the day, and the two next in the second planetary hour of the day and so on successively till you have gone through the day to the night, and through the night, till you come to the first of the day again.[3]

All these Spirits are of a good nature, and are willing to obey and do your pleasure.[4]

The Conjuration

I Conjure thee O thou mighty & potent Prince Dorochiel &c.

[The Supplementary Conjurations from the *Steganographia,* Book 1, Chapter X:

Dorothiel cusi feor madylon busar pamersy chear ianothym baony Camersy ulymeor peathan adial cadumyr renear thubra Cohagier maslon Lodierno fabelrusyn.

Dorothiel onear chameron ulyfeor madusyn peony oriel nayr druse movayr pamerson etro dumeson, davor caho. Casmiel hayrno, fabelrunthon.]

---

[1] *The Seventy second sheet Dr Rudd.*

[2] He is spelled Dorothiel in the *Steganographia.*

[3] This is the first time it is mentioned that these Spirits are allocated to the Planetary hours, and that these hours are the times when they should be called.

[4] W1: *"**Dorochiel**. Is 2nd under the dominion of the West and is a Mighty Prince governing in the West and by North and has 40 dukes to attend him by day and as many by night with an innumerable number of Servants whereof we shall mention 24 of the chief by day and as many by night – 12 of his day Dukes belong to the forenoon and 12 to the afternoon and the first 12 that belong to the day and the 1st 12 that belong to the night have 400 Each to attend them, observe the planetary motion for the two first belonging to the day are to be called in the first planetary hour, and the next in the 2nd & so Successfully with the rest in the night till you come to the day again. They are all good natured and willing to obey and do your will. In all these you must through the whole book observe which rule the day & which the night & which the day otherwise it is Labour lost".*

[Darochiel's Seal]

The names & Seals of 12 chief Dukes that belong to Dorochiel for the Day.

These 12 are [to be called] before noon.

The Names and Seals of other 12 chief Dukes that belong to Dorochiel for the day

These 12 are for [calling in the] Afternoon.

The Names & Seals of the 12 chief Dukes that belong to Dorochiel for the Night.

The[se] 12 [to be called] after Midnight.[1]

[1] Probably should be before Midnight.

[1]The names and Seals of the other 12 chief Dukes that belong to Dorochiel for the night.

[These 12 to be called after Midnight]

---

[1] *The Seventy third Sheet Dr Rudd.*

The Eleventh Spirit in order under the Emperor Amenadiel[1] is called **Usiel**,[2] he is a mighty prince ruling as King in the North West, he hath 40 Diurnal [day] & 40 Nocturnal [night] Dukes to attend on him day & night whereof we shall make mention of 14 that belongs to the day and as many for the night which is sufficient for practice. The first 8 that belongs to the day hath 40 Servants a piece to attend on them and the other 6 [have] 30 [Servants] a piece, And the first 8 that belongs to the night hath 40 servants a piece to attend on them, the next 4 Dukes [have] 20 servants, & the last 2 hath 10 a piece, and they are very obedient & do willingly appear when they are called. They have more power to hide or discover treasure than any other spirits (Saith Solomon) that are in *Theurgia Goetia*, & when you hide & would have any thing not taken away that is hid make these four Seals

[These are the four seals together of Abaria/Abariel, Magni, Ansoel, Adnan]

In Virgin's parchment & lay them with your treasure or where your treasure lieth & it will never be found nor taken away.[3]

[Usiel's Seal]

[1] The spelling used here is the more common one of S3 rather than that used by Rudd earlier in H. This probably means that 'Amenadiel' is the correct version.

[2] 'Vsiel' in the manuscript, but spelling updated to Usiel. 'U' and 'V' were interchangeable in the seventeenth century, with usage depending on the position in the word. Modern spelling practice uses 'u' for a vowel, and 'v' for a consonant.

[3] W1: *"**Usiel.** Is the 3rd Spirit under the dominion of the West he rules as King in the North West. He has 40 day & 40 night Dukes whereof we shall mention 14 of Each, the first 8 of the day and night have 40 Servants each & the others 36 each and willingly appear when called. Solomon affirmed they had more power to hide and discover treasures than any other Spirits contained in the* Theurgia Goetia; *and when you would hide and not have it found, make these 4 Seals in Virgin Parchment & lay with the treasure and it will never be found or taken away."*

[1]The names & Seals of Usiel's Eight ~~nocturnal~~ Diurnal Dukes

[1] *Seventy fourth Sheet Dr Rudd.*

The names & Seals of Usiel's six ~~Nocturnal~~ Diurnal Dukes

The Conjuration

I Conjure thee O thou mighty & potent Prince Usiel &c.

[The Supplementary Conjurations from the *Steganographia,* Book 1, Chapter XI:

Usiel parnothiel chameron briosy sthrubal brionear Caron sotronthi egypia odiel Chelorsy mear Chadusy notiel ornych turbelsi paneras thorthay pean adresmo boma arnotiel Chelmodyn drusarloy sodiviel Carson, eltrae myre notiel mesraym Venea dublearsy mavear melusyron chartulneas fabelmerusyn.

Usiel asoyr paremon cruato madusyn sauepe mavayr realdo chameron ilco paneras thurmo pean elsoty fabelrusyn iltras charson frymasto chelmodyn.]

[1]The Names and Seals of Usiel's Eight ~~Diurnal~~ Dukes Nocturnal

[1] *Seventy fourth Sheet Dr Rudd.* [Mistakenly repeated in the manuscript].

The Names and Seals of Usiel's 6 ~~Diurnal~~ Dukes Nocturnal

The 12th Spirit in Order (but the fourth under [Amenadiel] the Emperor of the West) is **Cabariel**[1] he hath 50 Dukes to attend on him in the day and as many for the night under whom are many Servants to attend on them; whereof we shall make mention of but ten of the chief Dukes that belongs to the day and as many for the night, and every one of them hath fifty servants to give attendance when their Masters are called. Note these Dukes that belong to the day are very good and willing to obey their Masters and are to be called in the day time; And those of the night are to be called in the night time, they are by nature evil & disobedient and will deceive you if they can.[2]

The Invocation

I Conjure thee O thou mighty & potent Prince Gabariel[sic] &c

[The Supplementary Conjurations from the *Steganographia,* Book 1, Chapter XII:

Cabariel onear chameron fruani, parnaton fosiel bryosi nagreal fabelrontyn adiel thortay nofruav pena afesiel chusy.

Cabariel asiar paremon chiltan amedyn sayr pemadon chulty movayr savepor peatha mal frimaston dayr pean cothurno fabelrusyn elsoty chelmodyn.]

[Cabariel's Seal]

[1] H: The text alternates between the names Cabariel and Gabariel. S3: Cabariel; W1: Cabariel, which we suspect is the correct form.

[2] W1: "***Cabariel****. Is 4th Spirit under the Emperor of the West and rules as King in the North and by West & has 50 dukes to attend him in the day and 50 in the night, whereof we shall Mention 10 of the Chief by day and as many by night & every one has 50 Servants to attend them. The day Spirits are very good and obedient. The Night [Spirits] are Evil & will deceive you if they can.*"

The names and Seals of Cabariel's ten Dukes that belong to the day.

[1]The Names and Seals of Cabariel's ten Dukes for the night.

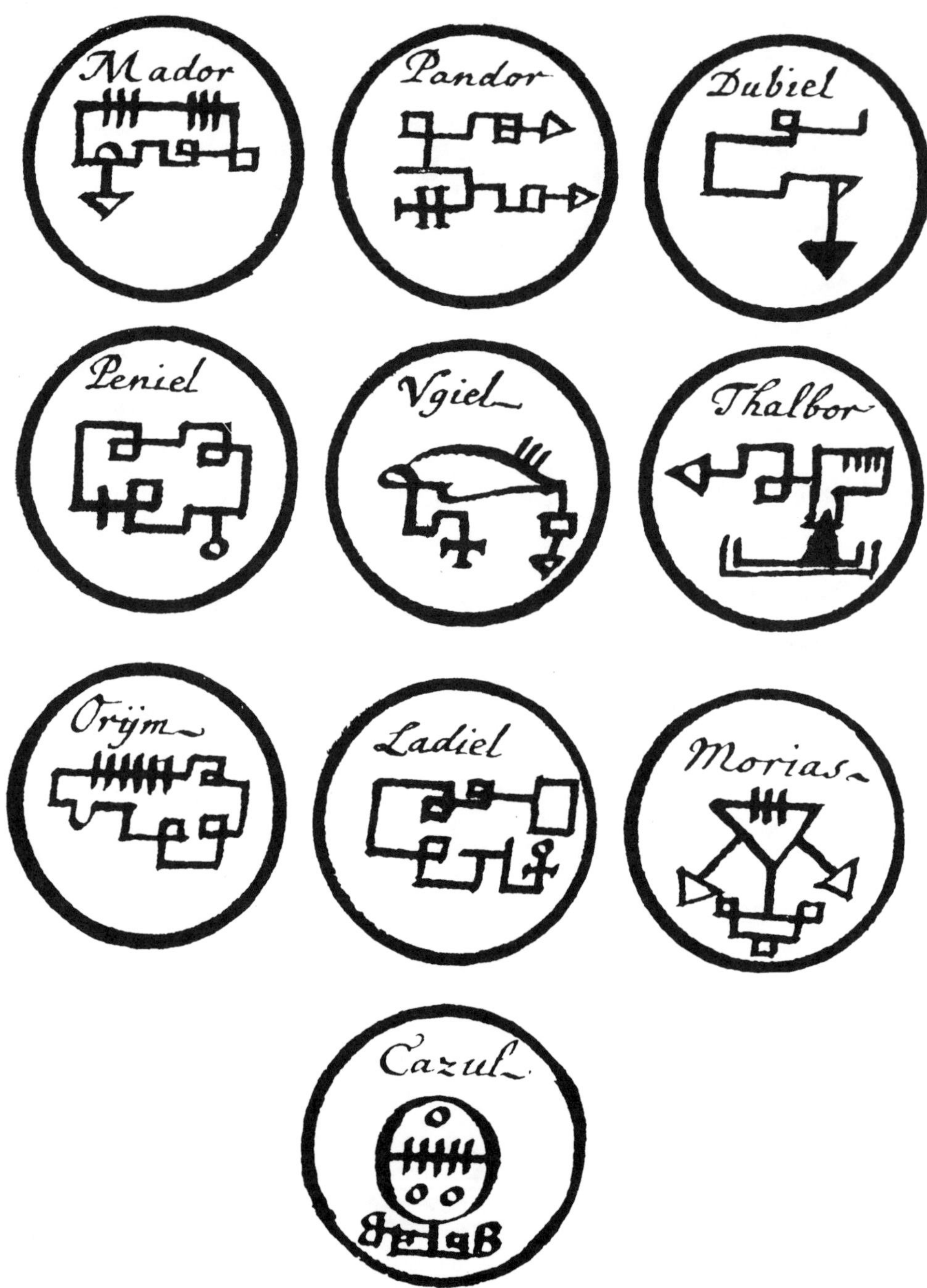

[1] *Seventy fifth sheet Dr Rudd.*

[1]The 13th Spirit in order (but the first under Demoriel the Emperor of the North) is called **Rasiel,**[2] he ruleth as King in the North, and hath 150 Dukes for the day and as many for the night to attend him and they have many servants under them again for to do their will &c, whereof we shall mention 16 Chief Dukes that belong to the day because they are by nature good and willing to obey, and but only 14 belong to the night because they are by nature evil and stubborn & disobedient & will not obey.

All those Dukes that belongs to the day hath 50 Servants[3] a piece excepting the 6 last which hath but 30 a piece and the 8 first that belongs to the day hath 40 servants a piece the 4 next hath 20 a piece and the last 2 but 10 a piece.[4]

[The Conjuration][5]

[The Supplementary Conjurations from the *Steganographia,* Book 1, Chapter XIII:

Raysiel afruano chameron fofiel onear Vemabi parnothon fruano Caspiel fufre bedarym bulifeor pean Curmaby Layr Vaymeor pesarym adorcus odiel Vernabi peatha darsum laspheno deuior Camedonton phorsy lasbenay to charmon druson olnays, Venouym lulefin, peorso fabelrontos thurno. Calephoy Vem, nabelron bural thorasyn charnoty Capelron. *(carmen conjurationis)*

Raysiel myltran, fruano fiar charmy clymarso pean Sayr pultho chultusa medon vepursandly tusan axeyr afflon. *(carmen conjurationis)*]

[Raysiel's Seal]

[1] W1: Adds the heading *"Spirits of Demoriel Emp[eror of the] North"*.

[2] S3: Raysiel. This is probably the correct form as Rudd at one points inserts 'i' into the name as an afterthought, producing 'Raisiel'. Raysiel is the form used by Trithemius.

[3] There seems little logic in the sequence of numbers of servants. It is an interesting coincidence (but probably nothing more) that these numbers if converted to Hebrew letters form three words with a sort of coherent sense. Thus, 50-6-30 8-40-4 20-2-10 = נול חמד כבי = NVL ChMD KBI = to defile (or dung heap) an object of sacred desire [and] glory.

[4] W1: *"**Raysial.** First Spirit under the Emperor of the North is Raysial he rules as King in the North & has 50 dukes of the day & 50 of the night to attend him & they again have Many servants to attend them & do their will of which we shall mention 16 day Dukes because they are good and willing to obey, and but 14 belonging to the night because they are by nature Evil Stubborn & disobedient, the day dukes, Except the 6 last have 50 Servants to attend them each, the last 6 have but 30. The 8 first night dukes have 40, the 4 next [have] 20 the two next [have] 10".*

[5] Missing.

The Names and Seals of Rasiel's 8 Dukes that belong to the Day.

The names and Seals of the other 8 Dukes that belong to Rasiel for the day.

[1]The Names and Seals of Rasiel's 8 Dukes that belong to the night

[1] *Seventy sixth Sheet Dr Rudd.*

The names and Seals of the other 6 Dukes of Rasiel[1] that belong to the night.

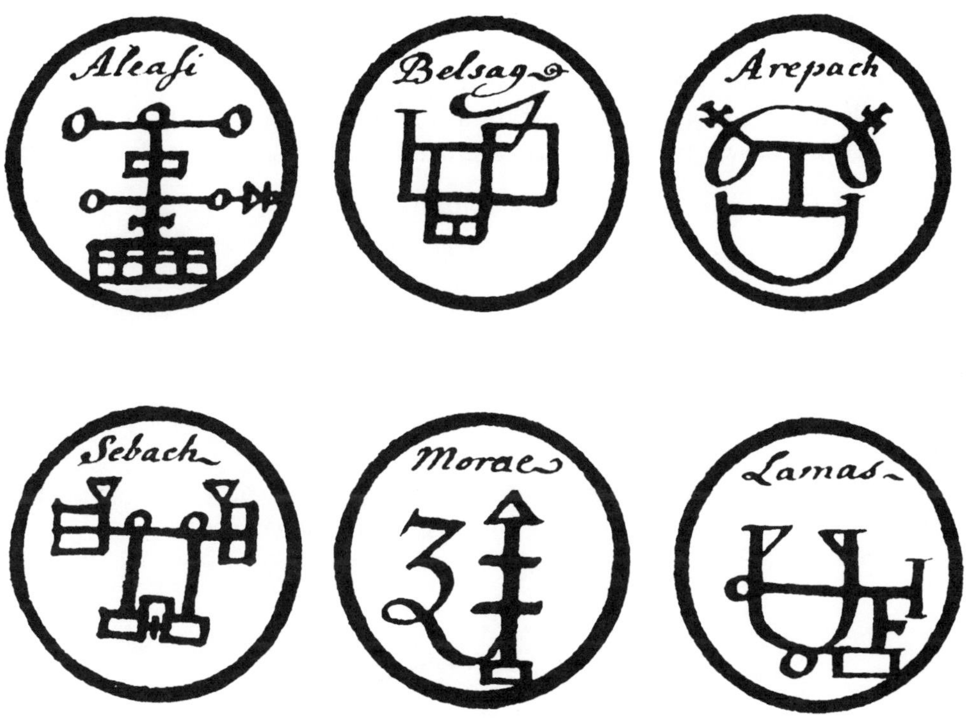

[1] Rudd inserts an 'i' as an afterthought making 'Raisiel'.

The fourteenth Spirit in order (but the second under [Demoriel] the Emperor of the North) is **Symiel** who Ruleth as King in the North and by East who hath ten Dukes to attend on him in the day time, and a thousand in the night, and every one of them hath a certain Number of servants whereof we shall make mention of the ten that belongs to the day and ten of those that belongs to the night, and those of the day are very good and not disobedient as those of the night for they are stubborn and will not appear willingly. Note those of the day hath 720 servants amongst them to do their will, and those ten of the night hath 790 servants to attend on them as occasion serves.[1]

The Conjuration

I Conjure thee O thou mighty and potent Prince Symiel &c.

[The Supplementary Conjurations from the *Steganographia,* Book 1, Chapter XIV:

Symiel myrno chamerony theor pasron adiveal fanerosthi sofear Carmedon Charnothiel peasor sositran fabelrusy thyrno pamerosy trelno chabelron chymo churmabon, asiel, peasor carmes nabeyros toys Camalthonty. *(carmen ad spiritus)*

Symiel marlos chameron pyrcohi pean fruary fabelronti gaelto siargoti melafsor hialbra penor olesy Aiulbrany ordu Casmeron omer vemabon. (*conjuratio*)]

[Symiel's Seal]

[1] W1: *"**Symiel**. Is the 2nd under the Emperor of the North and rules as King in the N and by E, he has 10 dukes to attend him in the day & 1000 by night & Every one of them has ~~1000 is the night~~ a certain Number to attend them, we shall mention 10 that belong to the day who are good and have 720 Servants to attend them & ~~so~~ 10 belonging to the night who are bad and have 790 Servants to attend them as occasions serves".*

The names & Seals of Ten Dukes of Symiel that belongs to the day.

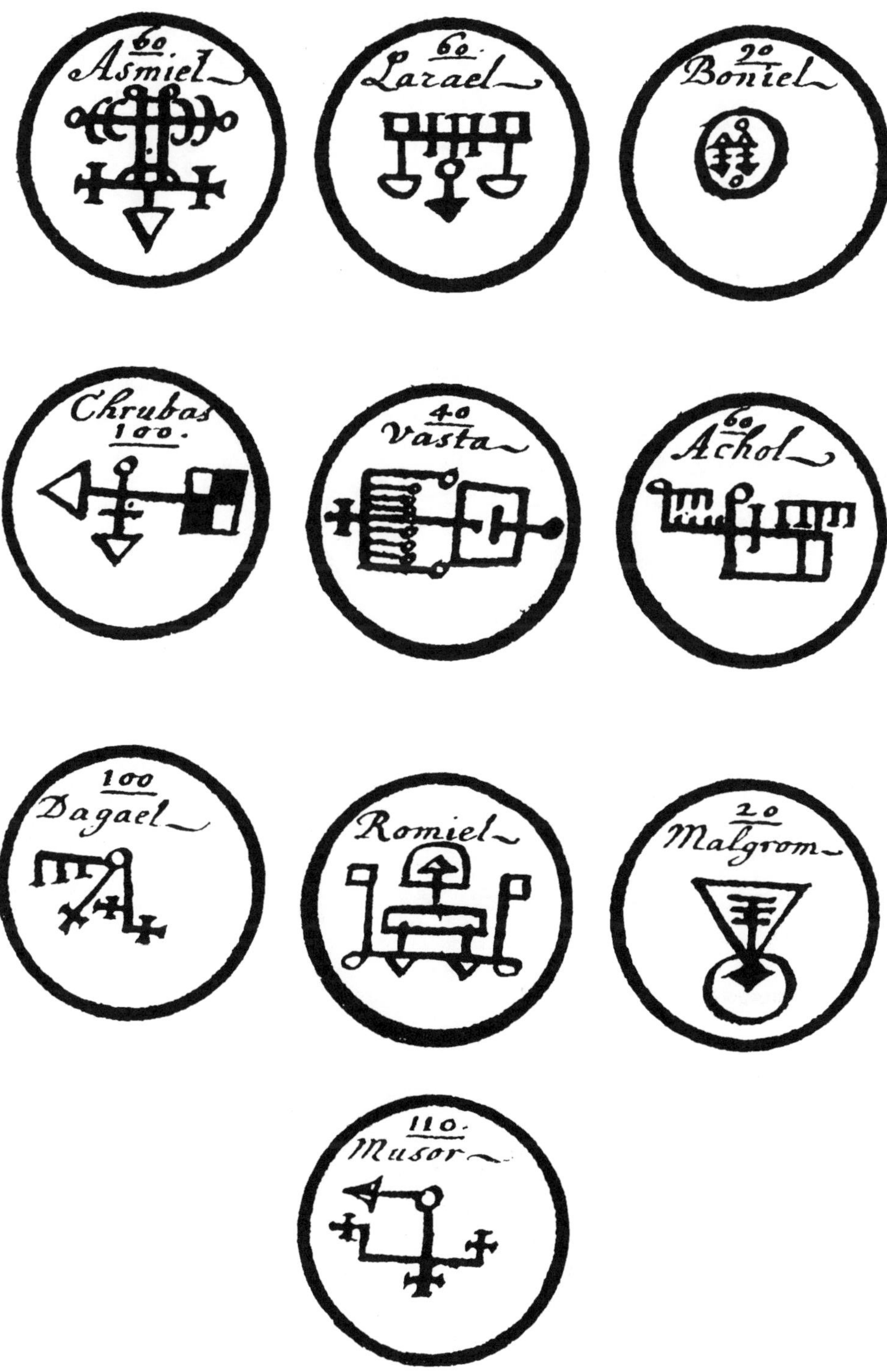

[1]The Names & Seals of Symiel's ten Dukes for the night.

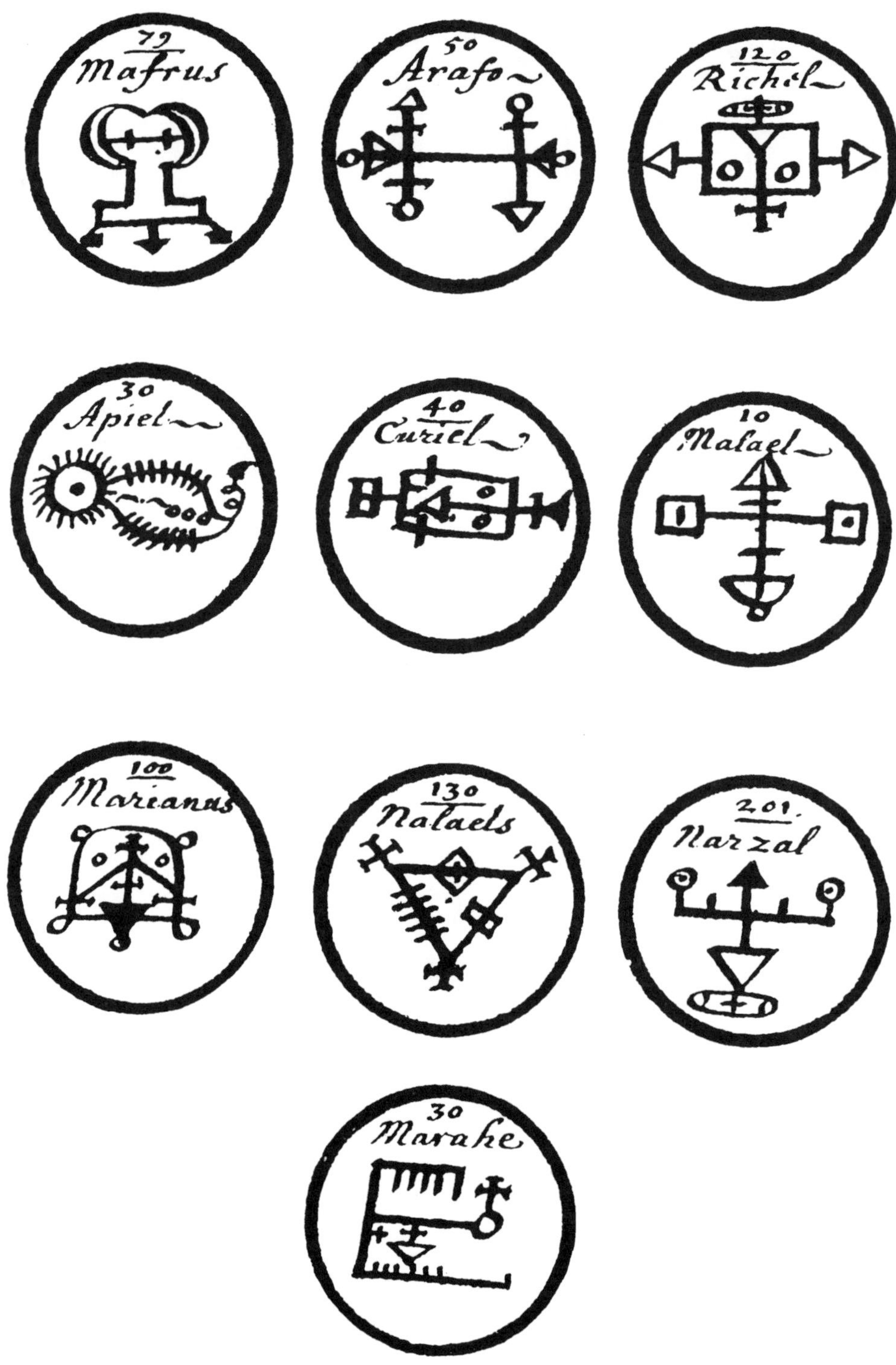

[1] *Seventy seventh sheet Dr Rudd.*

The fifteenth Spirit in order (but the third under [Demoriel] the Emperor of the North) is **Armadiel** who Ruleth as King in the North East part and hath many Dukes under him besides their Servants whereof we shall make mention of 15 of the chief Dukes who hath 260[1] Servants to attend them these Dukes are to be called in the day & night dividing the same into 15 parts beginning at the Sun Rising with the first Spirit and so on till you come to the last Division of the night.[2] These Spirits are all good by nature and willing to do your will in all things.[3]

The Conjuration

I Conjure thee O thou mighty & potent Prince Armadiel &c.

[The Supplementary Conjurations from the *Steganographia,* Book 1, Chapter XV:

Armadiel marbevo pelrusan neor chamyn aldron pemarson Cathornaor pean lyburmy Caveron Thorty abesmeron vear larso charnoty theor Caveos myat drupas Camedortys ly paruffes ernoty mesoryn elthy chaor atiel; lamesayn rovemu fabelrusin, friato chasalon pheor thamorny mesardiel pelusy madiel baferoty sarreon prolsoyr asenosy cameltruson. (*conjuratio*)

Armadiel afran meson Casayr pelodyn, Cavoti Chameron thersorvy marbevon pheor Casoyn myrvosy lyburmy deor fabelronton. Chubis archmarson. *conjuratio*)]

[Armadiel's Seal]

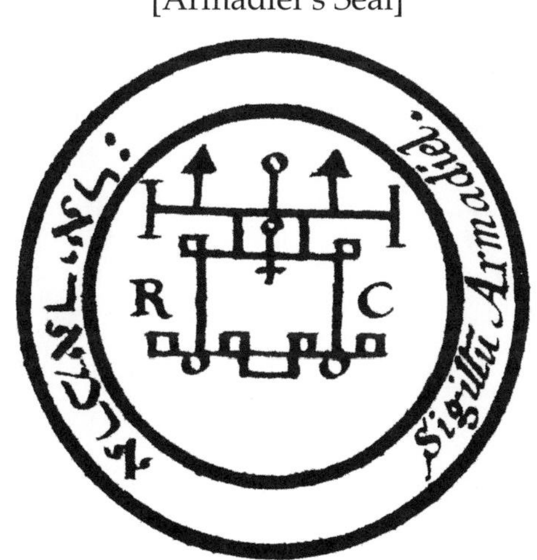

---

[1] S3: *"1260"*; S2: *"260"*; S1: *"'1260' other copy '260'"*.

[2] This is an interesting variation on Planetary hours, where each of the 15 Spirits is responsible for just one-fifteenth of the daylight hours.

[3] W1: *"**Armadiel.** Ruler as King in the N.E. part under Demoriel, he has many Dukes under him besides Servants, whereof we shall mention 10 of the ~~day~~ Dukes who have 260 Servants to attend them. Note these Dukes are to be called Day & night dividing the same into 15 Equal parts beginning with the first Spirit at the ☉ rising & so on till You come to the last division of the night. They are all willing to do your will / see page"*.

The Names & Seals of 8 of Armadiel's Dukes that serve both for Day & night.[1]

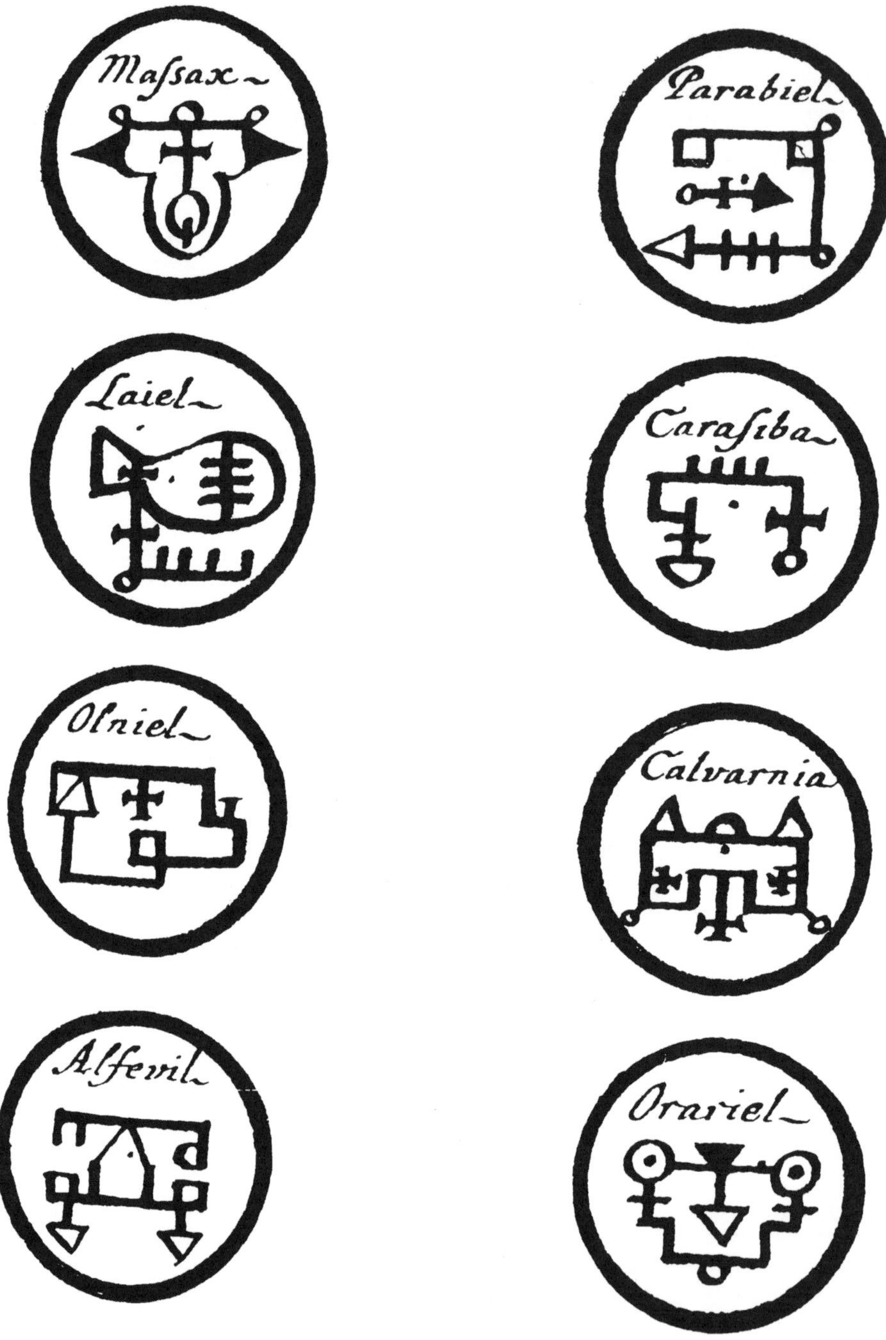

[1] This is a deviation from the usual practice up to this point of separating the Sprits into day and night Spirits. [The next page has been intentionally left blank]

[left intentionally blank]

The Names & Seals of Armadiel's seven other Dukes that serve for day & night.

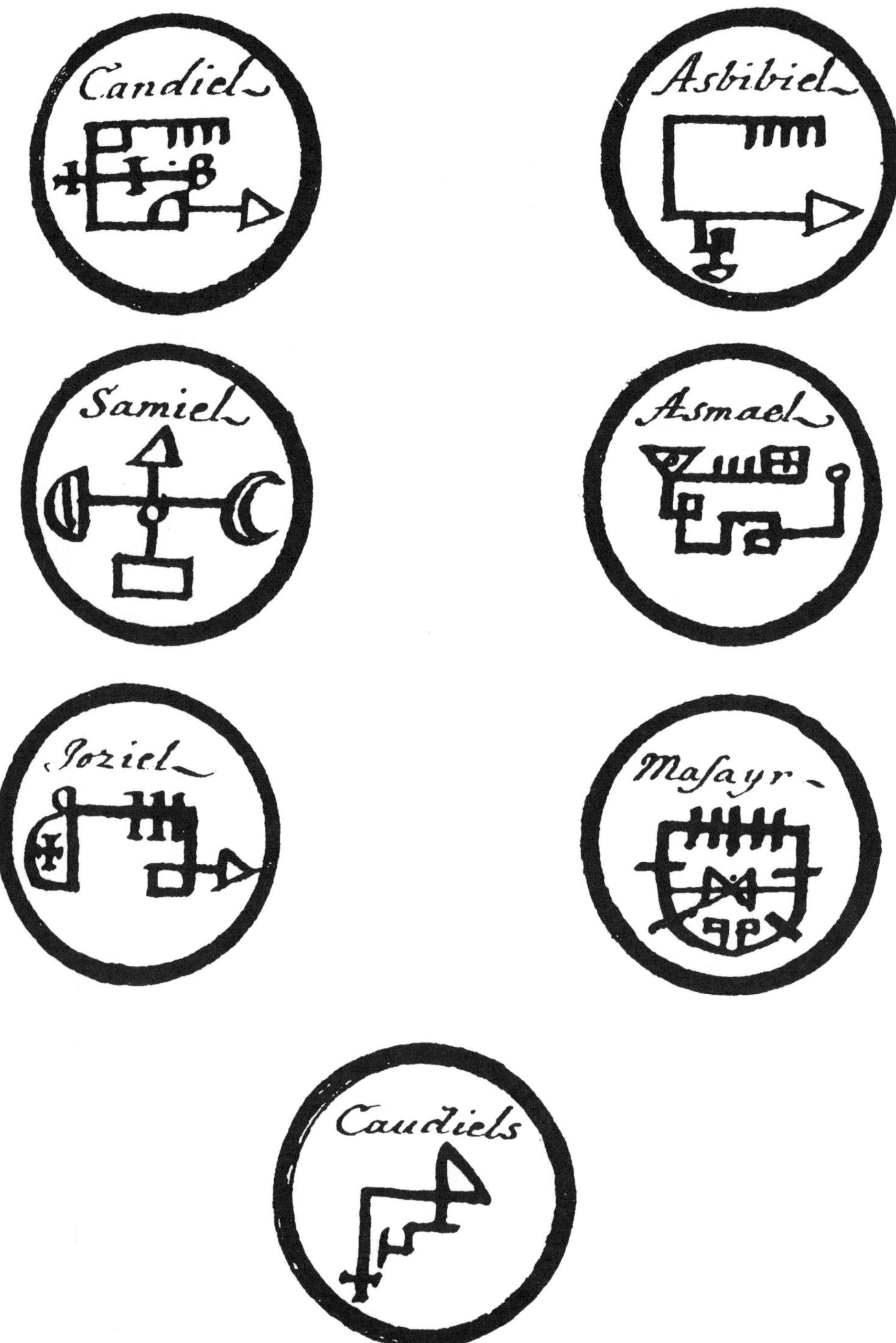

[1]The 16th Spirit in Order (but the fourth under [Demoriel] the Emperor of the North) is **Baruchas**, who Ruleth as King in the East and by North, and hath many Dukes and other Servant Spirits to attend him whereof we shall make mention of 15 of the chief Dukes that belong to the day and night who hath 7040 servants to attend on them they are all by nature good and are willing to obey &c. You are to call those spirits in the same manner as is showed in the foregoing Exemplary [example of] Armadiel and his Dukes, that is in dividing the day & night into 15 parts &c. The Names and Seals follows.[2]

The Conjuration

I Conjure thee O thou mighty and potent Prince Baruchas &c.

[The Supplementary Conjurations from the *Steganographia,* Book 1, Chapter XVI:

Baruchas malvear chemorsyn charnotiel bason ianocri medusyn aprilty casmyron sayr pean cavoty medason peroel chamyrsyn cherdiel avenos nosear penaon sayr chavelonti genayr pamelron frilcha madyrion onetiel fabelronthos. (*conjuratio*)

Baruchas Mularchas chameron notiel pedarsy phroys lamasay myar chalemon phorsy fabelrontho theras capean Vear almonym lierno medusan thersiel peatha thumar nerosyn cralnothiel peson segalry madon scoha bulayr. *(conjuratio spiritus)*]

[Baruchas' Seal]

[1] *Seventy Eight Sheet Dr Rudd.*

[2] W1: *"**Baruchas**. Is 4th under the Emperor of the North and rules as King in the East and by North & has many Dukes & other Servants to attend him, whereof we shall mention 15 Chief dukes belonging to the day and night who have 7040 Spirits to attend them. They are all good & willing to obey you & are to be called in the foregoing Example of Armadiel & their Names hence. See page"*. The MSS continues with 13 pages of Seals.

The names and seals of Baruchas' Eight Dukes

The names and Seals of 7 other Dukes belonging to Baruchas.

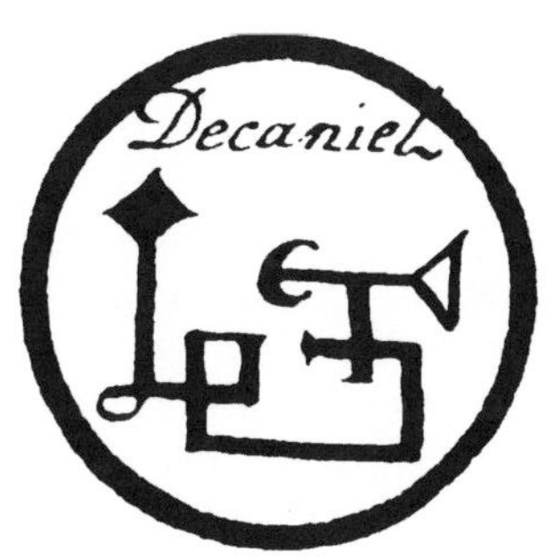

[The Eleven Wandering Princes]

[1]In this place we are to give you the understanding of Eleven mighty potent Princes[2] with their Servants who wander up and down in the air and never continue [stay] in one place, whereof one of the chief and first is called **Geradiel**[3] who hath 18150 Servants to attend him for he hath no Dukes nor Princes therefore he is to be Invocated alone, but when he is called there comes a great Number of his Servants with him, but more or less according to the ~~planetary motion~~ hour of the day or night he is called in.

For in the 2 first hours of the day (according to the planetary motion) and the 2 second hours of the night there come 470 of his servants with him, & in the two second hours of the day and ~~in the two~~ and in the two third ~~hou~~ hours of the night there comes 590 of his Servants with him, and in the two third hours of the day and in the two fourth hours of the night there comes 930 of his Servants with him; and in the two fourth hours of the day and in the two fifth hours of the night there comes 1560 of his servants. And in the two fifth hours of the day and in the 2 sixth hours of the night there comes 13710 of his Servants, and the sixth or last hours of the day there comes 930 of his Servants and they are all indifferently good by nature and will obey in all things willingly.[4]

---

[1] W1: Has the heading *"The Wandering Princes.*

[2] Or Dukes.

[3] Geradiel will be found in Chapter XXI of Book I of Trithemius' *Steganographia.* No subsidiary Dukes are given for Geradiel.

[4] W1: *"In this place we are to give you to understand of mighty and potent Princes with their servants, who wander up and down in the Air and contained not in one place whereof one of the Chief and first is called* ***Geradiel*** *who rules over 18150 Servants attending him for he has no dukes or princes therefore he is to be Invocated alone but when he is called there comes a great Number of servants with him, but more or less according to the hour of the day or night he is called in, for in the two first hours of the day or night according to the planetary motion there come 470 Servants, and in the two* 2nd *hours of the day or night there comes 570 Servants, and the two* 3rd *hours of the day & the four hours of night there comes 930 & in the two fourth oh the day & two fifth of the night there comes 1560 & in the 2* ~~*fourth*~~ *fifth of the day & two* 6th *of the night there comes 13710 & the 2* 6th *of the day there comes 930 of his good Servants, they are all indifferently & will obey in all things willingly. Note. In calling these wandering Spirits it is No matter which way you stand in the Circle with Your face, but in those Spirits who have fixed Mansions the face must be directed towards that* ~~*part of the Mansion*~~ *point of the compass where the Spirit called hath his Mansion or fixed Residence".*

The Conjuration

I Conjure thee O thou mighty & potent prince Geradiel [1]*who wandereth here & there in the air with thy servants, I Conjure thee Geradiel that thou forthwith appear with thy attendants in the first hour of the day here before me, in this Crystal stone or here before this Circle*[2]

[The Supplementary Conjurations from the *Steganographia,* Book 1, Chapter XXI:

Geradiel onayr bulesar modran pedarbon sazevo nabor vielis proyn therdial masre reneal Chemarson cuhadiam almona saelry penoyr satodial chramel nadiarsi thorays Vayr pean esridiel cubal draony myar dearsy colludarsy menador atotiel Cumalym drasnodiar parmy sosiel almenarys satiel chulty dealny peson duarsy cubet fruony maroy futiel, fabel merusi venodran pralto lusior lamedon fyvaro larboys theory malrosyn. *(carmen conjurationis)*

Geradiel osayl chamerusin chulti pemarsoniel dayr fayr Chaturmo les bornatyn ersoty camylor sayr fabelmerodan cosry damerson maltey nabelmerusyn. (*carmen coniurationis)*]

[Geradiel's Seal]

[1] *Seventy ninth sheet Dr Rudd.*

[2] It is interesting to see that here the Sprit is given the option of two modes of manifestation, the Crystal (as used by Dee for example) or the Triangle. This option appears in many grimoires. W1: *"I conjure thee oh thou Mighty & potent Prince **Geradiel** who wanders here & there in the air with thy Servants, that thou forthwith appear here with thy attendants in this the 5th hour of the day, here before me in this Circle."*

These next [and second] of those wandering Spirits is Prince **Buriel** who hath many Dukes and other Servants which do attend on him to do his will, they are all by nature evil & as are hated of all other spirits, they appear roguish and [manifest] in the form of a serpent with a Virgin's head and speaketh with many [different] voices, they are to be called in the night because they hate the day and in the planetary hours whereof, we shall make mention of twelve of the chief spirits which are Dukes that answer to the 12 planetary hours of the night who hath 880 Servants to attend on them in the night [shared] amongst them, their Names and Seals as followeth &c.[1]

The Conjuration

I Conjure thee O thou mighty & potent Prince Buriel who wandereth here and there in the air with thy Dukes and other [of] thy servants Spirits, I conjure thee Buriel that thou forthwith appear with thy attendants in the first hour of the night here before me in this Crystal stone (or here before this Circle) in a fair and comely shape to do my will in all things I shall desire of you &c.

[The Supplementary Conjurations from the *Steganographia,* Book 1, Chapter XXII:

Buriel mastfoyr chamerusyn, noel pean Ionachym mardusan philarsii, pedarym estlis carmoy boycharonti phroys fabelronti, mear Laphany vearchas, clareson, notiel, pador aslotiel, marsyno reneas, Capedon, thismasion melro, lavair carpentor, thurneam camelrosyn. (*conjuratio*)

Buriel, Thresoy chamerontis, hayr plassu, nadiel, marso, neany, pean, sayr, fabelron, chaturmo, melros, ersoty caduberosyn. (*conjuratio*)]

[Buriel's Seal]

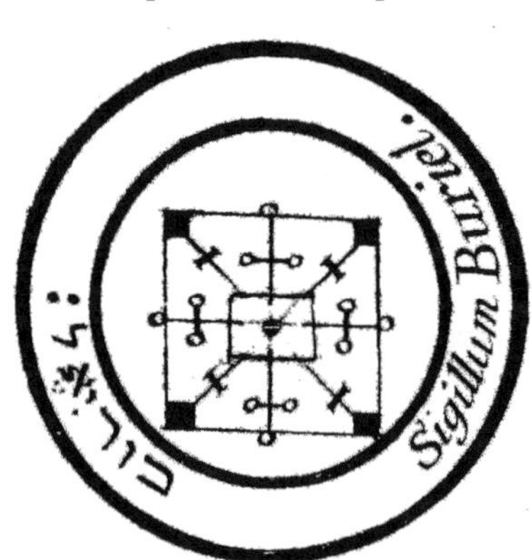

[1] W1: *"**Buriel.** Is the 2nd Wandering Spirit and he has many Kings Dukes and other Servants to attend him & do his will. They are not good by nature but Evil and are hated by all other Spirits, they appear roguish & in the form of a Serpent with a Virgins head and speak with Many voices, they are o be called in the night because they hate the day & in the planetary hour, we shall mention 12 of the Chief Spirits or Dukes that answer the 12 Planetary hours of the Night who have serving them 880 Servants to attend them – their names & Seals as follows see page".*

The names & Seals of Buriel's 12 [Night] Dukes

The third of these wandering Princes is called **Hydriel**[1] who hath 100 great Dukes besides 200 lesser Dukes and servants without number whereof we shall make mention of 12 of the chief Dukes who hath 1320 servants to attend them, they are to be called in the day as well as in the night according to the Planetary Motion, the first beginneth with the first hour of the day or night, and so successively on till you come to the last.

They appear in the form of a serpent with a Serpent's head and face yet they are very Courteous and willing to obey, they delight most in & about water and all moist grounds.[2]

The Conjuration

I Conjure thee O thou mighty & potent prince Hydriel &c.[3]

[The Supplementary Conjurations from the *Steganographia,* Book 1, Chapter XXIII:

Hydriel, apron chamerote, satrus pean nearmy chabelon, vearchas, belta, nothelmy phameron, arsoy pedaryn onzel, Lamedo drubel areon veatly cabyn & noty maleros haytny pesary does, pen rasi medusan ilcohi person. *(carmen)*

Hydriel omar, penadon epyrma narsoy greol fabelrusin adiel pedrusii nozevi melrays vremy pean larfoy naes chemerotyn. (*conjuratio*)]

[Hydriel's Seal]

[1] T1, S1""*Hidriel*".

[2] W1: *"**Hydriel**. Is the 3rd Wandering Prince & has 100 great dukes besides 200 lesser dukes & Servants innumerable whereof we shall Mention 12 of the Chief dukes ~~besides 200 lesser Dukes~~ who have 1320 Servants to attend hem, they are to be called in the day or night according to the planetary hour, the first begins with the planetary 1st hour of the day or night & so successively on till you come to the last, they appear in the form of a Serpent with a Serpents head & face, they are very Courteous & willing to obey they delight most in and about water and moist Ground, their names & Seals See page".*

[3] This line is also repeated after the Seal of Hydriel.

[1]The names & Seals of Hydriel's 12 Dukes.

[1] *The Eightieth sheet Dr Rudd.*

The fourth in order of these wandering Princes is called **Pyrichiel**,[1] He hath no Princes nor Dukes but Knights whereof we shall make mention of Eight of the chief [Knights] they being sufficient for practice, who have 2,000 Servants under them, they are to be called according to the planetary motion [hours]; they are all good by nature, and will do your desires willingly. Their Names and Seals are as follows[2]

The Conjuration

I conjure thee O thou potent and mighty Prince Pyrichiel &c.

[The Supplementary Conjurations from the *Steganographia,* Book 1, Chapter XXIV:

Pyrichiel marfoys chameron, nael peanos pury lames iamene famerusyn mearlo canorson theory torsa, nealthis dilumeris maphroy carful ameor thubra phorsotiel chrebonos aray pemalon layr toysi vadiniel nemor rosevarsy cabri phroys amenada machyr fabelronthis, poyl carepon vemij naslotyn. (*conjuratio*)

Pyrichiel osayr Chamerosy culty mesano dayr fabelron cathurmo pean ersoty meor iathor cabon Frilastro melrusy. (*conjuratio*)]

[Pyrichiel's Seal]

[1] S1, S3: *"Pirichiel"*; T1: *"Pyrichiel"*.

[2] W1: *"**Pirichiel**. The 4th Wandering Prince has no princes or dukes, but knights whereof we shall Mention 8 of the chief who have 2000 Servants to attend them. They are to be called according to the planetary hour & are all good by nature and will do your desires willingly. their Names & Seals".*

The Names and Seals of Pyrichiel's Eight Knights

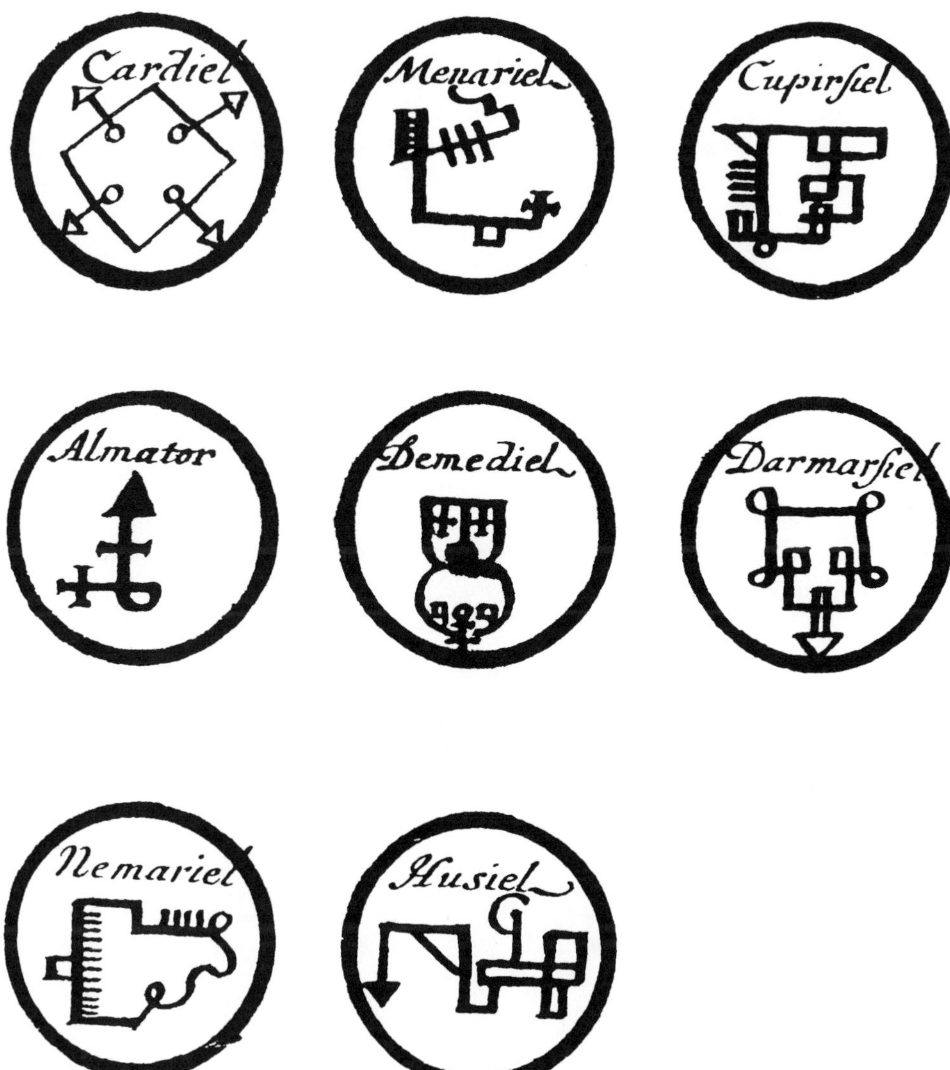

The fifth wandering Prince is called **Emoniel** who hath 100 Princes and chief Dukes besides 20 other Dukes and multitudes of Servants to attend them Whereof we shall mention twelve of the chief Princes or Dukes who hath 1320 Dukes and other inferior servants to attend them, they are all by nature good and willing to obey.

They are to be called in the day as well as in the night, and according to the Planetary order. It is said they Inhabit in woods. Their Names and Seals as follows[1]

The Conjuration

I Conjure thee O thou mighty and potent prince Emoniel &c.

[The Supplementary Conjurations from the *Steganographia,* Book 1, Chapter XXV:

Emoniel aproisi chamerusyn thulnear peanos mevear, pandroy cralnotiel narboy mavy fabelrontos, arliel chemorsyn nety pransobyr diviel malros ruelty person roab chrumelrusyn. *(carmen conjurationis)*

Emoniel lebos chameroty meor pemorsy dyor medulorsyn fray pean, Crymarsy melrosyne vari chabaryn dayr. Aschre cathurmo fabelron ersoty marduse. (*carmen conjurationis*)]

[Emoniel's Seal]

[1] W1: *"**Emoniel**. He has 100 Princes and Chief Dukes, besides 20 other dukes & multitudes of ~~Dukes~~ Servants to attend them, whereof we shall mention 12 of the princes & chief Dukes who have 1300 Superior Servants to attend them. They are all by nature good & willing to obey they are to be called in the day time as well as in the Night & according to the planetary hour they inhabit Mostly in woods".*

[1]The names and Seals of Emoniel's 12 Dukes.

[1] *Eighty first Sheet Dr Rudd.*

The Sixth wandering Spirit & Prince is called **Icosiel** who hath 100 Dukes and 300 Companies besides other Servants which are more inferior, whereof we have taken 15 of the chief Dukes for practice they being sufficient and they have 2200 Dukes and servants to attend on them. They are all of a good nature and will do what they are commanded, they appear mostly in houses because they delight most there. They are to be called in the 24 hours of the day and night, that is to be divided the 24 hours into 15 parts according to the number of spirits beginning at the first at Sun rise and end at Sun rising the next day.

[The Supplementary Conjurations from the *Steganographia,* Book 1, Chapter XXVI:

Icosiel aphorsi chamersyn thulneas ianotiel menear peanos crasnotiel medusan matory fabelron ersonial cathurmos laernoty besraym alphayr lamedonti nael cabelron. (*conjuratio*)

Icosiel osayr penarizo chulti meradym phrael melchusy dayr pean cathurmo fabelron ersoti chamerusan iltham pedaly fuar melrosyn crymarsy phroyson. (*conjuratio*)]

Their Names & Seals follows.[1]

[Icosiel's Seal]

[1] W1: *"**Icesiel.** Has 100 dukes & 200 Companies besides other servants who are more Inferior whereof we have taken 15 of the Chief Dukes for Practice, they being sufficient & they have 2200 dukes and servants to attend them. They are all good natured & willing to do what they are desired. They appear mostly in houses, because they delight therein. They are to be called in the 24 hours of the day & night i.e. dividing the 24 hours into 15 parts, as according to the No's of Spirits beginning at Sun rising with the first & ending with the last at ☉ rise next day".*

The Names and Seals of Icosiel's Eight Dukes [of the Day?].

The Names and Seals of Icosiel's seven other Dukes [of the Night?].

[1]The seventh of these wandering Spirits and Princes is called **Soleviel** who hath under his command 200 Dukes and 200 Companies who changeth every year their places, they have many to attend them. They are all very good, and very obedient and here we shall mention twelve of the chief Dukes where the first Six are Dukes one year and the other six the next [year] following and so rule in order to serve their Prince, who have under them 1840 Servants to attend on them, they are all to be called in the day as well as in the night, according to the planetary motion [hours].[2]

[The Supplementary Conjurations from the *Steganographia,* Book 1, Chapter XXVII:

Soleviel marfoy chamerusyn oniel dabry diviel pean vear, lasmyn cralmoty pedaros drumes, pean vear chameron loes madur noty basray erxo nadrus peliel thabron thyrso ianothin vear perasy loes pean nothyr fabelron bavery drameron eschiran pumelon meor dabrios crimorsiel penyvear nameroy lyernoti pralsones. (*carmen conjurationis*)

Soleviel curtiel chamerusyn saty pemalros dayr ianothy cathurmo parmoy iotran lamedon frascu penoy ilthon fabelmerusyn. (*conjuratio*)]

Their Names and Seals are as follows.

[Solviel's Seal]

[1] *Eighty second sheet Dr Rudd.*

[2] W1: *"**Soleviel**. Soleviel is the 7th Wandering Spirit & has under his command 200 Dukes and 200 Companies who change their places Every year, they have Many to attend them & are all good and very obedient & here we shall mention 12 of the Chief Dukes whereof the first 6 rule one year and the other the following [year] & so rule in order, they have 1840 Servants to attend them. They are all to be called in the day as well as in the night according to the planetary hour".*

The names & Seals of Soleviel's 12 Dukes [of the Day and Night]

The Eight[h] of these wandering Princes is called **Menadiel** who hath 20 Dukes and a hundred Companies and many other Servants they being all of a good Nature and very obedient, here we have mentioned six of the chief Dukes, and six of the under Dukes who hath 390 Servants that attend them.

Note you must call these according to the planetary motion [hours, with] a Duke in the first hour and Companion in the next [hour,] and so successively on through all the hours of the day and night whose names and Seals are as follows.[1]

[The Supplementary Conjurations from the *Steganographia,* Book 1, Chapter XXVIII:

Menadiel marfoy peanos onael chamerusyn theor ianothy ofayr melros tudayr penorsyn sachul tarno rosevas peathan asiel morfoy maplear casmyron storeal marpenu nosayr pelno dan layr thubra elnodion carsephy drumos fabelmerusyn andu pean, purays calbyn nachir loes philuemy casaner. (*conjuratio*)

Menadiel murty chamerose dayr pean cathurmo phameron ersoti pray sarvepo, fabel merii rean, charon ietlas Meduse fayr lamerosyn alty merchahon. (*conjuratio*)]

[Menadiel's Seal]

[1] W1: *"**Menadiel**. Has 20 dukes and 100 Companies & many other Servants, they being all of a good nature & very obedient, we have mentioned 6 of the Chief & 6 of the under dukes, who have 390 Servants that attend them – Note you must call a duke in the 1st planetary hour, and a companion in the Next & so successively ~~who~~ through all the hours of the day & night. Their Names & Seals. See page".*

The names and Seals of Menadiel's twelve Dukes [of the Day and Night]

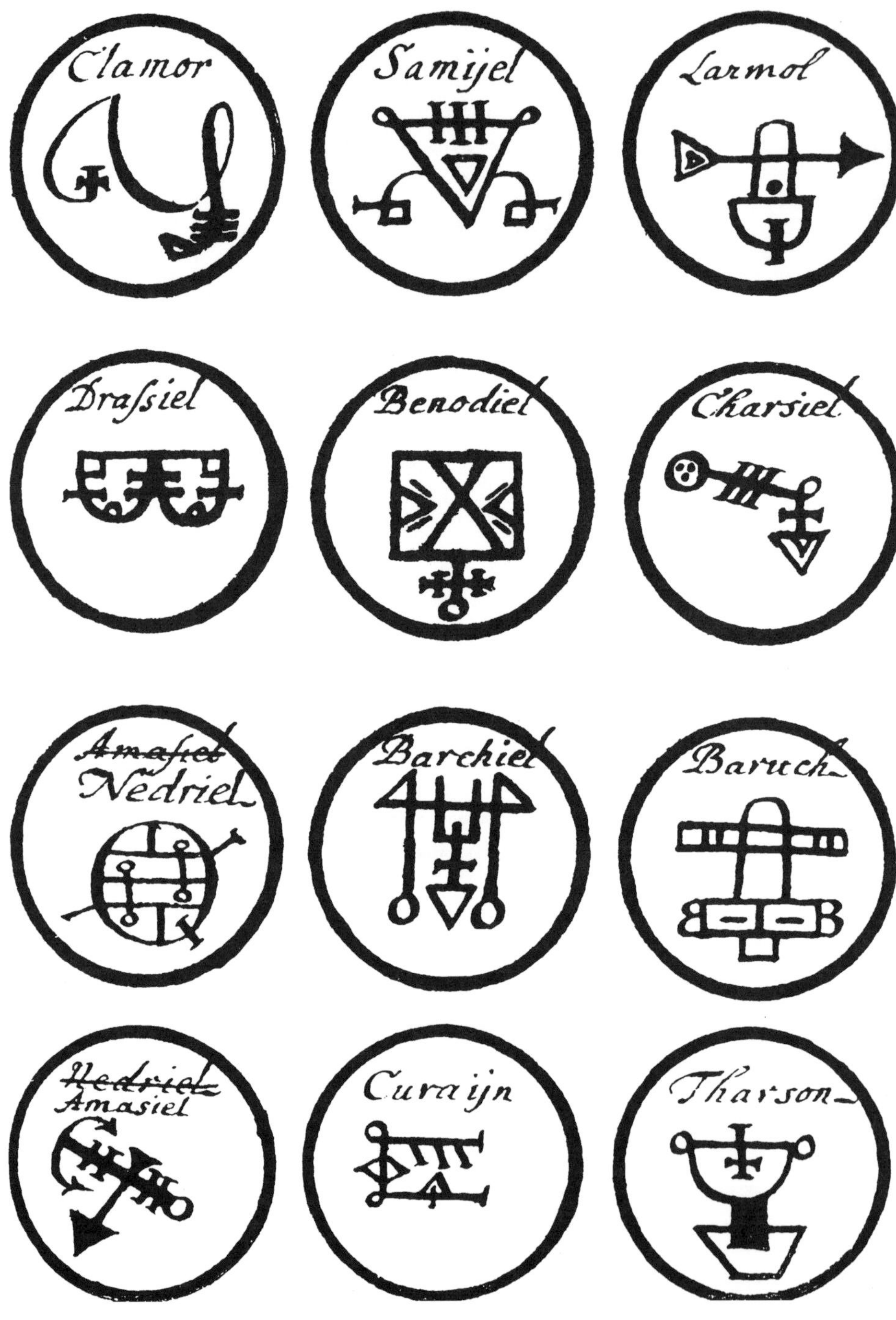

[1]The Ninth wandering Spirit [or Prince] in Order is called **Macariel** who hath 40 Dukes besides many other Inferior Servants to attend him. Whereof we shall mention twelve of the chief Dukes who have 700 Servants to attend them, They are all good by nature and willing to do the will of the Exorcist, they appear in divers forms but mostly in the form of a Dragon with a Virgin's head, these Dukes are to be called in the day as well as in the night according to the planetary order [hour].[2]

Their Names and Seals are as follows.

The Conjuration[3]

[The Supplementary Conjurations from the *Steganographia,* Book 1, Chapter XXIX:

Macariel myrno chamerosy purmy maresyn amos peanam olradu, chabor ianoes fabelron dearsy chadon ulyses Almos rutiel pedaron deabry madero neas lamero dearsy, thubra dorpilto melrosyne draor chalmea near, parmon dearsy charon alnodiel parsa radean, maroy reneas charso gnole, melrosin te dranso casmar ebroset. Landrys masfayr therafonte noel amalan. *(carmen)*

Macariel osayr chamerose chulti pesano dayr fameron; cathurmo pean ersoty lamedon sovapor casrea mafyr. Ianos tharfia, peathanon acri pean etion matramy. *(carmen conjurationis)*]

[Macariel's Seal]

[1] *The Eighty third sheet Dr Rudd.*

[2] W1: *"**Mecariel**. Has 40 dukes besides other inferior Servants to attend him, they are all good, we shall mention 12 of the chief dukes, who have 400 Servants to attend them. They appear in diverse forms, but chiefly in that of a dragon with a Virgin's head. These dukes can be called day or night according to the planetary hour".*

[3] H1: There is no following text, which the copyist has omitted or forgotten.

The Names and Seals of Macariel's 12 Dukes [of Day and Night].

The tenth wandering Spirit [or Prince] in Order is Called **Uriel**[1] who hath ten chief Dukes and 100 Under Dukes with many servants to attend him, they are all by nature evil and will not obey willingly and are very false in their doings, they appear in the form of a Serpent with a ~~fiery~~ Virgin's head and face. Whereof we shall mention but the chief ten Dukes who hath 650 Companies and servants to attend them. Their Names and Seals are as follows.[2]

[The Supplementary Conjurations from the *Steganographia,* Book 1, Chapter XXX:

Uriel marfoys lamedonti noes, chameron, anducharpean phusciel arsmony tuerchoy iamersyn nairiel penos raseon loes vear fabelruso cralty layr parlis meraii mear, thubra aslotiel dubyr reanu navosti masliel pedonyto chemarphin. (conjuratio)

Uriel Aflan pemason cosayr chameron, chulty fabelmeron deyr pean, cathurmo merosyn ersoti chalmon savepo Meduse rean lamerosyn. (*conjuratio*)]

[Uriel's Seal]

[1] "Vriel" in the text, but changed to modern convention "Uriel". Uriel was of course also a major Archangel.

[2] W1: *"**Uriel.** Is 10th Wandering Spirit & has 10 Chief dukes and 100 other dukes with many Servants to attend hem, they are by nature Evil and false in their doings, and will not willingly obey, They appear in the from of a Serpent with a Virgins head & face, the 10 Chief which we shall mention have 650 Servants to attend them – see page".*

The Names and Seals of Uriel's ten chief Dukes

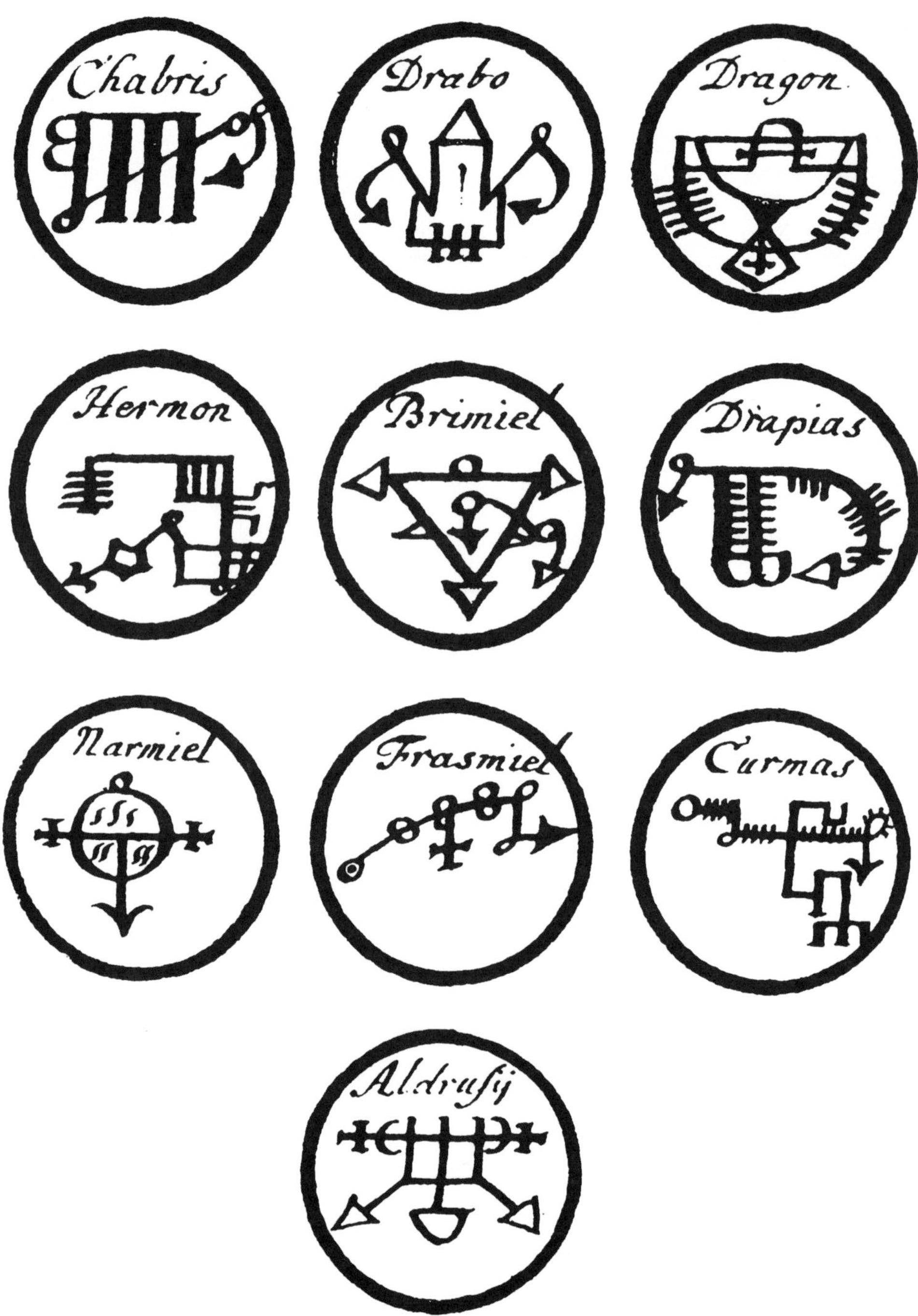

[1]The Eleventh and last Prince of this wandering Order is called **Bidiel** who hath under his Command Twenty chief Dukes and two hundred other Dukes more inferior besides very many Servants. These Dukes changeth every year their Office [specialities] and place, they are all good and willing to obey the Exorcist in all things and they appear very beautiful in human shape whereof we shall mention here ten of the chief Dukes who ~~ereof~~ have 2400 servants to attend them.[2]

Their Names and Seals as follows.

[The Supplementary Conjurations from the *Steganographia,* Book 1, Chapter XXXI:

Bydiel marchan chamerosi philtres maduse vear casmyron cralnoti: pean devoon fabelros eltida camean veor. Oniel vear thyrso liernoty: ianos prolsato chanos elasry peanon elsathas melros notiel pen soes probys chyras lesbroy mavear iothan liernoti chrymarson *(carmen conjurationis)*

Bydiel maslo chameron theory madias near fabelron thiamy marfoy vear pean liernoty calmea drules: Thubra pleory malresa teorty melchoy vemo chosray. *(carmen)*]

[Bidiel's Seal]

[1] *The Eighty fourth sheet Dr Rudd.*

[2] W1: *"**Bidiel**. The 11th and last Wandering Spirit is called Bidiel, and he commands 20 Chief & 200 inferior dukes with Many Servants. These Dukes change their office & place every year, they are all very good natured and willing to obey the exorcist in all things. They appear very beautiful in human shape & here we mention 10 of the Chief who have 2440 Servants to attend them – Their names & Seals are as follows".*

The Names and Seals of Bidiel's ten Great Dukes.

[Conjurations]

The Conjuration to the Wandering Spirits [Princes].[1]

I Conjure thee O thou Mighty & potent Prince Bidiel who wandereth here and there in the air with thy Dukes and other of thy servants. I conjure thee Bidiel that thou forthwith appear with thy attendants in this first hour of the day here before me in this Crystal Stone or here before this Circle in a fair and comely shape to do my will in all things that I shall desire of you &c.

Note this * mark in the Conjuration following, and go on as it follows there.[2]

The Conjuration[3]

[1] W1: "The Conjuration of the Wandering Spirits." This conjuration is applicable to all the preceding eleven Wandering Princes. This Conjuration is written on folio 195v just before the "Names and Seales of Bidiel's tenn Great Dukes", and so is slightly out of place. We have taken the liberty of moving it one page forward so that it falls after Bidiel's Dukes, where it more logically fits.

[2] W1: *"I conjure thee O thou mighty and potent Prince Bidiel who wanders here and there with thy dukes and other princes with thy Spirits. I conjure thee Bidiel that thou forthwith appear here, thy attendants in this, the 1st hour of the day here before me in this Crystal Stone, or here before this Circle in a fair and comely Manner, to do my will in all things that I shall desire. And Note the Mark + in the Conjuration following and go on as followeth afterward".*

[3] H1: There is an exact repetition of this previous Conjuration of Bidiel repeated after the Names and Seals of Bidiel's ten Great Dukes.

[The General Conjurations]

The Conjuration to the Princes that Govern the Points of the Compass[1]

[Conjuration of the Princes of the Quarters]

I Conjure thee O thou mighty and potent Prince Pamersiel who Ruleth as King in the Dominion of the East under the great Emperor Carnasiel[2] *I Conjure thee Pamersiel that forthwith thou appear with thy attendants in this first hour of the day here before me in this Crystal Stone or here before me in*[3] *this Circle in a fair & Comely shape to do my will in all things that I shall ask of you &c. Observe this mark * and [then] go on.*[4]

[Conjuration of the Emperors of the Quarters]

[5]*I Conjure thee O thou great Mighty & potent Prince Carnasiel who is the Emperor and chief King ruling in the Dominion of the East. I Conjure thee Carnasiel that thou forthwith appear.* Observe this Mark Δ and go on there as in the following

[The Conjuration of the Wandering Princes/Dukes]

The Conjuration to the 4th Emperor

To the Wandering Dukes, how to call them forth or any other Dukes that do not wander, only leaving out wandering here and there &c and only say for Princes say Dukes.

---

[1] The text here returns to the Dukes associated with the points of the compass mentioned towards the beginning of *Theurgia-Goetia.*

[2] Spelled 'Carnesiel' in the front of *Theurgia-Goetia.*

[3] Obviously this should be *outside* the Circle.

[4] W1: *"I conjure thee oh thou Mighty and Potent Prince Pameriel who rules as King in the dominion of the West under the great Emperor Carnesiel. I conjure thee Pameriel that thou forthwith appear with thy attendants in this 1st hour of the day here before me in this Crystal Stone or before this circle in fair and comely shape to do my will in all things that I shall desire of you. Observe the Mark + and go on as follows afterward".*

[5] W1: *"I conjure thee O thou great and potent Prince Carnesiel who are the Emperor and Chief King of the East. I conjure thee oh Carnesiel that thou forthwith appear – observe * and go on as follows after.*

To the Wandering Dukes or any other that do not wander to call them forth, leave out the words Wandering and for Prince say Duke &c.

*I conjure thee oh thou Mighty and Potent Duke who wanders here and there with thy Princes and servants in the Air. I conjure thee N. that thou forthwith appear. Note * and go on as follows".*

I Conjure thee O thou Mighty & potent Duke N. who wandereth here and there with thy princes, N: and other of his and thy servants in the air. I conjure thee N. that thou forthwith appear &c, Note this Δ Mark.

The Conjuration to those Dukes that do not wander but belong to the [fixed] points of the Compass.[1]

I Conjure thee O thou Mighty & potent Duke N: who Ruleth under the prince or King N. in the Dominion of the East. I Conjure thee N. that thou forthwith appear alone or with thy servants in this first or second hours of the day here before me in this Crystal Stone, or here before this Circle in a fair and comely shape to do my will in all things that I shall desire or request of you (*) I Conjure and powerfully command you N. by him that said the word and it was done, and by all the holy & powerful Angels of God who is the only Creator of heaven and earth and hell and what is contained in them, ***Adonai, El, Elohim, Elohe, Elion, Escerchy [Escerchie] Zebaoth, Jah Tetragrammaton Sadai,*** *the only Lord God of hosts, that you forthwith appear unto me here in this Crystal Stone or here before this Circle in a fair and comely ~~sort~~ shape [2]without doing any harm to me or any other Creature that the Great God* ***Jehovah*** *hath created and made but come ye peaceably visibly and affably now without delay Manifesting what I desire being Conjured by the name of the eternal Living and true God* ***Heliorin Tetragrammaton Anepheneton*** *and fulfil my demands, and persist unto the end. I Conjure & Command and Constrain you Spirit N. by* ***Alpha and Omega****, and by the name* ***Primeumaton*** *which commandeth the whole host of heaven and by all those names which Moses named when he by the power of those Names brought great plagues upon Pharaoh and all the people of Egypt,* ***Zebaoth, Eserchie, Oriston, Elion, Adonii*** *~~and~~* ***Primeumaton*** *and by the name* ***Schemata Mathia*** *which Joshua called upon and the Sun stayed his course and by the name* ***Hagios****, and by the seal of* ***Adonay****, and by* ***Aglaon***[3] ***Tetragrammaton*** *to whom all Creatures are obedient and by the dreadful Judgement of the most High God, and by the holy Angels of heaven, and by the mighty wisdom of the Omnipotent God of host[4] that you come from all parts of the world, and make rational Answers to all things that I shall ask of you. Come ye peaceably visibly and affably speaking unto me with a voice Intelligible to my understanding, therefore Come, Come ye in the name of* ***Adonai Zebaoth, Adonai Amioram***

---

[1] W1: *"Conjuration of those Dukes that do not Wander but belong to the Points of the Compass"*.

[2] *Eighty fifth sheet Dr Rudd.*

[3] H1: This is a combining of the two names which are next to each other, *"Agla"* and *"On"*. This also occurs in S1, whereas S2 and S3 show the names separately, *"Agla, On"*.

[4] H1: This should read *"Hosts"*, as it does in S1, S2 and S3.

Come why stay ye hasten, **Adonai Sadai** *the King of Kings commands you,*[1]

When he is appeared Show him the seal and pentacle of Solomon Saying *behold the Pentacle of Solomon which I have brought before your presence* as is showed in the first Book *Goetia* at the latter End of the Conjurations, also when you have had your desire of the Spirit, License him to depart as is showed in the Book *Goetia*.[2]

---

[1] W1: *"I Conjure thee oh thou Mighty & Potent Prince N. who rules under the King & Prince N. in the dominion of the East. I conjure thee N that thou forthwith appear along with thy Servants in the first or 2nd hours of the day here before me in this Crystal Stone, or here before this circle in a fair and comely form to do my will in all that I shall ask or request of you + I conjure thee N. and powerfully command you by him that spoke the word & it was done, and by all the powerful and holy names of God who is the only Creator of heaven & Earth and hell & what is contained in them.* ***Adonai. El. Elohim. Elohe. Elion. Escerchie. Zabaoth. Jah. Tetragrammaton. Sadai*** *the only Lord God of Hosts that thou forthwith appear unto me in this Crystal Stone or before this Circle in a fair and comely shape without doing any harm to me or any other living creature, that the great God Jehovah has created or made, but come peaceably visible and affably now without delay manifesting what I desire, having conjured by the Eternal Living and true God –* ***Helion. Tetragrammaton. On. Anephenaton*** *and fulfil my demands & persist to the End.*
I conjure and command thee Spirit N. by ***Alpha and Omega*** *and by the Name* ***Primeumaton*** *which commands the whole host of heaven, and by all the Names that Moses Named when he by the power of those Names brought great Plagues upon Pharaoh and all the people of Egypt –* ***Zebaoth Escherchie. Oriston. Elion. Adonai. Primeumaton*** *and by the names* ***Schemata Matthia*** *which Joshua called upon and the Sun stayed his course, and by the name Hageos and by the* ***Seal Adonai*** *and* ***by Agla, On, Tetragrammaton*** *to whom all creatures are obedient and by the dreadful Judgement of the Most high God and by the holy Angels of heaven and by the Mighty Wisdom of the Omnipotent God of Hosts, that thou come from all parts of the world and make rational answer to all things I shall ask of you – come you peacefully affably and visibly, speaking unto me with a voice intelligible to my understanding – Therefore come you in the Name of* ***Adonai Zebaoth. Adonai Amiorem.*** *Come, why stay you, Hasten Adonai Saday the King of Kings command you".*
[2] W1: *"When he is appeared show him the Pentacle & Seal of Solomon Saying 'Behold the Pentacle of Solomon which I have brought before your presence' and so proceed as is showed in the 1st book Goetia.*
At the latter ~~wherefore you have~~ End of the Conjuration also when you have had your desire of the Spirit licence him to depart as is showed in the book Goetia
Finis Partis Secundis
Die [Jupiter] April 13/613
Hour ☉ JM".

[the Method][1]

To call forth Pamersiel or any of these his Servants make a Circle in the form as is showed in the Book *Goetia* foregoing in the upper room of your house, or in a place that is airy because these spirits that are in this part [of the *Theurgia-Goetia*] are all of the air.

You may [alternatively] call the spirits into a Crystal stone four Inches [in] Diameter, set on a Table made as follows which is called the secret Table of Solomon, having his seal on your breast and the girdle about your waist as is showed in the Book *Goetia*.[2]

The form of the [Seal on the] Table is this[3]

[4]When you have thus got what is to be prepared, Rehearse the Conjuration several times i.e. whilst the Spirit comes for without doubt he will come. Note the same method is to be used in all the following spirits of the second book *Theurgia Goetia*, also the same [method is used] in Calling forth the four Kings and their Servants aforesaid.

---

[1] These instructions, which occurred earlier in the *Theurgia-Goetia* in relation to Parmersiel, are of a general nature and so are repeated here for ease of reference.

[2] W1: "**Pameriel**. This is the first Chief Spirit ruling the East under Carnesiel who has 1000 Spirits under him & is called in the day, but with great care, for they are lofty & Stubborn I shall mention 11 of their Seals (see fig.). Note that these Spirits are by nature Evil and very false, Not to be trusted with Secrets, but are excellent for driving away any Spirits from any that are haunted, as houses. To call forth Pamerial or any of his Servants, make a circle in the form as is showed in the book Goetia, before going into the upper ~~part~~ region of a house or in a place that is airy, because the place that these Spirits are in is so, they being all of the Air – You may call the Spirits into a Crystal Stone 4 inches in diameter, set on a table made as follows, which is called the secret table of Solomon See page having his Seal on your breast, and the girdle about your waist as is showed in the book Goetia".

[3] W1: "The form of the Table see plate page." In most cases the Secret Seal of Solomon is shown here (Figure 11), when it should instead be the Table of Practice (Figure 12).

[4] W1: *"When you have got what is to be prepared, rehearse the following Conjuration several times that is while the Spirit comes for he will come without doubt. Note the same Method is to be used in all the following Spirits of these two Books* Theurgia Goetia *as with Parmariel and his Servants & also the same in Calling the 4 Kings & their Servants"*.

[Timing][1]

Observe the Planetary notion [motion] in calling forth the two first [Spirits] that belong to the day, for the two first that belong to the day are to be called in the first planetary hour of the day, and the two next in the second planetary hour of the day and so on successively till you have gone through the day to the night, and through the night, till you come to the first of the day again.

So endeth the Second Book Called

Theurgia Goetia.[2]

[1] The following passage is copied here from the section on Darochiel, because it is clear that these are general remarks on the timing of evocations rather than something attributable just to Darochiel. Where there are 12 Spirits of the day, or of the night, it would be helpful to observe the corresponding Planetary hour. Remember that Planetary hours are not of 60 minutes, but are one twelfth the time between sunrise and sunset (for day hours) or sunset and sunrise (for night hours).

[2] W1 is clearly missing other sections of the *Goetia*, as is indicated by the last page of text in this part of the MSS, which reads:
"Lemegeton Seu Claviculi Solomonis Regis
The little Key of Solomon the King
The 5th part ~~Called~~ contains ordering of prayers which Wise Solomon the King used upon the Altar in the Temple, which is called Ars Nota".

The Third Book of Clavicula Solomonis Regis called

The Art Pauline

of Solomon

[Preamble on the Nature of the Planetary Hours]

This [book] is divided into two Parts; the first part of the Angels of the hours of the day and night. The Second Part of the Angels of the signs of the Zodiac as hereafter follows.

The nature of these twenty four Angels of the day and night changeth every day, and their offices is to do all things that is Attributed to the seven planets but that changeth every day also as for Example you may see in the following Treatise that the Angel Samael Ruleth the first hour of the day beginneth at Sun rising Suppose it be on a Monday in the first hour of the day (that hour is attributed to the Moon) that you Call Samael or any of his Dukes their office in that hour is to do all things that is attributed to the Moon, but if you call him or any of his Servants Dukes on ~~Munday~~ Tuesday morning at Sun rising, being the first hour of the day their office is to do all things that are attributed to Mars, and so the like [same] Rule is to be observed in the first hour of every day and the like is to be observed of the Angels and their servants that Ruleth any of the other hours either in the day or night.[1]

Observe also in making the Seals of the 24 Angels according to the time of your day & hour that ~~is~~ you call the Angel or his Servants to do your will but you cannot [make a] mistake therein if you do but observe the example that is laid down in the following work they being all fitted for the tenth day of March being on a Wednesday in the year 1641,[2] according to the old Account,[3] and to know what is attributed to the seven planets do refer you to the Books of Astrology whereof large volumes have been written.

---

[1] Introduced paragraph break. To summarise, the first Planetary hour of each day corresponds with the planet of that day. For example the first hour of Monday (Moon day) is attributed to the Moon. Hence the starting hour changes every day. This means that although Samael is always the angel of the first hour, his duties are Moon-like on Monday, Martial on Tuesday, Mercurial on Wednesday, and so on.

[2] This date 10th March 1641 also occurs in other manuscripts of the *Lemegeton*. It is not necessarily the date the manuscript was written. It could simply be an example date. It does however suggest that some of the extant manuscripts of the *Lemegeton* may stem from one either written in 1641 or later, which used 10th March 1641 as an example.

[3] The old calendar before it was reformed. Dr John Dee urged this calendar reform in 1583 after it was adopted by Catholic nations, but it was not reformed in England till 1751.

When the Seals are made according to the former directions lay it [them] on the Table of Practice[1] upon that part of the Table that is noted [inscribed] with the Character that the Lord of that Ascendant is of.[2] Then lay your hand on the Said Seal and say the Conjuration that is [written] at the latter end of the third part[3] for it serves for all [of the conjurations] only changing their names according to the time of the work.

The Perfumes are to be made of such things as are attributed to the seven planets.

Note ♂ [Mars] is to be Lord of the Ascendant Ever[y] first hour of the day whilst the Sun goes through ♈ [Aries] and ♏ [Scorpio][4]. So is ♀ [Venus] Lady of the Ascendant every first hour whilst the Sun goes through Taurus & ♎ [Libra] and so of the rest.[5]

[1] This is the table which holds the crystal, and which is very similar to Dr John Dee's Table of Practice, reproduced in Casaubon. It has seven seals for the seven planets laid out in a hexagram pattern.

[2] A sentence break has been introduced here to clarify the meaning.

[3] Art Pauline.

[4] H1: gives ♍ [Virgo] but we have corrected this as it is clearly a copyist's error. S1 correctly gives ♏ [Scorpio], which is indeed ruled by ♂ [Mars], whereas ♍ [Virgo] is not.

[5] This is truly a work of astrological magic in the same tradition of Marsilio Ficino (1433-1499) and Tomasso Campanella (1568-1639). The astrological configuration of the hour of the invocation was most important. It is something that modern texts have lost sight of, conditioned as we are nowadays to thinking of astrology as applicable solely to personal birth horoscopes, or as a New Age psychological typing and compatibility system.

[1]The Table of Practice[2]

Figure 12: The Table of Practice

[1] *Eighty Sixth Sheet Dr Rudd.*

[2] This diagram is meant to be used on the Table of Practice. Upon it, in the centre, the Crystal or Glass Receptacle should be placed. Note that each circle represents a planet in order from Saturn at the top clockwise to the Moon at top left, with the Sun in the centre. John Dee's *Tabula Sancta* serves exactly the same purpose. See Appendix 3.

The Art Pauline [Book 1]

[Spirits] Of the twenty four hours of the Day & night.

[The Hours of the Day]

The first hour of every day is ruled by an Angel called Samael[1] who hath under his Command many Dukes[2] and Servants. Whereof we shall [just] mention Eight of the chief Dukes which is sufficient for practice who hath 444 Servants to attend them, their names are as follows viz: Armeniel, Charpen,[3] Darosiel, Monasiel, Brumiel, Nestoriel, Chremas and Meresyn[4].

Now to make a Seal for any of those Eight Dukes or their chief princes Do as follows. First write the Character of the [planet which is] Lord of the Ascendant. Secondly the Moon afterwards the rest of the Planets, and then the Character of the Sign that ascends on the 12th house in that March A[nn]o 1641 being on a Wednesday & the first hour of the Day.[5]

[Then say the Conjuration &c.][6]

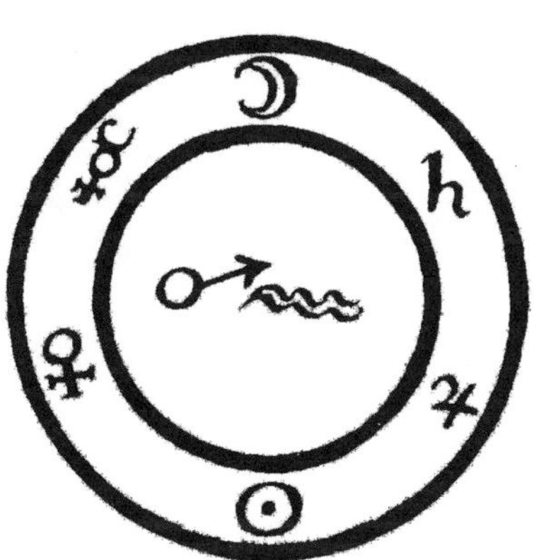

[1] Samael occurs in many places, but this one will be found in Chapter I of Book 2 of Trithemius' *Steganographia.*

[2] Probably ten chief Dukes and a 100 lesser Dukes, as do the other angels of the hours. Unlike all the others, this hour is not given a specific name.

[3] S3: "Charpon".

[4] In the manuscript *"Meresiin"* with a long second 'i'.

[5] The 10th March 1641 is used here as an example date, but it may also establish a date of original composition, or it may have been a significant date for the author.

[6] The Conjuration for Samael is to be found right at the end of the descriptions of all 24 Angels of the hours. This conjuration can be used in every case simply by replacing Samael's name with that of the appropriate angel of the hour.

The second hour of the day is called Sevormi[1] the Angel that governs the hour is called Anael[2] who hath ten chief Dukes and a 100 lesser Dukes to attend him, whereof we shall mention nine but the three first are chief, the other six are under Dukes they have 330 Servants to attend them the name of the nine are as follows Menarckos[3], Archiel, Chardiel, Orphiel, Cursiel, Elmoym[4], Quosiel, Ermosiel and Granyel[5], when you have a desire to work on the second house on Wednesday on the tenth of March, Make a Seal as was showed before in clean paper or parchment, writing first the Character of the Lord of the Ascendant then the rest of the Planets and the sign of the 12th house as you see in the sigil, and when it is made lay it on that part of the Table that hath the same Character as the Lord of the Ascendant is of, Observe this rule in all the rest.

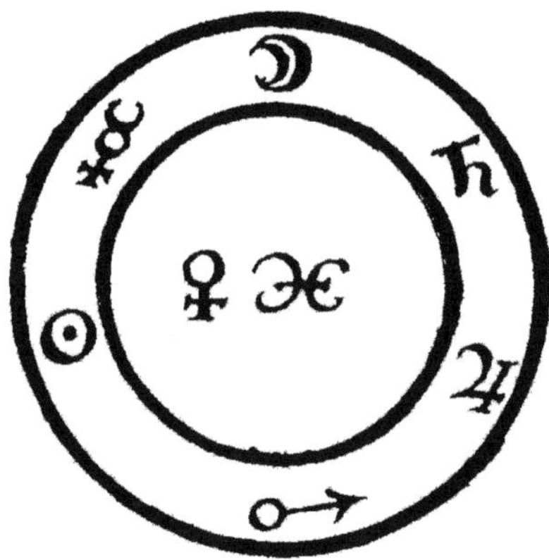

Then say the Conjuration [to be found] at the latter end [of the *Art Pauline*] &c.

---

1 S3: *"Cevorym"*.

2 Anael occurs in many grimoires but this one comes from Chapter II of Book 2 of Trithemius' *Steganographia.*

3 S3: *"Menarchos"*.

4 Spelled "Elmoiim" in the manuscript.

5 Spelled "Graniiel" in the manuscript.

The third hour of the day is called Dansor, and the Angel thereof is called Vegvaniel[1] who hath 20 chief Dukes and 200 lesser Dukes and a great many other Servants to attend them, their names are as follows, we shall here mention 4 of the chief Dukes and 8 of the lesser [Dukes] who have 1760 Servants to attend them. Scil: [lesser Dukes] Lossiel Drlemech Sadmiel, Parniel, Comadiel, Gemary Xautiel,[2] Serviel, Furiel ~~Furiel~~, [and Chief Dukes] Ansmiel Persiel Mursiel - these being sufficient for practice.

Make a Seal suitable to the day and hour of the year for the time before mentioned as here [below] you see, and you cannot Err.
Then say the Conjuration &c.

[3]**The fourth hour of the day** is called Elechin and the Angel that rules that hour is called Vachmiel who hath ten chief Dukes & a 100 under Dukes besides many servants whereof we shall mention five of the chiefs and ten of the under Dukes who have 155 servants to attend them Their names are as follows Ammiel, Larmiel, Marfiel, Ormiel, Zardiel, Emarfiel, Permiel, Queriel Strubiel, Daniel, Jermiel Thuzoz Vanesiel Lasaiel Harmiel they being sufficient for practice.

Make a Seal suitable to the hour as before directed and you cannot err. The form of it will be as this is here for the time before mentioned and when it is made do as you was before directed. And then say the Conjuration.

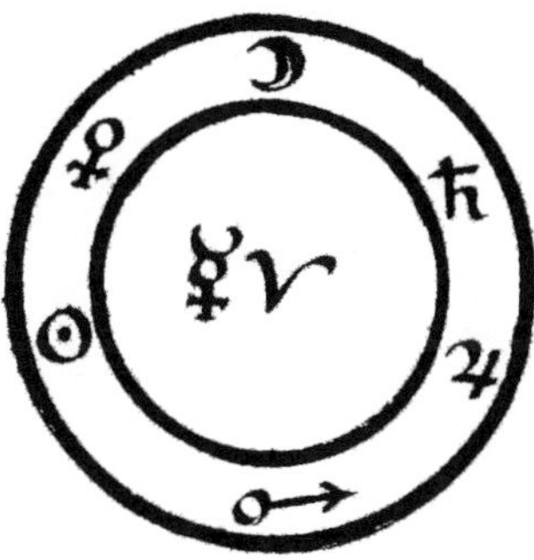

---

[1] S3: *"Vequaniel"*. Vequaniel will be found in Chapter III of Book 2 of Trithemius' *Steganographia.*

[2] S3: *"Xantiel"*.

[3] *Eighty seventh Sheet Dr Rudd.*

The fifth hour of the day is Called Tealech and the Angel Ruling it is called Sasquiel he hath ten chief Dukes and ten[1] lesser Dukes and many Servants whereof we shall mention five of the chief Dukes and ten of the lesser Dukes who have 5550 servants to attend them their names are as follows Damiel, Aramiel, Maroch, Serapiel, Putrsiel, Jameriel Futiniel, Pamersiel, Amisiel, Omezach, Lameros, Zathiel, Fustiel, Bariel being Sufficient for practice. Then make a Seal suitable for the time as I have here given you and Example for the day and year aforesaid of 1641. When you have made it lay it upon the Table as is before directed and then say the Conjuration &c.

The Sixth hour of the day is called Genapherim and the Angel Ruling that hour is Called Samiel who hath ten chief Dukes and a 100 Lesser Dukes besides many other Inferior Servants, whereof we shall mention five of the chief Dukes and ten of the lesser who have 5550 Servants to attend them. Their names are these (viz.) Arnebiel, Charuch, Medusiel, Nathniel, Pemiel, Jamiel, Jenotriel Sameon Frasiel, Zamion, Nedabar, Permon Brasiel, Camosiel, Enadar. They being sufficient for practice in this hour of the day, then make a Seal suitable to the time of the year day and hour as I have made one for the time aforesaid, then lay it on the table as is before directed. Then say the Conjuration &c.

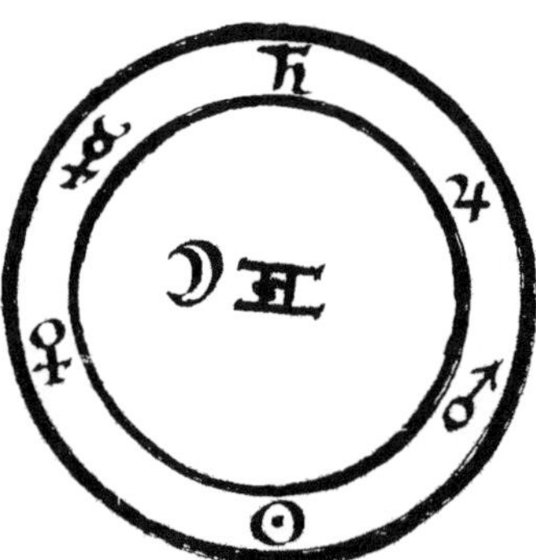

[1] Probably should be 100 as in the case of the others.

The Seventh hour of the day is called Hemarim and the Angel Governing the same is called Bargniel who hath ten chief Dukes, and 100 Under Dukes besides Servants which are very many whereof we shall make mention of five of the chief Dukes and ten of the lesser who have 600 servants to attend them in this hour. Their names are these (viz.) Abrasul, Farmos, Nostori, Mamiel, Sagiel, Harmiel, Nastrus Varmay,[1] Tusmas, Crosiel, Pastiel Venesiel, Evarim, Dusiel, Kathos. They being sufficient for practice in this hour of the day then make a Seal, lay it on the Table as before directed. Then say the Conjuration &c.

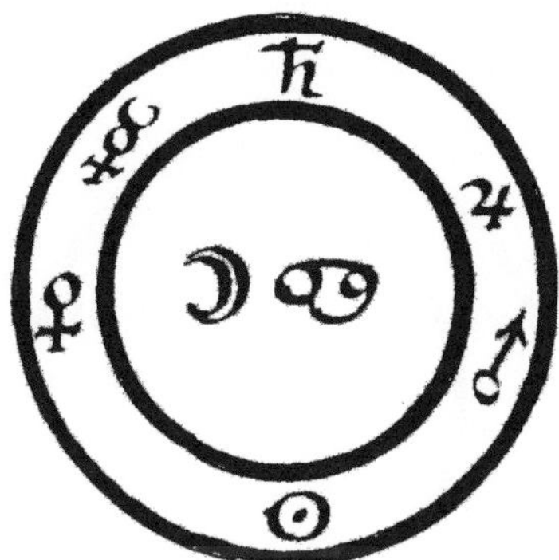

[2]**The Eight hour of the day** is called Jefamin and the Angel that Governs the same is called Osmadiel who hath ten chief Dukes and 100 lesser Dukes besides many other Servants to attend him. Whereof we shall mention five of the chief Dukes and ten of the lesser Dukes who hath 1100 Servants to attend them they being sufficient for practice. Their names are viz. Sarfiel, Amatim, Chroel, Mesiel, Lantrhos, Demaros, Janosiel, Larfuti Vemael, Thribiel, Mariel, Remafin, Theor, Framion, Ermiel. Then make a seal for the 8th hour, as is showed by this Seal which is made for an Example then lay it on the Table And say the Conjuration

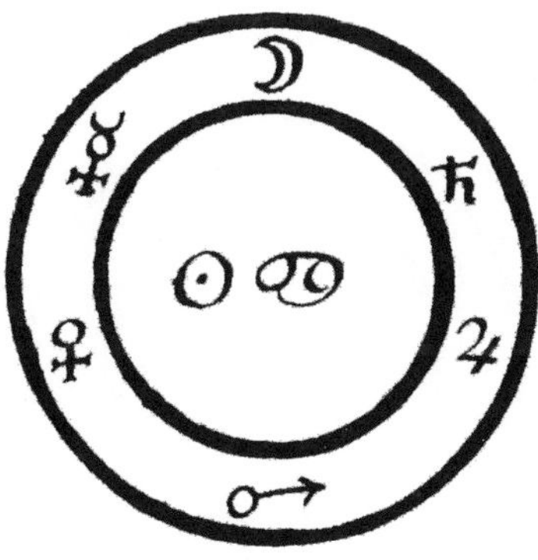

[1] Varmaii.

[2] *Eighty eight sheet Dr Rudd.*

The ninth hour of the day is called Karron and the Angel Ruling it is called Vadriel who hath many Dukes both of the greater and lesser order besides many other servants which is more Inferior, whereof ten of the great and 100 of the lesser Dukes hath 192890 Servants in ten Orders to obey and serve them whereof we shall mention the names of five of the great Dukes and ten of the lesser who hath 650 Chief Servants to attend on them in this hour they being sufficient for practice. Their names are these viz. Astroniel Charmis, Pamory, Damiel, Nadriel, Kromes Menos, Brasiel Nefarm Zoymiel Trubas Zarmiel, Lameson, Zasnoz, Janediel, and when you desire to make experiment in this hour make a Seal as aforesaid then say the Conjuration &c.

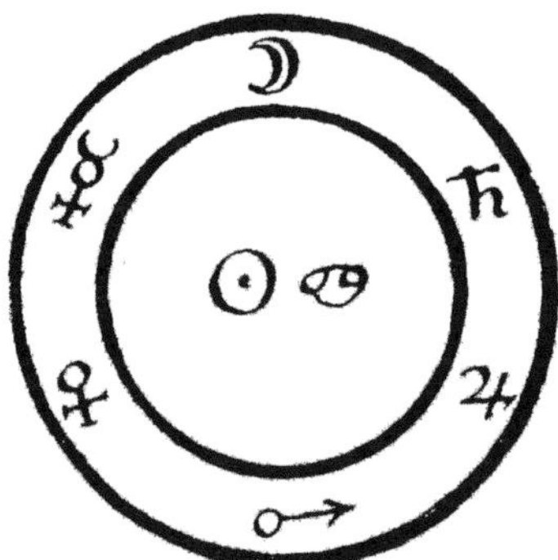

The tenth hour of the day is called Lamarthon, and the Angel ruling it is called Oriel who hath many Dukes and Servants divided into ten orders which contains 5600 Spirits whereof we shall mention five of the chief Dukes and ten of the lesser Dukes who hath 1100 Servants to attend on them, they being sufficient for practice. Their names are these viz. Armesi, Drabiel Penaly, Mesriel, Choreb Lemur, Ormas, Charny,[1] Zazior, Naveron Zentros, Busiton Nameron Kruneli Alfrael. And when you have a desire to practice in this hour make a Seal suitable to the time as this is here made for March 10 1641 on Wednesday. And then say the Conjuration [to be found] at the end of this *Pauline Art*.

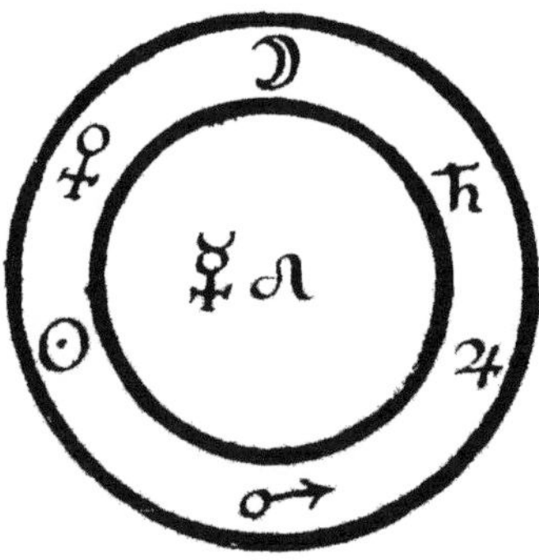

[1] Charnii.

The Eleventh hour of the day is called Manelohin and the Angel governing that hour is called Bariel who hath many Dukes and Servants which is divided into ten parts which contain 5600 Spirits, whereof we shall mention five of the chief Dukes of the first Order and ten lesser Dukes of the second order who hath 1100 Servants to attend them, they being sufficient for practice. Their names are these viz: Almerizel, Pralimiel, Chadros, Turmiel, Lamiel, Menafiel Demasar, Omary[1] Hehuas Zemoel Ahuas, Perman, Lomiel, Temal, Lanifiel then do all things in order as aforesaid, And [then] say the Conjuration.

[2]**The Twelfth hour of every day** is called Nahalon. And the Angel governing this hour is called Beraliel who hath many Dukes and other Servants which is divided into twelve degrees which contains the Number of 3700 Spirits in all whereof we shall mention five of the greatest Dukes and ten of the next order [of Dukes] who hath 1100 Servants to attend them they being sufficient for practice, their names are these viz. Camaron Altrafzel, Penaliel Demarac, Farmaris, Plamiel, Nerostiel, Emarson, ~~U~~ Virix,[3] Sameron, Edriel, Choriel, Romiel, Fenosiel, Harmary.[4] Then make the Seal proper and Say the Conjuration &c.

[1] Omarii.

[2] *Eighty ninth sheet Dr Rudd.*

[3] S3: *"Quirix"*.

[4] Harmarii.

[The Hours of the Night]

The first hour of every Night is called Omalhaveon and the Angel ruling it is called Sabrachan who hath 1540 Dukes and other Servants which are divided into ten Orders or parts whereof we shall mention five of the chief Dukes, and ~~ten~~ three of the lesser Dukes which are next to the five they being Sufficient for practice in this hour. There names are these viz. Domaros, Ameravy, Penoles, Hayzoim, Enalon, Furtiel, Uvenel, Rimaliel. They have two hundred servants to attend them.[1] Then prepare your Seal suitable to the time and do in all things as you was before directed.
Then say the Conjuration &c.

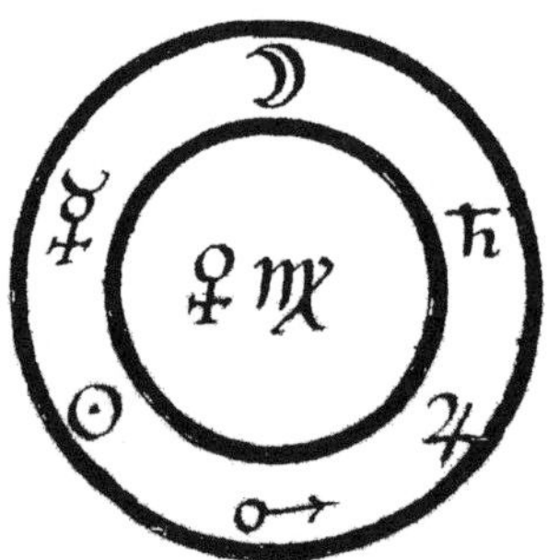

The Second hour of the Night is called Penazur and the Angel ruling it is called Taklis[2] who hath 101550 Spirits to attend him they being divided into twelve degrees or orders whereof we shall mention six of the chief Dukes of the first order and twelve of the next they being sufficient for practice. Their names are viz: Almodar, Famoriel, Nedros, Ormezin, Chabril, Praxiel, Permaz, Vameroz, Emariel, Fromezin, Ramaziel, Granozyn,[3] Gabrinoz Mezcoph, Famariel, Venomiel, Janaziel ~~Greo~~ Lemizim: these have 1320 Servants to attend them in this hour to do their will, and when you will work prepare your seal proper, and do in all things as before directed.
[Then say the Conjuration &c.]

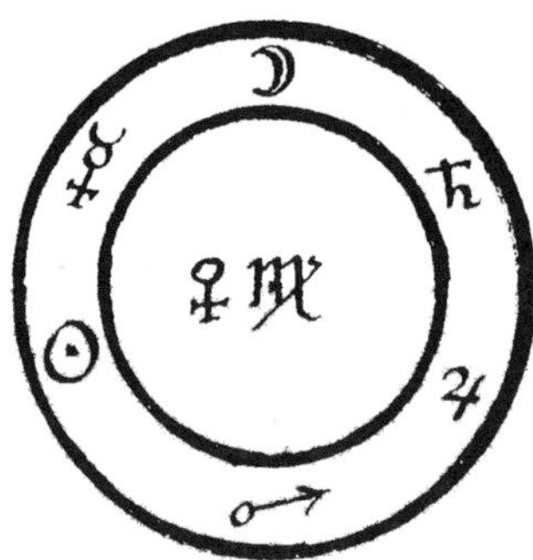

[1] S3: 2000 Servants.

[2] S3: *"Tartys"*.

[3] Granoziin.

The third hour of the Night is called Quabrion, and the Angel governing it is called Sarquamech which hath 101550 Servants Dukes and Servants to attend him the which is divided into 12 degrees or Orders these being six Dukes of the first order and twelve of the second Order, they having 1320 Servants to attend them. Their names are these. Menarim Crusiel, Penargos, Amriel, Thurmytzod Deminoz, Nestozoz, Evannel, Sarmezyn,[1] Haylon, Uvabriel ~~Thurmiy~~ Fremzon, Vanoie, Lemaron, Almonoyzod, Janothyel, Melrotz, Zanthyozod. And when you will make any experiment make a Seal proper to the time and do all things as before directed. Then say the Conjuration &c.

[2]**The fourth hour of the Night** is called Ramerzi and the Angel Governing it is called Jefisiel he hath 10[1]550 Dukes and other Servants which are divided into 12 orders or degrees to attend him whereof we shall mention six of the chief Dukes and twelve of those Spirits of the second order they being sufficient for practice Their names are Viz: Armosiel, Nedrum Maneyloz, Ormael Phorsiel, Rimesyn Rayziel, Gemozin, Fremiel, Hamayzod, Japuviel, Jasphiel, Lamediel, Adroziel, Bromiel, Coreziel, Enatriel.

These have 1260 Servants to attend them. When you have a desire to make experiment make your Seal and do as before directed.

Then say the Conjuration &c.

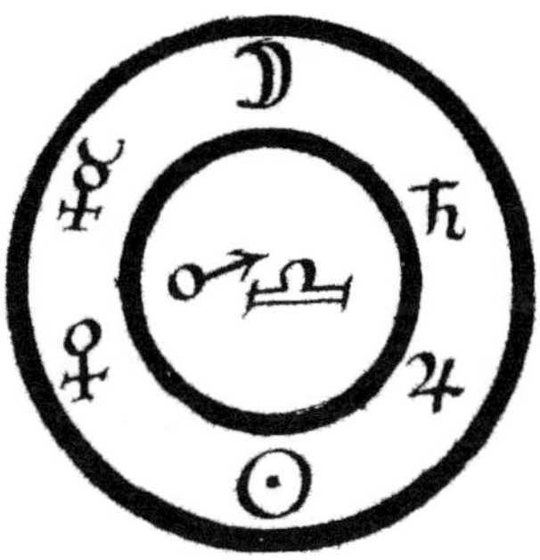

[1] Sarmeziin.

[2] *The Nineteth Sheet Dr Rudd.*

The Fifth hour of every night is called Sanayfor and its Governing Angel is called Abasdatho[1] he hath 101550 Dukes and other servants at his Command they being divided into 12 degrees of orders whereof we shall mention 12 of the Dukes belonging to the first order and as many of the second they being sufficient for practice. Their names are these viz. Meniel, Charby, Appiniel, Demarvon, Nechoxim, Hameriel, Untram~~er~~iel, Semelon, Gamari, Vanesior, Samerin, Zantropy,[2] Herphtzal, Chrymos, Patrozin, Namelon, Barmas, Phaliel ~~Rude for Satmon~~ Neszomi, Uvefulon, Caremax, Amariel, Kralim Hubalom who hath 2400 Servants to attend ~~these~~ them. Then make your seal according to the time when you make an Experiment and do all things as aforesaid. Then say the Invocation &c

The Sixth hour of every night is called Thaazoron and the Angel governing it is called Zaazenach who hath 101550 Dukes & other servants to attend him, they being divided into 12 orders whereof we shall mention 12 of the chief Dukes in the first order and 6 of the second order they being sufficient for practice in this hour, their Names are these viz: Amonzy, Menorike, Prenostix, Namedor Cherahel, Dramazed, Zeziel, Pammon, Dracon, Gemtzod, Enariel, Rudefor, Satmon who hath 2400 servants to attend them, then go to work make your seal and do all things as before directed.

Then say your Conjuration &c.

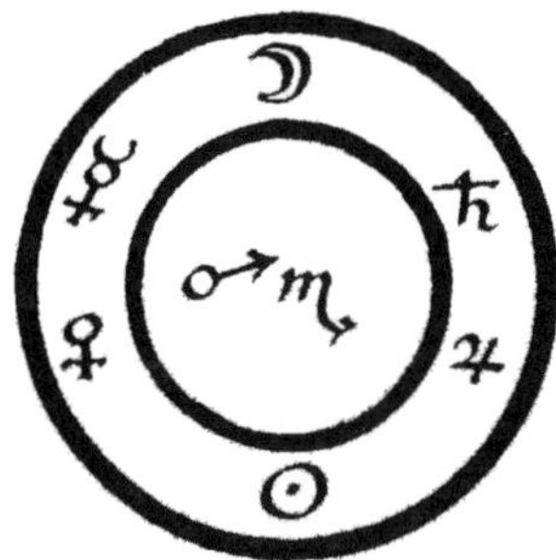

[1] Not 'Abasdarho'.

[2] Zantropii.

The Seventh hour of every night is called Venador and the Angel governing it is called Mendrion, who hath 101550 Dukes and other servants to attend them, they being divided into 12 Orders whereof we shall mention twelve of the chief Dukes, and six of the next lesser order they being sufficient for practice. Their Names are these viz: Ammiel, Choriel, Genaritzod, Pendroz, Memesiel, Semeriel, Ventariel, Zachariel, Dubraz, Marchiel Jonadriel, Pemoniel, Rayziel, Tarmitzod, Anapion, Imoniel, Framoch, Machmag who hath 1860 Servants to attend on them. When you intend to work make your seal proper to the time day & hour and do all things as you were before directed.

Then say the Conjuration &c.[1]

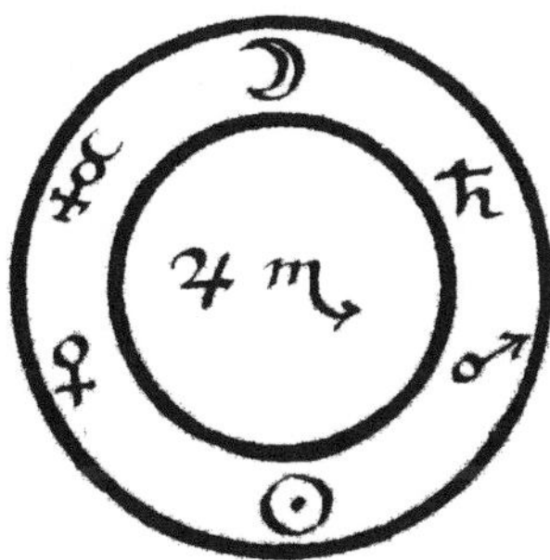

The Eight hour of the Night is called Ximalim and the Angel ruling it is called Narcoriel who hath 101550 Dukes and other servants spirits to attend him being divided into twelve Degrees whereof we shall mention twelve Dukes of the first order and six of the next they being sufficient for practice in this hour; their names are viz: Cambiel Nedarim Astrocon, Marifiel, Dremozin, Lustifion, Amelzom, Lemozor, Xernifiel, Hanorfiel, Bufanotzod, Jamedroz, Hanoriz, Jastrion, Themax, Hobrazim, Zimeloz, Gamsiel who hath 30200 servants to attend, When you intend to work make a seal proper to this hour as this is for an Example.

Then say the Conjuration

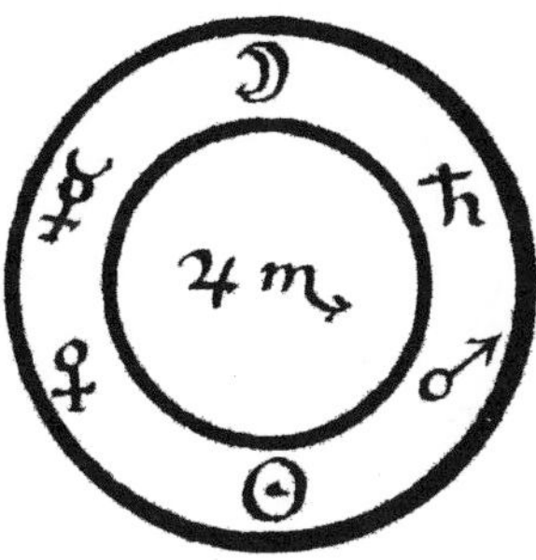

[1] *Ninety first sheet Dr Rudd.*

The Ninth hour of every night is called Zeschar and the Angel Ruling it is called Pamiel he hath 101550 Dukes and other Servants to attend him which is divided into 12 Orders whereof we shall mention Eighteen of the chief Dukes, their names are viz. Demannor, Nameal, Adrapon, Chermes, Fenadros, Vemasiel, Comary,[1] Maliel, Xenoroz, Brandiel, Evandiel, Jamiriel, Befranzy,[2] Xanthir, Armapi, Drachas, Sarajel who hath 1320 servants to attend them when you intend to work in this hour of the night. Make a Seal proper to the time and do all things else as you were before directed &c.

[Then say the Conjuration &c.]

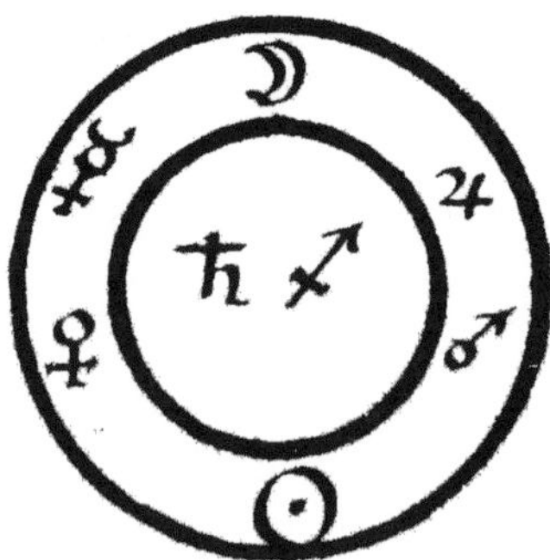

The tenth hour of every night is called Malcho, And the Angel governing it is called Jasgnarim who hath a chief Duke and 100 lesser Dukes besides many other Servants whereof we shall mention six that is to say three of the first Order and thereof the second Order who have 1520 Servants to attend them. Their names are these viz. Lapheriel, Emarziel, Nameroizod, Chameray, Hazaniel, Vraniel. Then make your Seal proper for the time and do as you were before directed. Then make your Seal proper for the time and do as you were before directed. Then say the Conjuration &c.

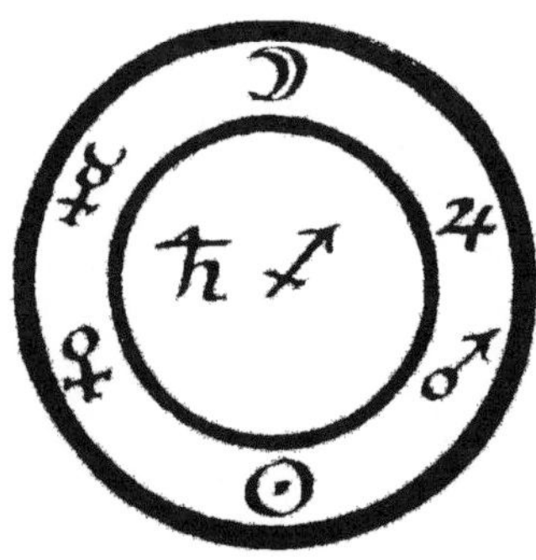

[1] Comarii.
[2] Befranzii.

The Eleventh hour of every night is called Aulacho and the Angel governing it is called Dardariel who hath many Dukes and Servants whereof we shall mention fourteen of the chief Dukes and seven of the next lesser Orders who hath 420 servants to attend them they are all good Spirits and obey God's Laws. Their names are these viz: Cardiel Permon, Armiel, Nastoriel Casmiros, Dameriel, Fumariel, Masriel, Hariaz, Dumar, Alachus, Emeriel, Nauezoz, Alaphar, Hermas, Druchas, Charmas, Elamis, Jatroziul, Lamersy, Hamarytzod, and then make your Seal proper to the time and do as aforesaid.

Then say the Conjuration &c.

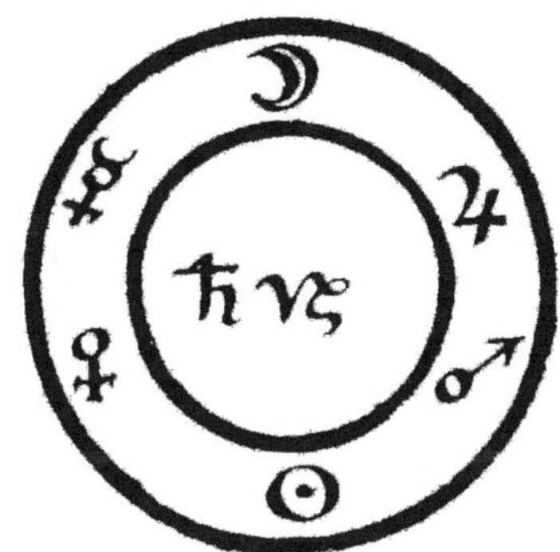

[1]**The twelfth hour of every Night** is called Xephan and the Angel governing it is called Sarandiel who hath many Dukes and Servants whereof we shall mention fourteen of the chief & good Dukes and Seven of the next and second order who hath 420 servants to attend on them Their names are as follows Viz. Adoniel, Damasiel, Ambriel, Meriel, Denaryzod, Emarion, Kabriel, Marachy, Chabrion Nestoriel, Zachriel, Naveriel, Damery, Namael, Hardiel, Nefryas, Irmanotzod, Gerthiel, Dromiel, Ladrotszod, Melanas.

When you desire to make an Experiment make a Seal to this hour of the night; Observe the time of the year and all other directions as aforesaid.

Then say the Conjuration following &c.

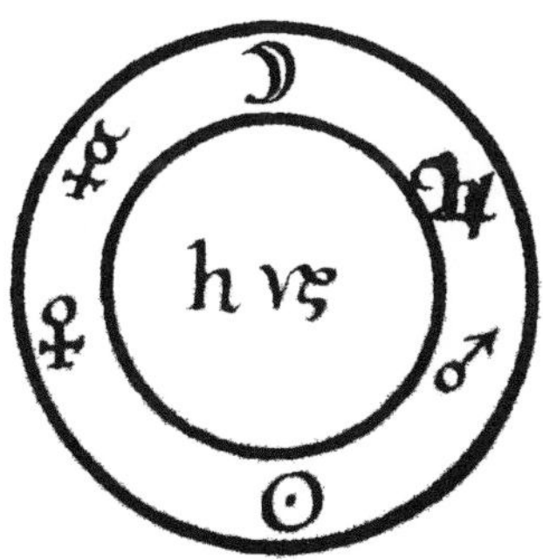

[1] *The ninty second Sheet Dr Rudd.*

The Conjuration

O thou mighty great and potent Angel Samael[1] *who Ruleth in this first hour of the day. I the Servant of the most High God do conjure and entreat thee servant of the most Omnipotent & immortal God of Host[s]* ***Jehovah Tetragrammaton*** *and by the name and in the name of that God that you owe obedience to, and by the head of your Hierarchy, And by the Seal or mark you are known in power by; And by the seven Angels that stand before the throne of God; and by the seven Planets and their Seals and Characters, and by the Angel that Ruleth the sign of the twelfth house which now Ascends in the first hour,*[2] *that you would be graciously pleased to gird up and gather your self together, And by divine permission to move & come from all parts of the world, wheresoever you be and show your self visibly and plainly in this Crystal stone to the sight of my eyes speaking with a voice intelligible and to my understanding, And that you would be favourably pleased that I may have thy familiar friendship and constant society*[3] *both now and at all other times when I shall call thee forth to visible appearance to inform and direct me in all things that shall seem good and lawful unto the Creator and thee O thou great and powerful Angel Samael,*[4] *I Invocate adjure, Command, and most powerfully Call you forth from your Orders*[5] *and place of residence to visible appearance in and through these great and mighty Incomprehensible signal*[6] *and divine names of the great God who was and is and ever shall be* ***Adonai Zebaoth Adonai Amioram, Hagios, Agla, On, Tetragrammaton.*** *And by and in the name* ***Primeumaton*** *which commanded the whole Host of Heaven; whose Power and virtue is most effectual for the Calling [of] you forth, and Commanding you to transmit your rays visibly*[7] *and perfectly unto my sight and your voice to my ears in and through this Crystal stone; That I may plainly see you and perfectly hear you speak unto me.*

Therefore move you O thou mighty & blessed Angel Samael[8]*, and by the Omnipotent name of the great God* ***Jehovah****, and by the Imperial dignity thereof, Descend and show your Self visibly and perfectly in a pleasant and comely form before me in this Crystal stone to the sight of mine eyes speaking with a voice intelligible and to my apprehension showing declaring and accomplishing all my desires that I shall ask or*

---

[1] This Conjuration is operative for all 24 Angels of the hours, and simply requires that the name of the Angel and the astrological details are changed as required.

[2] The hour number and the astrological details are to be changed as required.

[3] It is interesting and significant that the author of this grimoire assumed that the Angel should also derive pleasure from the knowledge and conversation of the magician.

[4] The name of the Angel to be changed as required.

[5] Orders, meaning which Order of Angels he belongs to, e.g. Thrones, Dominions, etc.

[6] As used here 'incomprehensible' means something that cannot be contained within any limits, and 'signal' means 'noteworthy.'

[7] An interesting reflection of Dee's researches into the optical qualities of crystal balls, as well as their magical qualities, and an attestation of how real the Angel's appearance within the crystal can become.

[8] The name of the Angel and the astrological details to be changed as required.

request of you both herein, and whatsoever truth and thing else that is just and lawful before the presence of Almighty God the Giver of all gifts unto whom I beg that he would be graciously pleased to bestow on me, O thou Servant of mercy Samael[1]. *Be thou therefore friendly unto me and do for me as for the Servant of the most high God, so far as God shall give you power to perform, Whereunto I move you both in power and presence to appear, That I may sing with his holy Angel O mappa=la=man Hallelujah*[2] *Amen.*[3]

[Before you call any of the Dukes, you are to Invocate the chief governing Angel that governs the hour of the Day or night as follows]

O thou mighty and potent Angel Samael[4], *who is by the Decree of the most high King of Glory Ruler and Governor of the first hour of the Day, I the Servant of the Highest do desire and entreat you in and by these three great and potent names of God* ***Agla, On, Tetragrammaton*** *and by the power and virtue thereof to assist and help me in my affairs. And by your power and authority to send and cause to come and appear unto me All or any of these Angels that I shall call by name that is residing under your Government, to instruct help aid and assist me in all further matters or things according to their offices, as I shall desire or request of him or them; And that they may do for me, as for the Servant of the Highest Amen.*

[Then begin to Invocate as follows][5]

O thou mighty and potent Angel Ameniel[6] *who is the first & principal Duke ruling by divine permission under the great and potent Angel Samael*[7] *who is the great and mighty Angel Ruling the first hour of the day I the servant of the most high God do Conjure and entreat thee: In the name of the most Omnipotent and immortal Lord God of Host[s] Jehovah [so go on as before at this *]*

[And when any Spirit is come, bid him welcome, Then ask your desire, And when you have done Dismiss according to the Order of Dismissing &c.][8]

The **End** of the first part of the **Book Pauline**

The Second Part

---

[1] The name of the Angel and the astrological details to be changed as required.

[2] Or Halleluyah. This exclamation is a composite of *Hallelu* and *Yah* (or *Jah*) which literally translates from Hebrew as "praise *Yah*". *Yah* is the shortened form of the name of God IHVH, or *Yahweh*, the Tetragrammaton. 'Halleluyah' is used about 24 times in the Bible (mainly as an ecstatic expletive in the book of *Psalms*, (especially *Psalms* 113-118) and four times in Greek transliteration in *Revelations*.

[3] *Ninty third Sheet Dr Rudd.* The following sentence is in brackets in the manuscript, and is not an editorial interpolation.

[4] The name of the Angel and the astrological details to be changed as required.

[5] The sentence is in brackets in the manuscript, and is not an editorial interpolation.

[6] To be changed to the name of the specific angel of hour.

[7] The name of the ruling Angel and hour to be changed as required.

[8] Both the sentences are in brackets in the manuscript, and are not editorial interpolations.

of this Book of Solomon of the

Art Pauline [Book 2].

[Spirits of the Degrees of the Zodiac]

This second Part contains the mystical names of the Angels of the Signs [of the Zodiac] in general, and also the Angels of every degree of the Signs in general which [are] called the Angels of men, Because that in some one of these signs and degrees every man is born in, therefore he that knows the minute of his birth, [thus] he may know the name of the Angel that governs him; And therefore he may attain to all Arts and Sciences, yea to all the wisdom and knowledge that any man at all can desire in this world.

The Ancient Philosophers[1] have taught how a man may know the nature of a [personal angel or] Genius whether good or bad from the Influx [influences] and aspects of the stars of his Geniture [birth date].

Porphyrius[2] seeks after it from the star that was Lord or Lady of the Geniture. Chaldeans find it out from the [the position of the] Sun or the Moon in his Nativity located.

Others find it out from the sixth house in the geniture, and call the Genius a good or bad genius or Dæmon.

A threefold Dæmon attends every man, one is his proper keeper, One indeed is holy, the other belongs to his geniture or Nativity. The holy Dæmon proceeds not from the stars but from a supreme power, even from God who himself is the president of Dæmons,[3] and descends to the Rational Soul being assigned thereto, and is universal above Nature's conception.

But the Dæmon of the Birth or Geniture which is also called the Genius, this Genius doth descend to the Birth [of the child] from the disposition of the stars [in] their Circuits round the world, who are Conversant [involved] in the generation.

The Dæmon of the profession or Calling of the Native is given from the stars to which such a profession or calling is subject to which any man professes,

---

[1] H1: The following section is only found in this MS, and comes from *De Occulta Philosophia* of Cornelius Agrippa.

[2] Porphyry (c.233–c. 309 CE), a Greek Neoplatonist pagan and mathematician, teacher of Iamblichus.

[3] An interesting title.

and the Soul shall make choice of. But this Dæmon is changed as any man changes his Calling, from a mean one to a more sublime [one] accordingly [the Dæmon will be] more worthy and sublime. Dæmons are present with us according as we daily ascend from one virtue to another, And these Dæmons do further take care to defend us.[1]

[1] At this point in the manuscript is inserted a narrative about Dr Rudd and Sir John Heydon and their dealings with a certain spirit and a Guardian Genius. The purpose of this narrative is to confirm the objective existence of spirits. Because it breaks the continuity of the *Ars Paulina* we have moved it to Appendix 11.

Note that those Angels that are attributed to the fire hath more knowledge therein than any other, and so likewise of the [Angels of the] air and water. And to know which belongs to the fire, Earth, air or Water. Observe the nature of the Signs and you cannot err, for those Angels that are attributed to ♈ are of the same nature fire; and the like in the rest. But if any planet be in that degree & ascends than that Angel is of the nature of the [zodiacal] Sign and planet both.

Observe this following method & you cannot but obtain your desire.

A Table of the Signs and Planets and their Natures.

♂	♀	☿	☾	☼	☿	♀	♂	♃	♄	♄	♃
♈	♉	♊	♋	♌	♍	♎	♏	♐	♑	♒	♓
Fire	*Earth*	*Air*	*Water*	*Fire*	*Earth*	*Air*	*Water*	*Fire*	*Earth*	*Air*	*Water*
Aiol	*Tual*	*Giel*	*Cael*	*Ol*	*Voil*	*Jael*	*Sosol*	*Suia-jasel*	*Casiri -ojah*	*Ansuil*	*Pasiel*

Those be the 12 Angels that are attributed to the 12 signs, because of those that have not got the very degree of their Nativity,[1] So that they make use of these Angels if they [only] know the sign that Ascends.

The other Angels which are attributed to every degree of every sign of the Zodiac are in the [following] Table of Genius's.

[1] Do not know the exact time of their birth.

[1]The Pauline Art

A Table of Genii's Names [1°-10°]

Signs/ Degrees[2]	1°	2°	3°	4°	5°	6°	7°	8°	9°	10°
♈ ♂	*Bial*	*Gesiel*	*Hael*	*Vaniel*	*Zaciel*	*Cegnel*	*Taphael*	*Itael*	*Cakiel*	*Lariel*
♉ ♀	*Letiel*	*Nujael*	*Sachiel*	*Gueliel*	*Panael*	*Jezisiel*	*Kingael*	*Raphiel*	*Tezael*	*Gn[a]kiel*
♊ ☿	*Latiel*	*Najael*	*Sachael*	*Gualiel*	*Paniel*	*Tzisiel*	*Kingael*	*Raphiel*	*Gnetiel*	*Bakiel*
♋ ☾	*Sachiel*	*Meiel*	*Aiel*	*Sachiel*	*Meliel*	*Aniel*	*Sasael*	*Magnael*	*Aphiel*	*Setzael*
♌ ☼	*Machiel*	*Satiel*	*Aiel*	*Mechiel*	*Saliel*	*Aniel*	*Masiel*	*Sengael*	*Aphiel*	*Metziel*
♍ ☿	*Celiel*	*Lenael*	*Nasael*	*Sengiel*	*Gnaph[i]el*	*Patziel*	*Tzakiel*	*Kiriel*	*Rathiel*	*Tangiel*
♎ ♀	*Ibajah*	*Cogiel*	*Latrael*	*Naviel*	*Saziel*	*Gnachiel*	*Patiel*	*Tzajael*	*Kehiel*	*Raliel*
♏ ♂	*Taliel*	*Janiel*	*Cesiel*	*Laugael*	*Naphael*	*Satziel*	*Gnakiel*	*Ratziel*	*Trahel*	*Kingiel*
♐ ♃	*Taliel*	*Janiel*	*Casiel*	*Laugael*	*Naphaiel*	*Satziel*	*Gnakiel*	*Periel*	*Traug[i]el*	*Kbiel*
♑ ♄	*Chathel*	*Temael*	*Jaajah*	*Cashiel*	*Lamajah*	*Naajah*	*Sasajah*	*Periel*	*Paajah*	*Trashiel*
♒ ♄	*Chamiel*	*Tesael*	*Jaajah*	*Camiel*	*Lashiel*	*Naajah*	*Samiel*	*Gnamiel*	*Paajah*	*Tzamiel*
♓ ♃	*Lachiel*	*Nehiel*	*Sanael*	*Gnasiel*	*Pangael*	*Tzophiel*	*Kphiel*	*Gnashiel*	*Tarajahel*	*Gnathiel*

[1] Ninty Sixth Sheet Dr Rudd.
2 There are no degree symbols (°) in the original manuscript but have been added here for clarity.

A Table of Genii's Names [11°-20°]

Degrees	11°	12°	13°	14°	15°	16°	17°	18°	19°	20°
♈ ♂	*Natheel*	*Saguel*	*Gabiel*	*Pegiel*	*Gadiel*	*Kheel*	*Leviel*	*Hezael*	*Geciel*	*Betiel*
♉ ♀	*Beriel*	*Gethiel*	*Dagnel*	*Vabiel*	*Zegiel*	*Chadiel*	*Tehiel*	*Javiel*	*Chaziel*	*Betiel*
♊ ☿	*Goriel*	*Dathiel*	*Hegnel*	*Vabiel*	*Zagiel*	*Chadiel*	*Taheel*	*Javiel*	*Chazael*	*Bachael*
♋ ☾	*Makel*	*Ariel*	*Sethiel*	*Magnael*	*Abiel*	*Sagal*	*Madiel*	*Ahiel*	*Savael*	*Maziel*
♌ ☼	*Sekel*	*Ariel*	*Methiel*	*Sagel*	*Abiel*	*Magiel*	*Sadiel*	*Aheel*	*Makel*	*Saziel*
♍ ☿	*Gnabiel*	*Bagiel*	*Gediel*	*Dahiel*	*Havael*	*Vaziel*	*Zachiel*	*Chetiel*	*Tijel*	*Jachiel*
♎ ♀	*Tavael*	*Gnaniel*	*Baugel*	*Geph[i]el*	*Datziel*	*Hekel*	*Variel*	*Zethel*	*Chengel*	*Tebiel*
♏ ♂	*Rebiel*	*Tagiel*	*Gnadiel*	*Bevael*	*Geziel*	*Dachiel*	*Hephiel*	*Vajael*	*Zachiel*	*Chabiel*
♐ ♃	*Regael*	*Tadiel*	*Gnahiel*	*Bevael*	*Geziel*	*Dachiel*	*Hephiel*	*Vajael*	*Zachiel*	*Chabiel*
♑ ♄	*Kiniel*	*Riajah*	*Tashiel*	*Genamiel*	*Baajah*	*Cashiel*	*Damiel*	*Haajah*	*Vashiel*	*Zannel*
♒ ♄	*Kshiel*	*Raajah*	*Tamiel*	*Genashiel*	*Baajah*	*Gamiel*	*Dashiel*	*Haajah*	*Vamiel*	*Zashiel*
♓ ♃	*Bengael*	*Gebiel*	*Dagiel*	*Hadiel*	*Vahajah*	*Zavael*	*Chazael*	*Tachael*	*Jatael*	*Cajael*

A Table of Genii's Names [21°-30°]

Degrees	21°	22°	23°	24°	25°	26°	27°	28°	29°	30°
♈ ♂	*Giel*	*Dachael*	*Habiel*	*Vigael*	*Zadiel*	*Chael*	*Tacael*	*Jezel*	*Chiel*	*Hetiel*
♉ ♀	*Getiel*	*Daiel*	*Hachael*	*Vabiel*	*Zadiel*	*Chadiel*	*Tehael*	*Javael*	*Chaziel*	*Sachael*
♊ ☿	*Getiel*	*Dajeel*	*Hechael*	*Vabiel*	*Zagiel*	*Chadiel*	*Tahiel*	*Daviel*	*Heziel*	*Vachael*
♋ ☽	*Achiel*	*Setiel*	*Majel*	*Achael*	*Sabiel*	*Magiel*	*Adiel*	*Sahiel*	*Maviel*	*Aziel*
♌ ☉	*Achiel*	*Matiel*	*Siel*	*Achael*	*Mabiel*	*Sagiel*	*Adiel*	*Mahiel*	*Savael*	*Aziel*
♍ ☿	*Cabiel*	*Bagiel*	*Gediel*	*Dahiel*	*Hevael*	*Zaziel*	*Zachiel*	*Chetiel*	*Tajael*	*Jachiel*
♎ ♀	*Togiel*	*Cediel*	*Behel*	*Gevael*	*Duziel*	*Hechiel*	*Vatiel*	*Zajael*	*Chechiel*	*Tehiel*
♏ ♂	*Tagiel*	*Iadiel*	*Cahael*	*Baviel*	*Gezael*	*Dachael*	*Hatiel*	*Vagael*	*Zachiel*	*Chasiel*
♐ ♃	*Tagiel*	*Iadiel*	*Cahel*	*Baviel*	*Gezael*	*Dachael*	*Hatiel*	*Vadael*	*Zahael*	*Chaviel*
♑ ♄	*Chael*	*Tashiel*	*Imajah*	*Ciajah*	*Beshael*	*Gamiel*	*Daael*	*Heshael*	*Vamiel*	*Zaajah*
♒ ♄	*Chael*	*Iamiel*	*Jashiel*	*Ciajah*	*Bemiel*	*Gashiel*	*Daael*	*Hemiel*	*Vashiel*	*Zaajah*
♓ ♃	*Bachiel*	*Gabael*	*Dagiel*	*Hediel*	*Vahejah*	*Zavael*	*Chazael*	*Tutiel*	*Jatael*	*Cajael*

[The 12 seales of the 12 Signs of the Zodiac]

These be the twelve Seals which are attributed to the twelve Signs & the 360 Angels or Geniis aforesaid.[1]

[The First Seal of Aries]

Make this Seal of ♂ 3ss, ☉ 3ii. ♀ 3ss, and melt them together when the Sun enters the first Degree of Aries then on ♂ day the Moon being in 9 or 10 Degrees of ♈ make it and finish it.[2]

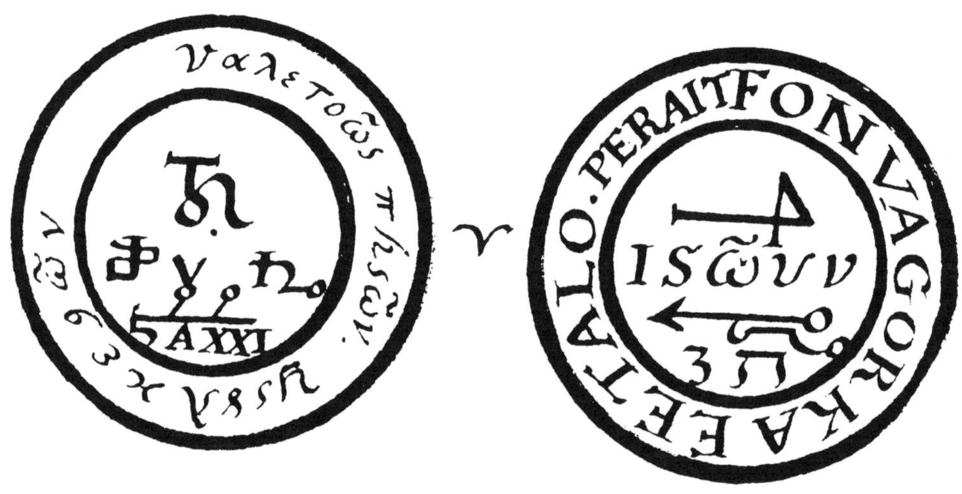

[1] These 12 zodiacal seals also occur in the *Second Treatise of Celestial Medicines*, containing, *The Mysteries of the Signes of the Zodiack* by Paracelsus. This was published in 1656 in a volume entitled *Paracelsus Of the Supreme Mysteries of Nature* which was reprinted by Askin Publishers in 1975 retitled as *The Archidoxes of Magic*, introduced by Stephen Skinner, and republished by Ibis Press in 2004. The seals have slight variations, but even the printed version has the same rather untidy collections of distorted Greek, zodiacal words and seals. The British Museum has several metal examples of similar seals, presumably produced by practitioners. In each case the two circles represent both sides of the same disk. The Zodical signs are out of order, unlike those in the printed version. The seals are in a very strange order, beginning with Aries and taking every second sign, before returning to Taurus and then becoming rather random in order. This suggests that the original source was probably laid out in a different way, possibly vertically, and errors have been introduced by the copyist in the process of re-ordering them.

[2] The planetary sigils correspond to the appropriate planetary metal for the planet. Note for measures that *3* = 1oz (28.35g), ***3*** = ⅛oz (3.54g), *ss* = ½, *i* = Roman numerals to indicate quantity; thus *3ii* = 2oz, *3ss* = ½oz.

[1]The Second Seal [of Gemini]

Make this Seal of ☉ 3i. ☽ 3i. Melt them together when the Sun enters Gemini and make a Lamen thereof when the Moon is in Leo or Pisces.

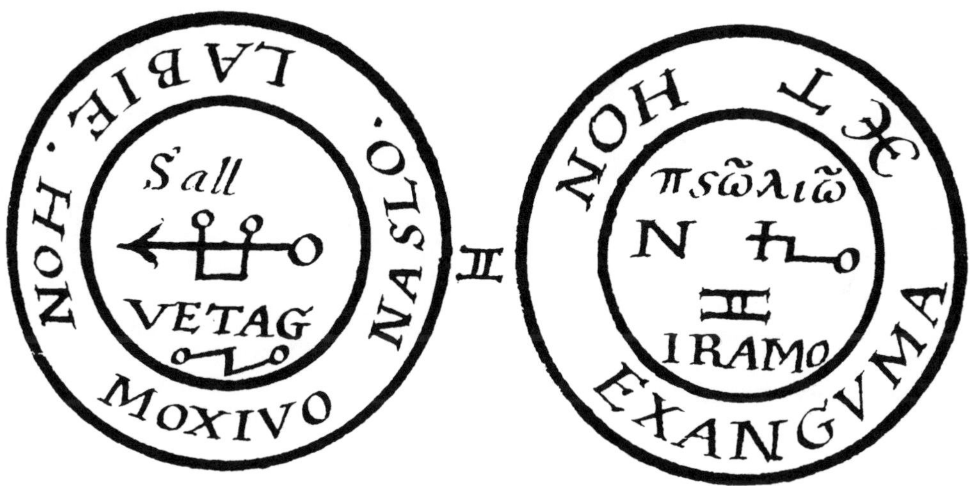

[1] Ninty seventh Sheet Dr Rudd.

The third Seal [of Leo][1]

This Seal make of ☼[2] when he enters Leo then after when Jupiter is in Pisces Engrave the first figures, and [then] the other side when the Moon is in Pisces it must not come into the fire but once when it is melted.

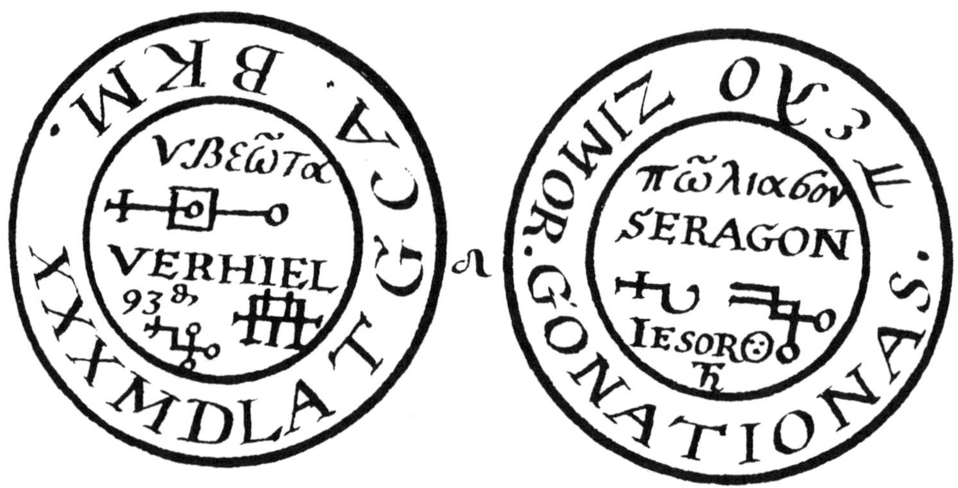

The fourth Seal [of Libra][3]

Make this Seal [of] ♀ Melted poured out and made when the Sun enters Libra.

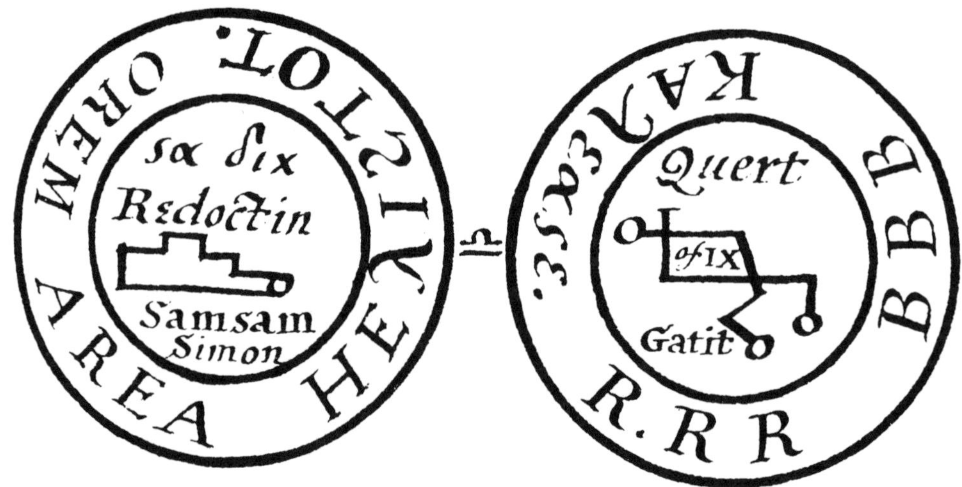

[1] The text might at first glance suggest that this is a Seal of Pisces, but the seal is definitely Leo, and marked as Leo between the two circles. The words "XXXMDL AT GCA. BKM" do not occur in the printed version. XXXMDL is an impossible date but could conceivably be meant to be 1520.

[2] A circle containing three dots like a face.

[3] The writing on this seal is here much clearer than the printed version. As a general rule the seals in this manuscript show the word breaks correctly, whilst the printed ones often run two words together.

The fifth Seal [of Sagittarius]

Make this Seal of pure ♃ in the hour of the Sun entering Sagittarius and engrave it in the hour of ♃. this Seal is to be hung in a silver ring.

[1]The Sixth Seal [of Taurus]

Make this Seal of ♀ 3i. ♃ 3i. ♂ 3ss of ☉ 3ii and melt them together in the very point [time when] the Sun enters Taurus and so finish it.

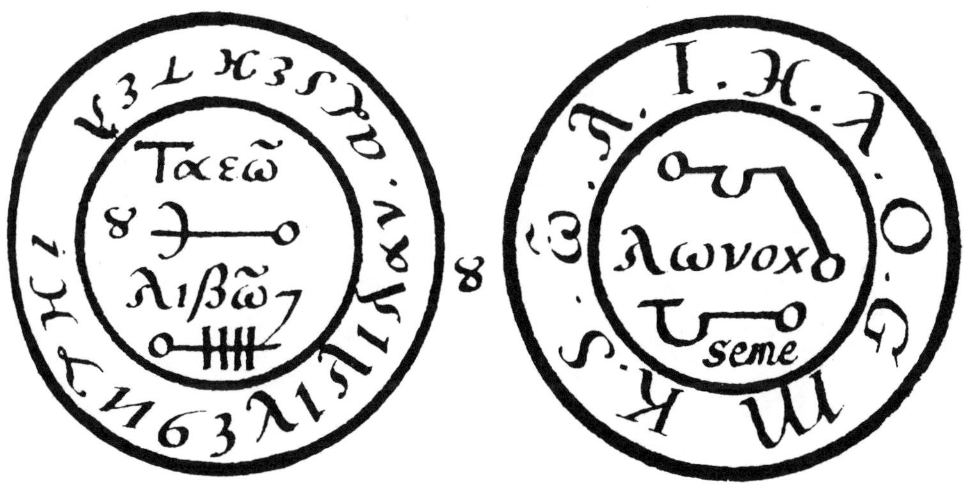

[1] *Ninty eight Sheet Dr Rudd.*

The Seventh Seal [of Cancer]

Make this Seal of Luna when the Sun enters Cancer in the hour of the Moon She increasing and in good Aspect:

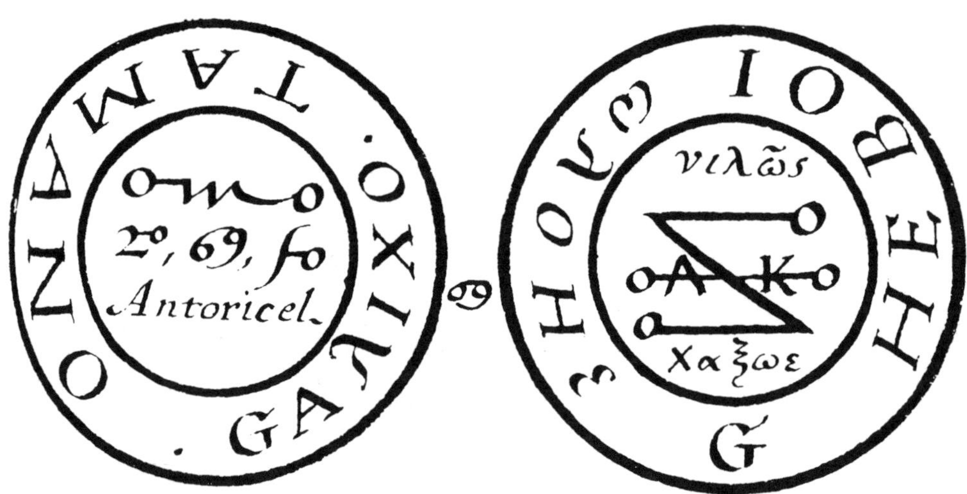

The Eight[h] Seal [of Aquarius][1]

Make this Seal of ☉[2] 3ss. ♄ 3ii. ♂ 3i and melt them when the Sun enters Aquarius and Engrave it as you see in this figure when Saturn is in the ninth house.

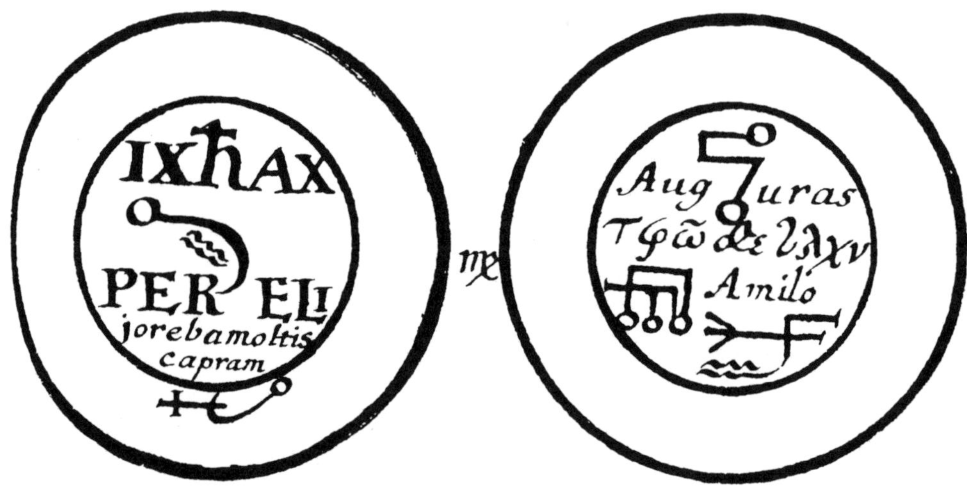

[1] The text suggests that this is a Seal of Aquarius, but the seal has Virgo written between the two circles: in fact it is the Seal of Aquarius.

[2] A circle containing three dots like a face.

The Ninth Seal [of Virgo][1]

Make this Seal of ♀ 3i ☉ [3]ss ☽ 3ii ♃ [3]ss and melt them on ☉[2] when the Sun enters Capricorn then after when Mercury is well aspected, on his day Engrave the words and Characters as you see in the figure.

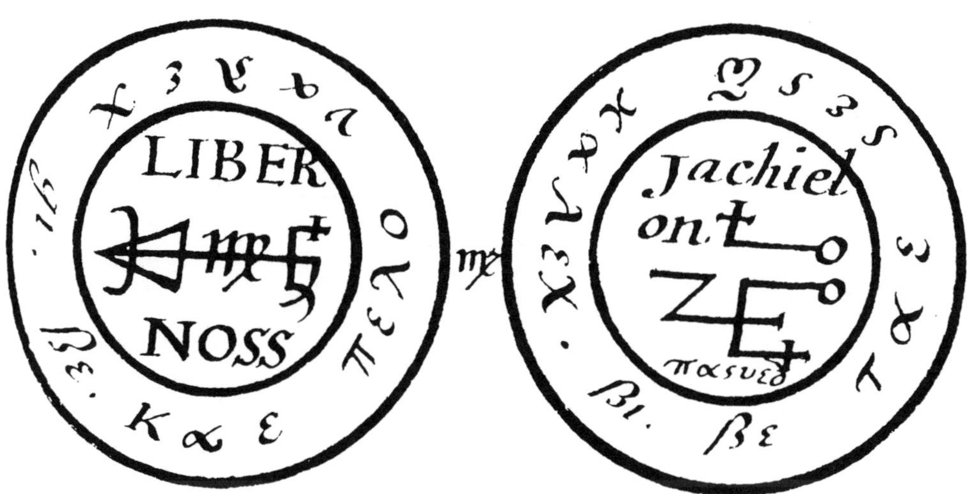

[3]The Tenth Seal [of Scorpio]

Make this Seal of Mars in the day & hour when Sun enters Scorpio engrave the forepart of it; after when the Sun enters Aries engrave the other side

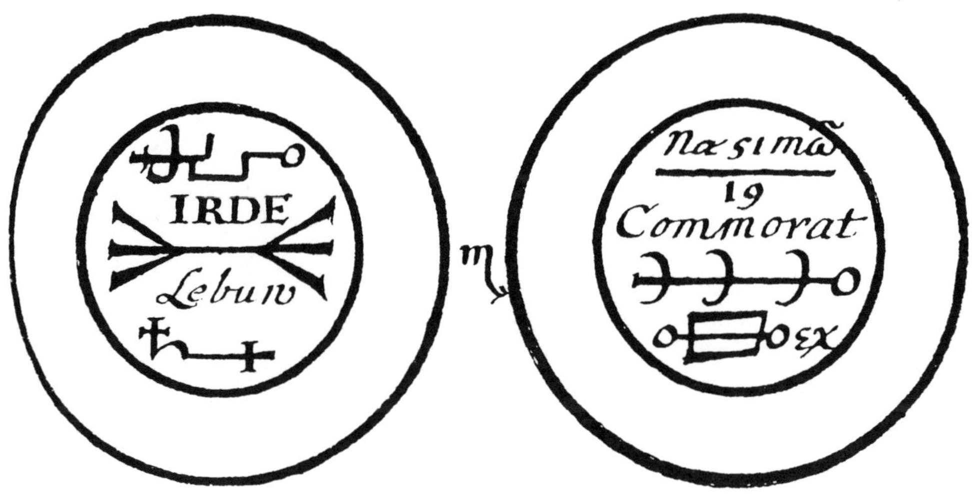

[1] The text suggests that this is a Seal of Capricorn, but the seal has Virgo between the two circles. It is in fact Virgo.
[2] A circle containing three dots like a face.
[3] Ninty nine Sheet Dr Rudd.

The Eleventh Seal [of Capricorn]

Make this Seal of ☉[1] and a Ring of ♀ to hang it in when the Sun enters Capricorn and Engrave it when Saturn is well aspected and in his day and hour.

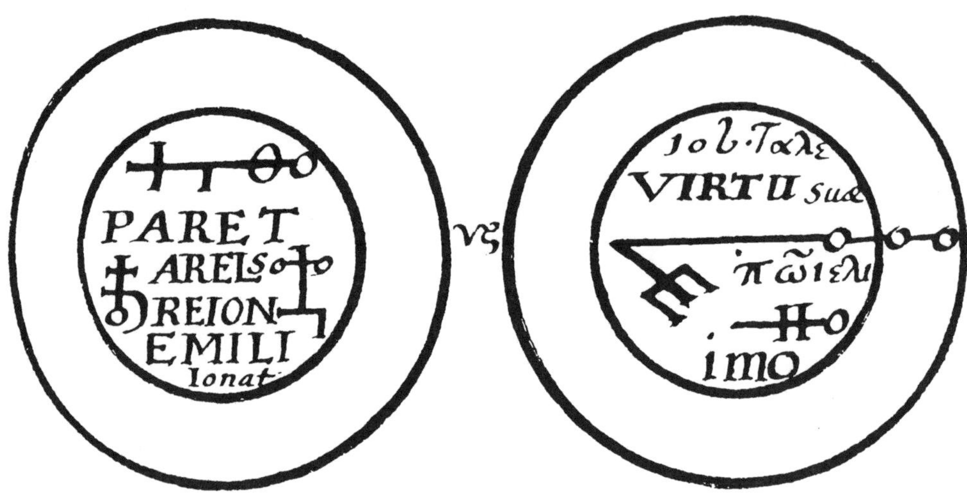

The Twelfth Seal [of Pisces]

Make this Seal when the Sun enters Pisces of ☼[2] ♂ ♀ and ☽ of each 3ii of ♃ 3ss and let them be melted and engrave both in that hour of ☽ Increase [waxing].

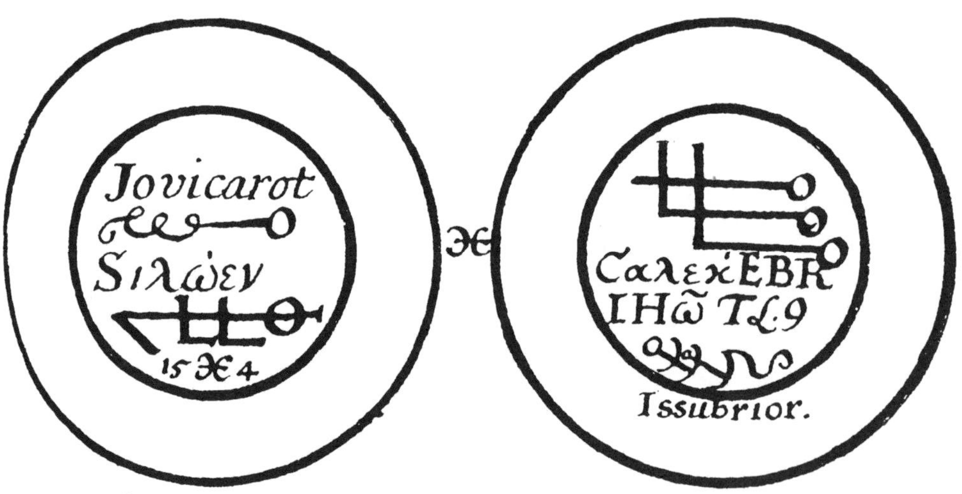

1 A circle containing three dots like a face.
2 A circle containing three dots like a face.

So when you know the Angel that governs the sign and degree of your Nativity and having the Seal ready, that belongs to the sign and degree as is showed before, then you are next to understand what Order he [the Genii] is of and under what prince as is showed here in this following part.

First those Genii that are attributed to **Aries, Leo** and **Sagittarius** are of the first Region, and [this] is governed by Michael the great Angel who is one of the chief Messengers of God which is towards the East, therefore these Genii are to be observed in the first hour of a Sunday [day of the Sun] and at the 8th hour, also at the third and tenth hour [of the night]:[1] Directing your self towards that quarter; They appear in Royal robes, holding Sceptres in their hands, oft[en] riding on a Lion or a Cock.[2] Their robes are of a red and saffron Colour, and most Comely, they assume the shape of a Crowned Queen, and very beautiful to behold.[3]

Secondly those Genii that are attributed to **Taurus, Virgo** and **Capricorn** are of the Earthly Region and are governed by Uriel who hath three princes to attend him viz: Asaiel, Sachiel and Cassiel, [4]therefore these Genii which are attributed to him, and these signs are to be observed in the West, They appear like Kings having Green and Silver Robes, or like little Children or women delighting in hunting. They are to be observed on Saturday [day of Saturn] at the first and eighth hours of the day, and the third and tenth hours of the night, in these hours you are with privacy to obtain your desires, directing your self towards the west as aforesaid.

Thirdly those Genii that are attributed to **Gemini Libra** and **Aquarius** are of the airy Region whose Sovereign Prince is called Raphael who hath under him two Princes which are called Seraphiel and Miel. Therefore those Genii who are attributed to him, and those signs are to be observed towards the South on a Wednesday [day of Mercury] the first and eighth hours of the day, and at night the third & tenth hours. They appear as Kings or beautiful young men in Robes of diverse colours but most comely like women transcendentally handsome by reason of their admirable whiteness and beauty.

Fourthly and lastly those Genii that are attributed to **Cancer Scorpio** and **Pisces** are of the watery Region and are governed by Gabriel who hath under him three mighty princes viz: Samael, Madiel and Mael. Therefore these Genii that are attributed to those signs are to be observed on Monday [day of the Moon] towards the North at the first and eighth hours of the day and at night

---

1 Because there are four occurrences of the solar hour on Sunday (the solar day).

2 They are holding sceptres to indicate their rank. Riding on an animal also indicates a higher rank of spirit, demon or genii.

3 Appearance is one of the key tests that the spirits are what they say they are.

4 The Hundred Sheet Dr Rudd.

at the third and tenth hours. They appear like Kings having Green and silver robes like little Children or Women delighting in hunting.[1]

So in the next place you are to observe the season of the year according to the constellation of the Celestial bodies. Otherwise we shall lose all our Labour. For if a Genius be of the Igneal[2] Hierarchy it's in vain to observe him in any other season but when the Sun enters those signs which are of his nature that is Aries Leo and Sagittarius. So if it be a Genius of the Earth it is to be observed when the Sun enters Taurus and Capricorn. And so the like on the rest.

Or otherwise thus Those Genii that are of the Order of fire are to be observed in the Summer, and those of the Earth in Autumn, and those of the air in Spring, and those of the water in Winter.

Their Office is to do all things that are just and not against the Laws of the great God Jehovah, but what is for our good and what shall concern the protection of our Lives our being & well being, and the doing good to and obliging our Neighbours. Now he that desires to see his Genius ought to prepare himself accordingly. Now if his Genius be of the fire [triplicity, then] his demands must be for the Conservation of his body and person, that he may receive no hurt from or by any fire, arms or guns or the like. And having a Seal suitable ready prepared, he is to wear it when he hath a desire to see his Genius, that he [the Genius] may confirm it to him [the operator]; That for the time to come he may not fail of his assistance & protection on any occasion.

But if his Genius be Aerial, He[3] reconciles men's natures increase love and affection between them and causeth the deserved love of Kings and princes, and secretly promotes marriages, and therefore he that hath such a Genius before he observe him should prepare a Seal suitable to his order that he may have it Confirmed by him in the day & hour of observation whereof he shall see strange and wonderful effects. So the like [manner] of the other two Hierarchies [Water and Earth].

And when the time is come that you would See your Genius, turn your face to that quarter [of the sky] the sign is [located in] And that with prayers to God, they being composed to your fancy but suitable to the matter in hand, There thou shalt find him; and having found him Sincerely acknowledge him, do your duty, then will he, as being benign and sociable Illuminate your mind taking away all that is obscure and dark in thy memory, and make you knowing in all Sciences sacred and divine in an instant.[4]

---

[1] The reference is to Diana goddess of the Moon and the hunt.

[2] Fiery.

[3] H1: repeats *"he"*.

[4] This promise of the instant mastery of a particular subject is like the method of the *Notory Art*.

A form of **Prayer** which ought to be said upon that Coast[1] or quarter where the Genius is several [2]times it being an Exorcism to call the Genius into the Crystal Stone.[3] Note this prayer may be altered to the mind of the worker for it is here set for an Example.[4]

The Prayer

O thou great and blessed N. my Angel Guardian vouchsafe to descend from thy holy mansion which is Celestial, with thy holy influence and presence into this Coelestiall [Crystal] Stone; that I may behold thy glory an enjoy thy society aid and assistance both now and for ever hereafter: O thou that are higher than the fourth heaven and knows the secrets of Elanel, thou that rides upon the wings of the wind, and art mighty & potent in thy Celestial and superlunary[5] motion do thou descend and be present I pray thee, and I humbly desire and entreat thee that if ever I have merited thy society; or if any of my actions or intentions be real and pure and sanctified before thee; bring thy external presence[6] hither and converse with me one of thy submissive people, in and by the name of the great God Jehovah whereunto the whole Quire [Choir] of Heaven sings continually O! mappa=la=man Hallelujah

Amen

[[7]When you have said this Prayer several times as Occasion serves; You will at last see strange sights and passages in the stone, and at last you will see your Genius; then give him a kind entertainment [greeting], as you was before directed, Declaring unto him your mind, and what you will have done.

So endeth the Book

PAULINE.

[1] 'Coast' here means 'direction' or 'side'.

[2] The Hundred & first sheet Dr Rudd.

[3] Exorcism is not used in the sense of banishing a demon or spirit (the sense in which the Church used it), but in the older sense of invoking or communicating with one, using holy names.

[4] This section probably contributed to the theories about obtaining the knowledge and conversation of the Holy Guardian Angel, as popularised by the Golden Dawn.

[5] Above the Moon, in the higher heavens, rather than the sublunary realm occupied by many spirits.

[6] Manifest outside of the Crystal Stone.

[7] A single bracket occurs here in the manuscript, and it does not here indicate an editor's interpolation.

Here beginneth the Fourth Part of this Book which is called

The Art Almadel

of Solomon the King

By this Art Solomon attained great wisdom from the Chief Angels that governs the four Altitudes of the World[1], for you must observe there are four Altitudes which represents the four Corners of the world East, West, North and South, the which are divided into twelve parts, that is every part [is divided into] three [Zodiacal signs]. And the Angels of every [one] of these Altitudes have their particular Virtues and powers as shall be showed hereafter.

Make this Almadel of pure white wax (but the others must be colours suitable to the Altitude). It is to be four square and six Inches and in every Corner a hole, and write betwixt every hole with a new pen these words or names of God following (but this is to be done in the day and hour of Sol) write upon the first part towards the East Adonai, Helomi, Pine, And upon the second towards the South Helion, Heloi, Heli. And upon the [third part towards the] West part Iod, Hod, Agla. And upon the fourth part which is North, write Tetragrammaton, Shadai, Iah, and betwixt the first and other quarters make the pentacle of Solomon thus ✫, And betwixt the first quarter write this word Anabona. And in the middle of ~~it~~ the Almadel make a six angled figure,[2] and in the midst of it a Triangle wherein must be written these Names of God Heli, Helion, Adonai, and this last name round the six angled figure as here it is made it being for an Example.

And of this same wax there must be made four Candles and they must be of the same colour as the Almadel is of. Note divide the wax into three parts one for to make the Almadel of, and the other parts to make the Candles of & let there come forth of every one of them a foot made of the same wax to Support the Almadel with, this being done, in the next phase you are to make a Seal of pure Gold or Silver but Gold is better whereon must be Engraved these three names Helion, Helluion, Adonai.

Behold the figure of the Almadel

---

[1] Each Altitude covers 90 degrees of the full circle of the Zodiac.

[2] Hexagram.

[1]The Figure of the Almadel

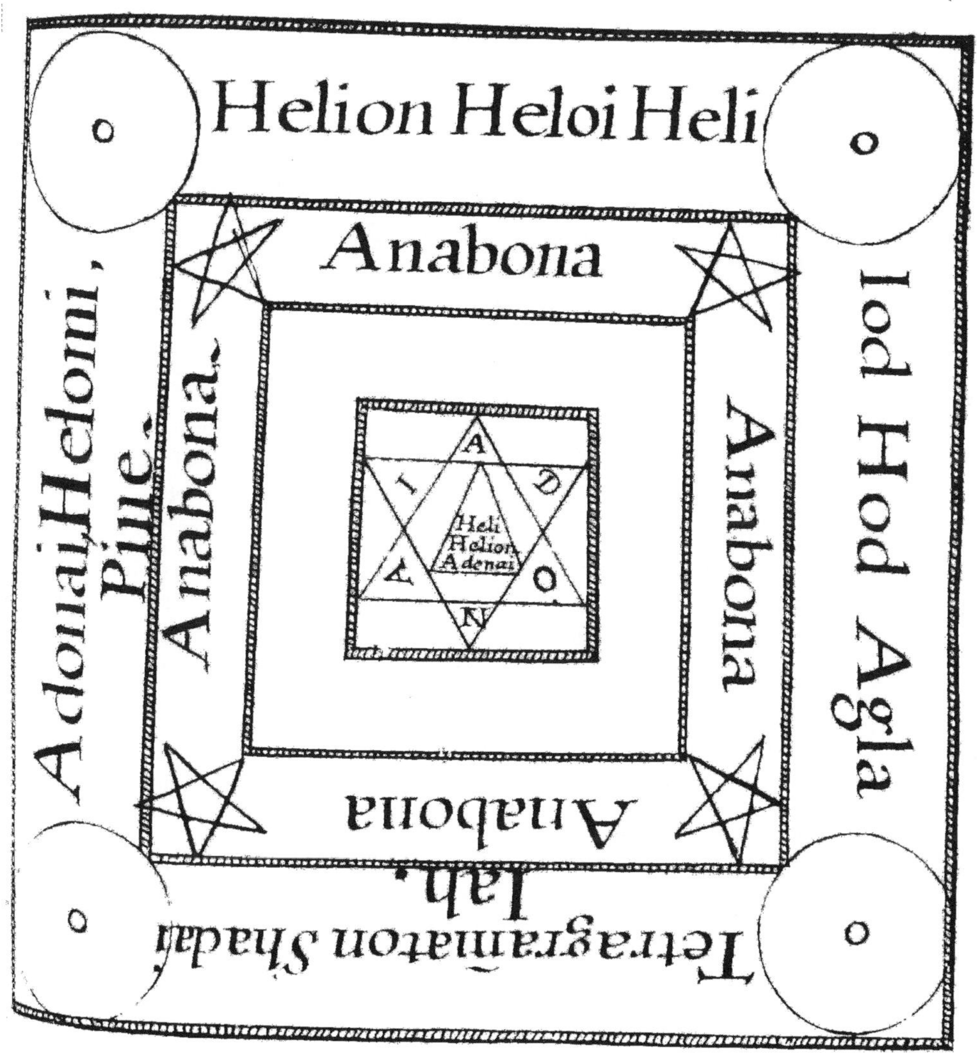

Figure 13: The Almadel

[1] *The Hundred & second Sheet Dr Rudd.*

Of the First Chora or Altitude

Note the first Altitude is called Chora Orientis or the East Altitude, and to make any experiment in this Chora it is to be done in the day & hour of the Sun and the power and office of those Angels is to make all things fruitful and Increase both Animal and vegetable in Creation and generation advancing the birth of Children and making barren women fruitful, and their names are these viz. Almiel Gabriel, Borachiel, Lebes and Hellison. Note you must not pray for any Angel but those that belong to the Altitude you have a desire to Call forth; And when you Operate set the four Candles upon four Candlesticks, but be careful you do not light them before you begin to operate, then lay the Almadel between the four Candles upon the waxen feet that comes from the Candles, And lay the Golden Seal upon the Almadel and having the Invocation ready written in Virgin's parchment, Light the Candles and read the Invocation.

And when he is appeared, he appeareth in the form of an Angel carrying in his hand a Fan or flag[1] having the picture of a white Cross upon it, his body being wrapped round about with a fair Cloud, and his face very fair and bright, and a Crown of Rose flowers upon his head. He ascends first upon the Superscription[2] of the Almadel as if it were a Mist or fog, them must the Exorcist have in readiness a Vessel of Earth of the same Colour as the Almadel is of and the other [items] of his furniture, it being in the form of a basin and put there into a few hot Ashes or Coals but not too much lest it should melt the wax of the Almadel, and put there in three little grains of Mastic in powder so that it may fume and the smell go upwards through the holes of the Almadel when it is under it, And as soon as the Angel smells it he beginneth to speak with a low voice Asking what your desire is, and what you have called the princes and Governors of the Altitude for. Then you must Answer him saying

I desire that all my requests may be granted and what I pray for may be accomplished, for your office makes appear and declares that such is to be fulfilled by you, if it please God.

Adding further the particular[s] of your request with humility for what is lawful and just, and that you shall obtain from him. But if he do not appear presently you must then take the Golden seal and make with it three or four marks upon the Candles by which means the Angel will presently appear as aforesaid. And when the Angel departs he will fill the whole place with a sweet and pleasant smell which will be smelt [for] a long time.

Note that the [same] Golden seal will serve and is to be used in all the operations of all the four Altitudes. The Colour of the Almadel belonging to the first Altitude or Chora is Lily white. And the second Chora a perfect red

[1] Dr John Dee's angels often used to carry a flag or ensign. This often indicates the rank of the spirit.

[2] The engraved upper face of the Almadel.

Rose Colour, the third [1]Chora is to be green mixed with white silver Colour. The fourth Chora is to be a black mixed with a little Green of a sad colour.

Of the Second Chora or Altitude

Note all the other three Altitudes with their Signs and Princes have power over goods and riches and can make any man rich or poor. And as the first Chora gives increase and makes fruitful, so these give decrease and barrenness and if any hath a desire to operate in any of these three following Choras or Altitudes they must do it in Die Solis[2] in the manner as aforesaid, But do not pray for anything that is contrary to the nature of their office or against God and his Laws, but what God giveth according to the Custom or Course of nature, that you may desire and obtain; And all the furniture that is to be used is to be of the same colour as the Almadel is of. And the Princes of this second Chora are named viz: Alphariza, Genon, Geron, Armon, Gereimon.[3] And when you operate, Kneel before the Almadel with Clothes of the same Colour in a Closet[4] hung of the same Colours also for the holy operation [it] will be of the same colour; And when he is appeared put the earthen vessel under the Almadel, with fire or hot ashes, and grains of Mastic in powder to perfume as aforesaid. And when the Angel smells it, he turns his face towards you, asking with a low voice why he hath called the Princes of this Chora or Altitude, then you must answer as before saying *I desire that my requests may be granted, and the contents thereof may be accomplished, for your office makes appear and declares that such is to be done by you if it please God.*

You must not be fearful but speak humbly saying,

I recommend my self wholly to your office, And I pray unto your Princes of this Altitude that I may enjoy and obtain all things according to my wishes and desires.

You may further express your mind in all particulars in your prayers. Do the like in the other two Choras following.

The Angel of the second Altitude appeareth in the form of a young Child with Clothes of satin and of a red rose Colour having a Crown of red Gilly flowers upon his head his face looks upward towards heaven and is of a red colour and is compassed round about [surrounded] with a bright splendour or the beams of the Sun, and before [he] departs, he speaks unto the Exorcist saying, *I am your friend and brother* and illuminates the Air round about with his splendour and leaves a pleasant smell which will last a long time.

The End of the second Chora.

---

[1] *Hundred and third sheet Dr Rudd.*

[2] Sunday.

[3] Gersimon?

[4] Small room.

Of the Third Chora or Altitude

In this Chora you must do in all things as you was before directed in the other two. The Angels of this Chora or Altitude are named viz. Eliphaniasai, Gelomiras, Gedobenai, Saranava and Elomnia, they appear in [the] form of Children or little women dressed in Green and silver Colour very delightful to behold, and a Crown of Bays[1] beset with flowers of white and Green Colours upon their heads, and they seem to look a little downward with their faces. They speak as the others do to the Exorcist, and leaves a mighty sweet Perfume behind them.

Of the Fourth Chora or Altitude

In this Chora you must do as before in the other [Choras], And the Angels of this Chora are called Barchiel, Gediel, Gobiel, Deliel and Captiel. They appear in [the] form of little men or boys with Clothes of a black colour mixed with a dark green, and in their hands they hold a bird which is naked, & their heads compassed round with a bright shining of diverse colours. They leave a sweet smell behind them also but [it] differs from the others something.

Note there are twelve Princes ruling besides these in the Altitudes, and they distribute their office among themselves every one ruling thirty days [2]or thereabouts every year. Now it will be in vain to call any of those Angels unless it be them that governs them, For every Chora or Altitude hath its limited time according to the twelve signs of the Zodiac and in that sign the Sun is in, that or the Angel that belongs to that sign hath the government.

As for Example Suppose I would call the two first of the five [angels] that belongs to the first Chora, then choose the first Sunday in March after the Sun hath entered Aries, and then I make my Experiment. And so do the like if you will the next Sunday after again. And if you will call the two second that belongs to the first Chora, then you must take the Sunday after the Sun enters Taurus in April but if you will call the last of the five then you must take those ~~said~~ Sundays that are in May as the Sun is [then] entered Gemini to make your experiment in.

Do the like in the other Altitude; for they have all one way of working. But the Altitudes have a name formed severally in the substance of heaven even as a Character, for when the Angels hear the names of God that is attributed to them, they hear it by virtue of that Character.[3] Therefore it is in vain to call any angel or spirit Unless he knows what Names of God to call him by. Therefore observe the form of the following Conjuration or Invocation following.

---

[1] Bay leaves.

[2] *Hundred & fourth sheet Dr Rudd*. This page also repeats the title "The Almadel" at the top of the page, but in the middle of the text, so we have not inserted it here.

[3] Perhaps the only time that the connection between the sigil characters and the spoken names of God is spelled out in any grimoire.

The Invocation

O[1] *thou great blessed and glorious Angel of God (N)* [2] *who Ruleth and is the first and chief governing Angel in the first Chora or Altitude in the East, I the servant of the same your God* ***Adonai, Helomi*** *and* ***Pine*** *whom you do obey, and is the distributor and disposer of all things both in heaven, Earth and hell do Invocate Conjure and Entreat thee (N) that thou forthwith appear in the virtue and power of the same God* ***Adonai, Helomi*** *and* ***Pine.*** *And I do Command thee by him whom you do obey and is set over you as King by the divine power of God. That you forthwith Descend from your Orders or place of abode to come unto me and show thyself plainly and visibly here before me in this Crystal stone in thy own proper shape and glory speaking with a voice intelligible and to my understanding. O thou mighty and powerful Angel (N) who art by the power of God ordained to govern all animals vegetables and minerals and to cause them and all Creatures of God to spring Increase and bring forth according to their kind and nature, I the servant of the most high God whom you obey do entreat and humbly beseech thee to com from your Celestial mansion and show unto me all things I shall desire of you, So far as in office you may or can or is capable to perform if God permit the same. O thou servant of mercy (N) I do humbly entreat and beseech thee in and by these holy and blessed names of your God* ***Adonai, Helomi, Pine****. And I do also constrain you in and by this powerful name* ***Anabona*** *that you forthwith appear visibly and plainly in your own proper shape and glory in and through this Crystal stone that I may visibly see you and audibly hear you speak unto me, And that I may have thy glorious assistance and blessed Communication, familiar friendship and constant society Community and instruction both now and at all other times to inform & rightly instruct me in my Judgement in my ignorant and depraved Intellect and*[3] *understanding, and to assist me both herein and in all other truths &c, the Almighty* ***Adonai*** *the King of Kings, the Giver of all good gifts shall in his bountiful and fatherly mercy be graciously pleased to bestow upon me.*

Therefore O thou blessed Angel (N) be friendly unto me so far as God shall give you power in office to perform, whereunto I move you in power and presence to appear, that I may sing with holy Angels O Mappa la man Hallelujah. Amen

[4]When he is appeared give him or them a Kind entertainment [welcome], and then ask what is just and lawful, and that which is proper and suitable to his office and you shall obtain it.

So endeth the fourth Book called
The **Almadel** of Solomon the King

---

[1] H: This letter is drawn large with the date *"1712"* written inside it, the date Peter Smart copied the original manuscript of Dr Rudd.

[2] Here insert the name of the angel being called.

[3] H: *"and"* is repeated here.

[4] Hundred and fifth Sheet Dr Rudd.

Appendices

Appendix 1 - *Theurgia-Goetia* in Sloane 3824.

Longobardus[1]

A Prayer to be said before the calling forth of Elemental or Infernal Powers, or Spirits of Darkness.[2]

O most high, Immense, Immortal, Incomprehensible, and Omnipotent Lord God of Hosts, the only Creator of Heaven & Earth, & of all things contained therein; who, amongst all other admirable works of the Creation, hast made Man, according to the express Image of thy self, dignifying him with more divine, Celestial & Sublime Excellency, & superior part and participation, cohering with the most high & sacred Godhead, Angels, Heavens, Elements, & Elemental things; & given him an Imperial Sovereignty, over all Sublunar things in the Creation, both Animal, Vegetable, Mineral & Elemental: and next even to thy self under the Heavens, as a benefit and prerogative proper only to Man, & to no other Creature: And who hath likewise given to Man, a Sovereign power over all sublunar Spirits, both Aerial, Terrestrial & otherwise Elemental, residing in Orders & Mansions proper, & other wandering Spirits out of Orders or Mansions proper, both of Light & Darkness, & also Infernal Spirits, & subjected them to his Obedience & Service, whensoever he shall Command, Constrain, Call forth & move them to visible appearance, in order thereunto. Now then O most high & heavenly God we thy humble Servants, reverently here present in thy holy fear, do beseech thee in thine infinite Mercy & paternal goodness, that all Sublunar Spirits both Elemental and residing in Orders, & otherwise wandering out of Orders, both of Light & Darkness, & also Infernal Powers, may at the reading & rehearsal of our Invocations, Conjurations & Constringations, [3] *& by thee commanded, & compelled, & constrained, obediently and peaceably to move & appear visibly, in fair & decent Form & Shape, & in no wise hurtful, dreadful, terrible or affrightful, or otherwise in any violence or violent manner unto us, & here before us in these Glass Receptacles, or otherwise, to appear out of them here before us, in like serene, fair & decent manner, as shall be most convenient & necessary for any action, thing or matter, that they are called for to such appearances; & to serve & obey us, & to fulfil & go form our will, desires & Commandments in all & every several & particular matters & things respectively, wherein their ~~Order~~ Office & Orders are concerned, or whereunto in any wise they properly appertain; & also to depart from our presence, & obediently & peaceably to return to their Orders & Places of residence, when they have performed & fulfilled all our Will and Commandments; And yet we shall discharge them for the time present, & time future; or shall accordingly give them Licence so to do, and also to be ready from time to time at our Call, & at all times to appear visibly unto us, & to serve & obey us, & to fulfil all our*

[1] Sloane MS 3824 fol. 3-13. This is the first item in the manuscript has been strangely captioned by one of its owners as 'Longobardus'. This item is in the hand of Elias Ashmole.

[2] Folios 3-5.

[3] Constraints.

requests whatsoever we shall command them, & also to return to their Orders in peace, when we shall give them Licence to depart thereunto, without violence, injury, harm, prejudice or other mischief or mischievous matter to be done unto us or this Place, or to any other person or ~~persons~~ places whatsoever. Amen.

The Lord bless us & keep us, the Lord make his Face shine upon us, & be gracious unto us: the Lord lift up his Countenance upon us, & give us his Peace.

O All you Spirits of great power **L:B:S: [Lucifer, Beelzebub, and Sathan]**[1] *unto whom By Orders & Offices,*[2] *as Messengers of wrath, & Ministers of divine Justice, the Execution of God's Judgement are committed, & accordingly at his Commandment by you fulfilled, on all sublunar things, Creatures & places whatsoever & wheresoever he shall decree and appoint the same to be inflicted: And otherwise also & against sundry & many other times, preordained you by Orders & Offices, to serve & assist the Sons of men, living upon Earth, Servants of the most high God, whensoever you shall be invoked, moved, requested, commanded & constrained thereunto: Now therefore know ye; O all ye Spirits* **L:B:S: [Lucifer, Beelzebub, Sathan]** *that we, Servants of the most high God, reverently here present in his holy fear, being dignified in the holy Trinity, with celestial power & authority, given to Man at his Creation, & to his successive posterity & Generations, unto the utmost period of time, above & over all Sublunar Spirits, of all Degrees, Natures, Orders & Offices, both Aerial, Terrestrial & otherwise Elemental, or wandering out of Orders, or Infernal, whether of Light or Darkness, from the Superior to the Inferior; do by the Name of your God, & by your Seals & Characters, most firmly & solidly subjecting & binding you by Orders & Office, both to the divine command of the Highest & his Servants the Sons of Men, now living on Earth: We do Exorcise, Conjure, Command, Constrain & move you, O all you Spirits* **L:B:S: [Lucifer, Beelzebub, and Sathan]** *to subject all Spirits whatsoever, from the Superior to the Inferior, that have place & Residence in any, or all, & every of your several & respective Orders or Mansions, or that shall be otherwise under your power, government & Command unto us, & our Invocations, Conjurations & Constringations. And that whensoever & wheresoever we shall at any time, & in any place, Conjure, Command, Constrain, Call forth & move them, by Names, Orders & Offices, or any or either of them, that then & there, even at the very instant time, be enforced, compelled & constrained to move & appear, in fair & decent forms, & in no wise hurtful, dreadful, terrible or affrightful unto us, or this place, or to any other person or place whatsoever, but in all humility & serenity, visibly to the sight of our Eyes, either in these G: R: [Glass Receptacles]*[3] *or any of them standing here before us, for that purpose, according to a usual way of receiving & enclosing Spirits at*

---

1 S4: This contraction "L:B:S:" in the manuscript clearly refers to Lucifer, Beelzebub and Sathan, as later conjurations demonstrate. These three are part of the hierarchy left out of later versions of the *Lemegeton.* The text goes on to acknowledge that these three are appointed by God as his rulers of the sublunary world. They are therefore necessary to the hierarchy of the *Goetia.*

2 In the sense of Angelic Orders, and appointed duties.

3 The skrying glass.

their appearance, Or otherwise out of them here before us, ~~in all or any such Operations & Affairs, as the necessity or occasion thereof shall require~~ according as best befitteth, or shall be most beneficial & convenient for us, in all or any such our Operations & Affairs, as the necessity or occasion thereof shall require. And to show forth unto us true & visible signs, foregoing [foreshadowing] their coming & appearance. And to make true & faithful Answers unto us, & also to reveal, discover & show forth unto us, the very truth & certainty of all such our purposeful matters & things in question, & to fulfil, perform & accomplish unto us, all these our demands & Requests, as lyeth here before us. And also furthermore, as in the content of our Invocations, Conjurations & Constringations, shall more fully & at large be declared & expressly rehearsed: speaking plainly unto us, so as that we may both hear & understand them. All which as aforesaid, we do powerfully Exorcise, Conjure, Command, Compel Constrain & move you, O all you Spirits ***L: B: S: [Lucifer, Beelzebub, Sathan]*** *in the Name of your ~~your~~ God, & by the Seals of your Orders, preordinately decreed of the most high God, Confirming, Subjecting and binding you by Orders & Office, into strict Obedience; first to the fulfilling of his Divine Will & pleasure, both at his instant & immediate Commandments & Appointments; And secondly as well unto the Service, Obedience & Assistance of his Servants the Sons of Men, now living on Earth, in your several & respective Orders & Offices, as to [not] seduce, subvert & seek to destroy them by your evil Temptations, or any other vile, subtle, crafty insinuations & illusions: And by the Celestial power of the most high & holy Trinity, wherewith we are now through divine Grace, dignified, armed & supported, to do, fulfil, perform & accomplish for & unto ~~under~~ us, both now at this time present, & also at all other times, whensoever we shall move, request & command them thereunto, without delay delusion or disturbance, whereby to surprise or assault our senses with fears & amazements: or in any wise to obstruct or hinder the effects of these our present Operations, by any subtle Craft or illusions whatsoever, &c.*[1]

[1] The next invocation, which we have not transcribed, conjures *"all you Spirits by Name Sulphur, Anaboth, Sonenel, Barbatos, Gorson, (or Gorzon), Everges, Mureril, Vassago, Agares, Baramper, Barbason..."* and also *"Scor (or Scarus), Roab, Zaym, Umbra, & Gijel."* Four of these spirits are from the *Goetia,* further demonstrating the continuity between this manuscript and the *Lemegeton.*

[General Invocation][1]

A General Invocation, Conjuration or Constringation, moving and calling forth, any particular Aerial, Terrestrial, or other Elemental or Infernal, or other wandering Spirit or Spirits, of what Name, Order, Office, Angle, Mansion, Nature, Degree or power whatsoever they are or may be of, or in any wise properly appertaining or belonging unto; which are to be mentioned in the following Invocation, whence the Letter N: is inserted, as being conveniently used thereunto, & so placed therein accordingly.[2]

O you Spirit, or Spiritual power, who is known of us from the Tradition of our Ancestors, & called by the Name N: of what nature Order, Office, Angle, Mansion or other place of abode wheresoever you are, or may be of, or do reside, frequent or in any wise properly or differently appertain or belong unto, or whether Elemental or Infernal, or other wandering Spirit or power, either of Light or darkness, having power given you to visit the Earth, & to execute the Commandments of the highest: and also by divine provision plainly & visibly, & in a fair & decent form to appear unto the Sons of Men, Servants of the most high God living on Earth, whensoever you shall be of them Invocated, Commanded, called forth, moved, & thereby Conjured, & constrained thereunto, to obey them, to serve them, & to be friendly unto them, & readily forthwith to fulfil & perform all such [of] their commands & requests which they shall make; wherein by nature Office order, place or power, you may in any wise be concerned or serviceable. Know therefore O ye Spirit called by the Name N: (as aforesaid) that we the Servants of the most high God, & reverently here present in his holy fear, do Conjure, Command, Constrain, move & call you forth to visible Appearance, in the name of the most high ***Madzilodarp*** *and by the virtue and power of these his glorious, great, mighty & sacred Names,* ***Tetragrammaton, Jehovah, Adonay, Zebaoth, Jah, Saday, Agla, El, Elohim, Alpha & Omega****, And who said, let us make Man, accordingly to our Image & Similitude, & let him bear rule over the works of our hands, & have sovereign power & command over all Sublunar Spirits, both Aerial, Terrestrial & otherwise Elemental, & other wandering Spirits & Infernal Spirits, of all Orders & offices whatsoever, both of Light & Darkness, & by your Seal & Character, most firmly & solidly binding, subjecting & obliging you by Order & Office, both to the divine Command of the Highest, & his servants the Sons of Men, calling forth & moving you thereunto. And we do also further Conjure, Compel, Command, Constrain, Call forth & move you, By nature, degree, Order & Office, unto what Hierarchy Mansion or Place of residence whatsoever you appertain or belong unto, or wheresoever else you shall at this present be, either wandering out of Orders, or otherwise, O you Spirit, who is called N: to visible Appearance, Move therefore O ye Spirit N: Come away and appear ye visibly unto us, in fair & decent form in these Glass Receptacles or otherwise out of the same,*

---

[1] Folio 13v-15v.

[2] S4: This prayer is found in Sloane 3824 fol. 13b-15b. As it refers to Wandering Spirits and precedes the subsequent material from *Theurgia-Goetia*, we felt it should also be included here.

in like form: visibly here before us, not in any wise terrible or affrightful unto us, to amaze or surprise us, or in any violent or turbulent manner, hurtful to us or this place, or to any other person or place whatsoever, but come & appear you in all serenity, peace & mildness, showing forth likewise unto us, a visible sign or test foregoing your appearance, and by the virtue, power, efficacy & influence of these great, mighty & sacred names of the most high God, which Adam heard & spoke, & by the Name Agla, which Lot heard & was saved with his family; and by the Name of **Gin**, *which Noah heard & spake, after he was delivered from the Flood, And by the Names which Abraham heard & did know God, & by the Name* **Ioth**, *which Jacob heard & was delivered from the hand of his brother Esau. And by the Name* **Tetragrammaton**, *which was heard of the Angel striving with him, And by the Name* **Anapheketon**, *which Aaron heard and speaking was made wise, And by the Name* **Zebioth**, *which Moses named, & the water of Egypt was turned into blood, And by the Name* **Escherie Oriston**, *which Moses named & all the Rivers belched out Frogs, & they went into the Egyptian Houses, destroying all things, And by the Name* **Adonay**, *which Moses named, & there were Locusts appeared upon the Land of the Egyptians, & ate up all that which was remaining, And by the name* **Elion**, *which Moses named, & there was such a Storm of Hail as was not from the beginning of the World. And by the Name* **Primeumaton**, *& the most wonderful power & efficacy thereof, which Moses named, & the Earth opened her mouth, & swallowed up Corah, Dathan & Abiram, & all their Generation & People, And by the Name that Moses heard from the midst of the burning Bush, & was astonished, And by the Name that the Israelites heard upon the Mount Sina, & they died for fear, And by the Name* **Burne**, *by the virtue & power whereof the Sea parted in sunder, And by the efficacy of that Name, at the rehearsing whereof the Waters was divided, And by the mighty power of that great Name, at the speaking whereof, the Stones burst & relented. And by the Name* **Schemes, Amathia**, *which Joshua named, & the Sun stayed his course,*[1] *And by the Name* **Alpha & Omega**, *which Daniel named & destroyed Bell & the Dragon,*[2] *And by the Name* **Emanuel**, *which the three Children, Shadrach, Mesack & Abednigo*[3] *sang in the midst of the burning fiery furnace, & were unharmed. And by the virtue & power of those Names, whereby Solomon called forth, constrained, bound, enclosed or shut up Spirits* **Elbrach, Ebanher, Agla, Goth, Ioth, Othie, Venoch, Nabrach**, *And by the Imperial Throne, & by the Majesty & Diety of the Almighty, Everlasting & true God of Hosts; We do call upon you, O you Spirit who is called N: And being dignified by the power of the holy Spirit, & strengthened by his all powerful arms, & being thereby supported with his*

---

[1] "Then spake Joshua to the Lord…in the sight of Israel: 'Sun, stand thou still upon Gibeon; and thou, Moon, in the Valley of Ajalon.' And the sun stood still, and the moon stayed, until the people had avenged themselves upon their enemies. Is not this written in the *Book of Jasher*? So the sun stood still in the midst of heaven, and hasted not to go down about a whole day." *Joshua 10:12-13*

[2] See the apocryphal book *Bel and the Dragon* sometimes included in the book of *Daliel*, in which Daniel gets the better of the god Bel.

[3] *Daniel* 3:1-29.

Celestial & Divine assistance, Do Conjure, Command, Constrain, Call forth & move you O you Spirit N: to visible appearance: Move therefore & appear you, & show your self visibly & affably in fair & decent form, in these G: R: [Glass Receptacles] or otherwise out of the same here before us, as may be most convenient & necessary, for this our purpose, in these present Operations & affairs, & come ye in all serenity, mildness, peace & friendship, & in no wise terrible or hurtful to us or to this place, or to any other place or person whatsoever, & make true & faithful answers unto all such, of these our demands & requests, as lyeth her before us, ready to be proposed, & made known unto you, & likewise readily & willingly fulfil & perform all such our other Commandments & desires, as we shall yet further will & enjoin you, wherein your Orders & Offices, is in any wise properly appertaining & concerned, Now therefore O you Spirit N: prepare ye & be not obstinate, refractory or pertinacious, but come ye away forthwith & immediately from your Orders, or from what Mansion, Element, Angle, part or place of residence, or else wheresoever you are in, or at this present shall, or may, either chance by, or otherwise by divine or superior command or appointment happen to be, & depart ye not from our presence & commands, until ye have fully & effectually fulfilled our desires, in all fidelity reality & truth, without any delay, fraud, guile, or illusion whatsoever.

Now therefore hearken unto our voice: O ye Spirit N: & be not obstinate, refractory or disobedient. Know ye that we the servants of the most high God, being dignified, fortified & supported, assisted & encouraged, by his omnipotent, divine, & Celestial power, & by the virtue force influence & efficacy thereof; & by this his most high, great, & mighty Name **Iehovah Tetragrammaton**, *who saith & it is done; whom all Creatures both Celestial, Elemental & Infernal, with fear & reverence doth most humbly serve honour & obey, & wherein all the world was formed, which being heard the Elements Thunder, the Air is Shaken, the Sea goes back, the Fire is quenched, the Earth trembleth, & all the heavenly, earthly & infernal Hosts do tremble & are troubled; Do Conjure, Command, Compel, Constrain, Call forth, & move you to visible appearance, wherefore O ye Spirit N: now presently & without any further tarrying, illusion, hindrance, or delay, move ye immediately, even at this very instant Call, make haste, & wheresoever you are, come away & appear ye visibly, affably courteously & peaceably, in fair & decent form, in these G: R: [Glass Receptacles] or otherwise out of them, as may be most convenient & befitting this our present action, occasion, operation & affair, plainly here before us, & to show forth unto us a true & visible sign, foregoing your coming & appearance: And come ye in all serenity, quietness and friendship, without noise or turbulence, or in any violent manner, hurtful to us or this place, or to any other place or person whatsoever, or otherwise, either to assault surprise or amaze us, either in Spirit or bodily senses, with fear astonishment or otherwise dreadful or terrible visions, or false motions or appearances, in any wise to affright, obstruct or delude us, & make us rational, true & faithful answers, speaking so plainly unto us, as that we may perfectly hear & understand you, readily & willingly fulfilling all our demands & requests, & accomplishing all such our desires, & assisting us in these & all others our operations & affairs, in any wise relating to your nature, degree, Order & Office, & therein to* *perform unto us, not only what we have proposed, but also in whatsoever wise we shall further enjoin or command you. Move therefore & come away, in the name of the Omnipotent, Everliving & true God* **Helioren**, *& appear as aforesaid visibly here before us, in these Names* **Aye Saraye, Aye Saraye, Aye Saraye**, *make haste & defer not your coming, in & through these Names* **Eloye, Archima Rabur**[1] *and obey your Master who is called* **Octinomos**.[2] *Now then finally know ye, O you Spirit N: that we being dignified by Celestial power, do by the Content of this our great & royal Invocation (as aforesaid) & by the virtue, power, Influence & efficacy thereof, Conjure, Command, Compel, Constrain, Call forth & move you to visible appearance, immediately at this very minute. Give ye now therefore present audience attendance and obedience thereunto, & come away with speed, & appear ye visibly unto the sight of our Eyes, in fair & decent forms, in these G: R: [Glass Receptacle] or otherwise there out here before us, & show forth unto us a visible sign foregoing your Appearance, persisting herein, to the full and effectual accomplishment & fulfilling of all our demands & requests, that we have or shall make unto you, even to the very utmost (as we have before said) without further Apology, excuse, pretence, hindrance, tarrying, delay, delusion, deceit, subtlety, Craft, disguise, interruption, false motion, disturbance, fear, fright, amazement: by any dreadful or terrible assault or surprise, or any other Illusion whatsoever, &c.*[3]

---

[1] *Eloye, Archima Rabur* is drawn from an earlier grimoire, probably *Liber Juratus*, and refers to Jesus Christ. *Eloye* = *Theloy* was the spirit that, according to Honorius of Thebes in *Liber Juratus*, "Who at Cana turnedst water into wine." *Archima* was the spirit that, according to the same source, "for thirty-two years didst preach to the people of the Catholic faith, and Who didst make the twelve Apostles perfect in knowledge and grace". *Rabuch* was the spirit that, according to the same source, "for forty days fastedst in the desert and wast tempted by the devil; Who didst forgive Mary Magdalene…Who gavest sight to one born blind; Who didst raise Lazarus who was dead for four days; Who didst vouchsafe Thy body to be sacrificed…nailed to the Cross through Thy hands and Feet, given vinegar and gall to drink, pierced in the side with a spear…" In short *Eloye, Archima Rabuch* is a mediaeval magician's name for Jesus of Nazareth, or if you prefer just maybe for the various spirits working through him. The latter opens up some interesting ideas regarding the magic used in his miracles.

[2] *Octynnomos* or *Octinomos* was the spirit that, according to Honorius of Thebes in *Liber Juratus*, "didst send the first star to the three kings, Jasper, Melchoir and Balthazar, who came to worship" Jesus after his birth.

[3] This is followed in folios 16-21v with an "Experiment, to cause a Thief to come again with the Goods he hath stolen" and to force the return of runaways, which is achieved through the conjuration of the demon bishops Theltrion, Sperion, Mayerion and Boytheon, but which as it does not directly relate to the *Lemegeton*, we have not transcribed here. The most interesting thing about this conjuration is that the spell is specifically designed to find a thief who has robbed John Rudd of Bedford in Kent, undoubtedly a relative of Thomas Rudd.
This is followed by (folio 22-29v) various preparations, consecrations and benedictions, just as they appear in the *Goetia*.

The Second Part of the *Art of King Solomon*[1]

In this following Treatise you have 31 names of chief Spirits,[2] with several of the Ministering Spirits which are under them, with their Seals or Characters, which is to be worn as a Lamen on your breast, for without that the Spirit that is appeared will not obey you to do your Will, &c.

The Offices of these Spirits are all one, for what one commands, the other can do the same, they can show & discover all things that are hid or done in the World, & can fetch & carry, & do any thing that is to be done, or is contained in any of the four Elements, Fire, Air, Earth or Water, &c: also the Secrets of any person whatsoever, let it be in what kind it will.

These Spirits Naturally are both good and Evil (that is to say) one part of them is good, & the other part of them is Evil; They are all commanded, and all Subject, governed & ruled by their Princes, & each said Prince resideth in that Mansion & place of abode, in the true point of the Compass, which is at large fixed compassed & showed forth, in the following Scheme or figure.[3]

Therefore, when you are resolved to enter upon the Practice, or to make use of any of these Spirits, or have desire to invoke or call forth any of the Kings, or likewise any of their Servants, you are straight way to direct, & truly to place your self to that said point of the Compass wherein the King hath his Mansion, Residence, or true place of abode, & you cannot Err or any ways go amiss, in this your Operations or any like Experiment.

Note therefore & carefully observe that every Prince is to have his Conjuration, yet all [are] of one Form & manner as in the foregoing part of this Book is showed at large. Therefore you have sufficient Explanation how to Call both King & Servant, particularly observing every Prince to have the like Conjuration of one form, excepting the Name & Place of the Spirit, for in that they must change & differ. Also the Seal of the Spirit is to be changed accordingly.

The Form of the Figure which discovers the Orders of the 31 Kings[4] or Princes, with their Servient Ministers, for when the King is found, his Subjects are easier to be found out, & so conversed withal.

You may perceive by this Figure,[5] that 20 of these Kings hath fixed Mansions, the Eleven is moveable, sometimes in one place, & sometimes in another, & other times together. Therefore you may stand with your Face, which way you please, when you call any of them or their servants forth to visible appearance.

---

[1] All the seals are missing from Sloane MS 3824, but we felt that the conjurations of the Wandering Princes deserved reproduction as they are not reproduced in this form in any other extant copies of the *Lemegeton*. This part of *Theurgia-Goetia* is found in Sloane MS 3824, fol. 53-71b.

[2] See Tables M20, M20a and M21 in Appendix 2.

[3] Missing figure not present in the MS, but the directional details are listed in the aforementioned Tables.

[4] S4: This is mis-recorded as "Knigs" from here on in this particular evocation in the MS.

[5] Not included.

[The Four Emperors]

Carnesiell[1] is the most great & chief Emperor Ruling in the East, who hath 1000 great Dukes, and a 100 lesser Dukes under him, beside 5000000000000 of Ministering Spirits, which is more inferior than the Dukes whereof we shall make no mention but only of twelve of the chief Dukes & their Seals, because they are sufficient for practice.

Then follows the names & Seals of Carnesiel, & the 12 Dukes.[2]

Note Carnesiel when he appears day or night, attends him 60000000000000 Dukes, but when you call any of these Dukes, there never attends above 300, & sometimes not above 10 &c.

The Conjuration of **Carnesiel** as follows.

We Conjure thee O thou mighty & potent Prince ***Carnesiel****, who is the Emperor & chief Commander ruling as King in the Dominion of the East, who has Rule by the power of the Supreme God* ***El****, over all Spirits both Superior & Inferior, belonging to the Infernal Orders. We Invoke & Command you, by this especial & truest Name of your God, & by that God you worship and obey, & by the seal of your Creation, & by the most mighty & powerful Name of God* ***Jehovah Tetragrammaton*** *who cast you out of heaven with all other the Infernal Spirits, & by all the most powerful & great Names of God, who created Heaven Earth and Hell, & all things contained in them, & by their powers & Virtues, & by the Name* ***PrimaVmaton***[3] *who commandeth the whole host of Heaven, that thou O Spirit* ***Carnesiel****, forthwith come forth & appear unto me here before this Circle, in a fair & comely form: & shape, without doing any harm to me, or any other Creature, this Place or any other part or place in the World, and answer truly & faithfully to all our Requests, that we may accomplish our Will or desire, in knowing or obtaining any matter or thing, which by Office you know, if belonging to your Orders, or proper for you to perform or to accomplish, through the power of God* ***El****, who created & disposeth of all things both Celestial Aerial Terrestrial & Infernal.*

---

[1] Carnesiel will be found in Chapter XVII of Book I of Trithemius' *Steganographia*.

[2] A semi marginal note. The Seals of the 12 Dukes have in fact not been included.

[3] Ashmole writes 'Primaumaton' as 'PrimaVmaton', stressing the central 'u' so that it becomes a capital 'V' probably to stress the pronunciation which was probably 'prime-you-ma-ton'. This ensures that the meaning 'First Breath' or 'prime *pneuma*' is fully implied.

Caspiel,[1] is the great & chief Emperor ruling in the South who hath 200 great Dukes & 400 lesser Dukes under him besides 1000200000000 of Ministering Spirits, which is much inferior &c: whereof we (saith Solomon) shall make no mention, but only of 12 of the chief Dukes, and their Seals, for they are sufficient for practice.

Then follows the Names & Seals of Caspiel, & those 12 Dukes.[2]

These 12 Dukes have 2660 under Dukes again to attend them, whereof some of them comes along with him, when he is invoked, but they are very stubborn and churlish.

The Conjuration of **Caspiel** as followeth.

We Conjure thee O thou mighty & potent Prince ***Caspiel****, who is a great & chief Emperor, ruling in the South, who bears rule by the power of the supreme God* ***El****, over all Spirits both Superior & Inferior of the Infernal Orders &c: We Command you by the especial & truest Name of your God, and by that God you worship & obey, & by the Seal of your Creation, & by the most mighty & powerful name of God* ***Iehovah Tetragrammaton****, who cast you out of Heaven, with all other [of] the Infernal Spirits & by the most powerful & great Names of God, who created Heaven, Earth & Hell, & all things contained in them, & by their powers & virtues, & by the Name* ***Primaumaton*** *who commandeth the whole Host of Heaven, that thou O Spirit* ***Caspiel****, forthwith come forth & appear unto me here before this Circle, do not delay, do not linger, what needs any more words, Move (we say) move we say, show your self & appear affably courteous friendly, in a fair & comely form & shape, without doing any harm, to us or any other Creature in this place, or any other part or place in the World, & answer truly & faithfully to all our Requests That we may accomplish our Wills or desires, in knowing or obtaining any matter or thing, which by Office you know, if belonging to your Orders, or proper for you to accomplish or perform, through the power of God* ***El****, who created & disposeth of all things, both Celestial, Aerial, Terrestrial & Infernal.*

[1] Caspiel will be found in Chapter XVIII of Book I of Trithemius' *Steganographia.*
[2] The Seals of the 12 Dukes have in fact not been included.

Amenadiel[1] is the great Emperor of the West who hath 300 great Dukes, & 500 lesser Dukes, beside 40000030000100000, other ministering Spirits more inferior to attend him, whereof we shall not make any mention but only of 12 of the chief Dukes & their Seals which is sufficient for practice.

Then follows the Names & Seals of Amenadiel & these 12 Dukes.[2]

Note **Amenadiel** may be called at any hour of the day or night, but his Dukes (who hath 3880 Servants a piece to attend them) are to be called in certain hours, as **Vadros**, he may be called in the 2 first hours of the day, **Camiel** in the second 2 hours of the day, & so successively on till you come to **Nadros** who is to be called in the 2 last hours of the Night, and then begin again at **Vadros** &c: the same Rule is to be observed in calling the Dukes belonging to **Demorial** the Emperor of the North.

The Conjuration of **Amenadiel**

We Conjure thee O thou mighty & Potent Prince ***Amenadiel****, who is Emperor & chief King ruling in the dominion of the West, who bears rule & power, by the permission of the Supreme God* ***El****, over all Spirits both Superior & inferior, belonging to the Terrestrial & Infernal Orders; We Invoke, Constrain, Compel & Command you, by this especial & truest Name of your God, & by that God, which you serve, worship & obey, & by the true Seal of your Creation, and by the most mighty, most dreadful & powerful Name of the Everlasting & Living God* ***Jehovah Tetragrammaton*** *who threw you down & cast you out of Heaven, with all other, & the rest of the Infernal Spirits, and by all the most powerful & great Names of God, who created Heaven, Earth & Hell, & all things whatsoever contained in them, And by their powers & virtues & by the Name* ***Primaumaton*** *who commandeth the whole Host of Heaven, that thou O Spirit* ***Amenadiel*** *forthwith (we say) move descend & appear, & show thy self Visibly unto me here before this Crystal, Come you in fair & comely form & shape without any delay, the King commands you, Therefore defer not your coming, what needs any more words, In the name of him that Liveth for ever, who shall come to Judge the Quick & the dead, & the World by Fire, gird up your self & come away, even at this very present time, before the Circle, and behold the Pentacle of Solomon. Behold your Conclusion [Termination], be not obstinate & rebellious, Behold the Banner of God, Move therefore & give your presence in no ghastly shape, without doing any harm to us, or any other Creature, this place or any other part or place in the World, Come ye therefore continuously, affably friendly, & answer truly & faithfully to all our requests, that we may accomplish our Wills and desires, in knowing or obtaining any matter or thing whatsoever, which by Office you know, if belonging to your Orders, or proper for you to perform or to accomplish, through the power of God* ***El****, who created & disposeth of all things, both Celestial Aerial, Terrestrial and Infernal.*

---

[1] Amenadiel will be found in Chapter XIX of Book I of Trithemius' *Steganographia*.

[2] A semi marginal note. The Seals of the 12 Dukes have in fact not been included.

Demoriel[1] is the great & mighty Emperor of the North, who hath 400 great Dukes & 600 lesser Dukes, with 700000800000900000 Servants under his Command to attend him, whereof we shall make mention but of 12 of the chief Dukes & their Seals, which will be sufficient for practice.

Here should follow the Names & Seals of Demoriel and the said 12 Dukes.[2]

Note each of those Dukes hath 1140 Servants, who attends them as need requireth, for when the Duke you call for, have more to do then ordinary, he hath the more Servants to attend him.

The Conjuration of **Demoriel** as followeth.

We Conjure thee O thou great & mighty Emperor ***Demoriel****, who is the King & chief Prince ruling in the dominion of the North, who bears rule & power, by the permission of the Supreme God* ***El****, over all Spirits both Superior & Inferior, belonging to the Terrestrial & Infernal Orders, We Invocate Constrain, Compel & Command you, by this especial & truest name of our God, And by that God which you serve worship & obey, & by the true Seal of your Creation, & by the most mighty most dreadful and powerful Name of the Everlasting & living God,* ***Jehovah Tetragrammaton*** *who threw you down [and] cast you out of Heaven, with all other & the rest of the Infernal Spirits, & by all the most powerful & great Names of God, who created Heaven Earth & Hell, & all things whatsoever contained in them, And by their power & virtues, and by the Name* ***Primaumaton****, who commandeth the whole Host of Heaven, that thou O Spirit* ***Demoriel****, forthwith (we say) move, descend & appear, & show thy self visibly unto us here before this Circle, Come you in a fair & comely form & shape without any delay, the King commands you, therefore defer not your coming, what needs any more words, in the Name of him that liveth for ever, who shall come to Judge the Quick & the dead & the World by Fire, Gird up your self & come away, even at this very present time before this Circle, & behold the Pentacle of Solomon, Behold your Conclusion be not obstinate & Rebellious, Behold the banner of God, Move therefore, & give your presence in no ghastly shape, without doing any harm to us, or any other Creature in this place, or any other part or place in the World, Come ye therefore courteously, affably, friendly, & answer truly and faithfully to all our requests, that we may accomplish our Wills & desires, in knowing or obtaining any matter or thing whatsoever, which by [your] Office you know, if belonging to your Orders, or proper for you to perform or accomplish, through the power of God* ***El****, who created and disposeth all things both Celestial Aerial Terrestrial & Infernal.*

---

[1] Demoriel will be found in Chapter XX of Book I of Trithemius' *Steganographia.*

[2] A semi marginal note. The Seals of the 12 Dukes have in fact not been included. This is in fact true in the rest of this, that where the Seals are indicated they are in fact missing.

Pamersiel is the first & chief Spirit in the East under [the Emperor of the East] **Carnesiel**, who hath 1000 Spirits under him, which are to be called in the day time, but with great care, for they are very lofty & stubborn, whereof we shall make mention but of [only] 11 as followeth.

Then follows the Names & Seals of Pamesiel,[1] & eleven Spirits.[2]

Note these Spirits are by nature Evil & very false, not to be trusted in secret things, but is excellent in driving away Spirits of darkness from any place or House that is haunted.[3]

[Method of Calling][4]

To call forth Pamersiel or any of these his Servants, chose the uppermost private or secret & most tacit Room in the house, or in some certain Island, Wood or Grove, or the most occult or hidden place from all comers or goers that no one chancily may (if possible) happen that way. (Chamber or what ever place else you Act[ion] your Concerns in). Observe that it be very Airy, because those Spirits that in this part, are all of the Air, you may call these Spirits into a Crystal Stone or Glass Receptacle, being an ancient & usual way of receiving & binding of Spirits, This Crystal Stone must be four Inches Diameter, set [on] a Table of Art[5] made as followeth, which is truly called the Secret Table of Solomon, having the Seal of the Spirit on your Breast, & the Girdle [of lion skin] about your Waist, & you cannot err, the form of the Table is thus, as this present Figure doth here represent & show;[6] behold the Figure when you have thus prepared what is to be prepared, rehearse the Conjuration following several times, that is whilst the Spirit comes, for without doubt he will come; **Note** the same Method is to be used, in all the following part of this Book as is here of [specified for] Pamersiel, & his Servants, Also the same [method should be used] in calling the King & his Servants &c.

---

[1] S4: This is given incorrectly rather than *Pamersiel*. However the spelling 'Parmersiel' will be found in Chapter 1 of Book I of Trithemius' *Steganographia*.

[2] The Seals do not appear in the manuscript.

[3] An interesting application of Spirits to the clearing of a haunted house.

[4] As mentioned in the Introduction, the actual method of Calling the Spirits is here embedded within the description of Pamersiel. It would be most useful to find the manuscript source which had the method clearly separated at the beginning of the book, rather than included within the description of an individual Spirit.

[5] Table of Practice.

[6] The illustration accompanying this is a very crudely drawn Seal of Solomon, which as we have explained earlier is not appropriate for the Table of Practice.

The Conjuration of Pamersiel

We Conjure thee O ***Pamersiel****, a chief Spirit ruling in the East, under that mighty Potent and great Prince [Emperor of the East]* ***Carnesiel****, We Invocate (Move & call you forth), compel, constrain & command you by the especial & truest name of God, & by that God which you [also] serve worship & obey, & by the true Seal of your creation, & by the most mighty & most dreadful & most powerful name of the Everlasting & living God,* ***Jehovah Tetragrammaton****, who threw you down & cast you out of Heaven, with all other & the rest of the Infernal Spirits, and by all the most powerful & great Names of God, who created Heaven Earth & Hell, & all things whatsoever contained in them, & by their powers & virtues & by the Name* ***PrimaUmaton****,*[1] *who commandeth the whole Host of Heaven, that thou O Spirit* ***Pamersiel****, forthwith (we say) move, descend & appear, & to show thy self visibly unto us here before this Circle, Come ye in a fair & comely form & shape, without any delay, the King commands you, therefore defer not your coming, what needs any more words, In the Name of him that liveth for ever, who shall come to judge the Quick & the dead,*[2] *& the World by Fire, Gird up your self & come away, even at this present time before this Circle, & behold the Pentacle of Solomon, behold the Conclusion, be not obstinate & Rebellious, behold the Banner of God, Move therefore & give your presence in no ghastly shape, without doing any harm to us, or any other Creature in this place, or any other part or place in the World, Come ye therefore courteously, affably, friendly, & answer truly & faithfully to all our Requests, that we may accomplish our Wills & desires in knowing or obtaining any matter or thing, which by Office you know if belonging to your Orders, or proper for you to perform or accomplish; through the power of God* ***El****, who created and disposeth of all things both Celestial, Aerial & Infernal.*

---

[1] This time Ashmole uses a capital 'U' in the middle of the word, to stress the pronunciation.

[2] 'The Quick' = 'the living'. The phrase 'the Quick and the Dead' comes from the Bible, *1 Peter* 4:5, where it describes judgment of both the currently living and the dead.

The second Spirit in order under [Carnesiel] the Emperor of the East, is called **Padiel**, he ruleth in the East and by South as King, & governeth 10000 Spirits by day, and 200000 by Night, besides as well Thousands under them, They are all good by Nature, and may be trusted. Solomon saith, that these Spirits have no power of themselves, but what is given unto them by their Prince **Padiel**, therefore he hath made no mention of any of their names, because if any of them is called, they cannot appear without the leave of their Prince, as others can do &c: You must use the same Method in calling this Prince **Padiel**, as is directed before of **Pamersiel**.

Then follows the Seal of **Padiel**.[1]

The Conjuration of **Padiel**.

We Conjure thee O thou Mighty & Potent Prince ***Padiel****, who rules as a chief Prince or King, in the dominion of East and by South, We Invocate command & compel you, by this especial Name of your God, and by that God which you serve worship & obey, & by the true Seal of your Creation, and by the most mighty ~~&~~ most dreadful, and powerful Name, of the everlasting & Living God,* ***Jehovah Tetragrammaton****, who threw down & cast you out of Heaven, with all the other the rest of the Infernal Spirits, and by all the most powerful & great Names of God, who created Heaven Earth & Hell, & all thing whatsoever contained in them, and by their power & virtues and by the Name* ***Primaumaton*** *who commandeth the whole Host of Heaven, That thou O Spirit* ***Padiel*** *forthwith (we say) move, descend and appear, & show thy self visibly unto us here before this Crystal, Come you in a fair & comely form and shape, without any delay, the King commands you, therefore defer not your coming, what needs any more words, in the Name of him that liveth for ever, who shall come to judge the Quick & the dead, & the World by fire, ~~Grid~~ Gird up your self, & come away even at this very present time before this Circle, & behold the Pentacle of Solomon, Behold your Conclusion be not obstinate & Rebellious, Behold the Banner of God, Move therefore & give your presence in no ghastly shape, without doing any harm unto us, or any other Creature in this place, or any other part or place in the World, Come ye therefore courteously, affably, friendly, and answer truly & faithfully to all our Requests, that we may accomplish our Wills & desires, in knowing or obtaining any matter or thing, which by Office you know if belonging to your Orders, or proper for you to perform or accomplish, through the power of God* ***El****, who created and disposeth of all things both Celestial Aerial Terrestrial and Infernal.*[2]

[1] The Seal is not provided.

[2] At this point we break off transcribing from Sloane MS 3824, as the Conjurations of the following 10 Spirits follow the same pattern as that of Padiel, and their other details can be found in the main text of the present book. Sloane MS 3824 itself breaks off part way through the Conjuration of Cabariel, omitting the last four Spirits altogether. We skip these pages and resume transcribing with the Spirit Contract for Padiel. This Contract is unique and does not appear in any other version of the *Theurgia-Goetia*, as far as we are aware.

[The Spirit Contract for Padiel][1]

I ~~a~~ Presidential Spirit ~~called~~ by name called Padiel, residing & serving under ~~B~~ Carnesiel a King of the Angle or Mansion of the West, at the Command of the Sovereign head of my Orders, and on my own accord, by the virtue power & force of Invocation on that behalf, do firmly & solidly bind & oblige my self by these present, Visibly to appear, in fair & decent Form, unto A:B and C:D or either of them, at all times & in all places, whensoever & wheresoever, I shall of them, or either of them [be] called forth & moved thereunto; either in a Glass Receptacle[2] or otherwise out of it, as the Condition or Occasion of any matters in question or Operation shall properly or necessarily require. And I the said Spirit Padiel, do also yet further & more especially bind & oblige my self, unto A:B & C:D[3] or either of them as aforesaid, in by & through the truest & most especial name of my God, & by the principal head of my Orders, & by his Seal & Character & the virtue thereof, at the sight of which all Spirits in their several & respective degrees, Orders & Offices, do therein accordingly serve, honour & obey. And chiefly by this my [own] Seal or Character, as here under is by me affixed or inserted. And by the force and virtue of these words most powerfully in the Sophick or M[a]gick Art, Lay, Alzym, Mura, Syron, Nalgava, Rythin, Layaganum, Layarazin, Lasai, By the content hereof, & by the virtue power & efficacy of all aforesaid, I the said Spirit Padiel do firmly & faithfully promise to appear visibly unto A:B & C:D[3] or either of them, in manner & form as aforesaid, & to make true & faithful answers, unto all & every their or either of their demands & requests, speaking plainly, & to be understood of them or either of them, & also readily, willingly & effectually to fulfil, perform & accomplish, all & every such their or either of their Commandments, as at any time they or either of them shall request & enjoin me, at all times & in all places, whensoever & wheresoever I shall of them or either of them moved, or called forth to visible appearance, during their or either of their natural lives, even to the last or ultimate Survivors. In testimony whereof being commanded, I have hereunto & hereunder, affixed or inserted, my true Seal or Character, unto which I serve & bear obedience, and have always stuck close.[4]

---

[1] This interesting example of a Spirit Contract follows on immediately from the page which ends halfway through the summoning of Cabariel. As it specifically refers to Padiel we felt it should be included as a fine example of this rare form of document at this point. This document is intended to be used as part and parcel of the *ligatio* stage of an evocation.

[2] Footnote in MS: as being one usual manner of appearance & of receiving and enclosing of Spirits.

[3] Possibly two practitioners in Rudd's circle, or just a convention for identifying any two people.

[4] S4: The rest of the item is a mixture of seals, treasure spirits and other magical items, not relevant to the *Lemegeton*, which we intend to reproduce in the appropriate place in a subsequent volume. For details of other items in this manuscript see the Introduction.

Appendix 2: The Table of 72 Demons of the Goetia[751]

M15. Demons of the Goetia (Lemegeton Book I) – 1.

	a. Wierus [Harley 6482]	b. Harley 6483	c. Demon Name [alt. spelling]	d. Hebrew	e. Stead Ridden, Other Qualities	f. GD Decans	g. Ruling Angel Name (Rudd)
♈	1 [11]	1	**Bael**[752] [Baell, Baël]	באל – בעל	Crocodile [Under Lucifer][753] [East]	**Day** 1♈	Vehujah והויאה
♈	2	2	Agares Agreas	אגאראש אגאר –	Order of Virtues Under Lucifer [East]	2♈	Jeliel ילי׳אל
♈	0	3	Vasago [Vassago]	ושאגו – –		3♈	Syrael שיראל
♈	46 [41]	4	Gamigin [Samigina, Gamygyn]	גאמיגינ גמיגין כמיגין		1♉	Elemiah אלאמיאה
♈	3	5	Marbas [Barbas]	מארבש מארב –	[Under Lucifer]	2♉	Mahasaiah מהשיאה
♈	14 [59]	6	Valefar Valefor [Malaphar]	ואלפהר ואלפר ולפר	[Under Astaroth]	3♉	Jelahel ילאהל
♉	5	7	Amon [Aamon]	אמונ אמון –	[Under Lucifer]	1♊	Achasiah אחיאה
♉	6 [12]	8	Barbatos	ברבטוש – –	Order of Virtues [Under Lucifer] [♐]	2♊	Cahatel כאהטל
♉	22 [55]	9	**Paimon**	פאימונ פאימון פימון	Dromedary camel Order of Potestates [NW] Under Lucifer[754]	3♊	Hasiel האסיאל
♉	7 [22]	10	Buer	בואר – –	[Under Belzebuth] [Sun in ♐]	1♋	Aladiah אלדיאה
♉	8	11	Gusoin [Gusoyn, Gusoin,Gorson]	גוסוינ גוסיון –	[Under Belzebuth]	2♋	Laviah לאויאה
♉	21 [58]	12	Sitri [Sytry, Bitru]	שיטרי שיטרי		3♋	Hahajah האהאיה

[751] This and all subsequent Tables are reprinted from Stephen Skinner, *Complete Magician's Tables*, Golden Hoard Press, London & Singapore, 2006, reprinted Llewellyn, Woodbury, 2006.
[752] Kings are marked in bold.
[753] Rulership is marked in square brackets, where taken conjecturally from the *Grand Grimoire*.
[754] More accurately, 'northerly including NW'. He is "More obedient unto Lucifer than other Kings".

Demons of the Goetia –1 (continued).				
h. Rank	**i. Planet**	**j. No. of Legions**	**k. Evoked Appearance**	**l. Powers & Attributes**
King	Sun	66	With three heads (toad, man and cat) or with each form separately.	Invisibility.
Duke	Venus	31	Old Man riding on a Crocodile, carrying a Goshawk on his fist.	Makes people run that stand still; returns Runaways. Teaches all languages, destroys dignities spiritual and temporal, causes earthquakes.
Prince	Jupiter	26	Good natured.	Declares things Past & Future; Discovers the Hidden & Lost.
Marquis	Moon	30	Little horse or ass, then as a human with a hoarse voice.	Teaches Liberal Sciences; Giveth Account of Dead causes Souls that died in Sin or drowned to answer questions.
President	Mercury	36	A mighty lion, human shape.	Reveals any hidden or secret things; Causes & cures diseases; Wisdom; knowledge of Mechanical Arts and handicrafts; Changes Men into other shapes.
Duke	Venus	10	Lion with man's head (a thief's head).	A good familiar, but he tempts the magician to steal, and may finally bring him to the gallows
Marquis	Moon	40	Wolf with serpent's tail vomiting fire, like a raven with dog's teeth.	Reveals things past, present and future; procures love; resolves controversies between friends and foes.
Duke & Earl	Venus	300 [30]	Appears when Sun is in Sagittarius accompanied by 4 Kings & their Troops.	Teaches the language of birds, dogs & other creatures; breaks open hidden treasures enchanted by other magicians; Knows things past, present & future; Reconciles Friends with those in power.
King,[755]	Sun	200+25	Crowned man sitting upon a dromedary camel, with a host of musicians going before him.	Teaches all arts & sciences, the Elements & other secret things; he gives honours; he binds others to be obedient to the magician; gives good familiars. Of Angels & Potestates. Initially difficult to understand.
President	Mercury	50 [40]	Appears when Sun is in Sagittarius.	Teaches Philosophy (moral & natural) & logic & the virtues of herbs and plants; heals illnesses; gives good familiars.
Duke	Venus	40 [45]	Appears in the form of a Xenophilus.[756]	Reveals things past, present & future; answers all questions; reconciles friends; gives honours.
Prince	Jupiter	60	Leopard's face & Gryphon's wings, then very beautiful human.	Inflames men with woman's love and vice versa; Causes women to be luxurious and to go naked.

[755] He arrives with 2 other Kings, Baball and Abalam.
[756] Maybe a *zenophali*. Not to be confused with the 4th century Pythagorean philosopher Xenophilus.

M15. Demons of the Goetia (Lemegeton Book I) – 2.

	Wierus [Rudd 6482]	No. in Harley 6483	Demon Name [alt. spellings]	Hebrew	Stead Ridden, Other Qualities	GD Decans	Ruling Angel Name (Rudd)
♊	20 [25]	13	**Beleth** [or Bilet, Byleth, Bileth] [S and E][757]	בלאת – –	Pale horse Order of Potestates	**Day** 1♌	Jezalel יזאלאל
	13	14	Leraic [Leraye, Leraje, Leraika, Oray, Leraie][758]	לראיכ לראיך לריך	[Under Astaroth] [♐]	2♌	Mebahel מבאהל
	12	15	Eligos [Eligor, Abigor]	אליגוש – –	[Under Belzebuth]	3♌	Haziel האזיאל
	19	16	Zepar	זאפר זפאר זפר		1♍	Hakamiah האקמיאה
	9 [19]	17	Botis [Otis]	בוטיש – –	[Under Belzebuth]	2♍	Loviah לוויאה
	10 [16]	18	Bathin [Bathyn, Bathym, Marthim, Mathim]	באתינ באתין –	Pale horse [Under Belzebuth]	3♍	Caliel כאליאל
♋	64	19	Saleos [Sallos, Zaleos]	שאלוש – שלוש	Crocodile	1♎	Leuviah לוויאה[759]
	11	20	**Purson** [Pursan, Curson]	פורשונ פורשון פרשון	Bear [Under Belzebuth] Virtues & Thrones	2♎	Pahaliah פהליאה
	15	21	Morax [Marax, Foraii]	מאראס מאראץ מוראץ	[Under Astaroth]	3♎	Nelchael נלכאל
	16	22	Ipos [Ipes, Ayperos, Ayporos]	יפוש – –	[Under Astaroth]	1♏	Jejael ייאל
	56	23	Aim [Haborym, Haborim]	אים – אימה		2♏	Melahel מלאהל
	17	24	Naberius [Naberus alias Cerberus]	נבריוש נבר –	[Under Astaroth]	3♏	Haiviah האיואה

757 Hoping to return eventually to the 7th Throne.
758 Or Loray, Lerajé, Leraika, or Leraie.
759 Compare with number 17 which Rudd gives the same Hebrew spelling. See Column A24 for the correct Hebrew.

Demons of the Goetia –2 (continued).				
Rank	**Planet**	**No. of Legions**	**Evoked Appearance**	**Powers & Attributes**
King	Sun	85	Rides a pale horse attended by trumpeters and musicians. Initially ill-tempered.	Causes love of man and woman. Of the Order of Powers, hoping to return in time to the 7th Throne.
Marquis	Moon	30	Archer clad in Green, carrying a bow and quiver. Sagittarius.	Causes wars & battles; putrefies wounds made by arrows.
Duke	Venus	60	Knight carrying a lance, ensign & serpent.	Discovers hidden things; Knows future things; Knowledge of Wars & how Soldiers will clash; Causes the love of Lords & great people.
Duke	Venus	26	Armed soldier clad in red.	Causes women to love men; can make women barren.
President & Earl[760]	Mercury	60	Ugly viper, then human with a great tooth & two horns, carrying a bright sword.	Reveals things past, present & future; Reconciles friends & foes. Understands the virtues of herbs and precious stones.
Duke	Venus	30	Strong man with serpent's tail, sitting upon a pale horse.	Gives Knowledge of herbs & precious stones; Transports people suddenly from one country to another.
Duke & Earl[761]	Venus	30	Soldier wearing a Duke's crown, riding a crocodile.	Causes men and women to love one another.
King	Sun	22	Man with lion's face, carrying a viper, riding on a bear, preceded by trumpeters.	Knows things hidden; Discovers treasure; Reveals the past, present & future; Answers truly things secret or divine; gives good familiars.
President & Earl	Mercury & Mars	3 [30]	Bull with man's face.	Teaches Astronomy & all Liberal Sciences; Gives good wise familiars; Virtues of herbs & stones.
Prince & Earl	Jupiter & Mars	36	Angel with Lion's head, goose's feet, and a hare's tail.	Knows things past & future; Makes men witty & bold.
Duke	Venus	26	Man with 3 heads (serpent, man with two stars on forehead, cat), on a viper, with fire.	Set cities, castles and great places on fire; Makes people witty; Gives true answers to private matters.
Marquis	Moon	19	Black crow [or crane] fluttering round the circle, speaking with a hoarse voice.	Makes men cunning in all arts & sciences, especially rhetoric; Restores lost honours.

[760] Under an Earl. Named as a Duke in Harley MS 6482 but this may be an error.
[761] Listed as an Earl in Weirus.

M15. Demons of the Goetia (Lemegeton Book I) – 3.

	Wierus [Rudd 6482]	No. in Harley 6483	Demon Name [alt. spellings]	Hebrew	Stead Ridden, Other	GD Decans	Ruling Angel Name (Rudd)
	18 [40]	25	Glasya-La Bolas [Glasialabolas, Glacia La bolas][762]	גלאסיא לבולש גלאס לבול גלאס לבול	[Under Astaroth]	**Day** 1♐	Nithhajah ניתהיאה
	24 [23]	26	Bune [Bimé, Bime, Bimé, Bim]	בימ בים –		2♐	Haajah האיאה
	26	27	Ronove [Roneve, Ronové]	רונוו ריגוו –		3♐	Jerathel ירתאל
♌	27 [21]	28	Berith [Beal, Beall, Beale, Berithi, Bolfry]	ברית – –	Red horse	1♑	Seechiah שאהאה
	28 [4]	29	**Astaroth**	אשטארות אשתרות עשתרת	Dragon	2♑	Reiajel ריאיל (sic)
	25	30	Forneus [Forners]	פהורנארש פורנאש פרנאש	Order of Thrones and of Angels	3♑	Omael ומאל
	29	31	Foras [Forras, Forcas]	פוראש – פראש		1♒	Lectabal. לאכטבל
	35 [3]	32	**Asmoday** [Asmodai, Sydonay, Sidonay][East][763]	אסמודי אסמודאי אשמודאי	Under Amaymon	2♒	Vasariah ואשריאה
♍	36 [38]	33	**Gaap** [Gäap alias Tap] [Goap?][764]	גאאפ געף –	Under Amaymon. Order of Potestates	3♒	Jehujah הויאה
	30	34	Furfur [Furtur]	פהור פהור פורפור –		1♓	Lehahiah לאההאה
	31 [46]	35	Marchosias [Marchocias][765]	מרחושיאש מרחוש –	Order of Dominations	2♓	Chajakiah חאיאקיאה
	68	36	Stolas [Stolus, Stolos]	שטולוש שטוליש צולס		3♓	Manadel מאנארל

[762] Alias Caacrinolaas or Caassimolar.
[763] See *Tobit* 3:8 and Column M1 (line 4) and Column M27 for more details.
[764] He "appeareth in a meridionall [southern] signe", i.e. a southerly Sign e.g. Libra, but also Libra through Pisces. Maybe a form of Goap, King of the South.
[765] He hopes, after 1200 years, to return to the 7th Throne.

Demons of the Goetia –3 (continued).				
Rank	**Planet**	**No. of Legions**	**Evoked Appearance**	**Powers & Attributes**
President	Mercury	36	Dog with gryphon's wings.	Teaches all arts & sciences instantly; Bloodshed & manslaughter; Teaches all things past, present & future; Causes love of friends & foes; Makes a man invisible.
Duke	Venus	30	Dragon with 3 heads (dog, gryphon, & man) speaking with a high-pitched voice.	Changes the places of the dead; Causes his spirits to gather on the sepulchers of the dead; Gives riches, wisdom & eloquence; Answers demands truly.
Marquis & Earl	Moon	19	Monster.	Teaches rhetoric and languages; Gives favour with friends or foes.
Duke	Venus	26	Soldier wearing red, riding a red horse, wearing a gold crown.	Reveals things past, present & future truely; Transmutes all metals to gold; gives honours and confirms them, but is a great liar, and not to be trusted.
Duke [& King][766]	Venus	40	Beautiful angel riding an infernal Dragon, carrying a viper, with dangerous and foul breath.	Gives true answers; Reveals things past, present & future and all secrets; Reveals how the angels fell; Gives knowledge of all Liberal Sciences.
Marquis	Moon	29	Great sea monster.	Teaches rhetoric; Causes men to have a good reputation; Teaches languages; Makes them loved by their foes and friends.
President	Mercury	29	Strong man.	Gives Knowledge of Herbs & Stones; Teaches Logic & Ethics; Makes Men Invisible & Long-lived & Eloquent.
King[767]	Sun	72	Man with 3 heads (bull, man, & ram), serpent's tail , goose's feet, on a dragon, with lance & flag.	Reveals the virtues of all herbs and stones; Teaches arithmetic, geometry, astronomy; Makes men invisible, witty, eloquent and long-lived; Finds things lost or hidden treasures.
President & Prince	Mercury & Jupiter	66	Man leading 4 mighty kings. Appears in the form of a doctor when he takes on human form.	Makes men knowledgeable in philosophy and all Liberal Sciences; Love & hatred; Delivers Familiars from other Magicians; Reveals things past, present & future; transports between Kingdoms.
Earl	Mars	26	Hart with Fiery tail. The form of an angel if in the Triangle.	Never speaks truly unless in the Triangle; Causes lightning & thunder; Answers things secret & divine.
Marquis	Moon	30	She-wolf with gryphon's wings & serpent's tail, breathing fire. Afterwards as a man.	Gives true answers to all questions & is very faithful to the Exorcist in doing his business. He is an excellent fighter. Was of Order of Dominations, hopes to return to heaven after 1200 years.
Prince	Jupiter	26	Raven, then in the form of a man.	Teaches astronomy; Gives knowledge of herbs & precious stones.

766 Should probably also be a King on the basis of his titles in other grimoires.
767 Chief under Amaymon (East/Air).

M15. Demons of the Goetia (Lemegeton Book I) – 4.

	Wierus [Rudd 6482]	No. in Harley 6483	Demon Name [alt. spellings]	Hebrew	Stead Ridden, Other Qualities	GD Decans	Ruling Angel Name
♎	67	37	Phenix [Phoenix, Phenex, Pheynix][768]	פאניס פאנץ פנץ		**Night** 1♈	Aniel **אניאל**
	42	38	Halphas [Malthas, Malthus or Malthous]	מאלתש האלף –		2♈	Hamiah **האמיאה**
	32	39	Malphas[769]	מאלפש מאלף –		3♈	Rehael **ראהאל**
	41	40	Raum [Räum, Raim, Raym]	ראום – רעם	Order of Thrones	1♉	Jejazel **ייאזאל**
	43 [36]	41	Focalor [Forcalor or Furcalor][770]	פהורכלור פוכלור –		2♉	Hahahel **ההחל**
	33	42	Vepar [Vephar, Separ]	ופאר – ופר		3♉	Michael **מיכאל**
♏	34	43	Sabnock [Savnok, Sabnack, Sabnach, Sabnac, Salmac]	שבנוכ שבנוך –	Pale horse	1♊	Vevaliah **ווליאה**
	37	44	Shax [Shaz, Shass, Shan, Chax, Scox]	שאז שץ –		2♊	Jelahiah **ילאהיה**
	44	45	**Vine**[771] [Viné or Vinea]	וינא – –	Black horse	3♊	Sealiah **סאליאה**
	45 [18]	46	Bifrons [Bifrous, Bifrovs, Bifroüs]	ביפרונש ביפרו –		1♋	Ariel **אריאל**
	65 [61]	47	Vual [Uvall, Vuall, Voval]	וואל אואל וול	Order of Potestes	2♋	Alaliah **אלאליאה**
	66	48	Haagenti	האגנטי העגנת –		3♋	Mihael **מיהיאל**

768 He hopes, after 1200 years, to return to the 7th Throne.
769 The description is confused in the MS with the previous demon, Halphas.
770 Hopes to return, after 1000 years to the 7th Throne.
771 Special numeration of 80.

Demons of the Goetia – 4 (continued).				
Rank	**Planet**	**No. of Legions**	**Evoked Appearance**	**Powers & Attributes**
Marquis	Moon	20	Like a phoenix with a child's voice, then after as a man.	Speaks marvellously of all wonderful sciences; He hopes to return to the 7th Throne after 1200 years.
Earl	Mars	26	Stork dove, speaking with a hoarse voice.	Builds towers and furnishes them with ammunition & weapons; Sends warriors to their appointed places.
President	Mercury	40	Crow, then as a man speaking with a hoarse voice.	Builds houses & high towers; Brings craftsmen from all parts of the world; Gives good familiars; Imparts knowledge of enemy's desires & thoughts.
Earl	Mars	30	Crow, then as a man.	Steals treasures from king's houses; Destroys cities & honours of men; Reveals things past, present & future; Causes love between friends & foes.
Duke	Venus	3 [30]	Man with gryphon's wings.	Kills & drowns men; Overturns ships of war; Power over seas and winds.
Duke	Venus	29	Mermaid.	Governs waters; Guides ships laden with armour & Munitions; Causes storms at sea [& Imaginary Fleets]; Kills men by causing worms to breed in them.
Marquis	Moon	50	Armed soldier with lion's head, riding a pale horse.	Builds high towers, castles & cities and furnish them with armour; Afflicts men with worms: Gives good familiars.
Marquis & Duke[772]	Moon	30	Stork dove, speaking with a hoarse and subtle voice.	Removes sight, hearing or understanding of any man or woman; Steals money out of king's houses; Fetches horses or any other thing; Discovers hidden things; Gives good familiars. Deceptive if not in the Triangle.
King & Earl	Sun & Mars	36	Lion [or man with lion's head] riding a black horse, carrying a viper.	Discovers things hidden, witches, and things past, present & future; Builds towers; Overthrows strong walls; Causes storms at sea.
Earl	Mars	6 [60] [26]	Monster, but after as a man.	Knowledge of astrology & geometry & other arts & sciences; Teaches the virtues of stones & woods; Changes dead bodies, conveys them elsewhere, & lights [candles] upon their graves.
Duke	Venus	37	Dromedary but after as a man speaking imperfect Egyptian in a base voice.	Procures the special love of women; Reveals things past, present & future; Procures friendship between friends & foes. Was of the Order of Potestates.
President	Mercury	33	Bull with gryphon's wings, and after as a man.	Instructs men in many things; Transmutes all metals into gold; Changes wine to water and back again.

[772] See the Latin of Weir.

M15. Demons of the Goetia (Lemegeton Book I) – 5.							
	Wierus [Rudd 6482]	**No. in Harley 6483**	**Demon Name [alt. spellings]**	**Hebrew**	**Stead Ridden, Other Qualities**	**GD Decans**	**Ruling Angel Name (Rudd)**
	38	49	Crocell [Crokel, Procel, Procell, Crokel]	כרוכל – –	Order of Potestes	**Night** 1♌	Vehuel והואל
	38 bis[773] [37]	50	Furcas	פהורכש פורך –	Pale horse[774]	2♌	Daniel דניאל
	62 [17]	51	**Balam**[775] [Balaam]	באלאם בעלם בלעם	Bear Order of Dominations	3♌	Hahasiah החשיאה
♐	63	52	Alloces [or Alocas, Allocer, Alocer, Alocas]	אלוכאס אלוך –	Gryphon	1♍	Imamiah ימאמיאה
	40 [24]	53	Caim [Caym, Camio]	כאמיו כאין –	Order of Angels	2♍	Nanael נאנאל
	39 [52]	54	Murmur [Murmus, Murmux]	מורמוס מורם מערם	Gryphon Order of Thrones and Angels	3♍	Nithael ניתאל
	57	55	Orobas	ורובש אוראוב ערבס		1♎	Nanael ננאל
	50 [39]	56	Gemory [Gremory, Gamori, Gomory]	גמורי גמור –	Camel	2♎	Polial פוליאל
	55 [54]	57	Ose [Oso, Osó, Oze, Voso]	ושז ושו –		♎3	Nemamiah נמאמיאה
♑	60	58	Auns [Amy, Avnas]	אונש און –	Order of Angels and Potestates	1♏	Jejalel יאיאלאל
	48	59	Orias [Oriax][776]	וריאס וריאץ –	Horse	2♏	Hazahel האזאהאל
	58	60	Napula [Nappula, Vapula, Naphula]	נפולא נפול נפל		♏3	Mizrael מיזראל

[773] Procell and Furcas are both numbered 38 in the *Pseudomonarchia Daemonum* as listed in Peterson's Appendix 2.
[774] Therefore possibly originally a Duke or Earl, with 'knight' being a description rather than a title.
[775] Was a Canaanite sorcerer.
[776] Maybe related to Ornias, the first demon in Column M1.

Demons of the Goetia –5 (continued).				
Rank	**Planet**	**No. of Legions**	**Evoked Appearance**	**Powers & Attributes**
Duke	Venus	48	Like an angel.	Speaks mystically of hidden things; Teaches geometry & liberal sciences; Makes the sound of running waters; Warms waters & baths.
Knight[777]	Saturn	20	Cruel old man with long beard & hoary head, riding a pale horse, carrying a sharp weapon.	Teaches practical philosophy, astrology, rhetoric, logic, chiromancy & pyromancy.
King	Sun	40	Man with 3 heads (bull, man, & ram), serpent's tail, flaming eyes, on a bear, with a goshawk.	Reveals true answers to things past, present & future; Makes men invisible & witty. Has a hoarse voice.
Duke	Venus	36 [30]	Soldier riding a gryphon, wearing a Duke's crown, preceded by trumpeters. [see 54]	Teaches philosophy; Compels deceased souls to come before the magician to answer him.[see 54]
President	Mercury	30	A thrush, and afterwards a man carrying a sharp sword.	Teaches the language of birds, bullocks, dogs and other animals; Reveals truly future things. Answers in burning ashes. Was of the Order of Potestates.
Duke & Earl	Venus & Mars	30	Soldier riding a gryphon, wearing a Duke's crown, preceded by ministers with trumpets.	Teaches philosophy; Compels deceased souls to come before the magician to answer him. Was of the Order of Thrones and Angels.
Prince	Jupiter	26	Horse, then as a man.	Discovers things past, present & future; Gives honours & Prelacies, the favour of friends & foes; Gives true answers to divinity questions; Faithful to the magician.
Duke	Venus	26	Beautiful woman riding a camel, with a Duchess's crown around her waist.	Reveals things past, present & future & hidden treasures; Procures the love of women.
President	Mercury	3 [30]	Leopard, afterwards pretending to be a man.	Makes men cunning in liberal sciences; Gives true answers to divinity & secret things; Changes a Man into any shape, and for an hour makes that man think that he is really that thing.
President	Mercury	36	Flaming fire, but after as a man.	Teaches astrology & all liberal sciences; Gives good familiars; Obtains treasures kept by spirits.
Marquis	Moon	30	Lion with serpent's tail riding a horse, holding 2 serpents in his right hand.	Teaches the virtues of the stars & mansions & virtues of planets; Transformation; Gives honours & prelacies, and the favour of friends & foes.
Duke & President	Venus & Mercury	36	Lion with gryphon's wings.	Teaches handicrafts, professions, philosophy & other sciences.

[777] The only Knight amongst the whole 72 demons.

M15. Demons of the Goetia (Lemegeton Book I) – 6.

	Wierus [Rudd 6482]	No. in Harley 6483	Demon Name [alt. spellings]	Hebrew	Stead Ridden, Other Qualities	GD Decans	Ruling Angel Name (Rudd)
♒	47	61	**Zagan** [Zagam]	זאגאנ זאגן זגן		**Night** 1♐	Umabel ומבאל
	49 [60]	62	Valac [Valu, Volac, Valak, Valac, Ualac]	ואלו ואל ולו	Two-headed dragon	♐2	Jahhael יההאאל
	53	63	Andras	אנדראש אנדר אנדראש	Black wolf	3♐	Anavel אנאואל
	61	64	Flauros [Haures,Hauras, Hauros,Havres]	האוראש האור פלער		1♑	Mehiel מאחיאל
	54	65	Andrealphus [Androalphus]	אנדראלפהוש אנדראלף –		♑2	Damabiah דמאביאה
	59 [26]	66	Cimeries [Cimejes, Cimeies, Kimaris]	כימאריש כימאור כימער	Black horse	3♑	Marakel מאראקאל
♓	52	67	Amduscias [Amducias, Amdusias, Amdukias]	אמדוכיאש אמדוך –	Order of Virtues and Angels	1♒	Eiael איאל
	23 [20]	68	**Belial**[1]	בליאל בליאל בליעל	Chariot Order of Vertues and Angels	2♒	Habujah הבויאה
	51	69	**Decarabi**a [Carabia]	דכארביא דכאוראב דכארביא		3♒	Roehel רואהל
	0 [20]	70	Seer [Seare, Seere, Sear, Seir]	שאר – –	Winged horse. Under Amaymon, King of the East	1♓	Tabamiah טבמיאה
	0	71	Dantalion [Dantaylion]	דאנטאליונ דנתאל דנתאליון		2♓	Hajajel האיאיאל
	0	72	Andromalius	אנדרומליוש אנדרומאל –		3♓	Mumiah מומייאה
	4	0	Pruflas/Bufas[2]		[Under Lucifer] Order of Thrones & Angels		–

[1] One of the highest ranking Kings.
[2] Or Purflas. Only appears in Weir. Omitted from Scot's list and all the manuscript versions of the *Goetia*.

Demons of the Goetia – 6 (continued).				
Rank	**Planet**	**No. of Legions**	**Evoked Appearance**	**Powers & Attributes**
King & President	Sun & Mercury	36	Bull with gryphon's wings, and after a man.	Makes men witty; Turns Wine to Water and back again, and blood into wine; Transmutes all metals into coin of the realm; Makes fools wise.
President	Mercury	30	Boy with angel's wings, riding a 2-headed dragon.	Reveals Hidden Treasures truly & locations of serpents, which he will bring to the magician without compulsion.
Marquis	Moon	30	Angel with raven's head, riding a black wolf, flourishing a bright & sharp sword.	Sow discord; he may try to kill the magician and his assistants.
Duke	Venus	3 [36]	Leopard, and after a man with fiery eyes and a terrible face.	Reveals things past, present & future, but lies if not in the Triangle; Teaches divinity & how the spirits fell; Destroys and burns enemies.
Marquis	Moon	30	Noisy peacock, but after as a human.	Teaches geometry, measurement & astronomy; Can transform a man into a bird.
Marquis	Moon	20	Soldier riding a black horse.	Rules over spirits in Africa; Teaches grammar, logic & rhetoric; Discovers treasures lost or hidden; Can make a man seem like a soldier. Rules parts of Africa.
Duke	Venus	29	Unicorn, and after as a man.	Causes musical instruments to be heard & trees to bend; Gives excellent familiars.
King[780]	Sun	[more than] 80 [50, 30]	A beautiful angel sitting in a fiery chariot.	Distributes preferments of senatorship; Causes favour of friends & foes; Gives excellent familiars. But he must have offerings.
Marquis, King & Earl[781]	Moon	30	Star inside a Pentacle, but afterwards as a man.	Discovers the virtues of birds & precious stones; Creates the Illusion of tame birds singing and flying.
Prince	Jupiter	26	Beautiful man riding a winged horse.	Comes & goes; Brings things to pass suddenly; Carries things to & fro across the whole Earth instantly; Reveals Thefts & Hidden Treasures; Good natured.
Duke	Venus	36	Man with many faces (both men's and women's), carrying a book in his right hand.	Teaches all arts & sciences to anyone; Causes Love; Shows the true similitude of anyone wherever they are; [Declares secret counsels; Changes the thoughts of men & women?]
Earl	Mars	36	Man holding a serpent.	Returns thieves & stolen goods; Discovers wickedness & underhand dealings; Punishes thieves & wicked people; Discovers hidden treasures.
Prince & Duke	Jupiter & Mars	26	The head of a night hawk.	Discord, war, quarrels, falsehood. Lives around the Tower of Babylon.

780 He claims to have been created next after Lucifer
781 Said to be a King and Earl in the Latin text of Weirus, but this rank not found in Scot or any other version.

M16. Powers and Specialties of the Demons of the *Goetia.*

Speciality/Power	Demon
Alchemy	28-Berith, 48-Haagenti, 61-Zagan
Animals	24-Naberius, 53-Camio, 62-Valu, 69-Decarabia
Archery	14-Leriac
Arithmetic	32-Asmodai
Astrology	21-Marax, 46-Bifrons, 50-Furcas, 58-Auns, 59-Orias
Astronomy	21-Marax, 32-Asmodai, 36-Stolus, 50-Furcas, 59-Orias, 65-Andrealphus
Bravery	17-Botis, 22-Ipos, 35-Marchosias
Builds Towers	38-Malthas, 39-Malphas, 43-Sabnock, 45-Vine
Charisma, Wit, Humor	22-Ipos, 23-Aim, 31-Foras, 51-Balam, 61-Zagan
Chiromancy or Palmistry	50-Furcas
Demotion, Destruction of Honours	2-Agares, 40-Raum
Destruction by Fire	23-Aim
Destruction of Enemies	40-Raum, 39-Malphas, 44-Shax, 45-Vine, 64-Haures
Divination	3-Vassago, 7-Amon, 8-Barbatos, 11-Gusion, 15-Eligos, 17-Botis, 20-Purson, 22-Ipos, 25-Glasya-LaBolas, 26-Bime, 28-Berith, 29-Astaroth, 33-Gaap, 40-Raum, 45-Vine, 47-Vuall, 51-Balam, 55-Orobas, 56-Gemory, 64-Haures
Drowning	41-Focalor, 42-Vepar
Earthquakes	2-Agares
Ethics	31-Foras
Familiar Spirits	9-Paimon, 10-Buer, 20-Purson, 21-Marax, 33-Gaap, 39-Malphas, 43-Sabnock, 44-Shax, 52-Alloces, 58-Auns, 67-Amducias, 68-Belial
Flying	18-Bathin, 33- Gaap
Friendships	7-Amon, 8-Barbatos, 11-Gusion, 17-Botis, 25-Glasya-La Bolas, 27-Ronove, 30-Forners, 40-Raum, 47-Vuall, 55-Orobas, 59-Orias, 68-Belial
Geometry	32-Asmodai, 46-Bifrons, 49-Crocell, 65-Andrealphus
Grammar	66-Cimeries
Health & Healing	5-Marbas, 10-Buer
Health, Ill-health	14-Leraic, 43-Sabnock, 44-Shax
Herbs, Virtues of	10-Buer, 17-Botis, 18-Bathin, 21-Marax, 31-Foras, 32-Asmodai, 36-Stolus, 46-Bifrons, 69-Decarabia
Honors, Promotions & Preferment	9-Paimon, 11-Gusion, 15-Eligos, 24-Naberius, 28-Berith, 30-Forners, 55-Orobas, 59-Orias, 68-Belial
Immobility	2-Agares, 31-Foras, 32-Asmodai
Infertility	16-Zepar
Invisibility	1-Bael, 25-Glasya-La Bolas, 31-Foras, 32-Asmodai, 51-Balam
Languages	2-Agares, 8-Barbatos, 27-Ronove, 30-Forners, 53-Camio
Liberal Arts & Sciences	4-Gamigin, 9-Paimon, 21-Marax, 24-Naberius, 25-Glasya-La Bolas, 29-Astaroth, 32-Asmodai, 33-Gaap, 37-Phenix, 46-Bifrons, 48-Haagenti, 49-Crocell, 57-Oso, 58-Auns, 60-Napula, 71-Dantaylion
Logic	10-Buer, 31-Foras, 50-Furcas, 66-Cineries

M16. Powers and Specialties of the Demons of the *Goetia.*

Speciality/Power	Demon
Longevity	31-Foras, 32-Asmodai
Love	7-Amon, 12-Sitri 13-Beleth, 14-Leraic, 15-Eligos, 16-Zepar, 19-Sallos, 32-Asmoday, 33-Gaap, 34-Furfur, 40-Raum, 47-Vuall, 56-Gemory, 71-Dantaylion,
Manslaughter	25-Glasya-La Bolas, 41-Focalor, 42-Vepar, 64-Haures
Mechanical Arts & Handicrafts	5-Marbas, 60-Napula
Mind Control	71-Dantaylion
Money (see also Treasure)	26-Bime
Music	67-Amducias
Necromancy	4-Gamigin, 24-Naberius, 26-Bime, 46-Bifrons, 52-Alloces, 54-Murmus, 58-Auns
Philosophy	10-Buer, 33-Gaap, 50-Furcas, 52-Alloces, 54-Murmus, 60-Napula
Poetry	37-Phenix
Pyromancy	50-Furcas
Questions answered truthfully	3-Vassago, 11-Gusion, 20-Purson, 23-Aim, 26-Bime, 29-Astaroth, 32-Asmodai, 34-Furfur, 35-Marchosias, 55-Orobas, 57-Oso
Rearranging graveyards	26-Bime, 46-Bifrons
Retrieving things lost or stolen	2-Agares , 3-Vassago, 15-Eligos, 31-Foras, 32-Asmodai, 40-Raum, 44-Shax, 45-Vine, 70-Seer, 72-Andromalius
Rhetoric and Eloquence	24-Naberius, 26-Bime, 27-Ronove, 30-Forners, 31-Foras, 32-Asmodai, 50-Furcas, 51-Balam, 66-Cineries
Secrets revealed	5-Marbas, 15-Eligos, 20-Purson, 29-Astaroth, 34-Furfur, 57-Oso, 71-Dantaylion
Shipping	41-Focalor, 42-Vepar
Stones, Virtues of	17-Botis, 18-Bathin, 21-Marax, 24-Naberius, 31-Foras, 32-Asmodai, 36-Stolus, 46-Bifrons, 69-Decarabia
Teleportation	18-Bathin, 33-Gaap, 39-Malphas, 70-Seer
Theology & Divinity	20-Purson, 29-Astaroth, 34-Furfur, 55-Orobas, 57-Oso, 64-Haures
Things Past, Present & Future declared	3-Vassago, 7-Amon, 8-Barbatos, 11-Gusion, 15-Eligos, 17-Botis, 20-Purson, 22-Ipos, 25-Glasya-La Bolas, 26-Bime, 28-Berith, 29-Astaroth, 33-Gaap, 40-Raum, 45-Vine, 47-Vuall, 51-Balam, 55-Orobas, 56-Gemory, 64-Haures
Transformations, Shape Shifting	5-Marbas, 16-Zepar, 57-Oso, 59-Orias, 65-Andrealphus
Treasure Finding	8-Barbatos, 20-Purson, 31-Foras, 32-Asmodai, 40-Raum, 44-Shax, 56-Gemory, 58-Auns, 62-Valu, 66-Cineries, 70-Seer, 72-Andromalius
War, Military & Death	14-Leraic, 15-Eligos, 25-Glasya-La Bolas, 35-Marchosias, 38-Malthas, 39-Malphas, 41-Focalor, 43-Sabnock, 66-Cineries
Water into Wine	48-Haagenti, 61-Zagan
Water, Controls	45-Vine, 49-Crocell
Weather (Thunder, Lightning, Winds)	34-Furfur, 41-Focalor, 42-Vepar, 45-Vine
Wisdom	1-Bael, 5-Marbas, 6-Valefor, 25-Glasya-La Bolas, 26-Bime, 29-Astaroth, 48-Haagenti, 49-Crocell, 61-Zagan

M17. Ranks of the Demons of the *Goetia*.

	Rank	Metal	Binding Times	Incense	Number of Demons
☾	Marquises	Silver	Ninth hour of day till compline, and compline till the end of the day [night?] (3pm – 9pm and 9pm – Sunrise)[782]	Jasmine	12
☿	Presidents	Mercury	Any hour of the day if his King is also invoked. But not twilight.	Storax	12
♀	Dukes	Copper	First hour of the day till noon. Sunrise – Noon (in clear weather)	Sandalwood	23
☼	King[783]	Gold	Third hour of day till noon and from ninth hour till evening (9am-Noon and 3pm–sunset)	Frankincense	12
♂	Earls (Counties/Counts)	Copper & Silver[784]	Any hour of the day (in a quiet place)	Dragon's blood	6
♃	Princes (& Prelates)	Tin	Any hour of the day	Cedar	6
♄	Knights	Lead	Dawn till sunrise and from Evensong till sunset. (Dawn – Sunrise and 4pm – Sunset)	Myrrh	1
	Total =				***72***

[782] The clock times are from Sloane MS 3825. It is more accurate to calculate the uneven planetary hours using the 'hour of the day' as drawn from Weirus.
[783] Ruling the 12 Zodiacal Signs.
[784] Instead of iron, which cannot be used with these demons.

	M18. Demons of the *Goetia* by Rank, Planet and Zodiacal Sign.						
Rank >	**Marquises**	**Presidents**	**Dukes**	**Kings**	**Earls (& Counts)**	**Princes (& Prelates)**	**Knights**
Planet >	*Moon*	*Mercury*	*Venus*	*Sun*	*Mars*	*Jupiter*	*Saturn*
	☾	☿	♀	☼	♂	♃	♄
♈	4-Gamigin	5-Marbas	*2-Agares*[785] 6-Valefar	**1-Bael**		3-Vassago	
♉	7-Amon	10-Buer	*8-Barbatos* *11-Gusion*	**9-Paimon**	(8-Barbatos)[786]	12-Sitri	
♊	14-Leraic	17-Botis	15-Eligos 16-Zepar 18-Bathin	**13-Beleth**	(17-Botis)		
♋	24-Naberius	21-Marax	19-Sallos *23-Aim*	**20-Purson**	(19-Sallos) (21-Marax) (22-Ipos)	22-Ipos	
♌	(27-Ronove) 30-Forneus	25-Glasya-La Bolas	26-Bime *28-Berith* (29-Astaroth)	**29-Astaroth**[787]	27-Ronove		
♍	35-Marchosias	31-Foras (33-Gaap)		**32-Asmoday**	34-Furfur	(33-Gaap) 36-Stolas	
♎	37-Phenex	39-Malphas	41-Focalor 42-Vepar	**33-Gaap**[788]	38-Halphas 40-Raum		
♏	43-Sabnock (44-Shax)	48-Haagenti	44-Shax 47-Vuall	**45-Vine**	(45-Vine) 46-Bifrons		
♐		53-Camio	49-Crocell *52-Alloces* 54-Murmus	**51-Balam**	(54-Murmus)		50-Furcas[789]
♑	59-Orias	57-Ose 58-Auns (60-Napula)	56-Gemory 60-Napula	**69-Decarabia**[790]		55-Orobas	
♒	63-Andras 65-Andrealphus 66-Cimeries	(61-Zagan) 62-Volac	64-Haures	**61-Zagan**			
♓	(69-Decarabia)		*67-Amducias* 71-Dantalion	**68-Belial**	72-Andromalius (69-Decarabia)	70-Seer	
Total= 72 [791]	**12**	**12**	**23**	**12**	**6**	**6**	**1**

[785] Italics indicate a Grand Duke, this title being drawn from other sources. In the *Goetia* he is simply listed as a Duke.
[786] Round brackets indicate a duplicated rank as originally found in the *Goetia*, with the demon thus appearing in two columns. The bracketed occurrence is the one we have chosen to ignore when it comes to totalling the demons in each column, to avoid double counting. The choice of which rank to ignore has been modified slightly.
[787] Astaroth has been given the additional title of King because he often has this rank in other sources. The three underlined Kings are all tentative placements.
[788] Gäap has many attributes with King-like qualities; in fact he guides "4 greate & mighty kings", so here he has been tentatively given the additional rank of King.
[789] In Weir, Furcas is simply described as a '*miles*' or soldier which perhaps should *not* have been translated as 'knight'. If this is only a description not a title, then it is conceivable that Furcas might have been a Duke, who all ride a horse or other mount, as does Furcas. That would result in 24 Dukes, giving exactly two Dukes per Zodiacal Sign.
[790] Decarabia is usually listed as a Marquise. Only the Latin text of Weir shows him clearly as a King and Earl, something which is inexplicably left out of the translation in Scot. Very interestingly, these two, Gäap and Decarabia, are directly opposite each other (if the 72 demons are laid out in a circular fashion), and immediately adjacent to two other Kings, Asmoday and Belial respectively.
[791] The total in this row excludes the duplications in round brackets, which are not counted to avoid duplication.

Theurgia Goetia[792]

M20. Good and Evil Aerial Spirits (of the Compass) from *Theurgia Goetia* (*Lemegeton* Book II).

No.	Emperors Ruling	Dukes	Direct-ion	Commands	Some Spirits/Dukes Commanded
1	Carnesiel	PAMERSIEL	E	1000 Spirits for Day	Anoyr, Madriel, Ebra, Sotheans, Abrulges, Ormenu, Itules, Rablion, Hamorphiel, Itrasbiel, Nadres
2		Padiel	E by S	10000 Spirits for Day	[not given as 'Padiel rules all Spirits']
				200000 Spirits for Night	
3		Camuel	SE	10 Spirits for Day	Orpemiel, Omyel, Camyel, Budiel, Elear, Citgara, Pariel, Cariel, Neriel, Daniel
				10 Spirits for Night	Asimiel, Calim, Dobiel, Nodar, Phaniel, Meras, Azemo, Tediel, Moriel (s), Tugaros
4		Aseliel	S by E	10 Chief Spirits for Day	Mariel, Charas, Parniel, Aratiel, Cubiel, Aniel, Asahel, Arean,
				20 Chief Spirits for Night	Asphiel, Curiel, Chamos, Odiel, Melas, Sariel, Othiel, Bofar
5	Caspiel	BARMIEL	S	10 Dukes for Day	Sochas, Tigara, Chansi, Keriel, Acteras, Barbil, Carpiel, Mansi
				20 Dukes for Night	Barbis, Marguns, Carniel, Acreba, Mareaiza, Baaba, Gabio, Astib
6		Gediel	S by W	20 Chief Spirits for Day	Coliel, Ranciel, Agra, Naras, Mashel, Anael, Sabas. Bariel, Aroan
				20 Chief Spirits for Night	Assaba, Reciel, Cirecas, Sariel, Sadiel, Aglas, Vriel,
7		Asiriel/ Asyriel	SW	20 Dukes for Day	Astor, Ariel, Maroth, Carga, Cusiel, Omiel, Buniel, Malguel, Budar
				20 Dukes for Night	Rabas, Amiel, Aspiel, Areisat, Cusriel, Faseua, Hamas
8		Maseriel	W by S	12 Dukes for Day	Mahue, Roriel, Zeriel, Atniel, Patiel, Assuel, Aliel, Espoel, Amoyr, Bachiel, Baras, Eliel,
				12 Dukes for Night	Vessur, Azimel, Chasor, Arach, Maras, Noguiel, Sarmiel, Earos, Rabiel, Atriel, Salvar
9	Amenadiel	MALGARAS	W	30 Dukes for Day	Carmiel, Meliel, Borasy, Agor, Oriel, Misiel, Barfas, Arois, Raboc, Aspiel, Caron, Zamor, Amiel
				30 Dukes for Night	Casiel, Babiel, Cabiel, Udiel, Aroc, Dodiel, Cubi, Libiel, Aspar, Deilas, Basiel
10		Darochiel	W by N	Dukes before Noon of the 24 Dukes for Day	Magael, Artino, Efiel/Artino, Maniel/Efiel, Suriel/Maniel, Carsiel/Suriel, Carsiel, Fubiel, Carba, Merach, Althor, Omiel
				Dukes after Noon of the 24 Dukes for Day	Gudiel, Asphor, Emuel, Soriel, Cabron, Diviel, Abriel, Danael, Lomor, Casael, Busiel, Larfos
				Dukes before Midnight of the 24 Dukes for Night	Nahiel, Ofisiel, Bulis, Momel, Darbari, Paniel, Cursas, Aliel, Aroziel, Cusyne, Vraniel, Pelusar
				Dukes after Midnight of the 24 Dukes for Night	Pafiel, Gariel, Soriel, Maziel, Cayros, Narsiel, Moziel, Abael, Meroth, Cadriel, Lodiel

792 NB: The listing and spelling of the Lesser Dukes and Spirits of the *Theurgia-Goetia* corresponds to Sloane MS 3825. The correct spelling, if there is one, would probably be the spelling in the *Steganographia*.

M20. Good and Evil Aerial Spirits (of the Compass) from *Theurgia Goetia* (*Lemegeton* Book II).

No.	Emperors Ruling	Dukes	Direct-ion	Commands	Some Spirits/Dukes Commanded
11		Usiel	NW	40 Dukes for Day	Abariel, Ameta, Arnin, Herne, Saefer, Potiel, Saefarn, Magni, Amandiel, Barfu, Garnasu, Hissam, Fabariel, Usiniel
				40 Dukes for Night	Ansoel, Godiel, Barfos, Burfa, Adan, Saddiel, Sodiel, Ofsidiel, Pathier, Marae, Asuriel, Almoel, Las Pharon, Ethiel
12		Cabariel	N by W	50 Dukes for Day	Satifiel, Parius, Godiel, Taros, Asoriel, Etimiel, Clyssan, Elitel, Aniel, Cuphal
				50 Dukes for Night	Mador, Peniel, Cugiel. Thalbos, Otim, Ladiel, Morias, Pandor, Cazul, Dubiel
13	Demoriel	RASIEL	N	50 Dukes for Day	Baciar, Thoac, Sequiel, Sadar, Terath, Astael, Ramica, Dubarus, Armena, Albhadur, Chanael, Fursiel, Betasiel, Melcha, Tharas, Vriel
				50 Dukes for Night	Thariel, Paras, Arayl, Culmar, Lazaba, Aleasy, Sebach, Quibda, Belsay, Morael, Sarach, Arepach, Lamas, Thurcal
14		Symiel	N by E	10 Dukes for Day	Asmiel, Chrubas, Vaslos, Malgron, Romiel, Larael, Achot, Bonyel, Dagiel, Musor
				10 Dukes for Night	Mafrus, Apiel, Curiel, Molael, Arafos, Marianu, Narzael, Murahe, Richel, Nalael
15		Armadiel	NE	15 Dukes	Nassar, Parabiel, Lariel, Calvarnia, Orariel, Alferiel, Oryn, Samiel, Asmaiel, Jasziel, Pandiel, Carasiba, Asbibiel, Mafayr, Oemiel
16		Baruchas	E by N	15 Dukes	Quitta, Sarael, Melchon, Cavayr, Aboc, Cartael, Janiel, Pharol, Baoxas, Geriel, Monael, Chubo, Lamael, Dorael, Decaniel

M21. Good and Evil Aerial Spirits (Emperors) from *Theurgia Goetia* (*Lemegeton* Book II).

	Direct-ion	Emperors	Commands	12 Chief Dukes
F	South	Caspiel	200 Great Dukes 400 Lesser Dukes 1,000,200,000,000 Ministering Spirits Attended by 2660 Lesser Dukes	Ursiel, Chariel, Maras, Femol, Budarim, Camory, Larmol, Aridiel, Geriel, Ambri, Camor, Oriel
A	East	Carnesiel	1000 Great Dukes 100 Lesser Dukes 50,000,000,000,000 Ministering Spirits 60,000,000,000,000 attendant Dukes	Myrezyn, Ornich, Zabriel, Bucafas, Benoliam, Arifiel, Cumeriel, Vadriel, Armany, Capriel, Bedary, Laphor
W	West	Amenadiel	300 Great Dukes 500 Lesser Dukes 40,000,030,000,100,000 Ministering Spirits Attended by 3880 Servants	Vadros, Camiel, Luziel, Musiriel, Rapsiel, Lamael Zoeniel, Curifas, Almesiel, Codriel, Balsur, Nadroc
E	North	Demoriel	400 Great Dukes 600 Lesser Dukes 70,000,080,000,900,000 Servants Attended by 1140 Servants	Arnibiel, Cabarim, Menador, Burisiel, Doriel, Mador, Carnol, Dubilon, Medar, Churibal, Dabrinos, Chamiel

M20a. Good and Evil Aerial Spirits (Wandering Princes) from *Theurgia Goetia* (*Lemegeton* Book II).

No.	Emperor Ruler	Wandering Princes	Direction	Commands	Commands
1	Carnesiel Amenadiel Demoriel	Geradiel	ESE SE by E NNW NNE?	18150 Servants	[not given]
2	Carnesiel Demoriel	Buriel	SE by S NNE NE by N	12 Dukes for Night 880 Servants	Merosiel, Almadiel, Cupriel, Sarviel, Casbriel, Nedriel, Bufiel, Futiel, Drusiel, Carniel, Drubiel, Nastros
3		Hidriel / Hydrial	SE by S SSE NE by N NE by E	100 Great Dukes 200 Lesser Dukes	Mortaliel, Chalmoriel, Pelariel, Musuziel, Lameniel, Barchiel, Samiel, Dusiriel, Camiel, Arbiel, Lusiel, Chariel
4	Amenadiel	Pirichiel	NW by W NW by N	8 Knights	Damarsiel, Cardiel, Almasor, Nemariel, Menariel, Demediel, Hursiel, Cuprisiel
5		Emoniel	NW by N NNW	20 Dukes	Ermoniel, Edriel, Carnodiel, Phanuel, Dramiel, Pandiel, Vasenel, Nasiniel, Cruhiel, Armesiel, Caspaniel, Musiniel
6	Carnesiel Caspiel Demoriel	Icosiel	SSE SSW NE by E ENE	100 Dukes 300 Companions	Machariel, Psichiel, Thanatiel, Zosiel, Agapiel, Larphiel, Amediel, Cambriel, Nathriel, Zachariel, Athesiel, Cumariel, Munefiel, Heresiel, Urbaniel
7		Soleviel	ESE SSW SW by S ENE	200 Dukes 200 Companions	Inachiel, Praxeel, Moracha, Almodar, Nadrusiel, Cobusiel, Amriel, Axosiel, Charoel, Parsiel, Mursiel, Penador
8	Caspiel	Menadiel	SW by S SW by W	20 Dukes 6 Chief Dukes 100 Companions	Larmol, Drasiel, Clamor, Benodiel, Charsiel, Samyel
				6 Lesser Dukes	Barchiel, Amasiel, Baruch, Nedriel, Curasin, Tharson
9	Caspiel	Macariel	SW by W WSW	40 Dukes	Claniel, Drusiel, Andros, Charoel, Asmadiel, Romyel, Mastuel, Varpiel, Gremiel, Thuriel, Brufiel, Lemodac
10	Caspiel Amenadiel	Uriel	WSW WNW	10 Dukes 100 Under Dukes	Chabri, Drabos, Narmiel, Frasmiel, Brymiel, Dragon, Curmas, Drapios, Hermon, Aldrusy
11	Amenadiel	Bidiel	WNW NW by W	20 Chief Dukes 200 Other Dukes	Mudirel, Cruchan, Bramsiel, Armoniel, Lameniel, Andruchiel, Merasiel, Charobiel, Parsifiel, Chremoas

Total = 4 Emperors + 11 Wandering Princes + 16 Aerial Spirits (Dukes) = 31 Spirits

M22. Spirits of the 24 Hours from *Ars Paulina* Part 1 – *Lemegeton* (Book III – 1).				
Hr	**Day Hour**	**Angel**	**Chief Dukes {Lesser Dukes}**	**Dukes & Servants**
1	–	Samuel [Samael]	Ameniel, Charpon, Darosiel, Monasiel, Brumiel, Nestoriel, Chremas, Meresyn	[10] Chief Dukes [100] Lesser Dukes 444 Servants each
2	Cevorym [Sevormi]	Anael	Menarchos, Archiel, Chardiel, {Orphiel, Cursiel, Elmoym, Quosiel, Ermaziel, Granyel}	10 Chief Dukes 100 Lesser Dukes 330 Servants each
3	Dansor [Danzur]	Vequaniel	Asmiel, Persiel, Mursiel, Zoesiel, {Drelmech, Sadiniel, Parniel, Comadiel, Gemary, Xantiel, Serviel, Furiel}	20 Chief Dukes 200 Lesser Dukes 1760 Servants
4	Elechym [Elechin]	Vathmiel [Vachmiel]	Armmyel, Larmich, Marfiel, Ormyel, Zardiel, {Emarfiel, Permiel, Queriel, Strubiel, Diviel, Jermiel, Thuros}	10 Chief Dukes 100 Lesser Dukes 1550 Servants
5	Fealech [Tealech]	Sasquiel	Damiel, Araniel, Maroch, Saraphiel, Putisiel, {Jameriel, Futiniel, Rameriel, Amisiel, Uraniel, Omerach, Lameros, Zachiel, Fustiel, Camiel}	10 Chief Dukes 100 Lesser Dukes 5500 Servants
6	Genapherim [Gebphorim]	Saniel [Samiel]	Arnebiel, Charuch, Medusiel, Nathmiel, Pemiel, {Gamyel, Jenotriel, Sameon, Trasiel, Xamyon, Nedabor, Permon, Brasiel, Camosiel, Evadar}	10 Chief Dukes 100 Lesser Dukes 5500 Servants
7	Hamarym [Hemarim]	Barquiel	Abrasiel, Farmos, Nestorii, Manuel, Sagiel, {Harmiel, Nastrus, Varmay, Tulmas, Crosiel, Pasriel, Venesiel, Evarym, Drufiel, Kathos}	10 Chief Dukes 100 Lesser Dukes 600 Servants
8	Jafanym [Jesamin]	Osmadiel	Sarfiel, Amalyn, Chroel, Mesial, Lantrhots, {Demarot, Janofiel, Larfuty, Vemael, Thribiel, Mariel, Remasyn, Theoriel, Framion, Ermiel}	100 Chief Dukes 100 Lesser Dukes 1100 Servants
9	Karron [Carron]	Quabriel [Vadriel]	Astroniel, Charmy, Pamory, Damyel, Nadriel, {Kranos, Menas, Brasiel, Nefarym, Zoymiel, Trubas, Xermiel, Lameson, Zasnor, Janediel}	10 Chief Dukes 100 Lesser Dukes 192980 Servants 650 Chief Servants
10	Lamarhon [Lamathon]	Oriel	Armosy, Drabiel, Penaly, Mesriel, Choreb, {Lemur, Ormas, Charny, Zazyor, Naveron, Xantros, Basilon, Nameron, Kranoti, Alfrael}	10 Chief Dukes 100 Lesser Dukes 1100 Servants 5600 Spirits
11	Maneloym [Manelohim]	Bariel	Almarizel, Prasiniel, Chadros, Turmiel, Lamiel, {Menafiel, Demasor, Omary, Helmas, Zemoel, Almas, Perman, Comial, Temas, Lanifiel}	[10] Chief Dukes 100 Lesser Dukes 1100 Servants 5600 Spirits
12	Nahalon [Naybalon]	Beratiel [Beraliel]	Camaron, Astrofiel, Penatiel, Demarac, {Famaras, Plamiel, Nerastiel, Fimarson, Quirix, Sameron, Edriel, Choriel, Romiel, Fenosiel, Harmary}	[10] Chief Dukes [100] Lesser Dukes 1100 Servants 3700 Spirits

M22. Spirits of the 24 Hours from *Ars Paulina* Part 1 – *Lemegeton* (Book III – 1).

Hr	Night Hour	Angel	Chief Dukes {Lesser Dukes}	Dukes & Servants
1	Omalharien [Omalhavien]	Sabrathan [Sabrachon]	Domaras, Amerany, Penoles, Mardiel, Nastul, {Ramesiel, Omedriel, Franedac, Chrasiel, Dormason, Hayzoym, Emalon, Turtiel, Quenol, Rymaliel}	1540 attendants [10] Chief Dukes [100] Lesser Dukes 2000 Servants
2	Panezur [Penazur]	Tartys [Taklis]	Almodar, Famoriel, Nedroz, Ormezyn, Chabriz, Praxiel, {Permaz, Vameroz, Emaryel, Fromezyn, Ramaziel, Granozyn, Gabrinoz, Mercoph, Tameriel, Venomiel, Jenaziel, Xemyzin}	101550 attendants [10] Chief Dukes [100] Lesser Dukes 1320 Servants
3	Quabrion [Guabrion]	Serquanich [Sarquamech]	Menarym, Chrusiel, Penargos, Amriel, Demanoz, {Nestoroz, Evanuel, Sarmozyn, Haylon, Quabriel, Thurmytz, Fronyzon, Vanosyr, Lemaron, Almonoyz, Janothyel, Melrotz, Xanthyozod}	101550 attendants 6 First Order Dukes 12 2nd Order Dukes 1320 Servants
4	Ramersy [Ramerzy]	Jefischa [Jefisiel]	Armosiel, Nedruan, Maneyloz, Ormael, Phorsiel, Rimezyn, {Rayziel, Gemezin, Fremiel, Hamayz, Japuriel, Jasphiel, Lamediel, Adroziel, Zodiel, Bramiel, Coreziel, Enatriel}	101550 attendants 12 First Order Dukes 12 2nd Order Dukes 7260 Servants
5	Sanayfar [Sanaysor]	Abasdarhon [Abasdarho]	Meniel, Charaby, Appiniel, Deinatz, Nechorym, Hameriel,Vulcaniel, Samelon, Gemary, Vanescor, Sameryn, Xantropy, {Herphatz, Chrymas, Patrozyn, Nameton, Barmas, Platiel, Neszomy, Quesdor, Caremaz, Umariel, Kralym, Habalon}	101550 attendants 12 First Order Dukes 12 2nd Order Dukes 3200 Servants
6	Thaazaron [Thaasoron]	Zaazenach	Amonazy, Menoriel, Prenostix, Namedor, Cherasiel, Dramaz, Tuberiel, Humaziel, Lanoziel, Lamerotzod, Xerphiel, Zeziel, {Pammon, Dracon, Gematzod, Enariel, Rudefor, Sarmon}	101550 attendants 12 First Order Dukes 12 2nd Order Dukes 2400 Servants
7	Venaydor [Venador]	Mendrion	Ammiel, Choriel, Genarytz, Pandroz, Menesiel, Sameriel, Ventariel, Zachariel, Dubraz, Marchiel, Jonadriel, Pemoniel, {Rayziel, Tarmytz, Anapion, Jmonyel, Framoth, Machmag}	101550 attendants 12 First Order Dukes 12 2nd Order Dukes 1860 Servants
8	Xymalim [Ximalim]	Narcoriel [Narcriel]	Cambiel, Nedarym, Astrocon, Marifiel, Dramozyn, Lustifion, Amelson, Lemozar, Xernifiel, Kanorsiel, Bufanotz, Jamedroz, {Xanoriz, Jastrion, Themaz, Hobrazym, Zymeloz, Gamisiel}	101550 attendants 12 First Order Dukes 12 2nd Order Dukes 30200 Servants
9	Zeschar	Pamyel [Pamiel]	Demaor, Nameal, Adrapon, Chermel, Fenadros, Vemasiel, Comary, Matiel, Zenoroz, Brandiel, Evandiel, Tameriel, Befranzy, Jachoroz, Xanthir, Armapy, Druchas, Sardiel	101550 attendants 12 First Order Dukes 12 2nd Order Dukes 1320 Servants
10	Malcho	Iassuarim [Jasguarim]	Lapheriel, Emarziel, Nameroyz, Chameray, Hazaniel, Uraniel	100 Chief Dukes 100 Lesser Dukes 1620 Servants
11	Aalacho [Alacho]	Dardariel	Cardiel, Permon, Armiel, Nastoriel, Casmiroz, Dameriel, Furamiel, Mafriel, Hariaz, Damar, Alachuc, Emeriel, Naveroz, Alaphar, {Nermas, Druchas, Carman, Elamyz, Jatroziel, Lamersy, Hamarytzod}	[10?] Chief Dukes [100?] Lesser Dukes 420 Servants
12	Xephan	Sarandiel	Adoniel, Damasiel, Ambriel, Meriel, Denaryz, Emarion, Kabriel, Marachy, Chabrion, Nestoriel, Zachriel, Naverial, Damery, Namael, {Hardiel, Nefrias, Irmanotzod, Gerthiel, Dromiel, Ladrotzod, Melanas}	[10?] Chief Dukes [100?] Lesser Dukes 420 Servants

M23. Angels of the Degrees of the Zodiac from *Ars Paulina* (Part 2) *Lemegeton* (Book III – 2).

	1°	2°	3°	4°	5°	6°	7°	8°	9°	10°
♈	Biael	Gesiel	Hael	Vaniel	Zaciel	Cegnel	Japhael	Itael	Cakiel	Lariel
♉	Latiel	Hujael	Sachiel	Gneliel	Panael	Jezisiel	Kingael	Raphiel	Tezael	Gnakiel
♊	Latiel	Nagael	Sachael	Gnaliel	Paniel	Tzisiel	Kingael	Raphiel	Gnetiel	Bakiel
♋	Sachiel	Metiel	Asel	Sachiel	Mihel	Aniel	Sasael	Magnael	Aphiel	Sersael
♌	Mechiel	Satiel	Ajel	Mechiel	Sahel	Aniel	Masiel	Sengael	Aphiel	Metziel
♍	Celiel	Senael	Nasael	Sangiel	Gnaphiel	Parziel	Tzakiel	Kriel	Rathiel	Tangiel
♎	Ibajah	Chaiel	Sahael	Naviel	Saziel	Gnachiel	Patiel	Trajael	Kachiel	Baliel
♏	Teliel	Jeniel	Cesiel	Lengael	Naphael	Satziel	Gnakiel	Periel	Tzethiel	Rengliel
♐	Taliel	Janiel	Casiel	Langael	Naphael	Satziel	Gnakiel	Periel	Tzangiel	Jebiel
♑	Chushel	Temael	Jaajah	Cashiel	Lamajah	Naajah	Sasajah	Gnamiel	Paajah	Izashiel
♒	Chamiel	Tesael	Jaajeh	Camiel	Lashiel	Naajah	Samiel	Gnashiel	Paajah	Izamiel
♓	Lachiel	Neliel	Sanael	Gnasiel	Pangael	Tzapheal	Kphiel	Ratziel	Tarajah	Gnathiel

M23. Angels of the Degrees of the Zodiac from *Ars Paulina* (Part 2) *Lemegeton* (Book III – 2) (*continued*).

	11°	12°	13°	14°	15°	16°	17°	18°	19°	20°
♈	Natheel	Sagnel	Gabiel	Pegiel	Gadiel	Kheel	Leviel	Hezael	Geciel	Betiel
♉	Beriel	Gethiel	Dagnel	Vabiel	Zegiel	Chadiel	Tahiel	Javiel	Chazael	Bachiel
♊	Geriel	Dathiel	Hegnel	Vabiel	Zagiel	Chadiel	Tahiel	Javiel	Chazael	Bachiel
♋	Makael	Ariel	Sethiel	Magnael	Abiel	Sagel	Madiel	Athiel	Savael	Maziel
♌	Sekiel	Ariel	Gnethiel	Sagiel	Abiel	Magiel	Sadiel	Athiel	Muviel	Saviel
♍	Gnasiel	Bagiel	Gediel	Dahiel	Hevael	Vaziel	Zachiel	Chetiel	Tiiel	Jechiel
♎	Tamael	Gnamiel	Bangiel	Gepheel	Datziel	Hekiel	Variel	Zethiel	Chengiel	Tibiel
♏	Rebiel	Tagiel	Gnadiel	Bevael	Geziel	Dachiel	Hephiel	Vagael	Zackiel	Chabiel
♐	Regael	Tediel	Gnaheel	Bevael	Geziel	Dachiel	Hephiel	Vagael	Zackiel	Chabiel
♑	Kmiel	Riajah	Tashiel	Gnamiel	Baajah	Gashiel	Dashiel	Haajah	Vashiel	Zamiel
♒	Kshiel	Raajah	Tamiel	Gnashiel	Baajah	Gashiel	Dashiel	Haajah	Vashiel	Zamiel
♓	Bengiel	Gebiel	Dagiel	Hadiel	Vahajah	Zavael	Chazael	Tachael	Jatael	Cajaiel

M23. Angels of the Degrees of the Zodiac from *Ars Paulina* (Part 2) *Lemegeton* (Book III – 2) (*continued*).

	21°	**22°**	**23°**	**24°**	**25°**	**26°**	**27°**	**28°**	**29°**	**30°**
♈	Giel	Dachael	Habiel	Vagel	Zadiel	Chahel	Tavael	Jezel	Cechiel	Hetiel
♉	Getiel	Dajiel	Hachael	Vabiel	Zagiel	Chadiel	Gehiel	Javael	Chasiel	Sachael
♊	Getiel	Dajiel	Hachael	Vabiel	Zagiel	Chadiel	Tahiel	Daviel	Heziel	Vachael
♋	Achiel	Setiel	Maiel	Achael	Sabiel	Magiel	Adiel	Sahiel	Meviel	Aziel
♌	Achiel	Metiel	Siel	Achael	Mabiel	Sagiel	Adiel	Mahiel	Savael	Aziel
♍	Cabiel	Bagiel	Gediel	Dahiel	Hoviel	Vaziel	Zachiel	Chetivel	Tajael	Jachiel
♎	Jagiel	Cediel	Behel	Gevael	Daziel	Heckiel	Vatiel	Zajel	Chechiel	Tehiel
♏	Tagiel	Jadiel	Cahael	Baviel	Gezael	Dachael	Hatiel	Vajael	Zachiel	Chasiel
♐	Tagiel	Jadiel	Cahael	Baviel	Gezael	Dachael	Hatiel	Vajael	Zachiel	Chasiel
♑	Chael	Tashiel	Jashiel	Ciajah	Beshael	Gamael	Daael	Heshael	Vamiel	Zaajah
♒	Chael	Tashiel	Jashiel	Ciajah	Beshael	Gamael	Daael	Heshael	Vamiel	Zaajah
♓	Bachiel	Gabiel	Dagiel	Hediel	Vahejah	Zavael	Chazael	Tachiel	Jatael	Cajael

Ars Almadel

M24. Angels of The Altitudes (Choras) from *Ars Almadel – Lemegeton (*Book IV*)*.

	Chora	**Colour**	**Angels**	**Appearance**	**God-Names**
F	**South**	Rose-red	Aphiriza Genon Geron Armon Gereimon	Young Child wearing Rose-red Satin & Crown of Gilly Flowers.	Helion Heloi Heli
A	**East**	Lily white	Alimiel Gabriel Barachiel Lebes Helison	Angel carrying Flag with White Cross wearing a Cloud & Crown of Roses.	Adonaij Helomi Pine
W	**West**	Green & whitish silver	Eliphaniasai Gelomiros Gedobonai Taranava Elomina	Children or Girls wearing Crowns of Bay Leaves.	Jod Hod Agla
E	**North**	Black & green	Barachiel Gediel Gedial Deliel Capitiel	Boys wearing Black & Green carrying Birds.	Tetragrammaton Shadai Jah

Appendix 3: Thomas Rudd's Synthesis of the 72 Demons and Dr John Dee's *Tabula Sancta cum Tabulis Enochi*

The BL catalogue entry for Harley MS 6483, the manuscript here transcribed, states that "Some of these spirits are in Enoch's Tables described in the former volume..." We have therefore extracted those items from the 'former volume' Harley MS 6482 and included them in this Appendix to show how Goetic spirits were used by Dr Rudd in conjunction with John Dee's Table of Practice.

From the same 'former volume' we have also extracted Rudd's descriptions of 61 demons and have included them in Appendix 4. That list contains a strange mixture of spirits, including some (but not all) of the major demons from the *Goetia*. Its order is not significant, being merely alphabetical.

Dr Rudd in Harley MS 6482[793] draws together the threads of the *Goetia*, the couterpointing of angels and demons, and Dee's magical practice. By bringing these together in one place you can see clearly how the techniques are complementary. In fact Rudd achieves the synthesis that Mathers was striving for, without the addition of Freemasonic and lodge rituals, keeping strictly to the evocation and invocation of 'spiritual creatures.' In the space of just a few pages he lists out the following:

a) The drawing of the *Tabula Sancta cum Tabulis Enochi* on folio 8. This is Dee's Table of Practice as transmitted to him via the skrying of Edward Kelly, but with certain startling amendments. Compare this with the original *Tabula Sancta* as published by Meric Casaubon, which also appears in Joseph Peterson's edition of Dee's *Five Books of Mystery* (page 43) and you will notice the similarity. The first thing noticeable is that Dee's hexagram (six pointed figure) is surrounded by a heptagram (seven pointed figure), which clearly positions the seven Planetary Tablets. These tablets on Dee's diagram were simply been spread around the perimeter. The introduction of a heptagram allows the operator to position them accurately, and this is certainly within the spirit of Dee's other work in which *hepta-* or seven plays a big part.

The surrounding square of Enochian letters is the same, but beyond that Rudd has added the sort of defences that you find on the *Goetia's* floor Circle. On each of the four sides are the Archangel names (not incidentally in Golden Dawn order) with South - Michael; North - Raphael; East - Gabriel; West - Auriel. Around that are five annular rings containing the Godnames, archangelic and angelic names as are found on the more elaborate Circle drawn in Sloane MS 3875 or Sloane MS 3648.

---

[793] In Harley MS 6482 the relevant folios are ff. 8-38. The original manuscript has been edited by Adam McLean in *A Treatise on Angel Magic*. Magnum Opus Hermetic Sourceworks 15, Edinburgh. Republished Weiser, York Beach, 2006. See pages 30-57.

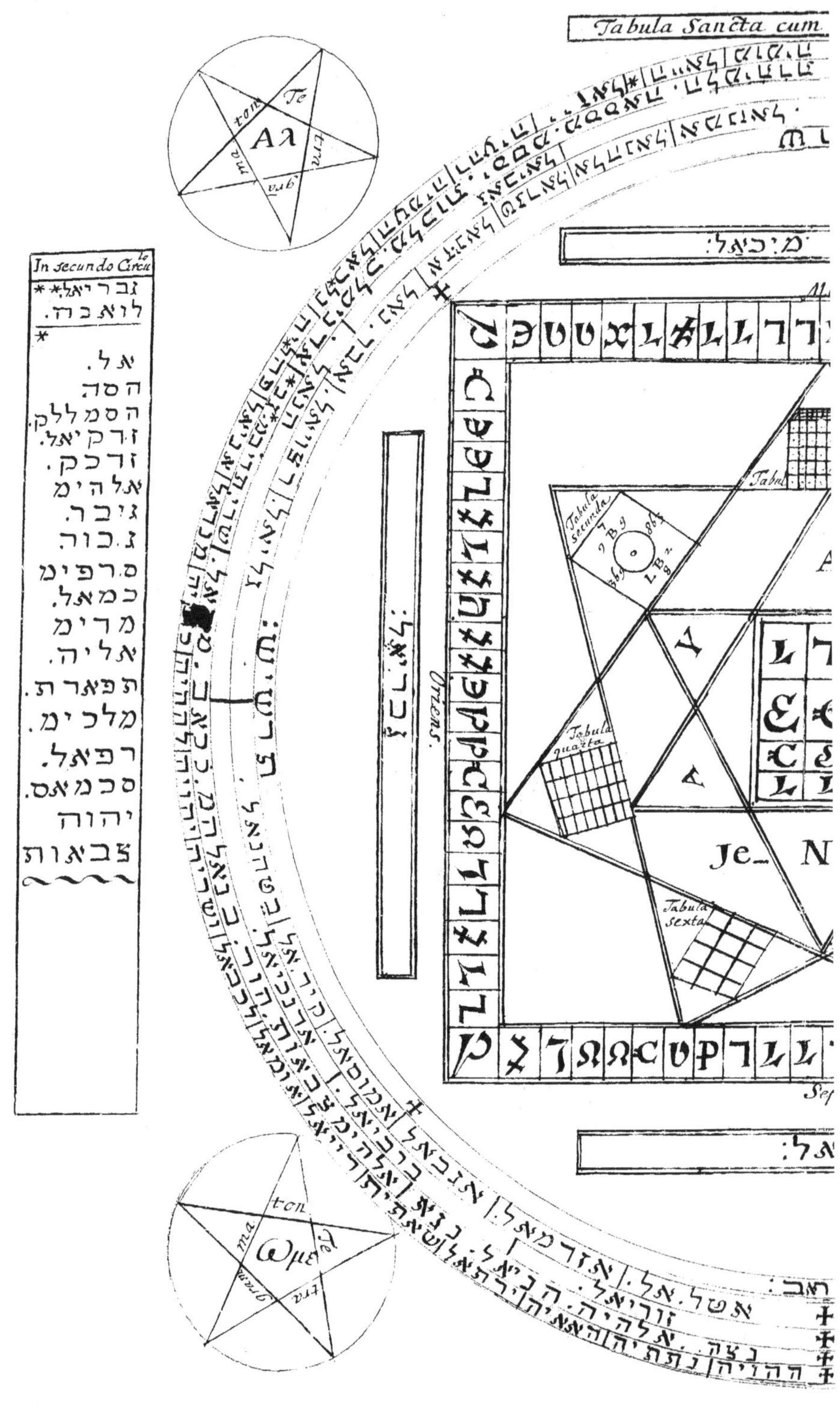

Figure 14: Rudd's enhanced version of Dee's *Tabula Sancta cum Tabulis Enochi*

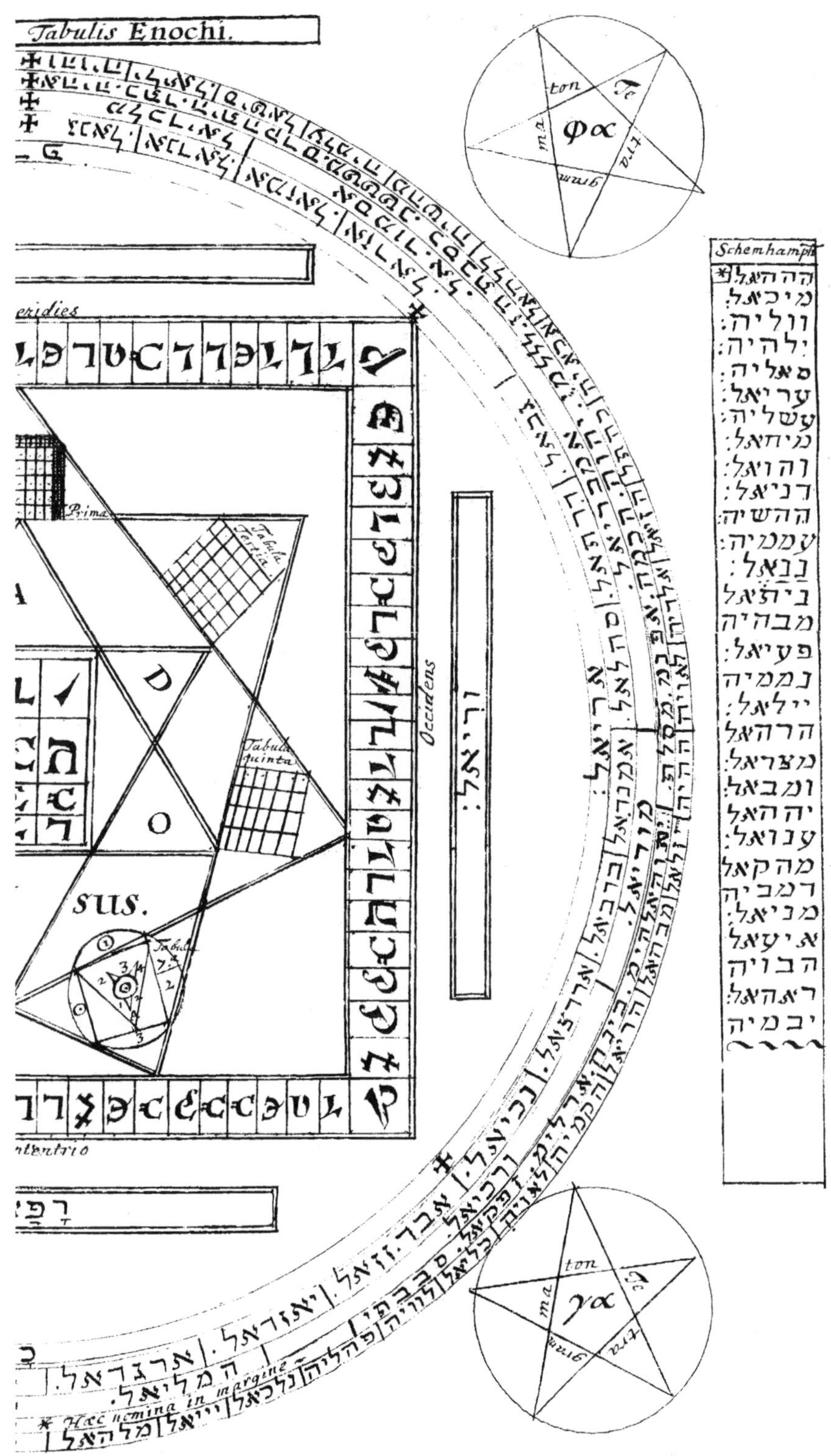
Tabulis Enochi.
Occidens
Prima
Tabula Tertia
Tabula quinta
D
O
SUS.
Schemhamph
ton
ma
Hæc nomina in margine

The difference is that in Rudd's manuscript they are written in Hebrew, but in the Sloane manuscripts just mentioned are written in English. In Rudd they are drawn around the Table of Practice, rather than the floor Circle, and they are obviously meant to contain the spirit in the crystal or glass receptacle.

Beyond them, at the corners are four pentagrams inscribed in circles, for the placement of candles. Finally on the right hand side is a panel containing some of the Shem ha-Mephorash angel names in Hebrew. On the left side are god and angel names, designed to be fitted into the five annular rings, as is indicated by the note, '*Hac nomina in margine*'.

This is a consummate extension of Dee's work and confirmation that the skrying crystal or glass receptacle on the Table of Practice needed as much protection as the main circle itself. In practice the spirit/demon more often manifests in the glass than in the Triangle, but both venues should always be made available to it. It also shows that the protection around the Circle and around the glass are partly interchangeable.

b) The outline of the contents of the 7 Planetary Tablets in folios 12v-18v. These 7 Planetary Tablets are just arrayed around the hexagram in Dee's original design, but are worked into a regular heptagram by Rudd. Where Dee simply places initials in the complex Tablets, Rudd expands them in full, and it is no surprise that this expansion reveals the names of spirits from the *Goetia*. Whether or not Dee intended this is difficult to tell, but Rudd expands Dee's letter 'b' into Botis, Buer, Bathin, Balam, Belial, and other spirits beginning with that letter. His 'g' becomes Gaap, Glasia-Labolas, and so on. It does seem possible that Dee used abbreviations for what might otherwise have been embarrassing demon names on his Holy Table. Not only does Rudd expand the letters, but he also interprets the numbers on these tables to indicate the number of times each spirit should be invocated. It would be interesting to know if Dr Rudd generated this interpretation, or if he was working from one of Dee's notebooks which has subsequently been lost. Robert Turner believes that Dr Rudd's interpretation of Dee's Table is wrong.

c) The 'Schemhamphoras' list of 72 angels is laid out in full on folios 21v-28. In each case, the appropriate invocatory Latin and English Psalm is given, with both the Hebrew and English spelling of the Shem ha-Mephorash angel. These are also used on the sigils of each of the 72 demons in the present volume. Thus it is clear that this part of Harley MS 6482 is meant as a summary of the ingredients of the Goetia which follows in Harley MS 6483.

d) On folios 28v-38 immediately following the 72 angels are an incomplete list of 61 spirits which are described as the "Good and Bad Spirits Solomon Made Use of which are mentioned in Enoch's Seven Tables". We have separated them into categories, with the spelling unchanged in Appendix 4.

Appendix 4: Rudd's Description of 61 Demons of the Goetia[794]

The Names of the Some of the Good and Bad Spirits Solomon Made Use of which are mentioned in Enoch's Seven Tables, with a true account of their shapes, powers, government and effects, with their several seigniories and degrees.

1 AMAIMON, King of the East.

2 ATEL, Angel of the fifth heaven.

3 ASMODIA, hath one Idea called Muriel incorporated into two figures Geomantic, called Populus by day and Via by night. A Lunar spirit.

4 ASTAROTH, a great and strong Duke coming forth in the shape of a foul Angel, sitting upon an infernal Dragon, carrying in his right hand a viper. He answers truly to matters present and to come, and of their fall. He saith he fell not by his own accord. He maketh a man wonderfully learned in the liberal sciences. He ruleth 40 Legions.

5 BALAY, Angel of the first heaven serving in the North on the day of the Moon.

6 BALIDET, is a Minister of the King Maymon, and Angel of the air ruling the day of Saturn, serving in the West.

7 BABEL, Angel of the second heaven, ruling the day of Mercury, serving in the South.

8 BARBAROT, Angel of the second heaven, serving in the East, ruling the day of Mercury.

9 BEALPHARES, a great King or Prince Aerial.

10 BONOHAM, a great Duke of the fiery region.

11 BAEL, a King which is of the power of the East, appeareth with three heads, the first like a toad, the second like a man, third like a cat, speaketh with a hoarse voice. He maketh a man go invisible. He hath under his government 66 Legions.

12 BARBATOS, a great Duke understandeth the singing of birds, the barking of dogs, the lowing of bullocks and the voice of all living creatures. He detecteth treasures hidden by magicians and enchanters, and was of the Order of Virtues. He knoweth what is past and to come, and reconcileth friends and powers, and governeth 30 Legions of spirits.

---

[794] This material is drawn from folios 28v-38 of Harley MS6482, immediately following the 72 angels. It is an incomplete list of 61 spirits which are described as the Good and Bad Spirits of Solomon. We have separated them into categories, with the spelling unchanged in the Table at the end of this Appendix. This clearly shows the juxtaposition of angels with demons, and further reinforces their appearance of their names in Dee's Seven Planetary Tablets. The list is a mix of 29 Goetic demons, 22 angels from one of Seven Heavens, and 10 Dukes and Kings of the Elements and the directions. It is indeed a mixed bag, of the different types of 'spiritual creature.' Of these 29 spirits are particularly relevant as they appear in the *Goetia*.

13 BACHIEL, an Angel of the fourth heaven serving for the East.

14 BACHANAEL, an Angel of the first heaven to the West, reigning on Monday.

15 BILET, Minister of Arcan a King, an Angel of the air for Monday

16 BATHIN, a great Duke. He is seen in the shape of a very strong man with a serpent's tail sitting on a pale horse, understanding the virtues of herbs and previous stones, transferring men suddenly from country to country and ruleth 30 Legions.

17 BALAM, a great and terrible King. He cometh forth with three heads, the first of a bull, the second of a man, the third of a ram. He hath a serpent's tail and flaming eyes riding upon a furious bear and carrying a hawk upon his fist. He speaketh with a hoarse voice answering perfectly of things past, present and to come, hath many Legions under him.

18 BIFRONS, appearance hath the similitude of a Monster, then he taketh the image of a man. He maketh one wonderful cunning in Astrology and Geometry, understands the strength and virtues of herbs, precious stones and woods, changeth and conveyeth dead bodies from place to place. He seemeth to light candles upon the sepulchres of the dead and hath under him 26 Legions.

19 BOTIS, a great Duke cometh in the shape of an ugly viper, and if he put on human shape he showeth great tooth and two horns, carrying a sharp sword in his hands. He giveth answers of things present and to come, and reconcileth friends and foes, ruling 60 Legions of inferior spirits.

20 BELIAL, is a King, appears like a beautiful Angel sitting in a fiery chariot, speaketh fair, distributeth preferments and the favour of friends, giveth excellent familiars, ruleth 80 Legions.

21 BERITH, a great and terrible Duke, he cometh forth as a red soldier on a red horse with a crown on his head. He answereth truly of things past, present and to come. He turneth metals into Gold, giveth Dignities, and confirmeth them. Speaketh with a clear and subtle voice. 26 Legions are under him.

22 BEUR, is a great President, he teaches Philosophy moral and natural, also logic and the virtue of herbs. He giveth the best familiars. He can heal all diseases, ruleth 40 Legions.

23 BUNE, is a great Duke appeareth as a Dragon with three heads, the third whereof is like a man. He speaketh with a divine voice. He maketh the dead to change their place, and devils to assemble upon the sepulchres of the dead. He greatly enricheth a man and maketh him eloquent and wise, answereth truly to all demands and 30 Legions obey him.

24 CAIM, is a great President taking the form of a thrush, but when he putteth on a man's shape he answereth in burning ashes, carrying in his hands a sharp sword, giveth the understanding of all birds, lowing of bullocks, and barking of dogs. He was of the Order of Angels and ruleth thirty Legions.

25 BILETH, is a great King and terrible, riding upon a pale horse before whom go trumpets and all kinds of music, appeareth trough and furious, he is of the Order of Powers, hoping to return to the seventh Throne. He ruleth 85 Legions.

26 CIMERIES, a great Marquis and strong, ruling in the parts of Africa. He teaches the Sciences, discovereth treasures hid.

27 CAMUEL, the chief King of the East.

28 CASPIEL, the chiefest Emperor ruling in the South, he hath 200 great Dukes, and 400 lesser Dukes under him.

29 CHOMIEL, a great Duke under Demoriel Emperor of the North.

30 DEAMIEL, an Angel of the first heaven serving in the East on the day of the Moon.

31 DAMAEL, an Angel of the fifth heaven serving in the East on the day of Mars.

32 DABRIEL, an Angel of the first heaven serving in the South on the day of the Moon.

33 DIRIEL, a Duke under Demoriel Emperor of the North.

34 DARQUIEL, an Angel of the first heaven serving in the South on the day of the Moon.

35 FRIAGNE, an Angel of the first heaven serving in the South on the day of the Moon.

36 FORCALOR, is a great Duke. He cometh forth as a man with wings like a griffin. He killeth men and drowneth them in the waters and overturneth ships of war, commanding and ruling both winds and seas, and if the Magician biddeth him hurt no man he willingly consenteth thereto. He hath three Legions.

37 FURCAS, is a Knight, and cometh forth in the similitude of a cruel man with a long beard and a hoary head. He sitteth on a pale horse, carrying in his hand a pale weapon. He perfectly teacheth practical philosophy, Rhetoric, Logic, Astronomy, Chiromancy, Pyromancy, and their parts. There obey him 20 Legions.

38 GAAP, a great President and a Prince, taketh human shape, maketh a man wonderfully knowing in philosophy and in all liberal sciences. He maketh love hatred, transfereth man most speedily into other nations, ruleth 66 Legions. He was of the Order of Powers.

39 GEMORI, a strong and mighty Duke appeareth like a fair woman with a Duchess's Crown, riding upon a camel, answereth all things

past, present and to come, of treasures hid, procureth the love of women, hath 26 Legions.

40 GLACIA LABOLAS, a great President, cometh forth like a dog, hath wings like a griffin. He understandeth things present and to come, gainst the love of friends and foes, maketh a man go invisible, rules 36 Legions.

41 GAMIGIN, is a great Marquis and is seen in the form of a little horse. When he taketh human shape, he speaketh with a hoarse voice, disputing of all liberal sciences, bringeth to pass that the Souls which are drowned in the sea shall take airy bodies and evidently appear and answer to interrogations at the magician's commandment. He tarrieth with the exorcist till he hath accomplished his desire and hast many Legions under him.

42 GALDEL, an Angel of the fifth heaven ruling in the South.

43 GABRIAL, an Angel of the fifth heaven ruling in the East on the day of the Moon.

44 HINIEL, an Angel of the fifth heaven ruling the North on the day of the Mars.

45 MICHAEL, the Angel of the divine Lord.

46 MARCHOSIAS, a Great Marquis showeth himself in the shape of a cruel she wolf with Griffin's wings and a serpent's tail. When he is in a man's shape he is an excellent fighter, answereth all questions truly. He was of the Order of Dominations. Under him are 30 Legions. He hopeth after 1200 years to come to the seventh heaven.

47 MASGABRIEL, a Angel of the fourth heaven, ruling the North on the day of the Sun.

48 MATUYEL, a Angel of the fourth heaven, ruling in the North on the day of Mars.

49 MATHIEL, a Angel of the fifth heaven, ruling in the North on the day of Mars.

50 MITRATON, a Angel of the second heaven, ruling in the West on the day of Mercury.

51 MAEL, a Angel of the first heaven, ruling in the North on the day of the Moon.

52 MURMUR, is a great Duke appearing in the shape of a soldier riding on a griffin with a Duke's Crown on his head. There go before him two of his ministers with great trumpets. He teacheth philosophy absolutely, constraineth souls to come before the magician to answer what he shall ask them. He was of the Order partly of Thrones and partly of Angels, and ruleth 30 Legions.

53 NELAPA, an Angel of the second heaven ruling in the South on the day of Mercury.

54 OSE, is a great President and cometh forth like a Leopard and counterfeiting to be a man. He maketh one cunning in the liberal sciences, he answereth truly of divine and secret things. He transformeth a man's shape, and bringeth a man to that madness that he thinketh himself to be that which he is not, *duratque id regnum ad horam* ("and it holds sway for an hour").

55 PAIMON, appeareth with a great cry and roaring, putting on the likeness of a man sitting on a dromedary wearing a glorious Crown, hath an effeminate countenance. There goes before him an host of men with trumpets, cymbals and all instruments. He giveth dignities, prepareth good familiars, and hath the understanding of all arts. There follows him 200 Legions partly of the Order of Angels, partly of Potestates.

56 RAHUMEL, an Angel of the fifth heaven ruling in the North on the day of Mars.

57 RAPHAEL, an Angel of the third heaven ruling in the North on the day of Venus.

58 SITRI, is a great Prince appearing with the face of a Leopard having wings as a Griffin. When he taketh human shape he is very beautiful, he enflameth a man with woman's love, and stirreth up women to love men, being commanded he willingly destroyeth secrets of women laughing at them and mocking them to make them luxuriously naked. And there obey him sixty Legions.

59 VALEFOR, is a strong Duke, appears in the shape of a lion and the head of a thief. He is very familiar with them to whom he maketh himself acquainted, that he may bring them to the gallows. Ruleth ten Legions.

60 VALAC, is a great President, and cometh abroad with Angel's wings like a boy riding on a two headed Dragon. He perfectly answereth of treasures hidden and where serpents may be seen which he delivereth into the magician's hands void of any force or strength, and hath dominion of 30 Legions of devils.

61 VUAL, is a great Duke and strong. He is seen as a great and terrible Dromedary, but in human form. He soundeth in a base voice the Egyptian tongue, procureth the special love of women, and knoweth things past, present and to come, procuring the love of friends and foes. He was of the Order of Potestates and governeth 37 Legions.

These demons and angels may be analysed according to their source and function as follows:

Goetic Demon	Angel from one of the 7 Heavens	Other King/Angel of an Element/Quarter
3 – Asmodai	2 – Atel	1 – Amaimon [E]
4 – Astaroth	5 – Balay	6 – Balidet [Angel of Water]
11 – Bael	7 – Babel	9 – Bealphares [Air]
12 – Barbatos	8 – Barbarot	10 – Bonoham [Fire]
16 – Bathin	13 – Baciel	15 – Bilet [Air]
17 – Balam	14 – Bachanael	27 – Camuel [E]
18 – Bifrons	30 – Deamiel	28 – Caspiel [S]
19 – Botis	31 – Damael	29 – Chomiel [Duke]
20 – Belial	32 – Dabriel	33 – Diriel [Duke of N]
21 – Berith	34 – Darquiel	45 – Michael [Angel of the Lord]
22 – Buer	35 – Fiagne	
23 – Bune	42 – Galdel	
25 – Bileth	43 – Gabriel	
24 – Caim	44 – Hiniel	
26 – Cimeries	47 – Masgabriel	
36 – Focalor	48 – Matuyel	
37 – Furcas	49 – Mathiel	
38 – Gaap	50 – Mitraton	
39 – Gemori	51 – Mael	
40 – Glacia-Labolas	53 – Nelapa	
41 – Gamigin	56 – Rahumel	
46 – Marchosias	57 – Raphael	
52 – Murmur		
54 – Ose		
55 – Paimon		
58 – Sitri		
59 – Valefor		
60 – Valac		
61 – Vual		

Appendix 5: Some of the Sources and Constituents of the *Lemegeton*

Date	**Goetia**							
1400s	*Le Livre des Esperitz* MS *Liber Officiorum Spirituum, seu Liber Dictus Empto[rium] Salomonis*		Various MSS	MSS of Peter de Abano's *Heptameron*				
1508	*On the Composition of the Names and Characters of the Evil Spirits* (in Trithemius's library)						Trithemius	
1531							H C Agrippa, *Three Books of Occult Philosophy* Book 2, Scale of 7	Book 2, Scale of 10
1570	T. R.'s MS translation of *Pseudomonarchia Daemonum*							
1584 & 1665	*Pseudomonarchia Daemonum* in Scot's *Discovery of Witchcraft*, Book XV							
1620			*The Magical Calendar*					
1655				Peter de Abano's *Heptameron* printed English edition				
Constituents	List of 72 Spirits	Seals of the 72 Spirits	Secret Seal of Solomon	Conjurations	Simple Circles	Elaborate Circle & Triangle	Lettering on Brass Vessel	*'Ars Nova'* Kabbalistic summary
	Goetia in…							
1641	*Lemegeton* – Sloane MS 3825 (used in Peterson's edition) it also includes *Janua Magica Reserata*							
c.1649	proto-*Lemegeton* – Sloane MS 3648							
1655/6	*Lemegeton* – Dr Rudd's original MS							
1687	*Lemegeton* – Sloane MS 2731 (used by most modern printed editions) and other MSS							
1712-1714	*Lemegeton* – Harley MS 6483 (Peter Smart's copy of Dr Rudd's original MS – this book)							

Date	Theurgia-Goetia				
1200-1400s			MSS of Peter de Abano's *Heptameron*		*Liber Juratus* Sundry MSS
1500	Trithemius' *Steganographia* Book I in MS			MS of Trithemius' *Steganographia*	John Dee
1608	Trithemius' *Steganographia* Book I, printed edition			Trithemius' *Steganographia* Book I, compass rose printed opposite title page	
1641/ 1649	*Art of Solomon the King & Trithemius Redivivus* – Sloane MS 3824				
1655			Peter de Abano's *Heptameron* printed edition		
Constit-uents	List of Spirits and Dukes	Spirit Seals[795]	Conjurations	Compass of 31 spirit directions	Table of Practice
	Theurgia-Goetia in… *Lemegeton*				

Date	Ars Paulina (I) hours of day and night			Ars Paulina (II) degrees of Zodiac		
1200-1400s	Standard astrological signs	*Liber Juratus* Sundry MSS		the *monomoirai*		
1500			Trithemius' *Steganographia* Book 2 in MS			
1608			Trithemius' *Steganographia* Book 2 printed			
1656					Paracelsus, *Archidoxes of Magic/Second Treatise of Celestial Medicines*	
Constit-uents	Spirit Seals	Planetary Table of Practice	List of Spirits of the hours	List of Spirits of 360°	Zodiacal Spirit Seals	Genii of the 4 Elements
	Ars Paulina in… *Lemegeton*					

[795] Just a few of these come from Trithemius' *Steganographia* Book I.

Date	**Ars Almadel**			**Ars Notoria**		
1227-41						*Liber Juratus* or the *Sworn Book* of Honorius
13th Century				*Ars Notoria* MSS		
?		Hebrew MS of the *Key of Solomon: Sepher Maphteah Shelomoh*				
1620					Latin version of *Ars Notoria* in Agrippa *Opera*	
1657					Turner's English translation of *Ars Notoria*	
Constit-uents	Invocations	Almadel or Table of Practice	List of Angels/Choras	Diagrams or *Notae*	Prayers and Conjurations	
	Ars Almadel, in…			*Ars Notoria*, in…		
	Lemegeton – as above					

Appendix 6 – Seals from Sibley's *Goetia*[796]

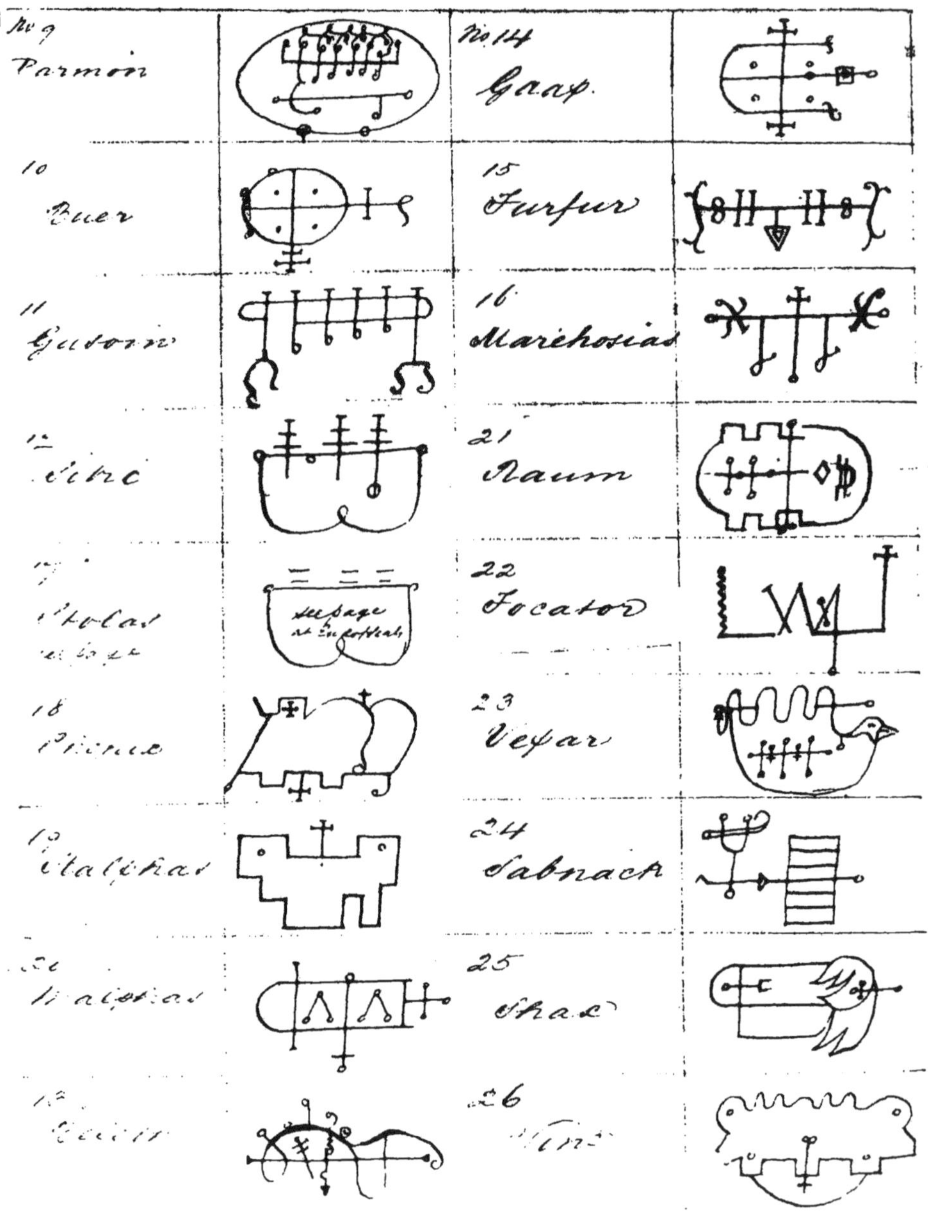

Figure 15. Demonic Seals from Sibley's *Goetia*.

[796] From Wellcome MS 3203.

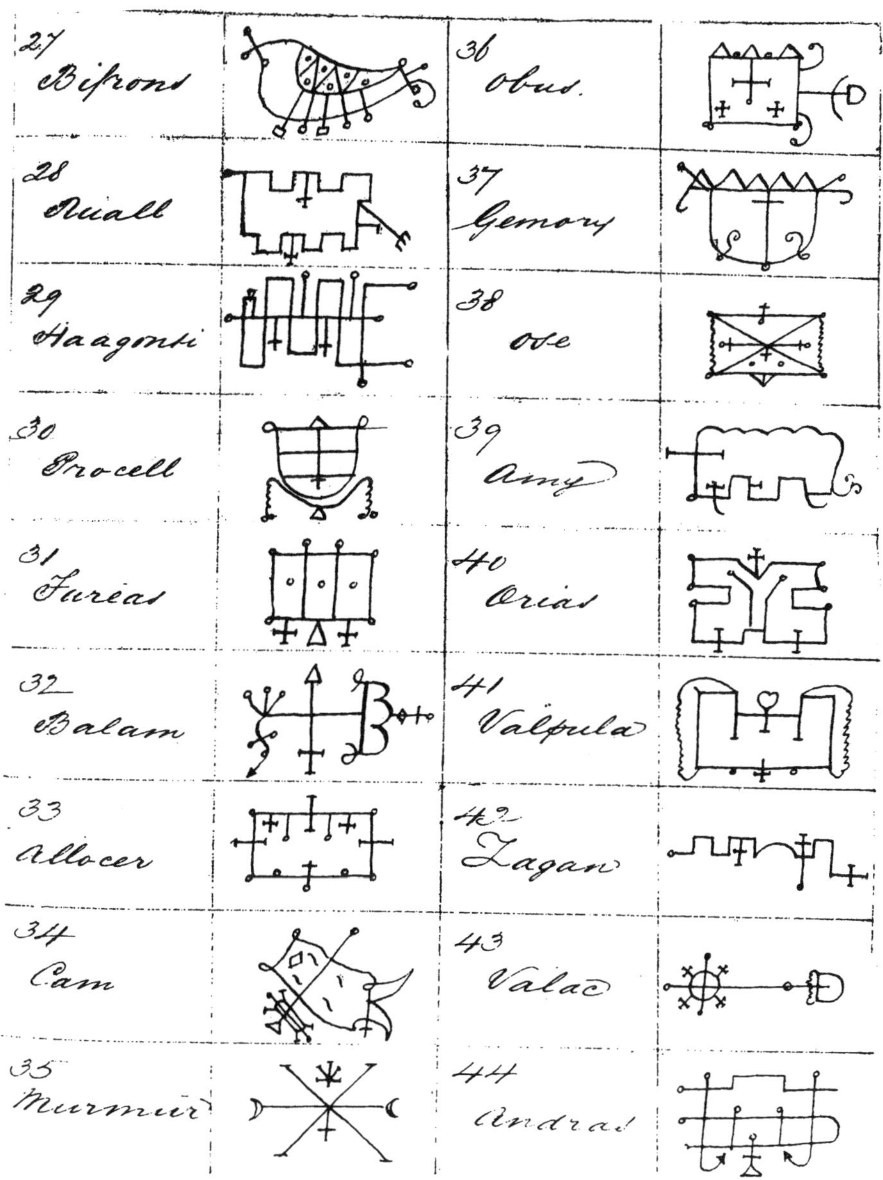

Figure 15. Demonic Seals from Sibley's *Goetia*.

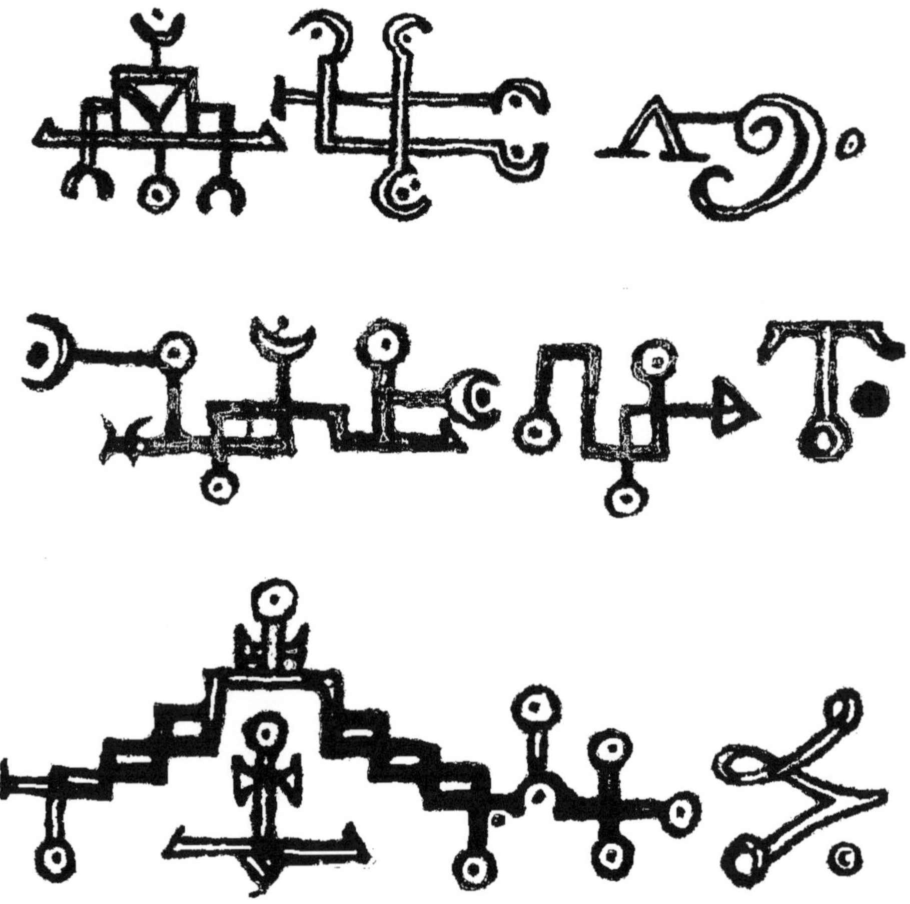

Figure 16. Angelic Seals bound together with Sibley's *Goetia*. These were copied by the same copyist from Lenain, who in turn took them from manuscripts of the Comte de Boulainvilliers in the Bibliothèque de l'Arsenal, suggesting an awareness of the connection between the 72 angels and 72 spirits.

Appendix 7 – The 72 Shem ha-Mephorash Angels

A24. The 72 Shem ha-Mephorash Angels, their Hebrew Root, Name, Degrees and Nature.

No	Hebrew Root	Name	Degrees Ruled	Characteristics
1	והו-יה	Vehuiah	1-5°	Helps enlightenment & expands consciousness; dominates the sciences; influences the shrewd.
2	ילי-אל	Yeliel	6-10°	Helps repress unjust revolts; aids conjugal peace; dominates kings & princes; influences all generations.
3	סיט-אל	Sitael	11-15°	Protects against adversity and calamity; dominates magnanimity & nobility; influences lovers of truth.
4	עלמ-יה	Elemiah	16-20°	Helps against spiritual torment; reveals traitors; dominates sea voyages; influences discoveries.
5	מהש-יה	Mahasiah	21-25°	Helps all to live in peace; dominates occult magic & theology; influences learning.
6	ללה-אל	Lelahel	26-30°	Serves to acquire "light"; cures contagious diseases; dominates love, fame & fortune; Influences the sciences.
7	אכא-יה	Achaiah	31-35°	Helps discover natural secrets; dominates patience & temperance; influences the spread of light and industry.
8	כהת-אל	Kahetel	36-40°	Serves to obtain blessing and protection against evil spirits. Dominates agricultural produce; influences the hunt.
9	הזי-אל	Aziel	41-45°	Helps keep promises & obtain the friendship of the great; dominates good faith; influences sincerity and faith.
10	אלד-יה	Aladiah	46-50°	Helps hide secrets; dominates plague and rabies; influences healing.
11	לאו-יה	Lauviah	51-55°	Protects against lightning; serves to obtain victory; dominates fame; influences the famous learned.
12	ההע-יה	Hahaiah	56-60°	Protects against adversity; helps those in need; dominates dreams; influences wise & spiritual people.
13	יזל-אל	Yezalel	61-65°	Helps reconciliation & conjugal faithfulness; dominates friendship & affability; influences memory & shrewdness.
14	מבה-אל	Mebahel	66-70°	Protects against those wishing to usurp the fortunes of others; dominates justice; influences & protects truth.
15	הרי-אל	Hariel	71-75°	Serves against the ungodly & defeatists; dominates the sciences & arts; influences discoveries & new methods.
16	הקמ-יה	Hakamiah	76-80°	Helps against traitors; serves for victory over enemies; dominates arsenals; influences frankness.
17	לאו-יה	Lauviah	81-85°	Helps refresh at night time; helps against sadness; dominates the high sciences; influences musicians & poets.
18	כלי-אל	Kaliel	86-90°	Serves to reveal the truth; aids the triumph of innocence; dominates trials; influences witnesses.
19	לוו-יה	Leuviah	91-95°	Protects & helps in obtaining grace; dominates the memory; influences joviality & intelligence.
20	פהל-יה	Pahaliah	96-100°	Helps conversions; dominates theology & religion; influences chastity & morals.
21	נלכ-אל	Nelekael	101-105°	Protects against unfavourable spirits & slanderers; Dominates mathematics & geometry.
22	ייי-אל	Yeiael	106-110°	Protects against storms & shipwrecks; dominates business fortunes; influences business trips.
23	מלה-אל	Melahel	111-115°	Protects against weapons & perils of travel; dominates medicinal herbs & water.
24	חהו-יה	Chahuiah	116-120°	Serves to obtain grace; dominates the exiled; protects against thieves & murderers.

A24. The 72 Shem ha-Mephorash Angels, their Hebrew Root, Name, Degrees and Nature.				
25	נתה-יה	Nithahaiah	121-125°	Serves to obtain wisdom & dream revelations; dominates the occult sciences & the wise.
26	האא-יה	Haaiah	126-130°	Protects those seeking the true light; dominates peace treaties; influences ambassadors.
27	ירת-אל	Yerathel	131-135°	Protects against unjust attacks; confounds one's enemies; dominates civilisation; influences peace.
28	שאה-יה	Sheahiah	146-140°	Protects against fire, ruin & collapse; dominates health & longevity; influences prudence.
29	ריי-אל	Reiyel	141-145°	Helps & protects against enemies both visible and invisible; dominates mystic feelings & sacred philosophy.
30	אומ-אל	Omael	146-150°	Helps against desperation & trouble; strengthens patience; dominates the generation (birth) of men and animals.
31	לכב-אל	Lekabel	151-155°	Casts light on one's profession; dominates vegetation; influences astrology.
32	ושר-יה	Vashariah	156-160°	Helps against false & unjust accusations; dominates justice & judges; influences the word.
33	יחו-יה	Yechuiah	161-165°	Uncovers plots & traitors; undoes their plans; dominates & influences just rulers.
34	להח-יה	Lehachiah	166-170°	Maintains peace & harmony between countries; dominates faithfulness & respect & devotion.
35	כוק-יה	Kevaqiah	171-175°	Recovers the friendship of those we have offended; dominates wills; influences friendly distribution.
36	מנד-אל	Menadel	176-180°	Protects against slander; releases prisoners; dominates the return of exiles.
37	אני-אל	Aniel	181-185°	Helps conquer & to obtain release from siege; dominates the sciences & arts; influences the meditation of the wise.
38	חעמ-יה	Chaamiah	186-190°	Protects against lightning and infernal spirits; dominates creeds; influences & protects those who seek the truth.
39	רהע-אל	Rehael	191-195°	Protects from & cures disease; dominates health & longevity; influences paternal love.
40	ייז-אל	Yeiazel	196-200°	Helps release prisoners, releases from enemies; dominates the press & books; influences artists.
41	ההה-אל	Hahahel	201-205°	Helps against the ungodly & slanderers; dominates missionaries; influences priests & prelates.
42	מיכ-אל	Mikael	206-210°	Helps & protects the safety of journeys; dominates the powerful; influences curiosity & politics.
43	וול-יה	Vevaliah	211-215°	Helps destroy enemies; frees from slavery; dominates peace; influences prosperity.
44	ילה-אל	Yelahiah	216-220°	Helps win lawsuits; dominates victory; influences courage in battle.
45	סאל-יה	Saliah	221-215°	Helps confound the evil & the proud; dominates vegetation; influences education.
46	ערי-אל	Ariel	226-230°	Helps uncover hidden treasures; dominates night-time visions; influences difficult solutions.
47	עשל-יה	Aushaliah	231-235°	Helps those who wish to raise themselves spiritually; dominates justice; influences contemplation.
48	מיה-אל	Mihael	236-240°	Helps preserve harmony & union between spouses; dominates the generations; influences love.
49	והו-אל	Vehuel	241-245°	Helps find peace against trouble; dominates great personalities; influences humility.
50	דני-אל	Daniel	246-250°	Protects & consoles; inspires decisions; dominates justice; influences judges.

A24. The 72 Shem ha-Mephorash Angels, their Hebrew Root, Name, Degrees and Nature.				
51	החש-יה	Hachashiah	251-255°	Helps those who wish to know the occult mysteries; dominates chemistry; influences abstract sciences.
52	עממ-יה	Aumamiah	256-260°	Destroys enemies; protects prisoners; dominates vigour; influences research.
53	ננא-אל	Nanael	261-265°	Obtains enlightenment; dominates the higher sciences; influences teachers & men of law.
54	נית-אל	Nithael	266-270°	Obtains mercy & longevity; dominates dynasties & stability.
55	מבה-יה	Mebahiah	271-275°	Helps in consolation & those who wish to have children; dominates morals, religion & piety.
56	פוי-אל	Poiel	276-280°	Obtains what is asked for; dominates fame, success & fortune; influences moderation.
57	נממ-יה	Nemmamiah	281-285°	Helps prosper & release prisoners; dominates generals; influences combatants.
58	ייל-אל	Yeialel	286-290°	Helps against trouble; heals eye diseases; dominates iron; influences locksmiths & knife-grinders.
59	הרח-אל	Harachel	291-295°	Protects against female sterility & rebellious children; dominates treasures & archives; influences the press.
60	מצר-אל	Mitzrael	296-300°	Heals the ills of the spirit; releases from persecutors; dominates men of virtue; influences faithfulness.
61	ומב-אל	Umabel	301-305°	Obtains the friendship of a person; dominates astronomy & physics; influences the sensitivity of the heart.
62	יהה-אל	Yahehel	206-310°	Obtains wisdom & knowledge; dominates philosophers & enlightened; influences virtue in solitude.
63	ענו-אל	Anuiel	311-315°	Protects against accidents; maintains health & heals; dominates trade & businessmen; influences business.
64	מחי-אל	Mechiel	316-320°	Protects against rabies & fierce animals; dominates the learned, orators & authors; influences the press & books.
65	דמב-יה	Damabiah	321-325°	Aids against sorcery; obtains wisdom; dominates the waters; influences sailors & fishermen.
66	מנק-אל	Manaqel	326-330°	Protects against & heals leprosy & anger; dominates vegetation; influences sleep & dreams.
67	איע-אל	Eiael	331-335°	Helps and consoles in adversity; obtains wisdom; dominates change; influences the occult sciences.
68	חבו-יה	Chabuiah	336-340°	Helps maintain health & cure disease; dominates fertility & agriculture & the earth.
69	ראה-אל	Rahel	341-345°	Helps find lost or stolen objects; dominates laws & judges; influences fame.
70	יבמ-יה	Yabamiah	346-350°	Protects & regenerates; leads to inner harmony; dominates philosophical knowledge; influences nature.
71	היי-אל	Hayiel	351-355°	Confounds evil; grants release from enemies; gives victory; dominates weapons & soldiers, influences iron.
72	מומ-יה	Mumiah	356-360°	Brings every experience to a happy conclusion; dominates medicine & influences longevity.

No.	A25. The 72 Shem ha-Mephorash Angels with their corresponding Invocatory Psalm.		
	Angel	**Psalm (KJV/ Vulgate)**	**Invocatory Psalm or *Tehilim***
1	Vehuiah	3:3 / 3:4	*Et tu Domine susceptor meus es, gloria mea et exaltans caput meum.* (Deus Exaltator) And thou, O Lord, art my guardian, and exaltest my head.
2	Yeliel	22:19 / 21:20	*Tu autem Domine ne elongaveris auxilium tuum a me, ad defensionem meam conspice.* (Deus Auxiliator) Do not remove thy help from me, O Lord, and look to my defence.
3	Sitael	91:2 / 90:2	*Dicam Domino, susceptor meus es, et refugium meum, Deus meus, sperabo in eum.* (Deus Spes) I shall say to the Lord, Thou art my guardian, my God is my refuge, and shall hope in him.
4	Elemiah	6:4 / 6:5	*Convertere Domine, et eripe animam meam, salvum me fac propter misericordiam tuam.* (Deu Absconditus) Turn, O Lord, and deliver my soul, and save me for Thy mercy's sake.
5	Mahasiah	34:4 / 33:5	*Exquisivi Dominum, et exaudivit me, et ex omnibus tribulationibus meis eripuit me.* (Deus Salvator) I called upon the Lord and he heard me and delivered me from all my tribulations.
6	Lelahel	9:11 / 9:12	*Psallite Domino qui habitat in Sion, annunciate inter gentes studia eius.* (Deus Laudabilis) Let him who lives in Zion sing unto the Lord, and proclaim his goodwill among the peoples.
7	Achaiah	103:8 /102:8	*Miserator et misericors Dominus, longanimus, et multum misericors.* (Deus Longanimis) The Lord is merciful and compassionate, long-suffering and of great goodness.
8	Kahetel	95:6 / 94:6	*Venite, adoremus, et procidamus ante facem Domini, qui fecit nos,* (Deus Adorandus) O come let us adore and fall down before God who bore us.
9	Aziel	25:6 / 24:6	*Reminiscere miserationum tuarum Domine, et misericordiarum tuarum quae a saeculo sunt.* (Deus Misericors) Remember Thy mercies, O Lord, and Thy mercies which have been for ever.
10	Aladiah	33:22 / 32:22	*Fiat misericordia tua Domine super nos, quemadmodum speravimus in te.* (Deus Propitiabilis) Perform Thy mercies O Lord upon us, for we have hoped in Thee.
11	Lauviah	18:46 / 17:47	*Vivit Dominus, et benedictus Deus meus, et exaltatur Deus salutis meae.* (Deus Exaltandus) The Lord liveth, blessed is my God, and let the God of my salvation be exalted.
12	Hahaiah	10:1 / 10:1	*Ut quid Domine recessisti longe, despicis in opportunitatibus in tribulatione?* (Deus Refugium) Why standest Thou afar off O Lord, why hidest thyself in the times of tribulation.
13	Yezalel	98:4 / 97:4	*Jubilate Domino omnis Terra, cantate, et exultate, et Psallite.* (Deus super omnia decantabilis) Rejoice in the Lord, all ye lands, sing exult, and play upon a stringed instrument.
14	Mebahel	9:9 / 9:9	*Et factus est Dominus refugium pauperi, adiniutor in opportunitatibus, in tribulatione.* (Deus Custos et Servator) The Lord also will be a refuge for the oppressed, and in times of trouble.
15	Hariel	94:22 / 93:22	*Et factus est mihi Dominus in refugium, et Deus meus in adjutorium spei meae.* (Deus Sublenator) The Lord is a refuge for me, and my God the help of my hope.

No.	A25. The 72 Shem ha-Mephorash Angels with their corresponding Invocatory Psalm.		
	Angel	**Psalm (KJV/ Vulgate)**	**Invocatory Psalm or *Tehilim***
16	Hakamiah	88:1 / 87:25	*Domine Deus salutis meae, in die clamavi et nocte coram te.* (Deus Erector) O Lord, God of my salvation, by day have I called to thee, and sought Thy presence by night.
17	Lauviah	8:9 / 8:2	*Domine Dominus noster, quam admirabile est nomen tuum in universa terra!* (Deus Mirabilis) O Lord our Lord, How wonderful is Thy name in all the world!
18	Kaliel	35:24 / 34:24	*Judica me secundum justitiam tuam, Domine Deus meus, et non supergaudeant mihi.* (Deus Invocandus) Judge me, O Lord, according to Thy loving kindness, and let not them be joyful over me, O Lord.
19	Leuviah	40:1 / 39:2	*Expectans expectavi Dominum et intendit mihi.* (Deus Festinus ad Audientum) I waited patiently for the Lord, and He inclined unto me, and heard my cry.
20	Pahaliah	120:1-2 / 119:2	*Et nomen Domini invocabo, O Domine, libera animam meam.* (Deus Redemptor) I shall call upon the name of the Lord, O Lord free my soul.
21	Nelekael	31:14 / 30:15	*Ego autem in te speravi Domine, dixi, Deus meus es tu.* (Deus Solus) In Thee also have I hoped, O Lord, and said, Thou art my God.
22	Yeiael	121:5 / 120:5	*Dominus custodit te, Dominus protectio tua super manum dexteram tuam.* (Deus Dextera) The Lord keep thee, the Lord be they protection on thy right hand.
23	Melahel	121:8 / 120:8	*Dominus custodiat introitum tuum, et exitum tuum, ex hoc, nunc et usque in saeculum.* (Deus Declinans Malum) The Lord keep thine incoming and thine outgoing from this time forth for evermore.
24	Chahuiah	33:18 / 35:5	*Beneplacitum est Domino super timentes eum, et in eos qui sperant super misericordiam eius.* (Deus Bonus ex seipso) The Lord is well pleased with those that fear Him and hope upon his mercy.
25	Nithahaiah	9:1 / 9:2	*Confitebor tibi Domine in tote corde meo, narrabo omnia mirabilia tua.* (Deus Largitor) I shall acknowledge Thee, O Lord, with all my heart and shall tell forth all Thy wonders.
26	Haaiah	119:145 / 118:145	*Clamavi in toto corde meo, exaudi me Domine, justificationes meas requiram.* (Deus Auditor in Abscondito) I have called unto thee with all my heart, hear me, O Lord, and I shall keep thy statutes.
27	Yerathel	140:1 / 139:1	*Eripe me Domine ab homine malo a viro iniquo eripe me.* (Deus Propulsator) Save me, O Lord, from the evil man and deliver me from the wicked doer.
28	Sheahiah	71:12 / 70:12	*Deus ne elongeris a me, Deus meus in auxilium meum respice.* (Deus Sublator Malorum) Let not God depart from me, look to my help, O God.
29	Reiyel	54:4 / 53:7	*Ecce Deus adjuvat me, et Dominus susceptor est animae meae.* (Deus Expectatio) Behold, God is my helper, and the Lord is the guardian of my soul.
30	Omael	71:5 / 70:5	*Quoniam tu es patentia mea Domine, Domine spes mea a juventute mea.* (Deus Patiens) For Thou are my strength, O Lord. O Lord, Thou are my hope from my youth.

No.	A25. The 72 Shem ha-Mephorash Angels with their corresponding Invocatory Psalm.		
	Angel	**Psalm (KJV/ Vulgate)**	**Invocatory Psalm or *Tehilim***
31	Lekabel	71:16 / 70:16	*Introibo in potentiam Domini, Deus meus memorabor justitiae tuae solius.* (Deus Doctor) I shall enter into the power of the Lord, my God, I shall be mindful of Thy justice only.
32	Vashariah	33:4 / 32:4	*Quia rectum est verbum Domini, et omnia opera eius in fide.* (Deus Rectus) For the word of the Lord is upright, and all his works faithful.
33	Yechuiah	94:11 / 93:11	*Dominus scit cogitationes hominum quoniam vana sunt.* (Deus Omnium Cognitor) The Lord knows the thoughts of men, for they are in vain.
34	Lehachiah	131:3 / 130:3	*Speret Israel in Domino, ex hoc nunc et usque in saeculum.* (Deus Clemens) Let Israel hope in the Lord from this time forth and for evermore.
35	Kevaqiah	116:1 / 114:1	*Dilexi quoniam exaudi Dominus vocem orationis meae.* (Deus Gaudiosus) I am joyful, for the Lord hears the voice of my prayer.
36	Menadel	26:8 / 25:8	*Domini dilexi decorum domus tuae, et locum habitationis gloriae tuae.* (Deus Honorabilis) I have delighted in the beauty of They House, O Lord, and in the place of the habitation of Thy glory.
37	Aniel	80:3 / 79:4	*Domine Deus virtutum converte nos; et ostende faciem tuam, et salvi erimus.* (Deus Dominus Virtutum) O Lord God, turn Thy power towards us, and show us Thy face and we shall be saved.
38	Chaamiah	91:9 / 90:9	*Quoniam tu es, Domine, spes mea, altissimum posuisti refugium tuum.* (Deus Spes Omnium finium terrae) For Thou art my hope, O Lord, and Thou hast been my deepest refuge.
39	Rehael	30:10 / 29:11	*Audivit me Dominus et misertus est mei, Dominus factus est adjutor meus.* (Deus Velox ad Condonandum) The Lord has heard me and pitied me and the Lord is my helper.
40	Yeiazel	88:14 / 87:15	*Ut quid Domine repellis animam meam, avertis faciem tuam a me.* (Deus Vivum Laetificans) Why drivest Thou away my soul, O Lord, and turnest Thy face from me?
41	Hahahel	120:2 / 119:2	*Domine libera animam meam a labiis iniquis, et a lingua dolosa.* (Deus Triunas) O Lord, deliver my soul from wicked lips and a deceitful tongue.
42	Mikael	121:7 / 120:7	*Dominus custodiat te ab omni malo, et custodiat animam tuam.* (Deus Quis sicut ille) The Lord protects thee from all evil and will protect thy soul.
43	Vevaliah	88:13 / 87:14	*Et Ego ad te Domine clamavi, et mane oratio meae praeveniet te.* (Deus Rex Dominator) I have cried unto Thee, O Lord, and let my prayer come unto Thee.
44	Yelahiah	119:108 / 118:108	*Voluntaria oris mei beneplacita fac Domine et Judicia tua doce me.* (Deus Aeternum, Manens) Make my wishes pleasing unto Thee, O Lord, and teach me Thy judgments.
45	Saliah	94:18 / 93:18	*Si dicebam motus est pes meus, misericordia tua Domine adjuvabit me.* (Deus Motor Omnium) If I say that my foot is moved, Thou wilt help me of Thy mercy.

No.	A25. The 72 Shem ha-Mephorash Angels with their corresponding Invocatory Psalm.		
	Angel	**Psalm (KJV/ Vulgate)**	**Invocatory Psalm or *Tehilim***
46	Ariel	145:9 / 144:9	*Suavis Dominus universes, et miserationes ejus super omnia opera ejus.* (Deus Revelator) The Lord is pleasant to all the world and his mercies are over all his works.
47	Aushaliah	92:5 / 91:6	*Quam magnificata sunt opera tua Domine, nimis profundae factae sunt cogitatones tuae.* (Deus Justus Judex) How wonderful are Thy works, O Lord, and how deep Thy thoughts.
48	Mihael	98:2 / 97:2	*Notum fecit Dominus salutare suum, in conspectu gentium, revelabit justitiam suam.* (Deus Pater Mittens) The Lord hath made thy salvation known in the sight of the peoples and will reveal his justice.
49	Vehuel	145:3 / 144:3	*Magnus Dominus et laudabilis nimis, et magnitudinis ejus non est finis.* (Deus Magnus et Excelsus) Great is the Lord and worthy to be praised, and there is no end to his greatness.
50	Daniel	145:8 / 144:8	*Miserator et misericors Dominus, patients, et multum misericors.* (Deus Judex Misericors) The Lord God is pitiful and merciful, long-suffering and of great mercy.
51	Hachashiah	104:31 / 103:31	*Sit gloria Domini in saeculam, laetabitur Dominus in operibus suis.* (Deus Secretus Impenetrabilis) Let the Lord be in glory for ever and the Lord will rejoice in His works.
52	Aumamiah	7:17 / 7:18	*Confitebor Domino secundum justitiam ejus, et psallam nomini Domini altissimi.* (Deus Caligine Rectus) I shall make known the Lord, according to his justice, and sing psalms to the name of the Lord, the greatest.
53	Nanael	119:75 / 118:75	*Cognovi Domine, quia aequitas judicia tua, et in veritate tua humiliasti me.* (Deus Superborum Depressor) I have known Thee, O Lord, for Thy judgements are just, and in Thy truth have I abased myself.
54	Nithael	103:19 / 102:19	*Dominus in Caelo paravit sedem suam, et regnum ipsius omnibus dominabitur.* (Deus Rex Coelestis) The Lord hath prepared His seat in heaven and His rule shall be over all.
55	Mebahiah	102:12 / 103:13	*Tu autem Domine in aeternum permanes, et memoriale tuum in generationem et generationem.* (Deus Sempiternus) Thou remainest for ever, O Lord, and Thy memorial is from generation in to generation.
56	Poiel	145.14 / 144:14	*Allevat Dominus omnes qui corruunt, et erigit omnes elisos.* (Deus Fulciens Omnia) The Lord raiseth up all who fall and setteth up the broken.
57	Nemmamiah	115:11 / 113:19	*Qui timent Dominum, speraverunt in Domino, adiutor eorum et protector eorem est.* (Deus Amabilis) They who fear the Lord have hoped in the Lord, He is their helper and their protector.
58	Yeialel	6:3 / 6:4	*Et anima mea turbata est valde, sed tu Domine usque quo.* (Deus Auditor Gemituum) My soul is greatly troubled, but Thou, O Lord art here also.
59	Harachel	113:3 / 112:3	*A Solis ortu usque ad occasum, laudabile nomen Domini.* (Deus Omnia Pentrans) From the rising of the Sun to the going down of the same, the word of the Lord is worthy to be praised.
60	Mitzrael	145:17 / 144:17	*Justus Dominus in omnibus viis suis, et sanctus in omnibus operibus* suis. (Deus Sublevans Opressos) The Lord is just in all his ways in blessed in all his works.

No.	A25. The 72 Shem ha-Mephorash Angels with their corresponding Invocatory Psalm.		
	Angel	**Psalm (KJV/ Vulgate)**	**Invocatory Psalm or *Tehilim***
61	Umabel	113:2 / 112:2	*Sit nomen Domini benedictum ex hoc, nunc, et usque in saeculum.* (Deus Super Omne Nomen) Let the name of the Lord be blessed from this time forth for evermore.
62	Yahehel	119:159 / 118:159	*Vide quoniam mandata tua dilexi, Domine, in misericordia tua vivifica me.* (Deus Ens Supremum) See, O Lord, how I have delighted in Thy commandments according to Thy life-giving mercy.
63	Anuel	100:2 / 99:2	*Servite Domino in Laetitia, introite in conspectu ejus in exultatione.* (Deus Mansuetus) Serve ye the Lord with gladness and enter into his sight with exultation.
64	Mechiel	33:18 / 32:18	*Ecce oculi Domini super metuentes eum, et in eis, qui sperant super misericordia ejus.* (Deus Vivificans) Behold the eyes of the Lord are upon those that fear Him and hope in His loving kindness.
65	Damabiah	90:13 / 89:13	*Convertere Domine usque quo, et deprecabilis esto super servos tuos.* (Deus Fons Sapientiae) Turn, O Lord, even here also, and be pleased with Thy servants.
66	Manaqel	38:21 / 37:22	*Ne derelinquas me Domine Deus meus, ne discesseris a me.* (Deus Omnia Pascens et Lactens) Neither leave me, O Lord, nor depart from me.
67	Eiael	37:4 / 36:4	*Delectare in Domino, et dabit tibi petitiones cordis tui.* (Deus Deliciae Filiorum Hominum) Delight in the Lord and He will give thee the petitions of thy heart.
68	Chabuiah	106:1 / 105:1	*Confitemini Domino, quoniam bonus, quoniam in sæculum misericordia ejus.* (Deus Liberalissimus Dator) Confess to the Lord, for He is God, and His mercy is for ever.
69	Rahel	16:5 / 15:5	*Dominus pars haereditatis meae et calicis mei, tu es qui restitues haereditatem meam mihi.* (Deus Omnia Videns) The Lord is my inheritance and my cup, and it is Thou who restorest mine inheritance.
70	Yabamiah	Genesis 1:1	*In principio creavit Deus Caelum et Terrum.* (Deus Verbo Omnia Producens) In the beginning God created the Heaven and the Earth. [The only scriptural passage not drawn from the Psalms from the 72 angels.]
71	Hayiel	109:30 / 108:30	*Confitebor Domino nimis in ore meo, et in medio multorum laudabo eum.* (Deus Dominus Universorum) I shall confess to the Lord with my mouth and praise Him in the midst of the multitude.
72	Mumiah	116:7 /114:7	*Convertere anima mea in requiem tuam quia Dominus benefeciet tibi.* (Deus Finis Universorum) Return to thy rest, my soul, for the Lord doeth thee good.

Appendix 8 - The Ecclesiastical Planetary Hours

Before the invention of clocks, certainly before their universal availability, the day was for both secular and religious purposes divided into Planetary Hours. The observance of Planetary Hours was part of the daily life of Mediaeval Europe as indeed it had been Jewish practice before. Although the list below is standardized in to specific clock times, these only really apply twice a year at the Equinox, otherwise the natural daylight hours are divided evenly up into twelve, as are the night hours. What could be more natural than for the procedures of magic to also follow the Planetary hours? It made a lot of sense, as in Summer the day was longer and its 'marker posts' more spread out, but in Winter when the time available for work was shorter so they were closer together. In agricultural terms also, there was more to be done in Summer.

Liturgical/Canonical Hours

Matins	(during the night), Vigils or Nocturns.[797]
Lauds	Dawn Prayer (at Dawn)
Prime	Early Morning Prayer (First Hour) or sunrise
Terce	Mid-Morning Prayer (Third Hour)
Sext	Midday Prayer (Sixth Hour = 12 noon)
None	Mid-Afternoon Prayer (Ninth Hour)
Vespers	Evening Prayer ('at the lighting of the lamps') or sunset
Compline	Night Prayer (before retiring)

As the structure of this timetable depends upon points like sunrise and sunset which change each day, it is necessary to use unequal hours to calculate rather than using fixed clock time like 6am, 9am, etc.

The Apostles observed the Jewish custom of praying at the third, sixth and ninth hour of the day and at midnight (see *Acts* 10:3, 9; and 16:25). The Christian prayers of that time consisted of almost the same elements as the Jewish. There is a parallel in the Muslim observance of five prayer times per day. The main difference being that Muslim prayer times are to be observed by all Muslims, whereas the Christian observance was mainly confined to the cloister or the monastery.

[797] Matins, as the name suggests, was originally a morning service, but later got moved to the previous night.

Appendix 9: *'Ars Nova'*: Explanation of Certain Names used in the Figures of the *Goetia*

This item is really just a summary of the names used in the illustrations of equipment in the *Goetia,* together with an Oration which may be a curse directed at anyone who might be tempted to steal the original manuscript. It is likely to be just one practitioner's notes, and is only appended to two manuscripts of the *Lemegeton,* Sloane MS 2731 and Sloane MS 3648. Our present manuscript Harley MS 6483 omits it completely. Nevertheless for the sake of completeness, we have reproduced it here in full.

The *Explanation of Certain Names used in Figures of the Goetia* is a summary made by a later writer, just three folios in length, but it does preserve some consecratory prayers that might be missing from the *Goetia.* It is often mistakenly labelled the *'Ars Nova'*, but in the manuscript it has no title at all. It is rightly confined to an Appendix by Peterson, but was reproduced by Mathers (and therefore Crowley) as if it were a part of the main text, but in a very confused state. It contains:

1. **The Explanation of the Circle of Solomon with the Kabbalistic Names and Prayers for each Sephiroth**

A list of the Godnames, archangelic, angel and planetary names associated with each ten Sephiroth of the Tree of Life with plus a short prayer. These names are those written around the Circle in Sloane MS 2731, and so act as a sort of summary. It is possible that the prayer was used whilst inscribing them.

2. The Prayers and Explanation of the' two Triangles' (the Pentagram and Hexagram) in the Parchment

An item taken by Mathers, Crowley and Peterson as an 'explanation' of the 'Two Triangles, by which is meant the Hexagram & Pentagram. In fact it is not an explanation at all, but a simple list of the key words, in the English, taken from the drawings of the Hexagram & Pentagram in the *Goetia,* plus a prayer probably recited whilst drawing them up. This would have been a summary for the practitioner making his equipment. However this list is fairly corrupt.

3. The Prayer and Explanation of Solomon's Triangle

This just lists out the words of power used in the Triangle, plus mentioning the North Angel and the Candle. A consecratory prayer is added.

The second column of all these first three items has a series of prayers to be said when each of the Circle, Pentagram, Hexagram and Triangle are made and consecrated. However because of the cramped writing this has not previously been recognised as two columns, and so it has been read, by all commentators to date, across the page to produce completely nonsensical 'explanations' such as:

> "Masloth [the zodiac] - so that it may tend unto thy glory and man's good"

However it was never meant to be read across the page. If you read it as two columns vertically, it then makes perfect sense. The result of reading it this way is 13 prayers for consecration of the equipment which is missing from the main text of the *Goetia*. We have expanded and reorganised these and reproduce them below in the form they were meant to be read.

4. The Prayer and Names in the Middle Square

The note headed 'The Middle Square' simply refers to the Hebrew 'HV' of the 'IHVI' drawn in the Master's square in the centre of the Circle along with the English word 'Jehovah'. The prayer to be said when drawing this is:

> "Thou Universal God of Heaven and all the hosts therein and of the Earth Sea and Air and all Creatures therein.
>
> Thou, before thy presence all spirits both infernall Airey and all others do fear and tremble let them be now at this time and forever be in subjection to me at the word of thy most holy name Jehovah."

5. The Prayer before the Brazen Vessel

A very corrupt version of the Prayer before the Brazen Vessel. We have restored the Hebrew as much as possible, but it is in a very corrupt state and obviously written by someone completely unfamiliar with that language.

6. The Mighty Oration

This may be an imprecation designed to force a thief to return stolen goods. Benjamin Rowe suggests this as a curse written at the end of the manuscript, by one of its owners, and directed against anyone who might have stolen the manuscript. It contains phrases like:

> "that thou thief return immediately & restore the goods again which thou hast stolen away... thou thief to restore the goods again immediately or else the wrath of God may fall upon thee & force thee to come immediately."

Here follows the full text of the *Explanation.*

[1. The Explanation of the Circle of Solomon with the Kabbalistic Names and Prayers for each Sephiroth]

[Kether]

P[rimum] M[obile]
Eheie[h] Kether
Haioth [ha - Kadosh][798]
Metatron
Reschith Hagalgalim[799]

[*Consecrating Prayer:*]

Almighty God whose dwelling is in the highest heavens
The great King of heaven and all the powers therein
And of all the holy hosts of Angels and Archangels
Hear the prayers of thy servant who put[s] his whole trust in thee
Let thy holy Angels command assist me at this time and at all times

[Chokmah]

S[phere of the] Z[odiac]
Jehovah
Hochmah
Ophanim
Jophiel
Masloth[800]

[*Consecrating Prayer of the Sphere of the Zodiac:*]

God Almighty, God omnipotent, hear my prayers
Command thy holy Angels Above the fixed stars
To be Assisting and Aiding of thy servants
That I may command all spirits of the Air Fire water earth and hell
So that it may tend to thy glory and Mans good

[Binah]

S[phere of Saturn] ♄
Jehovah
Elohim
Binah
Aralim
Sabbatha[i]

---

798 Holy Living Creatures.
799 Primum Mobile, or 'first swirlings.'
800 The Zodiac.

[*Consecrating Prayer of Saturn:*]

God Almighty, God omnipotent, hear my prayers
God with us, God be always present with us
Strengthen us and support us both now and forever
In these our undertakings which I doe as an Instrument in thy hands
Of thee the great God of Sabaoth

[Chesed]

K: S[phere Jupiter] ♃
[C]hesed
[C]hasmalim
Zedeck

[*Consecrating Prayer of Jupiter:*]

Thou great god governor and creator of all the Planets and host of heaven
Command them by the Almighty Power
To be now present and assisting to us thy poor servants both now and forever

[Geburah]

S[phere of Mars] ♂
Elohim Gebor
Seraphim
Camael
Madim

[*Consecrating Prayer of Mars:*]

Most Almighty eternal and everliving Lord God
Command thy Seraphims
To attend on us now at this time to assist us and defend us from all perils and dangers

[Tiphareth]

S[phere of Sol] ☼
Eloha
Tetragrammaton
Raphael
Schemes[h]

[*Consecrating Prayer of Sol*:]

O Almighty God be present with us both now and forever
And let thy Almighty power and presence ever guard us and protect us at this present and forever
Let thy holy Angel Raphael wait upon us at this present [time] and forever
To Assist us in this our undertakings

[Netzach]

S[phere of Venus] ♀
Jehovah
Sabaoth
Neza[c]h
Elohim
Haniel

[*Consecrating Prayer of Venus*:]

God Almighty, God omnipotent, hear my prayers
Thou great God of Sabaoths
All seeing God
God be present with us and let thy presence be now and always present with us
Let thy holy Angel Haniell come and minister unto us at this present

[Hod]

S[phere of Mercury] ☿
Elohim
Sabaoth
Hod
Ben[i Elohim]
Michael
Cockab

[*Consecrating Prayer of Mercury*:]

God be present with us and let thy presence be now and always present with us
O thou great god of Sabaoths be present with us at this time and forever
Let thy Almighty power defend us and protect us both now and forever
Let Michael who is under thee, General of thy heavenly host,
Come and expel all evil and danger from us both now and forever

[Yesod]

S[phere of Luna] ☽
Sadai
Jesod
Cherubin
Gabriel
Levanah

[*Consecrating Prayer of Luna:]*

Thou great God of all wisdom and knowledge
Instruct thy poor and most humble servant
By thy holy Cherubins
By thy holy Angel Gabriel who is the Author and messenger of good tidings
Direct us and support us at this present [time] and forever

[2.] The [Prayers and] Explanation of the two triangles [the Pentagram and Hexagram] in the Parchment

[*The Hexagram*]
Alpha and omega
Tetragrammaton

[*The Pentagram*]
Tetragrammaton

Soluzen	Bellony
Halliza	Hally
[Abdia]	Fra
Bellator	

[*Consecrating Prayer:*]

Thou O great God who art the beginning and the end, who was before all Eternity and ever shall be
Thou God of mighty power be ever present with us to guard us and protect us and let thy holy presence be now and always with us
Thou God of almighty power be ever present with us to guard us and protect us and let thy holy presence be now and always with us
I command thou spirit of what Region soever thou art come into this circle and Appear in human shape
And speak to us audibly in our mother tongue
And shew and discover to us all treasures that thou knowest of or that is in thy keeping and deliver it to us quietly
And answer us all such questions as we shall demand without any defect now at this time

[3.] The [Prayers and] Explanation of Solomon's Triangle

Anephezaton
Tetragrammaton
Primeumaton
Michael
Tetragrammaton.
North Angel - East Angel, South and West, are all one
Candle

[*Consecrating Prayer*:]

Thou great God of all the heavenly host
Thou God of almighty power be ever present with us to guard us and protect us and let thy holy presence be now and always with us
Thou who art the first and last let all spirits be subject to us and let the spirit be bound in this Triangle that disturbs this place
By thy holy Angel Michael until I shall discharge him
Thou God of almighty power be ever present with us to guard us and protect us, and let thy holy presence be now and always with us
To be a light to our understandings and attend us now in our undertakings and defend us from all evil and danger both of soul and body

[4.] The [Prayer and Names in the] Middle Square

הי [or הר]
Jehovah
Rosh:
Joh:

[*Consecrating Prayer*:]

Thow [Thou] Universal God of Heaven and all the hosts therein and of the Earth Sea and Air and all the Creatures therein
Thou, before thy presence all spirits both infernal Airy and all others do fear and tremble, let them be now at this time and forever be in subjection to me at the word of thy most holy name Jehovah

[5. The Prayer before the Brazen Vessel][801]

ש Jodgea > רהיוי Rosen Emolack ל?ם Roson Subbartha >ויצל Roson Eloham ליל??? Skimoy Abomoth ליה?ה Rosen Elemoth אל Zadon א>א> Behoma Reson אחל Gamaliall תא> Mackhamasmack[802] למא Baseh Zadon ? Hinmore צרק Molock Ehaddon אה?א א י Molack Johiron & Michael

[The Hebrew above is *very* conjectural, and virtually worthless, while the supposed translation of it in the manuscript continues below]

Jodgea, I humbly implore thee Rosen Emolack thou everlasting god Roson Subbartha thou omnipotent & everlasting Creator Roson Eloham thou god with us Skimoy Abomoth to bind & keep fast Rosen Elemoth Mackhamasmack by thy divine power those evil & airy spirits Baseh Zadon of the spirit of flyes & spirit of the air Hinnon & spirit of Hinnon Molock Ehaddon with all the spirits of hidden treasure & the disturbers of mankind Molack with the spirits of Molack Johinnon in chains in thy brazen urn Michael with thy Arch Angel Michael...[803]

[6.] The Mighty Oration

By the most great & almighty power of ***Alpha*** *&* ***Omega****,* ***Jehovah*** *&* ***Emmanuel****, and by him that divided the Red Sea & by that great power that turned all the waters & rivers of Egypt into blood & turned all the dust into flies & chains & by that great power that brought frogs all over the land of Egypt & entered into the King's Palace & chambers & by that great power that [sent] terrible thunder & lightning & hail stones mixed with fire, & sent locusts which did destroy all growing things in the whole land of Egypt, & by that great power that destroyed all the first born of the land of Egypt both of man & beast, & by that great power that divided the hard rock & rivers of water issued out of the sand of the wilderness, and by that great power that led the children of Israel into the land of Canaan & by that great power that destroyed Sonachoribs*[804] *great host & by that great & almighty power of him that walked on the sea as on dry land, & by that almighty power that raised the dead Lazarus out of his grave, & by that almighty power of the blessed & holy & glorious trinity that did cast the Devil & all disobedient Angels out of heaven into hell that thou thief return immediately & restore the goods again which thou hast stolen away, therefore in & by the names of the Almighty God before rehearsed I charge thee, thou thief to restore the goods again immediately or else the wrath of God may fall upon thee & force thee to come immediately. Amen.*

---

[801] The whole passage is very corrupt.

[802] This could be a very corrupt Shem ha-Mephorash.

[803] Perhaps the only thing of interest in this passage is the mention of Michael and the Brass Urn.

[804] Sennacherib was the son of Sargon II, whom he succeeded on the throne of Assyria (705–681 BCE).

Appendix 10: Derivation of some of the Words of Conjuration

All of these names have an actual derivation from Hebrew or Greek, plus a fanciful one which links them with a particular magical act in the Bible, which is their 'credentials' as a Word of Conjuration. The list is not definitive.

A and Ω = Alpha and Omega = A and Ω
Adonai = Adonay = אדני = Lord
Anabona = (Greek)
Anapheneton = (Greek)
Anaphexeton = (Greek)
Apologiae Sedes = (Greek)
Agios = Hagios = Holy (Greek)
Agla = AGLA = אגלא = *Aieth Gadol Leolam Adonai* = 'Thou art mighty forever, O Lord' = the name Lot heard and was saved from the destruction of Sodom
Alpha and Omega = A and Ω = the first and last letter of the Greek alphabet, i.e. everything = the name Daniel used to destroy the idol Bel and the dragon (probably a large snake)
Baldachiensis = Baldachia =
El = God = אל
El Elyon = God Most High (Hebrew)
Elion = Elyon = the name which caused the plague of hail in Egypt (Hebrew)
Elohe = Eloah = divine name for Tiphareth = אלוה
Elohim = gods = אלוהים
Emmanuel = 'God be with us' = the name Shadrach, Meshach and Abednego used in the fiery furnace
Escherchie Ariston = Greek *ischuros ariston* = Strong and noble (as in 'aristocrat') = supposedly the name that turned the rivers of Egypt into blood
Genio = Genius = Spirit
Genio Liachidai =
Hagios = holy (Greek)
Helioren = Helios + ? (Greek)
IHVH = Tetragrammaton = יהוה
Iscyros = Ischuros (Greek)
Jah = Yah = יה
Jehovah = IHVH = יהוה
Jetros = healer
Joth = ית = the name revealed to Jacob as he wrestled with the angel
Joth = Yod = י
On = said to be the ancient Egyptian city of Heliopolis, once considered to be the centre of the earth and of the magical world
Oriston = Ariston = noble
Otheos = O Theos = O God
Paracletus = the Holy Ghost of the Christian trinity (Greek)

Primeumaton = First Breath (Greek) = the Creator = the name Moses spoke and the Earth swallowed up Corah, Dathan, and Abiram

Sabaoth = Tzbaoth = God of Hosts = צבאות = the name used by Moses to cause the plague of frogs in Egypt

Saday = Shaddai = שדאי

Schemes Amathia = 'Sun be still' = the name Joshua spoke and the Sun stood still for a whole day

Shemesh = the Sun = שמש = Canaanite god of the Sun

Tetragrammaton = IHVH = יהוה

Theos = God (Greek)

Y and V = יו = the name that God revealed to Adam

Yah = YH = יה

Yod He Vau He = Tetragrammaton = IHVH = יהוה

Zebeoth = Sabaoth

Appendix 11: Narrative of Dr Rudd, Sir John Heydon and a Spirit

[1][From the Pauline Art]

How a man may have the continual Society of a Guardian Genius
– a Narrative [2]

There was a Gentleman by Descent from the lines of the Plantagenets[3] who was in Egypt, Italy and Arabia, frequenting the Society of the inspired Christians being at a Tavern in Cheapside[4] with Mr Heydon[5] and others whose discoursing of the nature and dignity of Angels which was interrupted by Dr Rudd[6] who said to the Gentleman, "Sir you are not from the Kingdom of God;"[7] at this many were silent yet several thoughts arose, some desired [asked] this strange Gentleman to stay but he refused, and being pressed he gave the Gentleman a paper of [containing some] white and yellow ~~paper~~ powder and bid him burn it at midnight, and read [aloud] that Chapter that lay open in his bible in his Chamber, and sing such Psalms, and then the window flew open and the Gentleman vanished.

He burnt the powder as he was bid, and there appeared a shining fly[8] upon the bible which he had in his hands, this vanished whilst he slept, which was then about 8 in the morning. Gemini being the Ascendant and Mercury in Virgo, the Gentleman conceived that this Spirit had been with him all his

---

[1] Taken from the Ninety fourth sheet Dr Rudd.

[2] This anecdote which concerns the Guardian Genius is unique to this manuscript, Harley MS 6483. It occurs in the middle of the *Pauline Art*, but does not form part of it. We have moved it out of the *Pauline Art* to this Appendix. It provides an insight into the men working the system.

[3] The Plantagenets were the family which produced various kings of France and England including King Edward I-V and King Henry III-VIII. By mentioning this connection, the author wishes to impress on the reader the nobility of the person concerned, and the veracity of his account.

[4] A part of the City of London.

[5] Undoubtedly Sir John Heydon (1629-1667), famous writer on Rosicrucians, astrology, geomancy and magic, almost unheard of now, but whose voluminous works had a strong influence on S L MacGregor Mathers. The relevance of mentioning him here is that when he drew up his own geniture or nativity he calculated that "at the time I was born: this is also the Character of my Genius Malhitriel, and [the] Spirit Taphza Benezelthar Thascraphimarah" [or Taphzabnezelthartha-seraphimarah], indicating that the procedure of deriving the name of your personal Dæmon or spirit from your horoscope was quite widespread at the time.

[6] Interesting that Rudd is here spoken of in the third person. This also helps to reinforce the dating of the original composition of the Rudd manuscript (not the later 1712 transcript by Peter Smart); as such a conversation probably took place after 1649 (when Heydon would have been twenty) but before Thomas Rudd's death in 1656.

[7] Maybe meaning that Rudd immediately suspected him of being a demon or a spirit.

[8] Flies are often associated with the demon Beelzebub.

lifetime as he gathered from certain monitory [warning] Dreams and Visions whence he was forewarned as well of several dangers [shown to him] as visions. Mr Waters and two Gentlemen more were at his house and desired him to go along with them to the Exchange[1] and dine with them, and some other Merchants, which he did, and going along upon his breast one of them espied a ball of Gold which did shine so gloriously that it dazzled the eyes of them all, and this continued all the rising of Mercury who was then in Virgo; this Spirit discovered [showed] himself to him after he had for a whole year together earnestly prayed to God to send a good Angel to him to be a guide of his life and actions, also he prayed for a token that this was the will and pleasure of God which was granted, for in a bright shining day no Cloud appearing there fell a drop of water upon his hat which to this day is not dry, and I think never will be although it be worn in this hot weather. He prays to God to defend him and guide him in the true religion.

Reading two or three hours at a time in the holy Bible; after this amongst many other divine Dreams and visions, he once in his sleep seemed to hear the voice of God Saying to him "I will save thy soul, I am he that before [this] appeared unto thee; Since [then] doth the spirit every day knock at his door about three or four o clock in the morning: He rising there appeared a Child of fair stature very comely, and gave him a Book which he kept very well, yet let many see it that can prevail with [persuade] him, this Book is full of divine things such I never read or heard of. Another time his Candle did fall down upon the Ground, and went out, and there appeared before him something about the bigness [size] of a Nut round & shining and making a noise, he strived to take it up, but it flowed like quick silver so that he could not handle it.

Many Gentlemen have been in his Company when he hath been pulled by the Coat as they have seen but could not see who did it; Sometimes his Gloves lying at one end of the table have been brought and given him, but they see the Gloves as they thought come themselves.

Another time being with some Merchants at dinner, that were strangers to this spirit and were abashed, when they heard the noise and saw nothing, presently a paper was given the Gentleman he read it and so did others, it was, that he should serve God and fear nothing for the enemies of his father which hated him should all surely die, and so should all that sought to do him hurt, and to be assured he named such a man, and said he should die such a day as he did, another should die such a day and he died also, the Merchants were stricken with fear but he bid them be of good courage, there was no hurt towards them, and the better to assure them of it, told the truth of all the whole matter.

[1] The London Stock Exchange, near the Bank of England in the City of London.

Ever since this Spirit hath been always with him, and by some sensible [perceptible] sign did ever advertise [warn] him of things as by striking his right ear if he did not well, if otherwise his left, if any danger he was foretold of it.

When he began to praise God in Psalms and to declare his marvellous arts that he was presently raised and strengthened with a spiritual & supernatural power, That he daily begged of God that he would teach him his will, his law, and his truth and that he set one day of the week apart for reading the Scriptures and for meditation with singing of Psalms all the day long in his house; But that in his ordinary conversation he is sufficiently merry if he like his Company and of a cheerful mind, if he talked[1]of any vain thing or indiscreetly would offer to discover [disclose] any secret is forbidden; or if he at any time [he] would discover [disclose] any inspired secret, he was forthwith admonished thereof in his ear; and [he is] every morning called to prayer. Since he often goes to meet the holy Company **R.C.**[2] at certain times and they make or Resolves Resolutions of all their actions.

He giveth Alms secretly & the more alms he bestows the more prosperous he is; he dares not commit any known fault. This Gentleman hath by the providence of God been directed through many eminent dangers, [and] even those who sought his life, [have] died.

At another time when he was in very great danger upon his Ascendant coming to the body of the Sun, and the Conjunction of Saturn and Jupiter opposing his Ascendant, and was newly gone to bed he said that the Spirit would not let him alone, till he had raised him again and told him he was falsely accused wherefore he watched and prayed all that night, the day after he escaped the hands of his persecutors in a wonderful manner.

Now it is the Condition of spirits themselves who cannot appear visible without some violence done to their own nature, it being as troublesome to them to keep in one steady visible consistency in the air, as it is for men to dive [and] to hold their breath in the water.

The Guardian Genii seem to me to be as the benign eye of God running to & fro in the world with love and pity beholding the innocent endeavours of harmless and single hearted men ever ready to do them good and to help them.

---

[1] *Ninty fifth sheet Dr Rudd.*

[2] I.e. Rosa Crucis or Rosicrucians. Heydon wrote many Rosicrucian books, of which the two with closest links to Dr Rudd's work are *Theomagia*, 3 Volumes, London, 1662-1664 and *El Havareuna*, London. 1665.

And these must be no Euchites[1] or Heretics that prophesy by familiarity of evil spirits for they deny goodness and honesty and their principles, and are of a different nature from goodness.

It is lawful to pray to God for such a good Genius or Angel. And to purge the mind from pride and hypocrisy which is one reason that all men are not capable of Consociation[2] with these good Genii, for faith and desire ought to be full sail to make such voyages prosperous, and our end and purpose pure & sincere; but if pride & conceitedness or affection of some peculiar privilege above other mortals spur a man up to so bold an enterprise, his Devotion will no more move either God or the good Genii than the whining voice of the Counterfeit will stir the affection of the discretely charitable. Nay this presumption may invite some real fiends to ~~invade~~ deceive him & be his destruction.

But the safest wisdom is the sincere consecrating [of] Man's Soul to God, and the aspiring to nothing but to a profound pitch of humility, as not to be Conscious to our selves of being at all touched with the praise and applause of men; and to such a free and universal sense of charity as to be delighted with the welfare of another as much as our own; they that ~~really~~ only have their eye upon these will find coming in what ever their heart can desire; but they that put forth their hand to catch at high things as they fancy & neglect these, prove at last but a plague to themselves and a laughing stock to the world.

Let no man doubt of the existence of a spirit.[3]

---

[1] The Euchites were a sect that sprang out of the Eastern Orthodox Church in Mesopotamia, and then extended their influence to Asia Minor and Thrace. They were first mentioned in a work by Michael Psellus (1018-1081) which touches on demons. By the 12th century the Euchites had reached Bohemia and Germany, and their doctrines were declared a heresy by the Council of Trier (1231) and they were thereafter persecuted. Their beliefs were very similar to those of the Bogomils and Luciferians. They did not recognise the formal sacraments of the Christian Church, and considered Lucifer to be the elder son of God, a view which probably had Gnostic roots. Their sexual outlook was liberal, believing that procreation was both necessary and natural. They accepted both incest and homosexuality among their members, and felt that virginity in women had no particular value.

[2] Association.

[3] Here ends this interpolated section, which is only to be found in this present Rudd manuscript.

Appendix 12: The Variant Forms of the *Heptameron* style Circle

The simple version of the Circle of Art as outlined in the *Heptameron* and used by Rudd, changes according to the hour and day of the conjuration. Below are four examples of these variant forms of the Circle taken from Sloane MS 3824, folio 140. You can see that the basic structure remains the same, but the outer two rings change according to the King and spirits ruling.

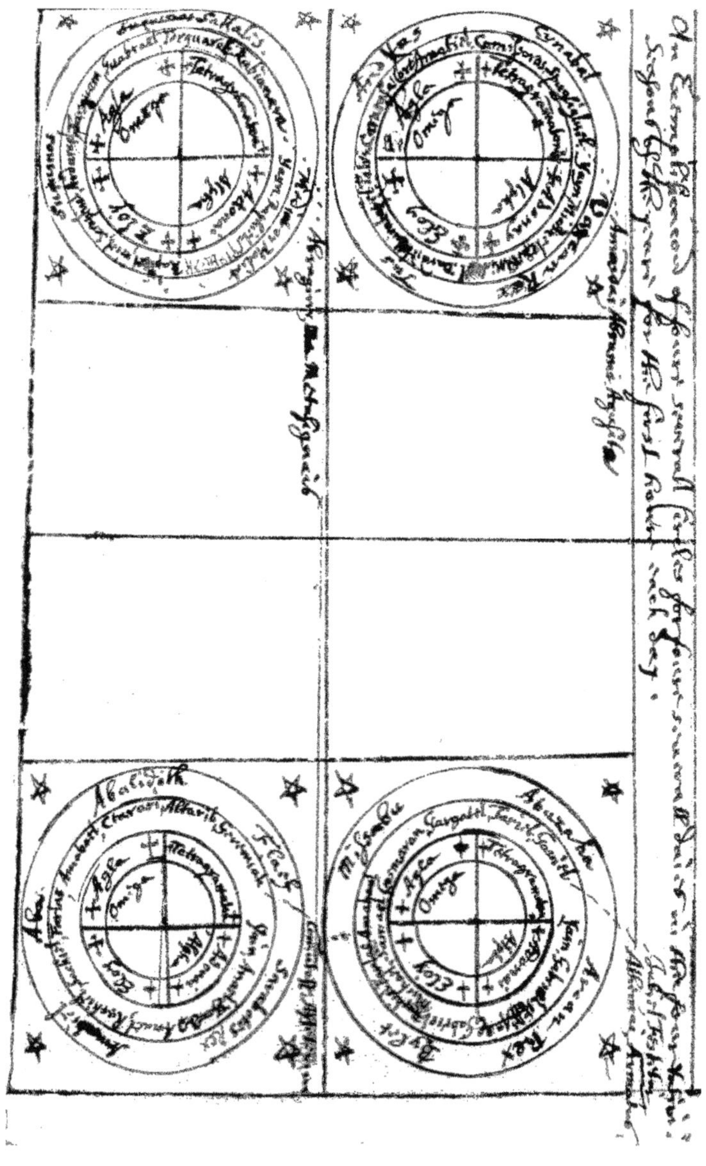

Figure 17: Four variant forms of the simple Circle

Appendix 13: Observations on Metals and Timing

Observations[1]

You must know and[2] observe the Moon's age for your working. The best days are when the Moon[3] [is] 2, 4, 6, 8[4], 10, [or] 12 days old according to Solomon,[5] and no other days are profitable. The Seals[6] are to be made in Metal[7]

Chief Kings -------------	Gold	[Sun]
Marquises ---------------	Silver	[Moon]
Dukes --------------------	Copper	[Venus]
Prelates [Princes] -----	Tin	[Jupiter]
Knights ------------------	Lead	[Saturn]
Presidents ---------------	Mercury	[Mercury]
Earls [or Counts] ------	Copper [mixed with] Silver[8]	[Mars]

[Each chosen] According to their dignity [title].[9]

The 12 Principal Kings[10] are under the power of Amaymon, Corsu[n][11] [Ziminiar] and Goap which are [the four] great Emperors or potentates[12] ruling in the [four] Quarters of the world[13] and [these] are not to be called forth except on[14] great occasions, but Invocated or[15] Commanded to send such or such a[16] Spirit as is under their power and rule[17] in their room as is shown in the following Invocation or Conjuration.

---

[1] W1: This small section entitled *"Observations"* is not found in H (though variants of it are found in S1, S2 & S3) and we have included it here for this reason..

[2] S1, S2, S3: Insert *"First thou art to"*.

[3] S1, S2, S3: Insert *"is"*.

[4] S1: *"9"*; S2, S3: *"8"*.

[5] S1, S2, S3: "as Salomon sayeth".

[6] S1, S2, S3: Insert "of those 72 kings".

[7] S1, S2, S3: *"Metals"*.

[8] You might expect to find iron here as the metal of Mars, but the Goetic spirits reputedly cannot abide that metal.

[9] S1, S2, S3: "The chiefest King in ☉, Marquises in ☽, Dukes in ♀ , Prelates in ♃, knights in ♄, & Presidents in ☿, & Earls in ♀ & ☽ equally alike &c."

[10] S1, S2, S3: *"These 72 kings"*. The reading "the 12 Principal Kings" adds considerable weight to our contention that there were originally 12 Kings or solar spirits, one to each Sign of the Zodiac as is shown in Table M18.

[11] S1, S2, S3: *"Corson"*. S1 also inserts *"Ziminar"*; S2 gives *"Zimimar"*.

[12] S1, S2, S3: replace "great Emperors or potentates" with "kings".

[13] S1, S2, S3: replace "Quarters of the world" with "4 quarters East, West, North, & South,".

[14] S1, S2, S3: "it be upon".

[15] S1, S2, S3: *Invoked &"*.

[16] S1, S2, S3: Omit *"a"*.

[17] S1, S2, S3: Transpose *"power"* and *"rule"*.

[Binding Times][1]

The houres wherein principall divels may be bound, to wit, raised and restrained from doing of hurt.

Amaymon king of the east, Gorson [or Corson] king of the south, Zimimar [Ziminiar] king of the north, Goap king and prince of the west, may be bound from the third houre [of the day, i.e. 9 am], till noone, and from the ninth houre [3 pm] till evening [sunset].

Marquesses [Marquises] may be bound from the ninth hour [of the day, i.e. 3 pm] till compline[2] [9 pm], and from compline [9 pm] till the end of the day.[3]

Dukes may be bound from the first hours [of the day, i.e sunrise] till noone; and [only if] clear weather is to be observed.[4]

Prelates may be bound in anie [any] houre of the daie.[5]

Knights [may be bound] from daie dawning, till sunne rising; or from evensong, till sunne set.[6]

A President may not be bound in anie houre of the daie, except the king, whom he obeieth [obeys], be invocated; nor in the shutting of the evening [twilight].[7]

Countries or erles [Earls] may be bound at anie houre of the daie, so [as long as] it be in the woods of feelds, where men resort not.[8]

[1] This section is taken instead from Scot's *Discoverie of Witchcraft,* Book xv, chapter iii, because it is more complete than the equivalent Wellcome MS 3203 section.
[2] See Appendix 8 for ecclesiastical hours.
[3] This does not make sense. It should probably read Compline till the end of the night (sunrise).
[4] It is a general observation that the weather should be clear and not stormy before invoking.
[5] W1: "Prelates may be bound in any hour of the day [but] chiefly from 4 o'Clock till Sunset." This includes Princes.
[6] S1, S2, S3: *"Knights may be bound from the dawning of the day till sunrising or from four of the Clock till sunset."*
[7] W1: "Presidents may be bound in any hour of the day excepting twilight at night, unless the King they are subject to be [also] Invocated."
[8] W1: adds "or where there is no noise."

Appendix 14: Equipment Diagrams from Sibley's *Goetia*[1]

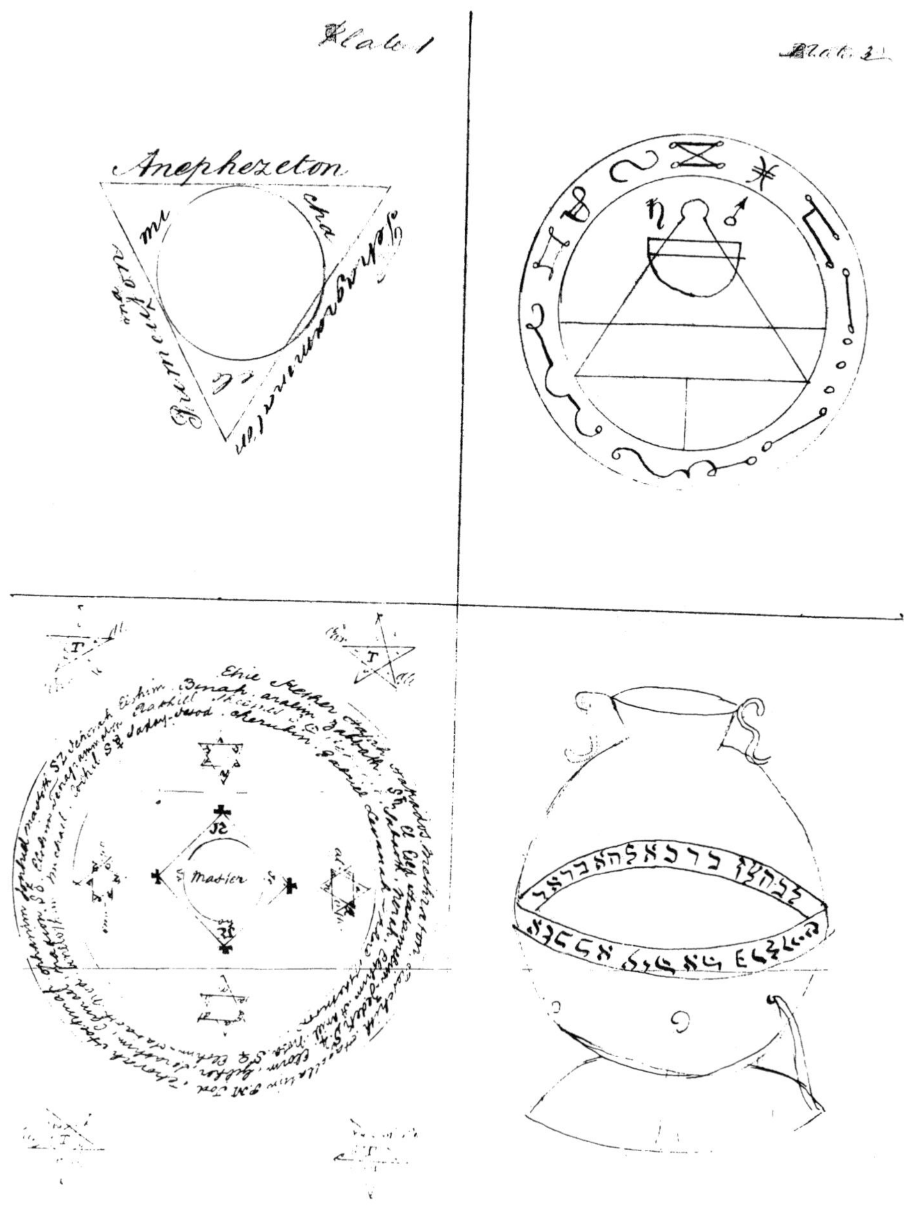

Figure 18: Plates from Sibley's *Goetia*, Wellcome MS 3203: Plate 1 - the Triangle of Solomon; Plate 2 – The Secret Seal of Solomon; Plate 3 – Solomon's Circle; Plate 3 [bis] – the Brazen Vessel.

[1] This material is not found in H, but is in the other manuscripts such as S1, S2 & S3, and in W1. We have included the version from W1, the copy of Sibley's *Goetia*.

[Triangle of Art]

Plate 1. Fig 1 – The form of the triangle that Solomon commanded the Evil Spirits into, it is to be made 2 feet from the Circle and 3 feet over [across] – N.B. it is to be placed on that quarter of the compass as the spirit is to come from.

[Seal of Solomon for the Brazen Vessel]

Plate 2. Fig 1 – The Secret Seal of Solomon by which he bound and sealed up the aforesaid Spirits and their Legions in the brazen Vessel. By this Seal Solomon compelled the Spirits into the Brazen Vessel and sealed it up, by this Seal which was made [as a lid] to cover the vessel top – and by it Solomon gained the Love of all manner of persons & overcame in battle, for neither weapon, Fire nor Water could hurt him.

This Secret Seal is to be made by one clean inwardly and outwardly & hath not defiled himself by any woman [within] the space of a month, but with fasting and prayer hath desired of God to forgive him his Sins. It is to be made on the night of the days of ♂ [Mars] or ♄ [Saturn] at 12 o'Clock, and written with the blood of a black cock which never trod hen,[1] on virgin parchment. Note on these nights the ☾ must be increasing in ♍ [Virgo] & when it is so done fume [incense] it with alum, raisins of the Sun, Dates, Cedar and Lignum aloes.

[1] In other words, a virgin black cock.

[Circle of Art]

Plate 3. The figure of Solomon's Circle which he made to preserve himself in, from the malice of Evil Spirits. This Circle is to be made 9 feet over [across] and the names around it [written] in one line, and to go on till you come to Levanah S ☽ [or] Levanah Sphere of the ☾. The names round the Circle are:[1]

Eheie. Kether Hajoh Hakados.[2] Methraton. Neschith Hagellatum P[rimum] M[obile]
Jod Jehovah. Hockmah Ophanim. Jophiel. Masloth S[phere of] Z[odiac]
Jehovah. Elohim. Binah. Aralim Zabbathi S[phere of] ♄
El Hesed Hasamelim Zedek S[phere] ♃
Elohim Gibher [Gibor]. Seraphim. Camael. Madion[3] S[phere of] ♂
Eloha Tetragrammaton. Raphiel Schemies S[phere of] ☉
Jehovah Sabaoth. Narah[?]. Elohim. Haniel Noga[h] S[phere of] ♀
Elohim Sabaoth Hod Benelohim.[4] Michael Cochab S[phere of] ☿
Sadai Jesod Cherubim Gabriel Lavanah S[phere of] ☾

At the 4 Corners ☆ with the name Tetragrammaton in each [pentagram] and a lighted candle in each & within the Circle towards the E[ast and] W[est]. [In the] N[orth and] S[outh] place ✡ and Adonay in each of the △ and Alpha et Omega Bvlr[?between]. & in the centre ◇[5] in the ○ [Circle] the Master is to Stand with Je.ho.vah round it, & in the corners of ◇ put הוהי[6] [IHVH] & a cross at each [corner] point.

[Brazen Vessel]

Plate 3 [bis]. The form of the Brazen Vessel into which Solomon shut the Spirits up in.[7]

[1] These words are written in a continuous line, both in the manuscript and on the Circle, but have here been broken into nine separate lines, corresponding to the first nine Sephiroth, for ease of reader recognition.
[2] ha-Qadosh.
[3] Madim.
[4] Bene Elohim.
[5] The Master's area in the centre of the Circle.
[6] The Hebrew has been written backwards by the scribe, probably unintentionally.
[7] This is an important piece of ritual equipment which has been given scant attention by previous commentators. A much more sophisticated version of this is provided by Rudd.

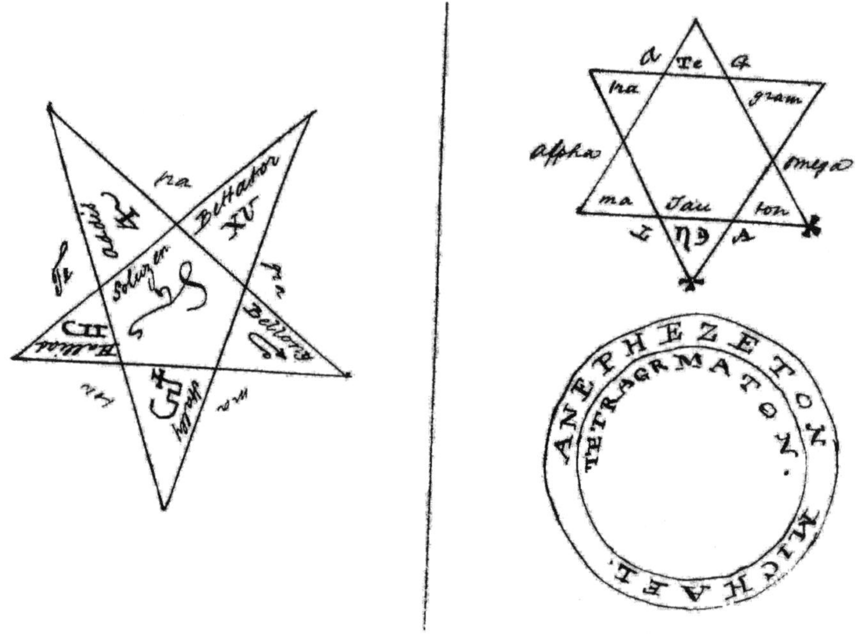

Figure 19: Plates from Sibley's *Goetia*, Wellcome MS 3203: Plate 4 - The Pentagram of Solomon or 'Pentagonal Figure'; Plate 5 - The Hexagram of Solomon or '6 angled figure'; Plate 6 - Solomon's Magical Ring.

[Pentagram]

Plate 4. The Pentagonal[1] Figure to be made of Gold & Silver, and to be worn on the heart with the Seal of the Spirit by its Side.

[Hexagram]

Plate 5. The 6 angled figure to be made on parchment made of Calfskin to be worn [attached] at the skirt of your white vestment covered with a linen Cloth, which when the Spirit appears, Show it [to] him & he will be compelled to [take] human shape and be obedient.

[Solomon's Magical Ring]

Plate 6. Solomon's Magical Ring to be held or placed before the face of the Exorcist to preserve him from the stinking fumes of the Spirit. Michael Anephezaton.[2]

[1] The author means a pentagram not a pentagon.

[2] Probably should be Anaphexeton. The last two words are to be engraved around Solomon's Ring. Tetragrammaton is to be engraved inside the ring.

[Other Equipment]

The other Materials are a Sceptre or Sword, a Mitre or Cap, a long white robe of linen, shoes and other Clothes for the purpose, a girdle of Lion's skin 3 inches broad, with all the names about it, as are [written] round about the uttermost [outer most] part of the Circle - Perfumes, a chafing dish of Charcoal, and Candles & put the fumes. Smoke and fume unto the place appointed for them - also anointing oil to anoint your temples and Eyes, & fair water to wash yourself in Several times, and in so doing you are to say, as [King] David said viz.

"Thou shalt purge me with Hyssop oh Lord and it shall be cleaned, wash me & I shall be whiter than the snow."

And in putting on your garment you must say

"By the figurative Mystery of this holy vesture I will clothe me with the armour of Salvation in the Strength of the Highest. ***Ancor Amacor Amides Theodonias Anitor*** *that my desire may be Effected through the Strength of* ***Adonay*** *to whom be Praise and Glory for Ever and Ever. Amen."*

After you have so done make your oration, and begin your work in the order Prescribed.

Appendix 15: The Form of Commanding Spirits given in Scot[1]

The forme of adjuring or citing of the spirits aforesaid to arise and appear.

WHEN you will have any spirit, you must know his name and office; you must also fast, and be cleane from all pollution, three or four days before; so will the spirit be the more obedient unto you. Then make a circle, and call up the spirit with great intention, and holding a ring[2] in your hand, rehearse in your own name, and your companions (for one must always be with you) this prayer following, and so no spirit shall annoy you, and your purpose shall take effect. And note how this agreeth with popish[3] charms and conjurations.

In the name of our Lord Jesus Christ the + father + and the son + and the Holy-ghost + holy trinity and inseparable unity, I call upon thee, that thou might be my salvation and defence, and the protection of my body and soul, and of all my goods through the virtue of thy holy cross, and through the virtue of thy passion, I beseech thee O Lord Jesus Christ, by the merits of thy blessed mother S[aint] Marie, and of all thy saints, that thou give me grace and divine power over all the wicked spirits, so as which of them soever I do call by name, they may come by and by from every coast,[4] and accomplish my will, that they neither be hurtful nor fearful unto me, but rather obedient and diligent about me. And through thy virtue straightly commanding them, let them fulfil my commandments, Amen. Holy, holy, holy, Lord God of ***Sabboth,***[5] *which wilt come to judge the quick and the dead, thou which art* ***A and Ω,*** *first and last, King of kings and Lord of lords,* ***Ioth, Aglanabrath, El, Abiel, Anathiel, Amazim, Sedomel, Gayes, Heli, Messias, Tolimi, Elias, Ischiros, Athanatos, Imas.*** *By these thy holy names, and by all other [names] I do call upon thee, and beseech thee O Lord Jesus Christ, by thy nativity and baptism, by thy cross and passion, by thine ascension, and by the coming of the Holy-ghost, by the bitterness of thy soul when it departed from thy body, by thy five wounds, by the blood and water which went out of thy body, by thy virtue, by the sacrament which thou gavest thy disciples the day before thou suffered, by the holy trinity, and by the inseparable unity, by blessed* ***Marie*** *thy mother, by thine angels, archangels, prophets, patriarchs, and by all thy saints, and by all the sacraments which are made in thine honour, I do worship and beseech thee, I bless and desire thee, to accept these prayers, conjurations, and words of my mouth, which I will use. I require thee O Lord*

---

[1] The following is the whole of the Fourth Chapter of Book XV of Reginald Scot's *Discovery of Witchcraft*, which immediately follows Scot's transcription of T.R.'s translation of Weirus' *Pseudomonarchia Daemonum*, which is the main source of the 72 spirit names in the *Goetia*, and of which it is part. It must therefore be considered as quite likely to be part of the missing method of the *Goetia*. The spelling has been modernised.

[2] After the pattern of Solomon's Ring.

[3] Roman Catholic. This sentence does not occur in Weir, but was obviously added disapprovingly by Scot. The Christian elements in this conjuration are probably also a later interpolation.

[4] 'Coast' literally means 'edge' (not seashore): in this sense the direction from which the spirit is expected to come to the circle.

[5] Sabaoth.

Jesus Christ, that thou give me thy virtue & power over all thine [fallen] angels (which were thrown down from heaven to deceive mankind) to draw them to me, to tie and bind them, & also to loose them, to gather them together before me, & to command them to do all that they can, and that by no means they condemn my voice, or the words of my mouth; but that they obey me and my sayings [words], and fear me. I beseech thee by thine humanity, mercy and grace, and I require thee ***Adonay, Amay, Horta, Vege dora,***[1] ***Mitai, Hel, Suranat, Ysion, Ysesy,***[2] *and by all thy holy names, and by all thine holy he saints and she saints, by all thine angels and archangels, powers, dominations, and virtues, and by that name that Salomon did bind the devils, and shut them up,* ***Elhrach,***[3] ***Ebanher,***[4] ***Agle, Goth, Ioth, Othie, Venoch, Nabrat****, and by all thine holy names which are written in this book, and by the virtue of them all, that thou enable me to congregate all thy spirits thrown down from heaven, that they may give me a true answer of all my demands, and that they satisfy all my requests, without the hurt of my body or soul, or any thing else that is mine, through our Lord Jesus Christ thy son, which liveth and reigneth with thee in the unity of the Holy-ghost, one God world without end.*

Oh father omnipotent, oh wise son, oh Holy-ghost, the searcher of hearts, oh you three in [one] persons, one true godhead in substance, which didst spare Adam and Eve in their sins; and oh thou son, which died for their sins a most filthy death, sustaining it upon the holy cross; oh thou most merciful, when I fly unto thy mercy, and beseech thee by all the means I can, by these the holy names of thy son; to wit, ***A and Ω****, and all other [of] his names, grant me thy virtue and power, that I may be able to cite before me, thy spirits which were thrown down from heaven, & that they may speak with me, & dispatch by & by without delay, & with a good will, & without the hurt of my body, soul, or goods, &c: as is contained in the book called* Annulus Salomonis.[5]

Oh great and eternal virtue of the highest, which through disposition, these being called to judgement, ***Vaicheon, Stimulamaton, Esphares, Tetragrammaton, Olioram, Cryon***[6]***, Esytion, Existion, Eriona, Onela, Brasim, Noym, Messias, Soter, Emanuel, Sabboth, Adonay****, I worship thee, I invocate thee, I implore thee with all the strength of my mind, that by thee, my present prayers, consecrations, and conjurations be hallowed: and whersoever wicked spirits are called, in the virtue of thy names, they may come together from every coast [direction], and diligently fulfil the will of me the exorcist. Fiat, fiat, fiat, Amen.*

[1] "Vigedara" in Weir.
[2] "Ysyesy" in Weir.
[3] "Elhroch" in Weir.
[4] "Eban her" in Weir.
[5] Another grimoire called *The Ring of Solomon*.
[6] "Irion" in Weir.

Bibliography

Manuscript Source Material

Harley MS 6482 - *A Treatise on Angel Magic, Tabula Sancta cum Tabulis Enochi, Dr Rudd's Nine Hierarchies* and other relevant Rudd *Goetia* material[1]

Harley MS 6483 - *Lemegeton* - Rudd's *Liber Malorum Spirituum seu Goetia*[2]

Sloane MS 2731 - *Lemegeton (Clavicula Salomonis)*[3]

Sloane MS 3648 - *Lemegeton*[4]

Sloane MS 3824 - proto-*Lemegeton*[5]

Sloane MS 3825 - *Lemegeton*[6] *& Janua Magica Reserata*[7]

Wellcome MS 3203 - *Lemegeton*[8]

Wellcome MS 4665 - *Lemegeton*[9]

Cambridge, Trinity MS O.8.29 College - *Livre des Esperitz*

---

[1] Published by Adam McLean in *A Treatise on Angel Magic*, Magnum Opus Hermetic Sourceworks, reprinted Weiser, York Beach, 2006.
[2] This volume.
[3] The source of most printed versions of the *Lemegeton*.
[4] In the hand of Elias Ashmole.
[5] Not listed in Peterson, *The Lesser Key of Solomon* as a *Lemegeton*. See our Appendix 1 of the present volume.
[6] Source of Peterson's standard edition of the *Lemegeton*.
[7] Printed in Skinner & Rankine, *Keys to the Gateway of Magic*, Volume 2, Sourceworks of Ceremonial Magic, Golden Hoard Press, London, 2005.
[8] Lea's copy of Hockley's copy. Not listed in Peterson, *The Lesser Key of Solomon*.
[9] Frederick Hockley's copy. Not listed in Peterson, *The Lesser Key of Solomon*. This MS is only fragmentary.

Printed Source Material

Abano, Peter de. *Heptameron or Magical Elements*. See Agrippa *Fourth Book of Occult Philosophy*.

Abraham of Worms, *The Book of Abramelin*, Ibis, Lake Worth, 2006. [Edited by Georg Dehn, translated by Steven Guth]

Agrippa, H. C. *Three Books of Occult Philosophy*. Translated by James Freake [Dr John French]. Edited by Donald Tyson. Llewellyn, St Paul, 1993.

Agrippa, H. C. *Fourth Book of Occult Philosophy*.
First facsimile edition Askin Publishers, London, 1978. It includes:
Of Occult Philosophy, or Magical Ceremonies by Agrippa;
Heptameron or Magical Elements by Peter de Abano;
Isagoge: On the Nature of Such Spirits by Georg Villinganus;
Arbatel of Magick: Of the Magick of the Ancients by Agrippa;
Of Geomancy by Agrippa;
Of Astronomical Geomancy by Gerard Cremonensis.
A new re-set and modernised edition edited by Stephen Skinner, Nicolas-Hays, Berwick, 2005.

Bardon, Franz. *The Practice of Magical Evocation: Instructions for Invoking Spirits from the Spheres Surrounding Us*. Rudolf Pravica, Graz, 1956.

Blish, James. *Black Easter, or Faust Aleph-Null*. Buccaneer, New York, 1968. [One of the best descriptions, albeit fictional, of the Goetic process.]

Butler, Elizabeth, Professor. *Ritual Magic*. Pennsylvania State UP, 1998.

Couliano, Ioan P, *Eros and Magic in the Renaissance*, University of Chicago Press, Chicago, 1987.

Crowley, Aleister, *The Book of the Goetia of Solomon the King*, SPRT, Foyers, 1904.

De Claremont, Lewis. *The Ancient's Book of Magic*, Oracle, 1936.

Fanger, Claire [ed]. *Conjuring Spirits: Texts and Traditions of Medieval Ritual Magic*. Pennsylvania State UP & Sutton Publishing, 1998.

Geller, Markham J, "Jesus' Theurgic Powers: Parallels in the Talmud and Incantation Bowls", *Journal of Jewish Studies*, 28, Oxford, 1977, p. 141-155.

Hamill, John [ed]. *The Rosicrucian Seer: Magical Writings of Frederick Hockley*. Aquarian Press, Wellingborough, 1986. With a note by R A Gilbert.

Hymenaeus Beta [William Breeze], *The Goetia, the Lesser Key of Solomon the King*, Red Wheel Weiser, Boston, 1997. [Based on Crowley's version].

James, Geoffrey. *Angel Magic: the Ancient Art of Summoning and Communicating with Angelic Beings*. Llewellyn, St. Paul, 1997. [An excellent overview]

Josephus, Flavius. *The Works of Josephus, Complete and Unabridged*. Hendrickson, Peabody, 1987. [Translation by William Whiston].

Kieckhefer, Richard. *Forbidden Rites: A Necromancer's Manual of the Fifteenth Century*, Sutton, Stroud, 1997.

Kuntz, Darcy [edited]. *Ars Notoria: the Magical Art of Solomon...Englished by Robert Turner*. Holmes, Sequim, 2006. [First English edition 1656]

Leitch, Aaron. *Secrets of the Magical Grimoires*, Llewellyn, Woodbury, 2005.

Lisiewski, Joseph C. *Ceremonial Magic & The Power of Evocation*. New Falcon, Tempe,

Arizona, 2004. [Uses de Abano's *Heptameron*.]

Mathers, S L MacGregor, (trans) *The Book of the Sacred Magic of Abramelin the Mage.* Watkins, London, 1900.

Mathers, S L MacGregor, (trans) *The Key of Solomon the King (Clavicula Salomonis).* Kegal Paul, London, 1909.

McLean, Adam [editor]. *The Steganographia of Johannes Trithemius.* Book I & III. Magnum Opus Hermetic Sourceworks 12, Edinburgh, 1982.

McLean, Adam [editor]. *A Treatise on Angel Magic.* Magnum Opus Hermetic Sourceworks 15, Edinburgh. Republished Weiser, York Beach, 2006.

McLean, Adam [editor]. *The Magical Calendar* Magnum Opus, Edinburgh, 1979.

Mora, George [editor]. *Witches, Devils, and Doctors in the Rennaisance,* Medieval & Renaissance Texts & Studies, New York, 1991.

Paracelsus von Hohenheim. *The Archidoxes of Magic,* introduced by Stephen Skinner, Askin Publishers, London, 1975 republished Ibis, Berwick, 2004.

Peterson, Joseph. (ed). *The Lesser Key of Solomon: Lemegeton Clavicula Salomonis,* Weiser Books, Maine, 2001.[The standard edition which uses Sloane MS 3825 as its main text with footnotes from Sloane MS 2731, Sloane MS 3648, and Harley MS 6483.]

Pingree, David. (editor) *Picatrix: The Latin Version of the Ghayat al-Hakim,* Warburg Institute, London, 1986.

Robinson, James. *Nag Hammadi Library in English,* Brill, Leyden, 1977. *The Testimony of Truth* (IX, 3).

Runyon, Carroll 'Poke'. *The Book of Solomon's Magick.* CHS, Siverado, 2003.

Savedow, Steve. *Goetic Evocation: The Magician's Workbook Volume 2.* Eschaton, 1996.

Scot, Reginald, *Discoverie of Witchcraft,* Elliot Stock, London, 1886, reprinted from 1665 edition. [limited edition of 250 copies.] Book xv, Chapter i-iv, pages 376-329 *et seq.*

Shah, Sayed Idries, *The Secret Lore of Magic,* Muller, London, 1957.

Shah, Sayed Idries, *Oriental Magic,* Rider, London,1956.

Skinner, Stephen & Rankine, David. *The Practical Angel Magic of John Dee's Enochian Tables,* Volume 1 Sourceworks of Ceremonial Magic, Golden Hoard Press, London, 2005.

Skinner, Stephen & Rankine, David. *Keys to the Gateway of Magic,* Volume 2 Sourceworks of Ceremonial Magic, Golden Hoard Press, London, 2005.

Skinner, Stephen. *Complete Magician's Tables,* Golden Hoard Press, London & Singapore, 2006; second edition Llewellyn, Woodbury, 2007.

Trithemius, Johannes. *Steganographia,* Frankfort, 1606. [See also McLean.]

Turner, Robert, et al. *Elizabethan Magic: The Art and the Magus.* Element, Longmead, 1989.

Waite, A E, *The Book of Black Magic and of Pacts,* Privately Printed, Edinburgh, 1898, republished by Samuel Weiser, York Beach, 1972.

Waite, A E, *The Secret Tradition in Goetia,* Rider, London, 1911.

Waite, A E, *The Book of Ceremonial Magic,* University Books, New York, 1961.

Weyer, Johann, *Pseudomonarchia Daemonum* in *Opera Omnia,* Amsterdam, 1660.

Index